THE PAN BOOK OF OPERA

ARTHUR JACOBS was born in Manchester in 1922 and educated at Oxford. He has been a music critic for various newspapers, principally the *Financial Times*, and since 1964 has been on the editorial board of the magazine *Opera*. Formerly a professor at the Royal Academy of Music, he is now head of the music department at Huddersfield Polytechnic. Well known as a translator of French, German, Italian and Russian operas, he has also written an original libretto for an opera, *One Man Show*, by Nicholas Maw. He is the author of *A New Dictionary of Music* and of *Arthur Sullivan, a Victorian Musician*.

STANLEY SADIE was born in London in 1930 and studied music at Cambridge where he took the PhD in 1958. Best known as editor of the widely acclaimed *New Grove Dictionary of Music and Musicians* (1980), he was a music critic for *The Times* for seventeen years and has been editor of the *Musical Times* since 1967. His books include studies of Mozart and Handel; he is editing a series of music studies arising from *The New Grove* and a History of Music series in connection with the Granada music history television programmes, for which he is music consultant. He was appointed CBE in 1982.

Arthur Jacobs and Stanley Sadie

The Pan Book of Opera

enlarged edition

Pan Original
Pan Books London and Sydney

First Pan Books edition published 1964
This revised and enlarged edition published 1984 by Pan Books Ltd,
Cavaye Place, London SW10 9PG
9 8 7 6 5
© Arthur Jacobs and Stanley Sadie 1964, 1984
ISBN 0 330 26843 0
Photoset by Parker Typesetting Service, Leicester
Printed and bound in Great Britain by
Cox & Wyman Ltd. Reading

CONTENTS

INTRODUCTION

Opera is a complex, strange and ever-fascinating art. In combining the form of a visual drama with that of a musical work, composers had been influenced not only by the musical means at their disposal but by theatrical practice and by the theatrical and literary tastes of their audiences. The musical scores which now delight us are the result of an encounter between the composer's genius and a variety of other factors – even, as in the case of *Rigoletto* and other Verdi operas, the hand of the political censor.

Yet the composer dominates. He dominates so strongly as to please not merely the audiences of his own time but the audiences of times to come – whose attitude to theatrical and other matters may have changed considerably. Beaumarchais's *Le mariage de Figaro* and Sardou's *La Tosca* have retreated into the historian's cupboard: Mozart's and Puccini's operas are the continuing delight of operatic audiences from Montreal to Moscow.

Opera is fully captured only in the theatre, and normally – unless we wish to assume that composers did not know what they were doing – only when the words are fully understood, either by performance in the audience's language or by full comprehension of the original. Accordingly, where the original text is not English we give quotations in English translation as well as in the original.

But we give the textual quotations in the original language too, not least in order to aid those who come to opera by the many fine recordings now available, and we depart from most previous books on opera in listing the characters not in order of importance in the drama but in order of singing.

As a general rule we name our characters in the language used by the composer himself. But where the plots are classical or biblical or based on English literary sources we use the accepted English form: and we allow certain eminent historical figures also to keep their well-known English forms, e.g. King Philip of Spain. In the theatre, the opera-lover must be prepared for occasional changes: for instance, as the action of *La traviata* takes place in France and is based on a French play, a production of the opera in English may prefer French names to those Italian ones which the composer, in accordance with Italian theatrical usage, substituted.

Our synopses cover in detail eighty-seven of the recognized classics of opera by forty-one composers from Purcell to Britten. Many other operas and composers are mentioned in passing. Of those operas treated in detail, each is discussed in three parts: General introduction – Synopsis – Musical commentary. The operas are grouped under their composers, and composers arranged in roughly chronological order within their countries. A narrative links each composer with the one preceding.

We are conscious, of course, of having had to restrict our choice in order to keep the book within its bounds; and we have excluded operetta altogether (even a work as fully a part of the opera-house repertory as *Die Fledermaus*). We offer our apologies to those whose favourites have had to be omitted – as, indeed, have been some of our own! The musical comments do not attempt the impossible task of reproducing all the principal tunes: they are chosen with the particular purpose of illuminating each composer's typical way of working on the intimate fusion of music and drama. In addition, our pages provide – by means of the linking narrative, a prologue ('The Beginnings') and an epilogue – a compressed history of opera itself. Throughout the book, a date against an opera is, unless otherwise indicated, the date of first production, not necessarily of composition.

Permission to use copyright musical and literal quotations was kindly granted by the following:

Ascherberg, Hopwood & Crew Ltd (Mascagni); Boosey & Hawkes Ltd (Richard Strauss, Stravinsky, Prokofiev, Shostakovich, Britten); G. Ricordi & Co. (London) Ltd (Verdi's *Otello* and *Falstaff*, Puccini); Schott & Co. Ltd (Henze, Tippett); Universal Edition Ltd, Alfred A. Kalmus Ltd (Janáček, Berg, Weill); G. Schirmer Ltd (Menotti); Chappell Music Ltd (Gershwin).

ARTHUR JACOBS
STANLEY SADIE
London 1984

PROLOGUE: THE BEGINNINGS

The word *opera* is Italian, derived from the plural of the Latin *opus*, meaning 'work'. The form that is the topic of this book originated in Italy at the end of the sixteenth century, though it had many antecedents. The use of singing as an element in drama dates at least back to the Greeks, and was important in the medieval mystery plays (like the twelfth-century *Play of Daniel*, which is among those to have been revived in modern times). Its more immediate ancestors were such early semi-dramatic forms as the madrigal comedy, the pastoral, the masque and the *intermedio*. Most were mixtures of singing (mainly solo but some ensemble), instrumental music, declamation and dance, in various proportions; almost all were designed as courtly entertainment, usually for special occasions such as royal weddings.

It was in Florence that the most brilliant and lavish of such entertainments took place, and there too that a group of intellectuals called the Camerata flourished in the late years of the sixteenth century – a group dedicated to the Renaissance ideal of recapturing the spirit of Greek drama. So it is not surprising that it was also in Florence that what is generally reckoned the first 'real' opera, *Dafne*, was produced; that was in 1597–8. The words were by Ottavio Rinuccini, the music mainly by Jacopo Peri (1561–1633), with Jacopo Corsi (1561–1602). This was a private performance for a group of Florentine noblemen and their friends, as were all the opera performances of these years, which also saw other works by Peri (*Euridice*, 1600) and Giulio Caccini (*Euridice*, 1600). The style soon spread elsewhere in Italy, notably to the Gonzaga court at Mantua, with Claudio Monteverdi's *Orfeo* (1607; in full, *La favola d'Orfeo*, 'The Story of Orpheus') and Marco da Gagliano's *Dafne* (1607–8). Sacred operas such as the *Rappresentatione di Anima, et di Corpo*

('Representation of the Soul and the Body'), by Emilio de' Cavalieri (1600), began to be performed in Rome, and this was eventually to lead to a rather different genre, the oratorio. It is significant that the early secular operas always took classical mythology as their basis. This was partly because of its familiarity to audiences and its many layers of allegorical meaning; also partly because its creators were striving for kinship with the Greeks. It is important too that many of these operas were based on stories specifically connected with the power of music to arouse human emotions.

Monteverdi's *Orfeo* is the earliest opera to be given fairly regularly in the professional theatre today. It still remains a late – and magnificent – example of a Renaissance court entertainment, compounded of singing in the new *stile rappresentativo* (the expressive 'representational style'), madrigalian choruses and dance. It is with Monteverdi's operas, written for a wider public, that this book begins: for in 1637 the first public opera house opened, in Venice (to be followed by three more over the next four years, so successful was the enterprise), and Monteverdi was among those to supply the repertory. Before looking more closely at his most famous opera, *L'incoronazione di Poppea* ('The Coronation of Poppaea', 1642), we should glance at operatic developments outside Italy in the seventeenth century. For the form spread, partly with the composition of operas in other tongues.

The first important composer of French opera was Jean-Baptiste Lully (1632–87), born Giovanni Battista Lulli in Florence, chief court composer to Louis XIV. He had to devise a musical language that was compatible with the great French theatrical traditions (this was the age of Racine, Corneille, Quinault and Molière) and did not violate the cherished declamatory and structural principles of the French stage, reconciling it at the same time with the traditional *ballet de cour*. In Germany, the first opera to be given was *Dafne*, by Heinrich Schütz (1585–1672), an adaptation of the Rinuccini text set by Peri; performed at Torgau in 1627 for a royal wedding, it is now lost. Schütz had studied in Venice under Giovanni Gabrieli, and was later to return to study with Monteverdi. But the structure of German society and the religious outlook of much of the country provided poor soil for opera, and it was slow to flourish. The first public opera house, giving mainly German-language opera, was opened at Hamburg in 1678. In England, the court masques performed in the early seventeenth century, under James I and Charles I, were close to opera. In 1656, although the public theatres were closed by Cromwell's ban on spoken drama, a dramatic work called *The Siege of Rhodes* with music by five different composers was sung 'in recitative musick' (according to the librettist): this is generally reckoned to be the first English opera. Here opera was even slower to establish itself: Purcell composed only one (and that for amateurs), apart from masque-like sections to be given within plays (sometimes called 'semi-operas'). It was not in fact until the present century that full-length, all-sung English opera became other than a rarity.

COMPOSERS AND
THEIR OPERAS

CLAUDIO MONTEVERDI

1567–1643

The operas of Claudio Monteverdi are the earliest works that the operagoer may expect to encounter fairly regularly. Monteverdi composed nine operas, embarked on but left incomplete three more, and wrote several shorter stage works of an operatic character. Six of the nine are lost; we have only *Orfeo* (1607), *Il ritorno d'Ulisse in patria* ('The Return of Odysseus to his Fatherland', 1641) and *L'incoronazione di Poppea* (1642). The two latter were written for the Venetian opera houses of Monteverdi's time, and their fame, and their composer's, ensured that they were soon given in other Italian centres and possibly elsewhere.

A word needs to be said about the texts of these operas. *Orfeo* is relatively straightforward: Monteverdi listed the instruments he wanted to accompany the vocal line, and specified when each should play, but left exactly *what* each should play to the imagination and understanding of his musicians. The same basic principle applies to all three works: the melody instruments in the orchestra (violins, recorders, trumpets, etc.) play exclusively in the ritornellos (the brief instrumental interludes between verses or scenes), and the solo voice is supported only by continuo – harmony instruments (lutes, harpsichords, organs) with a sustaining bass instrument (such as a viol or cello). For the other two operas we do not know precisely what instruments Monteverdi expected, except by such inferences as can be drawn from the surviving accounts of the theatre musicians, which show that only a few string players and a harmony group were used. The preference in the 1960s and early 1970s for a rich accompaniment and a highly colourful continuo realization has more lately tended to give way to a simpler and more faithful style in which the solo vocal line – the main expressive agent – receives the chief emphasis.

L'INCORONAZIONE DI POPPEA
(The Coronation of Poppaea)
Libretto by G. F. Busenello

First performed: Venice, 1642
Prologue and Three Acts

Cast in order of singing:

GODDESS OF FORTUNE (Fortuna)	*soprano*
GODDESS OF VIRTUE (Virtù)	*soprano*
GOD OF LOVE (Amore)	*soprano*
OTHO (Ottone), POPPAEA'S FORMER LOVER	*male mezzo-soprano*
TWO SOLDIERS OF NERO'S BODYGUARD	*tenors*
POPPAEA (Poppea)	*soprano*
NERO (Nerone), EMPEROR OF ROME	*male soprano*
ARNALTA, POPPAEA'S OLD NURSE	*contralto or tenor*
OCTAVIA (Ottavia), NERO'S EMPRESS	*mezzo-soprano*
OCTAVIA'S NURSE	*contralto*
SENECA, A PHILOSOPHER	*bass*
OCTAVIA'S PAGE (*valletto*)	*(male) soprano*
PALLAS ATHENÉ, GODDESS OF WISDOM	*soprano*
DRUSILLA, OCTAVIA'S LADY-IN-WAITING	*soprano*
MERCURY	*tenor*
CAPTAIN OF THE PRAETORIAN GUARD (a freed slave; *liberto*)	*tenor*
OCTAVIA'S MAID (*damigella*)	*soprano*
LUCAN (Lucano), A POET	*tenor*
LICTOR	*bass*
VENUS	*soprano*

Seneca's friends, Consuls, Tribunes
The scene is laid in Rome about AD55

This is an opera about love: about the power of love between two
people to alter the lives of several others (indeed to terminate two of
them prematurely), about its triumph over morality – and, we in the
audience may think, about its ability, when clothed in Monteverdi's
music, to persuade us that its values override all others. That is what
the composer and librettist intended, as the allegorical prologue – a
normal feature in these early operas – makes clear. The subtle and

finely constructed text by Giovanni Francesco Busenello, lawyer and intellectual as well as poet, has a realism, in the way it portrays none of the characters as black or white but all in shades of grey, that escaped many a more famous, later librettist.

In the cast list above, the characters are shown with their original voice pitches. Most of the men, it will be seen, are sung by males at female pitch (castratos) – a tradition that persisted in Italian serious opera to the end of the eighteenth century and even beyond. These roles, or some of them, are now often put down an octave to add greater realism for modern audiences; though today's operagoers have increasingly come to accept the convention of high voices in male roles – which is asking no more of them than numerous other conventions that we take for granted in opera. To cast Nero as a tenor does in fact seriously distort the musical effects Monteverdi was aiming at; the part can be persuasively sung by a woman, and some of the lower-pitched male parts, like Otho's, fit well on the male alto voice.

★   ★   ★

PROLOGUE: The goddesses of Fortune and Virtue dispute as to which of them has greater influence over the affairs of men. Then the god of Love claims to exceed either in his power; and to prove his case he offers the story of Nero and Poppaea.

ACT I: Otho, who has been away, returns joyfully to Poppaea's house. But then he sees two of Nero's soldiers on guard outside – and at once realizes that his beloved now lies in the Emperor's arms. He goes, and the soldiers, who have been dozing, wake; they express themselves cynically about Nero and the state of Rome. Now Nero and Poppaea emerge, she begging him not to leave her, and, when she sees that he must, pressing him to return soon; they bid each other a loving farewell. He goes, and she is joined by her old nurse, Arnalta, to whom she expresses her ambitions; Arnalta has few hopes of their fulfilment.

Now we meet Octavia, the Empress, bewailing her situation as rejected queen ('Disprezzata regina'). Her old nurse suggests that she seek love elsewhere, but she firmly rejects the idea. Seneca and her page (*valletto*) enter and Seneca counsels philosophic resignation; the page, however, offers livelier support and charges Seneca with uttering empty platitudes. Octavia tells Seneca that Nero plans to repudiate her. Alone, Seneca is visited by the goddess of Wisdom (the goddess herself? or a vision of her? or just his own wise thoughts? – there is an intentional ambiguity); she warns him that the omens are bad and he should be prepared for death. Nero enters, and tells his old mentor that he proposes to discard Octavia; he is infuriated by Seneca's admonitions of the wrongness, political as well as moral, of what he intends.

Back in Poppaea's house, Nero and she are embracing; he talks of her becoming his empress, and she talks of Seneca in a way designed to turn Nero more strongly against him by hinting that he boasts of his authority over Nero. Nero summons an officer and orders him to tell Seneca he must die that very night.

Otho mourns his dispossession of Poppaea's favours. She tells him to spare his reproaches; she has higher aims. He says he will try to forget her, and when the loving Drusilla comes he expresses his desire for her. She goes; and, alone, he confesses that although Drusilla's name is on his lips, it is Poppaea's that is in his heart.

ACT II: Seneca, alone, contemplates high ideals, away from the troubled world of the court. Mercury appears to him to say that his death sentence is imminent; he welcomes the news, and when, a moment later, the captain of Nero's guard (*liberto*) comes to tell him he must die, he contentedly accepts. The distressed captain bids him die happy. Now Seneca summons his 'famigliari' – which may mean his family, his friends or his pupils, or a combination: classical sources hold that his wife and two pupils were with him, and that would correspond with Monteverdi's three-part setting (the customary chorus is implausible, unless he were holding a seminar). He tells them he is to die, and they try to persuade him not to; but he cannot be moved, and calls for the bath to be readied in which his innocent blood will flow.

The page and the maid (*damigella*) are found together; he talks of a certain indescribable feeling she arouses in him, and they tease and play, singing of their mutual desire. They depart, and Nero appears with his friend Lucan; they sing a joyful duet to celebrate the death of Seneca, and Lucan, a poet, serenades the individual charms of Poppaea at Nero's prompting. Left alone, Nero continues to give voice to his passion.

Otho, alone, thinks of the possibility of killing Poppaea, but dismisses the idea. But then Octavia enters and, commanding his obedience on the grounds of his indebtedness to her ancestors, instructs him to murder Poppaea. In anguish, he is compelled to agree. They depart, and Drusilla enters singing of her joy at her and Otho's love. The page and the old nurse enter, and the page teases her about her amorous feelings. When they leave, Otho returns and tells Drusilla his intentions, and that (at Octavia's suggestion) he wishes to disguise himself in women's clothes to avoid detection; she readily proffers help, not displeased at the idea of her rival's death.

Poppaea, with Seneca dead, prays that love will realize her ambitions; Arnalta soothes her to sleep ('Oblivion soave'). As she sleeps, the god of Love descends and watches over her. Otho, wearing Drusilla's clothes, enters; cursing his own deed, he moves to kill her – but Love (the god standing guard, or his own emotions?) intervenes. He flees; Poppaea wakes and sees Drusilla (she thinks), knife in hand. Arnalta sets off in pursuit. Love celebrates his triumph and resolves to make Poppaea empress.

ACT III: Drusilla eagerly looks forward to Otho's successful return. But instead Arnalta, with a lictor and other officials, arrives, and denounces her as Poppaea's would-be murderess. She is arrested. Nero enters; in response to her pleas of innocence he condemns her to torture and death. Then – presumably realizing that only thus can she save her beloved – she admits guilt. But now Otho enters and claims the attempted crime. The two compete in guilt, then Otho tells Nero that it was at Octavia's bidding that he had gone in Drusilla's clothes to kill Poppaea. Nero decides to spare Otho, but banishes him; Drusilla chooses to share his exile. They leave, and Nero announces his decision – which now has more obvious justification – to repudiate Octavia. Poppaea, entering, is told of the events that have just passed; she and Nero sing of their love. Then Arnalta sings with delight and a typical touch of everyday philosophy about her prospects as the Empress's attendant.

Octavia, who is to be cast off in a ship at the mercy of the winds, bids farewell to her country and bitterly laments her fate ('A Dio, Roma').

Nero bids Poppaea ascend the throne, and she is crowned Empress of Rome. After a formal orchestral sinfonia, the consuls and tribunes sing in tribute to her; there are interventions too from the god of Love and from Venus. There, in the original printed libretto, the opera ends; but there exists a final duet (some scholars think it to be the composition of Francesco Cavalli, Monteverdi's greatest pupil and successor, rather than Monteverdi's own) in which the couple rejoice in the triumph of their love ('Pur ti miro').

★　★　★

The basic texture of *L'incoronazione di Poppea*, like all operas of its
date, is single voice with continuo accompaniment – that is, with a
bass line and harmonic filling-in on instruments like the lute or the
harpsichord but not with a full texture of melodic instrumental
parts. The vocal line varies greatly in speed, in rhythm, in style; the
older idea (of the 1590s) of imitating the ancient Greeks' heightened
speech still survived, but by this time a more naturally lyrical
musical expression was admitted. The most lyrical music – the love
duets, the lullaby, Otho's outpourings and all the warm expressions
of emotion – is cast in sweetly flowing triple metre; the exceptions
are the two big monologues of Octavia which are essentially expressions of grief and affronted dignity. The stiffness of her opening
music (ex. 1: 'Despised queen, afflicted wife of the Roman
emperor') contrasts revealingly with the supple, sensuous lines

Ex. 1

assigned to the lovers, where it is hardly too fanciful to see the
intertwining soprano voices as symbolizing the intertwining of
amorous limbs (ex. 2: 'No more shall delay be suffered; the glance of
your lovely eyes has robbed me of the heart in my breast').

There are two other distinct styles in the score. The secondary
characters, the manservant and maidservant, ·conduct their lighter
affairs in tones quite different from those proper to emperors and

Ex. 2

(would-be) empresses – the tones, in fact, of Monteverdi's lightweight madrigal-type works, the *Scherzi musicali*; quick-moving, in duple rather than triple rhythms, with vivacious lines and rapidly changing harmonies (ex. 3) – appropriate to the words, referring to 'a certain something' that 'tickles and delights'. Then,

Ex. 3

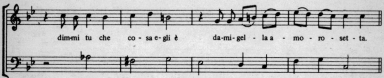

just occasionally, Monteverdi uses a true madrigal style; the pleas of
Seneca's 'famigliari' are couched in the strong musical language used
by Monteverdi and the other madrigalists, for example. These styles
were used by Monteverdi, in rather a different admixture, in *Il
ritorno d'Ulisse*, and by his successors, especially Cavalli, in the
operas composed in the decade or so after Monteverdi's death. There
is a hint of doubt, in fact, as to whether Monteverdi was truly the
composer of *Poppea* (the evidence that he was is from just one
unreliable source); whatever is the truth, this opera stands as beyond
question the greatest product – for its human insight and the sheer
beauty of its music – of the first half-century, perhaps even the first
century, of opera.

HENRY PURCELL

1659–95

Among the earliest operas holding the stage, especially in English-speaking countries, is an English one: *Dido and Aeneas*. It might be imagined that this is, so to speak, the choicest flower of a whole garden of English opera cultivated by Henry Purcell and his contemporaries. This is not so. *Dido and Aeneas* is a freak growth, standing almost on its own.

Purcell's teacher, John Blow (1649–1708), had written a short, all-sung musical drama, *Venus and Adonis*, presented at court about 1684; and to some extent this served as a model for *Dido and Aeneas*. But except in this work Purcell followed the taste of the town and provided 'operas' which we should rather call spectacular plays with music. Not all the characters sang. In *King Arthur* (1691), with libretto by Dryden, King Arthur himself does not sing a note. Such works have reasonably been termed 'semi-operas' by later historians. But *Dido and Aeneas*, despite its brevity (it plays for less than an hour) is a real, all-sung opera.

DIDO AND AENEAS
Libretto by Nahum Tate, after Virgil

First performed: Chelsea, London, 1689
Three Acts

Cast in order of singing:

BELINDA, LADY-IN-WAITING TO DIDO	*soprano*
DIDO, QUEEN OF CARTHAGE	*soprano*
ANOTHER LADY-IN-WAITING	*mezzo-soprano*
AENEAS, A TROJAN PRINCE	*tenor (or high baritone)*

A SORCERESS   *mezzo-soprano*
TWO WITCHES   *two sopranos*
A SPIRIT   *soprano*
A SAILOR   *tenor*

Chorus of courtiers, people, witches and sailors
The scene is laid in ancient Carthage

Josias Priest was a dancing-master who presumably met Purcell
when both were working in the London professional theatre. Priest
also ran a school for 'young gentlewomen' at Gorges House in
Chelsea (which was reckoned, at that time, near London but not
within London), and it was for this school that Purcell wrote *Dido
and Aeneas* – perhaps for an out-of-doors performance.

It is not known whether 'young gentlewomen' sang all the solo
roles except that of Aeneas and the sailor, or merely undertook the
top line of the chorus, plus the dancing. Professional singers must, to
a greater or lesser extent, have aided them. Aeneas's part is often
sung by a baritone today, but Purcell intended a tenor. The composer himself probably directed the performance from a harpsichord, as was then customary. Strings alone form the rest of the
orchestra.

The climax of the opera is Dido's farewell song, 'When I am laid in
earth'. With it, Dido, having been deserted by Aeneas (who has been
tricked into his desertion by witchcraft), dies – whether of a broken
heart or by suicide the text leaves in doubt. The emotional power of
this song, which has become a classic of the concert hall too, is partly
responsible for the success of the opera in both professional and
amateur performances.

★   ★   ★

ACT I: Belinda is endeavouring to cheer her royal mistress. The
courtiers recognize that love for Aeneas (who, having fled from the
sack of Troy, is a guest at the court) is making Dido unhappy; they
urge her to marry him and thus to unite the thrones of Carthage and
Troy. Aeneas enters and declares his love, and the music celebrates
the triumph of love as the courtiers depart on a hunting party.

ACT II: In a cave, a sorceress is conjuring up her witches. They hate
Dido and resolve to strike her by sending a false spirit, disguised as
Mercury, to make Aeneas leave; in the meantime they will raise a
storm to spoil the hunt. The spell is worked to an echo-chorus ('In

our deep vaulted cell' . . . '-ted cell'). A rapid dance movement, also using the echo principle, follows.

The scene changes to a grove, where the hunt is taking place. An air is sung by Belinda, and another ('Oft she visits') by the lady-in-waiting. Dido's women dance to entertain Aeneas, who displays the head of a boar he has killed. A storm arises and all flee back to town – all except Aeneas, to whom the false Mercury appears, announcing that Jove commands him to abandon the delights of love and sail away that very night. Aeneas laments but accepts the command. [Here should follow a scene and dance for the sorceress and witches: see below, page 32.]

ACT III: Aeneas's sailors, at the ships, are preparing for their departure; they sing, with one of them as soloist, a song with lines immemorially suited to their trade:

> Take a boozy short leave of your nymphs on the shore,
> And silence their mourning
> With vows of returning
> Though never intending to visit them more.

The sorceress and witches observe the spectacle with glee, their vengeful chorus alluding to Dido by her alternative name of Elissa:

> Destruction's our delight,
> Delight our greatest sorrow;
> Elissa bleeds tonight,
> And Carthage flames tomorrow.

The witches and sailors dance simultaneously.

Dido enters, heartbroken that Aeneas proposes to leave her. He says he will stay after all, but now Dido will have none of him. She dismisses him and he heads for his ships. A brief, grave chorus of courtiers leads to Dido's recitative, 'Thy hand, Belinda', preceding the air 'When I am laid in earth', in which the words 'Remember me' are instinctively repeated. Dido dies, a chorus mourns her; and the opera is over.

★　★　★

Purcell's marvellously apt musical setting of the English language shows itself particularly in recitative – and Aeneas, incidentally, has nothing but recitative to sing. The other numbers range, within one unified style, from the 'popular' idiom of the sailors' chorus to the 'learned' construction of a ground bass. Dido's first song, 'Ah,

Belinda', for example, is built on a regularly repeated four-bar phrase in the bass; so, too, is 'Oft she visits'. More subtle, because the repeated phrase is not four but five bars long, is the ground bass of 'When I am laid in earth' itself (ex. 1).

Ex. 1

[upper parts omitted]

There is a particular puzzle about the score of *Dido and Aeneas* as it has come down to us. A study of the rather complicated key structure of the opera suggests that some music is missing at the end of Act II; moreover, Purcell normally ends each scene of a major work with a chorus, which is not the case here. Suspicion grows more positive with the discovery that a contemporary printed libretto shows the act ending with six more lines (for the sorceress and witches) plus a dance. The probability is that Purcell did compose music for this – music which has now been lost. The practice of many modern editors and conductors is to supply music in its place from other works by Purcell.

JEAN-PHILIPPE RAMEAU

1683–1764

Rameau, born in Dijon, settled finally in Paris in the early 1720s, and was known as an organist, harpsichord composer and theorist; but his real ambitions lay in the opera-house. Not until he was fifty, however, did he actually have an opera given on the stage – belonging to the genre *tragédie lyrique*, the standard French form of serious opera. This, *Hippolyte et Aricie*, was a great success and Rameau was quick to follow it up. In 1735 *Les Indes galantes* was given – an *opéra-ballet*, a type of stage work usually in three or four *entrées* or acts connected by only a very slender thread of plot, often in spectacular and exotic settings, with dancing and choral as well as solo singing. More *tragédies* followed, of which *Castor et Pollux* (1737) and *Dardanus* (1739) are the best known. Of his other stage works, the *comédie-lyrique Platée* (1745) has been the most often revived. Rameau continued composing for the stage right up to the year of his death (when *Abaris, ou Les boréades* was in rehearsal), and he remained a centre of controversy – partly because of his depart-ures (which in fact were slight) from the revered model established by Jean-Baptiste Lully (1632–87), partly because, although he was deeply influenced by Italian music, he always represented in his day the French school as opposed to the Italian, at a time when Italian opera, and especially *opera buffa* (notably Pergolesi's *Le serva padrona*, given there in 1752 and 1756), became fashionable in Paris. Several Rameau operas have been revived since the 1960s, including some at the Paris Opéra (*Les Indes galantes* and *Dardanus*), and a number have been recorded. Unlike Italian operas of this period, French operas do not have clearcut divisions into recitative and aria; rather, the texture glides between a relatively lyrical kind of recitative, which strictly follows the syllabic quantities of the text in its free rhythm, and shorter *ariettes* or medium-length *airs* (these sometimes follow the *da capo* form, very common in Italian opera, in which the first part of an aria is repeated, perhaps with embellishment, after a middle section).

There are duets, too, and choruses and dances; almost every act of a French opera of this period has some kind of 'divertissement', a spectacular choral and balletic episode usually drawn into the main action only by an obvious contrivance – like a dream scene when a character is sleeping, or a nautical one when the action touches on the sea.

HIPPOLYTE ET ARICIE
(Hippolytus and Aricia)
Libretto by Simon–Joseph Pellegrin

First performed: Paris, 1733
Prologue and Five Acts

Cast in order of singing:

DIANA (Diane), THE GODDESS	*soprano*
CUPID (Amour), GOD OF LOVE	*soprano*
JUPITER	*bass*
A FOLLOWER OF CUPID	*contralto*
ARICIA (Aricie), A CAPTIVE ATHENIAN PRINCESS	*soprano*
HIPPOLYTUS (Hippolyte), SON OF THESEUS	*tenor*
A PRIESTESS OF DIANA	*soprano*
HIGH PRIESTESS OF DIANA	*soprano*
PHAEDRA (Phèdre), THESEUS'S SECOND WIFE	*soprano*
OENONE, PHAEDRA'S NURSE	*soprano*
ARCAS	*tenor*
THESEUS (Thésée), KING OF ATHENS	*baritone*
TISIPHON (Tisiphone), A FURY	*tenor*
PLUTO (Pluton), GOD OF THE UNDERWORLD	*bass*
THREE FATES	*countertenor, tenor, bass*
MERCURY (Mercure), MESSENGER OF THE GODS	*tenor*
A SAILOR	*soprano*
A HUNTRESS	*soprano*
NEPTUNE, GOD OF THE SEA	*bass*
A SHEPHERDESS	*soprano*

Chorus of nymphs and priestesses of Diana, inhabitants of the forest, infernal spirits, sailors, people of Troezen, hunters and huntresses, shepherds and shepherdesses
The scene is laid in Troezen in ancient Greece

While Italian opera plots were often historical (or at any rate pseudo-historical), and set in ancient Rome or medieval times, French ones usually drew on Greek mythology. France had a great tradition of classical theatre; the age of Racine, Corneille and Molière was only just past, and the playwrights and librettists of Rameau's day naturally leant on those writers. For *Hippolyte et Aricie*, the Abbé Simon-Joseph Pellegrin drew on Racine, whose *Phèdre* (1677) would have been well known to Rameau's audiences, and via him back to Euripides. But while Greek tragedies may end tragically, eighteenth-century operas had to end happily, for this was a world where reason was supposedly enthroned, where drama shows the triumph of right and the reward of virtue.

Like so many eighteenth-century operas, *Hippolyte et Aricie* underwent a certain amount of revision during its career on the stage. Rameau was keenly intellectual, even theoretical, in his approach to the theatre and continued to seek ways of improving his work. Sometimes, however, it was a matter of trimming it to the abilities of his singers: thus he removed Phaedra's air in Act III after the first performance, and later he excised the scene following it. In a revival of 1742 he removed the role of Arcas, the beginning of Act III, and the huntsmen's chorus in Act IV; and in a revival later still, in 1757, he removed the allegorical prologue – though that was more a matter of conforming with the new attitudes of the time, for these prologues (which in France had tended to be tributes to the king as much as true allegories about the ancient gods or abstract qualities) were no longer appropriate to the circumstances under which operas were performed. Rameau also made changes in the disposition of the dances.

There is one particularly interesting change between the original 1733 text and the 1742 one. At the end of Act III, Theseus, returning home, sees what he takes to be his son assaulting his wife; has to witness a welcoming ceremony with songs and dances; and only then can he vent his outrage. In the later version he gives expression to his feelings *before* the ceremony of welcome, which accordingly loses the dramatic irony it possesses in the first version; and the act ends with an unwonted (and uncontradicted) cheerfulness. It seems that the original audiences missed the effect of irony and Rameau accordingly separated tragedy and entertainment instead of boldly interleaving them. The synopsis below follows the original 1733 version.

★   ★   ★

PROLOGUE: In the forest, Diana's praises are sung by her nymphs; they are joined by the forest dwellers, whom Diana addresses, bidding them to chastity. Then Cupid appears, and the two dispute whether Cupid should enter Diana's sacred domain. Diana invokes Jupiter himself to give a ruling ('Arbitre souverain du ciel et de la terre' – 'Supreme arbiter of the heavens and the earth'); Jupiter descends, and rules that Fate cannot be defied and that Cupid must be permitted to enter Diana's forests for one day each year. He returns to the heavens, and Diana, admitting defeat, follows. Cupid celebrates his victory, and his followers dance a rondeau (sung by one of them), a gavotte, a pair of *menuets* and a march.

ACT I: Aricia, dressed as a huntress – and thus as a devotee of Diana – is alone in a temple dedicated to the goddess; as daughter of the late Athenian king, Pallas, she is to take a vow of chastity so that Theseus, who killed Pallas and others of his family, can eliminate his line. She bewails her situation and particularly her love for Hippolytus, Theseus's son ('Temple sacrée – 'Sacred temple'). Hippolytus enters, learns what is afoot and pleads with Aricia not to proceed; they reveal their mutual love, the fulfilment of which Aricia despairs of. Diana's priestesses arrive, and sing and dance two airs in Diana's honour. Now Phaedra (acting as regent in Theseus's absence) enters with Oenone and orders Aricia to take her vow; but Aricia declines to offer an unwilling heart to the goddess, and the priestesses agree with her sentiment. Phaedra demands that the ceremony go forward and asks Hippolytus to help, but he refuses; accordingly, she threatens to have the temple destroyed in face of this rebellious act. The High Priestess calls for thunderbolts from the gods, and thunder is duly heard. Diana appears, frees Aricia and reproaches Phaedra. Hippolytus leads Aricia off, and Phaedra expresses her anger, disclosing as she does that she herself loves Hippolytus. Arcas, a lieutenant of Theseus's, now arrives, and relates that he has seen Theseus (who is on an expedition to the underworld to abduct Proserpine, Pluto's consort) swallowed up in the earth; he must be presumed dead. He departs. Oenone points out to Phaedra that her passion for Hippolytus is now no longer adulterous and may be disclosed; perhaps Hippolytus will be tempted by union with a queen.

ACT II: Theseus is not in fact dead; we find him struggling with Tisiphon at the gates of Hades. His friend Peirithous has been killed, and he pleads for death. The gates open to reveal Pluto and the Three Fates. Pluto promises him only eternal torment, and sends him off in

Tisiphon's charge; he calls on the powers of the underworld to avenge him ('Qu'à servir mon courroux' – 'To serve my rage'). The infernal spirits echo him and dance two *airs infernels*. Theseus, searching for Peirithous, returns with Tisiphon. The Three Fates remind him that his destiny is in their hands. Now Theseus decides to call on his father, Neptune, for help ('Puisque Pluton est inflexible' – 'As Pluto is unyielding'). Mercury arrives, conveying from Neptune a request that Pluto forgive Theseus his crime; at first he refuses, but Mercury argues that the gods must exercise mutual goodwill, and he softens. He commands that Theseus be freed, and that the Three Fates tell him his destiny; in the famous 'Trio des Parques' they tell him that he can leave the underworld to find another hell in his own home.

ACT III: Phaedra, in a part of Theseus's palace by the sea coast, prays to Venus for forgiveness ('Cruelle mère des amours' – 'Cruel mother of our loves'). Oenone announces Hippolytus, who enters apologizing for his intrusion. Phaedra tells him his presence is by no means odious to her; he takes this to mean that she consents to his love, and swears to strengthen his father's throne – which she takes to mean that he is eager to succeed his father as her consort too. He, failing to grasp what she is saying, refers to his love for Aricia; she is enraged (duet: 'Ma fureur va tout entreprendre' – 'My fury shall undertake all'). Hippolytus, uncomprehending, asks why she threatens Aricia, and at last she discloses her love. He is appalled and calls on the gods to destroy her evil passion; and she, horrified at the situation, seizes his sword to kill herself. He snatches it back; and at this moment Theseus enters. He asks Phaedra to explain; she says only that love has been outraged, and departs. He turns to Hippolytus, who can only beg leave to withdraw. So he asks Oenone what has happened, and her hints lead him to think that his son was forcibly demanding Phaedra's love. Oenone leaves, and now a troupe of sailors and loyal subjects come to sing and dance in celebration of Theseus's safe homecoming ('Que ce rivage retentisse' – 'Let the shore resound'). The sailors dance airs and *rigaudons*, and eventually leave Theseus alone, to invoke Neptune's aid in the punishment of Hippolytus's incestuous crime ('Puissant maître des flots' – 'Mighty master of the waves'). The sea furiously surges as he sings.

ACT IV: Hippolytus is alone in a wood sacred to Diana, by the sea; he is in exile and laments his fate. Aricia joins him, and infers the reasons for his wretchedness. They reaffirm their love ('Nous allons nous jurer une immortelle foi' – 'We shall pledge an eternal troth').

Hunters enter; they sing and dance (an air, a gavotte and two *menuets*). Suddenly the wind rises, the sea rages, and a terrible monster emerges. All call on Diana for help, but none comes, and Hippolytus goes to challenge the monster; he is consumed by flames. Aricia falls unconscious; the hunters mourn Hippolytus's death; and Phaedra enters, to learn what has happened. She expresses her bitter remorse and begs the gods to spare her until she has told the true situation to Theseus.

ACT V: Theseus, who has learnt the true course of events from Phaedra as she died (by her own hand), is filled with remorse, and determines to die by throwing himself into the sea. But Neptune, appearing, prevents him, and tells him that Hippolytus still lives – though Theseus will never see him again.

The scene changes to a garden in Aricia's forest. She mourns her lost lover. Diana appears, with shepherds and shepherdesses; Aricia expresses her homage to the goddess. Diana tells her that she is to become queen of this domain and is to be married to a chosen king; the idea is hateful to Aricia. Hippolytus now arrives, transported by zephyrs; the lovers are happily reunited. All, including the forest dwellers, sing and dance in honour of the event (march and *chaconne*), a shepherdess sings a nightingale song ('Rossignols amoureux'), and there is further dancing (two gavottes).

★   ★   ★

All the characteristics of Rameau's operatic style are to be found in *Hippolyte et Aricie*: the brilliantly unorthodox dance music, often orchestrated in sharp and highly original colours; the intense mono-logues, usually with turbulent orchestral accompaniment to convey the anguish of the singer; the picturesque choral writing; the intel-lectual control. Rameau had a carefully calculated vocabulary of musical expression, with particular harmonic or melodic formulae representing particular emotions, though one is not aware of this while listening. But the listener familiar with Italian opera may be puzzled by the way he never yields to musical demands. For example, the reunion of Aricia and Hippolytus in Act V would, in an Italian work, call forth an extended, rapturous, lyrical number, a duet or an aria; here Rameau supplies thirty bars of dialogue in recitative, then a cool eighteen-bar duet. Anguish drew from him music of a more passionate kind, as in Theseus's monologue at the beginning of the act, where the restless and jerky rhythms in the orchestra underline his feelings (ex. 1) as he speaks of the remorse

Ex. 1

that tortures him and of the death of the perfidious Phaedra. Another
remarkable scene comes at the end of Act IV, when Phaedra,
entering, is told by the assembled people that Hippolytus has been
killed by a raging monster from the waves and owns her respon-
sibility for what has happened (ex. 2: the music continues with
distant thunder and an impassioned declamatory solo for Phaedra,
stricken with remorse).

Ex. 2

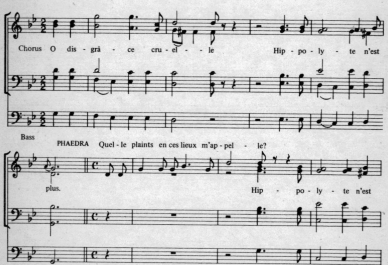

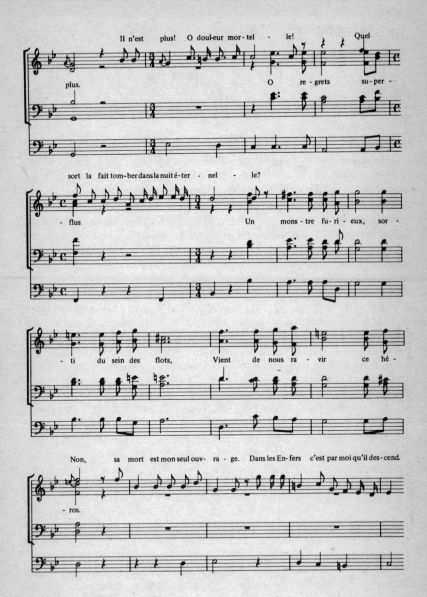

GEORGE FREDERICK HANDEL

1685–1759

Fifteen years after Purcell's death Handel first set foot in England; he was naturalized there in 1726. Though his larger works later took the form of English oratorios (on religious subjects) and other (non-religious) dramatic music not intended for the stage, his first years in London were chiefly devoted to establishing himself there as a composer of Italian opera. This type of opera – all sung, without spoken dialogue, using recitative accompanied by harpsichord to link the formal numbers – had captured fashionable taste all over Europe.

Meanwhile English native opera languished. The only English work of the period to achieve lasting success was *The Beggar's Opera* (1728); it is classified by historians as a 'ballad opera' because it uses well-known tunes of the day (set to new words, by John Gay) though it is basically not an opera in the usual sense but a play, calling for actors who can manage to deliver simple, short songs. Later versions, notably Frederic Austin's (1920) and Benjamin Britten's (1948), are considerably more 'operatic' than the original.

Serious Italian opera of Handel's type was long considered drama-tically stiff, largely because of the series of conventions by which it was governed: the clearcut separation of recitative and aria, with narrative and action in the former, contemplation in the latter; the use of the rather static *da capo* form (an *A–B–A* pattern) for the arias; the rule whereby each singer left the stage after an aria; the elaborate use of similes (a character comparing himself, for example, to a ship on a stormy sea, seeking a harbour); the allocation of the heroic roles to castrato singers; the hierarchical rules that dictated how many arias went to each singer; and the often contrived plots – mostly based on ancient or medieval tales, commonly involving dynastic struggles and amorous intrigue. More recently, audiences have come to accept the conventions for what they are, partly because of the growing historical awareness about baroque opera and its original performing circumstances – before an audience that (like many today) went partly to hear the most famous singers of the day, that followed the text in a bilingual libretto in a lighted theatre, and that did not subscribe to post-Verdi and post-Wagner ideals of dramatic realism but brought to the idiom considerable intellectual sophistication.

Handel was not a typical *opera seria* composer. On the European mainland, serious opera became dominated in his day by the Italian poet known as Metastasio (1698–1782), who was long 'imperial poet' in Vienna, and whose exquisitely polished texts, exalting the virtues of moral rectitude and its reward at the hands of the established order (the socio-political system dominated by the Catholic Habsburg monarchy), were regarded everywhere as a model, and were repeatedly set by such composers as Leonardo Vinci (*c*. 1690–1730), Leonardo Leo (1694–1744) and J. A. Hasse (1699–1783). But for English audiences, impatient of lengthy recitatives in a foreign tongue, and unlikely to appreciate the subtlety of Metastasian language, Handel had his librettists shorten the texts they used as their basis. Like most composers, Handel sometimes bent the conventions from time to time; but to call him a great dramatist on that account is to misunderstand him. His serious operas are the greatest of their day simply because the music itself is better – grander, more vivid, more characterful, more deeply felt – than that of any other opera composer of his time.

It is sometimes suggested that Handel's oratorios and similar works in English, to which the operatic conventions did not apply, gave fuller scope to his dramatic genius. Several of them have been revived on the stage, including *Samson* (1743; Covent Garden, 1959) and, with particular success, the secular works based on classical mythology (*Semele*, 1744; *Hercules*, 1745). But the importance of the chorus, and the ambiguity of its role (as commentator or participant), raises almost insuperable problems; Handel would have composed the works quite differently had he envisaged stage performance.

Among his true operas, which number close on forty (the early ones written in Hamburg and Italy, but the vast majority for London), the most often revived is *Giulio Cesare* ('Julius Caesar'), which indeed inaugurated the modern Handel revival in Germany in 1922 (admittedly in a corrupt edition); others to have made much impression include his first London opera, *Rinaldo* (1711), *Orlando* (1733), *Alcina* (1735) and the rather lighter *Serse* ('Xerxes', 1738 – the work from which 'Handel's Largo' comes).

GIULIO CESARE
Libretto by Nicola Haym, after G. F. Bussani

First performed: London, 1724
Three Acts

Cast in order of singing:

JULIUS CAESAR (Giulio Cesare)	*male alto*
CURIUS (Curio), A TRIBUNE	*bass*
CORNELIA, WIFE OF POMPEY	*contralto*
SEXTUS (Sesto), SON OF POMPEY AND CORNELIA	*male soprano*
ACHILLAS (Achilla), EGYPTIAN GENERAL,	
PTOLEMY'S ADVISER	*bass*
PTOLEMY (Tolomeo), KING OF EGYPT, CLEOPATRA'S	
YOUNGER BROTHER	*male alto*
CLEOPATRA, QUEEN OF EGYPT	*soprano*
NIRENUS (Nireno), CLEOPATRA'S ATTENDANT	*male alto*

Chorus of Romans, Egyptians
The scene in laid in Alexandria in 48BC

No opera of Handel's has been more successful, in his own day or in ours, than *Giulio Cesare*. Handel himself directed thirty-eight performances in London; most of the later ones included new arias to suit new singers who took over certain roles, for it was normal to modify an opera on revival so that it would be effective with the new cast. One particular change is of interest. The part of Sextus was composed for a female soprano, but at the revivals Handel used instead a tenor (at this period a voice rarely used for heroic roles, as it later came to be); Handel transposed some arias down an octave, but rewrote others completely. Like all of Handel's operas, it disappeared from the stage soon after his time. It was first revived in modern times at Göttingen in 1922, in a heavily corrupt edition, but was a success and was widely taken up elsewhere. A more authentic version was given by the Handel Opera Society in London in 1963; but the traditions of rewriting Handel were well established, and the famous New York City Opera production of 1966 (with Beverly Sills as Cleopatra and Norman Treigle, a baritone, as Caesar; subsequently recorded) used a new score prepared by the conductor Julius Rudel. The opera, a very long one, is usually cut. The English

National Opera brought it into their repertory in 1979, conducted by Charles Mackerras, with Janet Baker as Caesar.

Handel's operas rarely have a true chorus; the 'choral' items in this work (that is, the first number and the final one, and four bars in Act II) are intended to be sung by the principals, probably from offstage. The heroic role of Caesar is assigned to a castrato, originally the famous alto, Senesino; in modern times it has often been given to a baritone, but that is very damaging to the textures of the music (the voice keeps getting tangled up with the bass line in the orchestra) and far from properly heroic in effect. Ptolemy, too, is sometimes sung by a bass, in which case the character's shiftiness is apt to be forfeited; so, occasionally, is the small part of Nirenus, Cleopatra's eunuch attendant.

★ ★ ★

ACT I: Julius Caesar has just defeated Pompey and has thus in effect established himself as unchallenged dictator of Rome and its empire. He and his legions land by the Nile, to be acclaimed by the Egyptians. Pompey's wife and son, Cornelia and Sextus, come to plead for clemency for Caesar's rival; but then Achillas, Ptolemy's general, enters with a casket containing Pompey's head – Ptolemy had sought to ingratiate himself with this act of treachery, but Caesar is revolted and denounces his 'impious' act ('Empio, dirò, tu sei') before he leaves. Curius tries to console Cornelia with loving words, but she declares herself beyond consolation ('Priva son d'ogni conforto'). Sextus swears vengeance on his father's murderer ('Svegliatevi nel core').

In the royal palace, Cleopatra is planning to use her beauty to secure Caesar's help against her brother. Now Achillas tells Ptolemy of Caesar's reaction to his gift and offers, at the price of Cornelia's hand, to kill Caesar; Ptolemy, alone, vows revenge on the 'impious, treacherous' Caesar ('Empio, sleale').

By a memorial to Pompey (an urn with the ashes of his head and various trophies), Caesar contemplates his dead rival. A woman arrives; it is Cleopatra, but she is disguised as her maid and calls herself Lydia. Captivated by her beauty, Caesar agrees to help Cleopatra's cause. He leaves, but she conceals herself, as Cornelia comes, with Sextus, to her husband's memorial. 'Lydia' offers them help, and Sextus expresses pleasure at the prospect of revenge. Cleopatra looks forward to her success ('Tu la mia stella sei').

In the atrium of his palace, Ptolemy receives Caesar; neither trusts the other, and Caesar expresses his caution using a metaphor of the chase – the successful hunter is he who goes 'silent and concealed' ('Va tacito e nascosto'). He departs, and Cornelia – whose beauty now attracts Ptolemy himself as well as Achillas – enters with Sextus. Zealous for his father's honour, Sextus challenges Ptolemy to single combat, but Ptolemy promptly orders the arrest of both mother and son, sending Sextus to prison, Cornelia to the harem. They bid each other farewell, with Cornelia seeing herself as 'born to weep' ('Son nata a lagrimar').

ACT II: Cleopatra (as Lydia still) is attempting the seduction of Caesar: in a fanciful tableau she appears to him as Virtue, enthroned upon Parnassus, with her nine muses, and sings to him with an exotic accompaniment ('V'adoro, pupille'). Captivated, he follows her off, guided by Nirenus.

In the harem garden, the unhappy Cornelia is approached first by Achillas, and then by Ptolemy, who calls her 'pitiless' and threatens her ('Sì, spietata') when his suit too is rejected. Sextus enters and she encourages his determination to pursue revenge, in which Nirenus has offered to assist; Sextus vows his implacable resolve in an extravagant metaphor about an injured serpent who cannot rest ('L'angue offeso mai riposa').

Cleopatra awaits Caesar, and invokes Venus, goddess of Love ('Venere bella'). But no sooner has he arrived than Curius comes to warn him of the approach of Ptolemy's soldiers. Cleopatra discloses her true identity and urges him to flee, but he resolves to show the 'lightning-flash of arms' ('Al lampo dell' armi'). Caesar goes out to face his enemies as their shouts are heard; Cleopatra, alone, expresses her despair over her situation and the fate of the man she now finds she loves ('Se pietà').

Ptolemy, in his harem, is brought news by Achillas of Caesar's leap from a palace window into the sea and his apparent death by drowning. Cornelia is present with Sextus, and helps him screw up his courage.

ACT III: Achillas, because of Ptolemy's betrayal of him over Cornelia, decides to transfer his allegiance to Cleopatra. Sounds of battle are heard; Ptolemy's forces have triumphed, and Cleopatra is her brother's prisoner. She laments her situation and fate ('Piangerò la sorte mia').

Caesar is still living, having swum to safety from the 'peril of the waves' ('Dall'ondoso peroglio . . . Aure, deh, per pietà'). He conceals himself as the mortally wounded Achillas arrives with Sextus, to whom he hands his ring, the symbol of his authority by which Sextus should be able to gain entry to the palace. Caesar discloses himself and takes charge ('Qual torrente, che cade del monte'). Sextus looks forward to the just punishment of Ptolemy.

Cleopatra is mourning her situation when she hears a clash of arms and, to her astonished delight, Caesar bursts in; she compares herself to a storm-beaten ship that has found a haven ('Da tempeste il legno infranto').

Ptolemy again tries to press his love upon Cornelia; she threatens him with a dagger, but now Sextus enters and kills him.

To ceremonial music, Caesar and Cleopatra enter, with Egyptian followers; then come Curius and Nirenus, Sextus and Cornelia, and a page bearing Ptolemy's crown and sceptre. Caesar and Cleopatra sing of their love, he crowns her Queen of Egypt, and all celebrate the happy outcome.

★　★　★

Most of the arias in Handel's operas, like those of other composers of the time, are accompanied just by the string instruments (often the violins in unison) and a bass continuo line; sometimes the wind instruments are called in to double the strings. But occasionally, for special effect, the wind instruments are used colourfully, for example when recorders imitate birds in *Rinaldo*, or in *Giulio Cesare* when a horn evokes the hunt in Caesar's 'Va tacito'. Probably the most picturesque piece of orchestral writing in Handel's entire

Ex. 1

output appears in the Parnassus scene, Cleopatra's entertainment designed to entrance Caesar, in this opera, where the orchestra includes, besides strings, oboes and bassoons, a harp, a theorbo (a large lute) and a viola da gamba – all on or behind the stage to provide a sensuous instrumental halo to her song (ex. 1).

Macbeth, it is sometimes said, ought to have been called *Lady Macbeth*; and *Giulio Cesare* might well have been called *Cleopatra*, for her character is so richly and fascinatingly drawn in the music. Usually the idea of developing characterization is alien to baroque opera, but it is clear that Handel had in mind her starting as a spirited,

Ex. 2

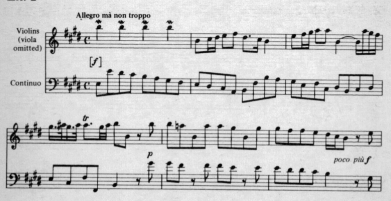

ambitious young woman (as in her first aria, ex. 2, where she ironically tells her brother not to despair), then, falling prey to her own scheming as well as to the power of Caesar's personality, gradually falling in love with him, so that the emotion she expresses in her penultimate aria is deeply felt (ex. 3), as she vows lifelong mourning for the cruelty of her fate. Her sequence of arias (she has eight in all) represents one of Handel's greatest achievements in terms of insight into human character and integrity in its portrayal. Incidentally, it is amusing to note that the singer for whom the role

Ex. 3

vi - ta in pet - to a-vrò;

was written, Francesca Cuzzoni, was famed for her ringing top E, and that Handel set three of her eight arias in the rare key of E major and three in A major or its relative minor, where the note would always figure prominently.

ALCINA
Libretto by an unknown author, adapted from 'L'isola di Alcina', an opera given in 1728, based on an episode in Ariosto's 'Orlando furioso'

First performed: London, 1735
Three Acts

Cast in order of singing:

MORGANA, ALCINA'S SISTER	*soprano*
ALCINA, AN ENCHANTRESS	*soprano*
RUGGIERO, A KNIGHT, BETROTHED TO BRADAMANTE	*male alto*
BRADAMANTE	*contralto*
ORONTE, ALCINA'S GENERAL	*tenor*
MELISSO, BRADAMANTE'S GUARDIAN	*bass*

Chorus of Alcina's attendants and her former lovers
The scene is laid on Alcina's magic island

Handel's operas are sometimes categorized, very roughly, into three groups: the heroic, the anti-heroic, and the magic. Most of the heroic ones date from the 1720s or early 1730s, the time when opera in London was underwritten by a company called, in imitation of the

Académie Royale de Musique in Paris, the Royal Academy of Music (unconnected, of course, with the later institution of that name). They include *Giulio Cesare* and several others of the particularly fine group composed around that time, like *Tamerlano* (1724), *Rodelinda* (1725), *Scipione* (1726) and *Admeto* (1727). The anti-heroic ones mostly came towards the end of his time of composing operas, that is, the late 1730s, and prominent among them is *Serse* (1738), though other, earlier operas whose libretto sources have Venetian connections tend to fall into this class, like *Partenope* (1730). The magic operas, a fairly small group, are mostly based on the epic Italian poetry of Ariosto or Tasso, and depend on some transformation or similar happening for their dénouement or indeed for other events in their plots. This means, generally, that they are less concerned with dramatic realism than with providing situations that give rise to strong and varied emotions (and thus allow the composer wide scope) and with the exploitation of the baroque theatre's capacity for the spectacular – spectacle was an important part of the attraction to audiences at this period. All this applies to *Alcina*, the tale of a sorceress on an enchanted island. *Orlando* is another example of the 'magic' type.

Unlike most of Handel's operas, *Alcina* includes ballet – not because of inner dramatic need but because Handel, eager to outshine the rival opera company that had lately been established, was working with the famous French dancer Marie Sallé and her troupe during the 1734–5 season (it is quite possible that their availability led him to this particular plot, where they could serve a good dramatic purpose). The opera is also exceptional in calling for a true chorus, not just an ensemble of soloists. *Alcina* is a fairly long opera, and in most modern performances the character of Oberto is omitted; the episodes concerning him are excluded from the synopsis below, as are other sections that are generally left out. The last aria in Act I is sometimes – unsuitably, although Handel himself provided the precedent – assigned to Alcina rather than her sister Morgana. The opera has had numerous revivals over the last few decades, not only for the striking quality of its music but also for the brilliant and demanding central role of the sorceress Alcina herself.

★   ★   ★

ACT I: Bradamante (in male attire, as a warrior) and her guardian Melisso have been searching for Ruggiero, Bradamante's betrothed, and are shipwrecked on an island ruled by the enchantress, Alcina. They are met by Alcina's sister, Morgana, who is attracted to Bradamante and begins to fall in love with 'him'.

Suddenly there is lightning and thunder, and the scene dissolves. Alcina is seen in her palace with Ruggiero. Her attendants sing in praise of the delights of her island; a ballet follows. Alcina welcomes the strangers and bids Ruggiero entertain them; she herself sings of her love for him: 'Di, cor mio' ('Say, my heart').

Alcina goes, and Bradamante and Melisso try to remind Ruggiero of his duty towards his betrothed, Bradamante (Bradamante herself poses as Ricciardo, her own brother), but he says that he now loves only Alcina. Oronte, Alcina's general, enters, he loves Morgana and denounces 'Ricciardo', who seems to be his rival. Bradmante addresses Oronte and Morgana alternately in an aria about jealousy: 'È gelosia'.

Oronte tells Ruggiero that Alcina herself is attracted by 'Ricciardo', and that he (Ruggiero) may soon join Alcina's former lovers in their various forms as wild beasts, trees and the like, to which she has transformed them. He warns Ruggiero that only a simple person would believe a woman: 'Semplicetto! a donna credi'.

Alcina joins Ruggiero and denies his charge that she is fickle. She leaves. Bradamante tells Ruggiero of her true identity, although Melisso tries to stop her. Ruggiero, however, does not believe she is other than 'Ricciardo': 'La bocca vaga' ('A sweet mouth').

Melisso and then Morgana try to persuade Bradamante to leave the dangerous island. But Bradamante is still determined to reclaim Ruggiero, and will not. Morgana, still believing that Bradamante is 'Ricciardo' and in love with her, promises to intercede with Alcina, who will be furious on finding that 'Ricciardo' evidently prefers another to her. Morgana sings of her love for 'Ricciardo', bidding him return and captivate her: 'Tornami a vagheggiar'.

ACT II: In a hall of Alcina's palace, Ruggiero sings of his love for her. Melisso enters in the form of Atlante, Ruggiero's former tutor. Ruggiero is confused. Melisso puts a magic ring on Ruggiero's finger, breaking Alcina's spell. The splendid hall becomes an empty desert, and Ruggiero returns to his senses and no longer feels love for Alcina. Melisso (now also in his normal form) reminds him of his betrothed, Bradamante, and 'consider the one who weeps for him': 'Pensa a chi geme'.

Bradamante herself enters. But still Ruggiero is not convinced of her identity, suspecting some further plot on Alcina's part. Bradamante sings angrily of Ruggiero's faithlessness and her desire for revenge: 'Vorrei vendicarmi'. Ruggiero, alone, expresses his confusion mixed with delight: 'Mi lusinga'.

Near her gardens, Alcina is about to transform the uncompliant 'Ricciardo' into a 'brutal shape', but Morgana interrupts her. Ruggiero enters and assures the doubting Alcina of his love (with asides making it clear that his love is really no longer for her).

Oronte comes to Alcina and tells her that Ruggiero intends to leave her. She is both heart-broken and determined on vengeance: 'Ah! mio cor!' ('Ah, my heart!'). Oronte then tells Morgana that her 'lover' is also unfaithful. But she still rejects the love which Oronte himself offers; she goes, and he sings 'È un folle' ('It is mad').

Bradamante and Ruggiero (at last free of illusions) enter and embrace, but are seen by the jealous Morgana who angrily goes off to Alcina. Ruggiero bids farewell to the 'verdant meadows' of the enchanted island: 'Verdi prati'.

Alcina, alone in an underground room, sings of her desertion by the cruel Ruggiero: 'Ah! Ruggiero crudel'. She tries to summon her evil spirits to her aid, but they do not appear: 'Ombre pallide' ('Ye pale ghosts'). She goes off in a rage.

ACT III: Morgana too is now free of illusion. She realizes that 'Ricciardo', whom she loved, is a woman, Bradamante. In a court of the palace, she asks her former suitor, Oronte, to believe in her grief: 'Credete al mio dolore'. She departs; before he follows, Oronte admits that he still loves her.

Alcina reproaches Ruggiero for leaving her and swears revenge: 'Ma quando tornerai' ('But when you return'). She leaves and Bradamante enters with Melisso. They talk of the danger of leaving the island: Ruggiero, having to part momentarily from Bradamante, compares his situation to that of a tigress having to leave its young: 'Sta nell' Ircana'. Bradamante determines to restore the bewitched former lovers to life: 'All'alma fedel' ('To a faithful soul').

Alcina learns from Oronte that Ruggiero and Bradamante are conquering the island before leaving. She expresses her grief, saying that her tears remain: 'Mi restano le lagrime'.

Ruggiero and Bradamante enter, intent on breaking Alcina's spell before they leave the island. Alcina tries to dissuade them by friendship, in a trio: 'Non è amor, nè gelosia' ('This is neither love nor jealousy'). Ruggiero breaks the urn in which Alcina's magical

powers are vested; she, with Morgana, vanishes. Alcina's former
lovers return to life. Their choruses of joy, and a ballet, end the
opera.

★   ★   ★

One of the strongest weapons in Handel's musical and dramatic
armoury was his fertile and apt melodic gift. At Ruggiero's farewell
to Alcina's enchanted island, the melody in which he recalls its
'verdant meadows and pleasant woods' (whose beauty will vanish as
the magic spell is removed) is not merely intensely beautiful in itself,
but also serves to convey the mixed feelings – a twinge of nostalgic
regret as well as joy and relief – which he experiences (ex. 1).

In a style whose musical patterns are mostly very regular, a
notable dramatic effect is made by deliberately breaking these patterns. Handel does this several times. One splendid example is at the
beginning of Act II, where Ruggiero's aria trails off into recitative on
the sudden entry of the disguised Melisso. Another example occurs
in Alcina's 'Ah! mio cor'. In an aria of this period it is normal for the
singer to enter with the same music as has just been heard in the
orchestral introduction; here Alcina enters with an unaccompanied
'sighing' phrase ('Ah! my heart'), and then goes on with a new
counter-theme ('You [my heart] are scorned!') to the original introduction, heard again in the orchestra. The effect is both arresting and
moving (ex. 2).

One customary pattern running through all opera of this kind is the sequence of recitative (accompanied by harpsichord) followed by aria (accompanied by orchestra). This pattern could be broken by using 'accompanied recitative' – recitative in which the orchestra (not just the harpsichord) accompanies, usually in dramatic and illustrative style. There is one such movement in *Alcina*, in the scene at the end of Act II where Alcina tries to conjure up her evil spirits. Oddly enough, the most striking part of this so-called 'accompanied recitative' is entirely unaccompanied. Alcina's agitation is expressed by the chromaticism and the wide 'skips' in her music. 'I seek you, yet you hide? I command you, yet you are silent? Has my magic wand no power?' she complains; and the utter emptiness and silence around her phrases conveys her solitude as the spirits fail to respond (ex. 3).

Ex. 3

CHRISTOPH WILLIBALD VON GLUCK

1714–87

Gluck, a Bohemian–German who settled in Vienna, greatly admired Handel but rebelled against the formal conventions of the kind of Italian opera which Handel wrote. His aim – in the latter part of his career – was to make opera more truly and more naturally dramatic, more concerned with the powerful representation of emotion and less with displaying singers' virtuosity.

But because the abuses which Gluck rebelled against are largely unfamiliar today, the extent of his reforming zeal is now not too evident, and even Gluck's own operas seem sometimes a little formal and stiff. In particular the appearances and miracles of classical deities introduce a note of artificiality. Such appearances mark his two most celebrated 'reform' operas, *Orfeo ed Euridice* and *Alceste* (written to Italian texts in 1762 and 1767 respectively, later revised with French ones), as well as the later French operas *Iphigénie en Aulide* and *Iphigénie en Tauride* (1774, 1779). None the less, all these are heard today, the two first particularly.

ORFEO ED EURIDICE
(Orpheus and Eurydice)
Libretto by Ranieri Calzabigi

Italian version first performed: Vienna, 1762
French version (*Orphée et Euridice*) first performed: Paris, 1774
Three Acts

Cast in order of singing:

ORPHEUS	*male alto*
EROS	*soprano*
A BLESSED SPIRIT	*soprano*
EURYDICE	*soprano*

Chorus of Shepherds and shepherdesses, furies, demons and blessed spirits
The scene is laid in Ancient Greece, Hades and the Elysian Fields

The story of Orpheus and Eurydice has appealed to many composers of opera – from Peri and Monteverdi (already mentioned) to Haydn (1791) and on to Darius Milhaud (1892–1974), who, in *Les malheurs d'Orphée* ('The Sorrows of Orpheus', 1926) transposed the action to modern times. According to legend, Orpheus's magical power as a musician enabled him to regain his wife from the dead on condition that he did not look at her on the journey back from Hades – a condition it proved impossible to fulfil. In Gluck's opera a further miracle then happens so that Eurydice is resurrected and joins him after all.

Despite the artificiality of this resurrection, Gluck's *Orfeo* is felt as deeply expressive of real emotion – human love, the terror of hidden dark forces, the vision of unearthly bliss. Chorus and orchestra are fully used by Gluck to deepen the pathos suggested by the plight of the protagonist.

In most modern productions, the role of Orpheus is sung by a contralto. (The practice was established with the historic revival of the opera in 1859 by Berlioz, an ardent champion of Gluck.) This was not Gluck's intention. He wrote the role for a castrato male alto, and later rewrote it with a tenor for the Paris production in French in 1774 because the French would not countenance *castrato* singers. This rewriting of the title-role, with some consequent shifts in the keys, was not the only change Gluck made in the French version. Modern performances generally adopt some features of the original (Italian) score, some of the French one.

The god of Love appears in the original score under his Latin name, Amor; proper English usage, alongside the other Greek names, is Eros.

★   ★   ★

ACT I: Orpheus and his friends are weeping at the tomb of Eurydice. When he dismisses them, Orpheus sings of his passionate grief, calling on his beloved: 'Chiamo il mio ben'. In answer to his cries Eros, the god of Love, appears. He tells Orpheus that Zeus has had pity on him and will allow him to go down to Hades, charm its guardians by the power of his music, and bring Eurydice back – provided he does not look at her on the way (or explain why he cannot). Orpheus, confident, sets out.

ACT II: At the mouth of Hades, the furies and demons at first violently resist Orpheus's coming, with repeated shouts of 'No!'. He seeks to soothe them ('Deh placatevi'), and eventually they give way to the new emotion they feel ('Ah, quale incognito affetto'). The furies and demons disappear; the gates of the Elysian Fields open and the Dance of the Blessed Spirits is heard. Led by one of their number, the Spirits sing of their joyous existence in this beautiful place ('Questo asilo').

Orpheus himself now enters the Elysian Fields: 'Che puro ciel' ('What a clear sky'). Eurydice is led to him, and he (not looking at her, in obedience to the command) leads her away, as the Blessed Spirits look on and encourage her to return ('Torna, o bella').

ACT III: Eurydice, uncomprehending, grows restive and suspicious; it seems that Orpheus no longer loves her: 'Che fiero momento' ('What a terrible moment'). He tries vainly to soothe her. At length he can no longer resist Eurydice's urging, turns, and embraces her; immediately she dies.

Orpheus gives way to his grief: 'Che farò' senza Euridice?' ('What shall I do without Eurydice?'). He is on the point of joining his wife in death when Eros again appears, tells Orpheus that his constancy has been tested enough, and restores Eurydice to him. A chorus and ballet in praise of love formally seal the opera.

★   ★   ★

It is in this opera that Orpheus sings Gluck's most famous air, 'Che farò senza Euridice?' It is a strange air because, despite its pathetic words and the sense of agonized loss which it supposedly expresses, its straightforward, major-key tune has none of the purely musical features which normally convey pathos or agony (see ex. 1).

The use of the chorus as a main participant in the drama was a revolutionary step on Gluck's part. So was his dispensing with so-called 'dry recitative' (accompanied only by the harpsichord, as in Handel's operas) and having all recitative accompanied by the

Ex. 1

orchestra, thus helping to make recitative and aria sound more nearly homogeneous and avoiding breaks in continuity. Equally individual is Gluck's imaginative use of the orchestra. The furies and demons call on Cerberus (the three-headed dog who according to mythology stands guard at the entrance to Hades) to destroy the interloper, and the terrifying barking of the monster is represented by a weird orchestral sound which sends cellos and double-basses sliding up to repeated, emphatic high notes (ex. 2).

Ex. 2

There are other remarkable instrumental effects in *Orfeo*, for example the cornett (a near obsolete instrument, of wood but akin to a trumpet) and the chalumeau (a lowish clarinet-like instrument) in Orpheus's Act I lament. But the most famous one is the flute solo in the Dance of the Blessed Spirits, written for the Paris version – this 'celestial' melody, with its expressive sighs, could belong to no other instrument.

WOLFGANG AMADEUS MOZART

1756–91

In contrast to serious eighteenth-century Italian opera, with its plots concerning lofty heroes and heroines in remote times, there grew up a type of Italian comic opera which dealt with the present day and put dramatic emphasis on intrigue and absurdity. This type of opera (often referred to as *opera buffa*, which is just the Italian for 'comic opera') was originally often performed as an interlude in the performance of a serious opera (*opera seria*). Like its serious relative, *opera buffa* used recitative and not spoken dialogue to link the songs.

The centre of this type of Italian comic opera was Naples, and it was there in 1733 that the most famous example (and almost the only one still performed today) had its first performance: *La serva padrona* ('The Maid as Mistress') by Pergolesi (1710–36). Later in the century, however, the initiative in comic opera passed to Venice, stimulated by the deft and ingenious librettos of Carlo Goldoni (1707–93).

Comic opera of this type – especially in its device of putting all the characters on the stage together so that by singing 'against' each other they can represent a point of maximum dramatic complexity – is an important ingredient in the operatic style of Mozart, as in *Le nozze di Figaro*. He also used the 'lofty' style of serious Italian opera in two mature works, *Idomeneo* and *La clemenza di Tito*. His German operas, *Die Entführung aus dem Serail* and *Die Zauberflöte* differ from his Italian not merely in language but in using elements of a more popular musical style and in using spoken dialogue in place of recitative. This type of German opera was of recent origin: in its simpler form it was called *Singspiel* (literally, a singing play).

IDOMENEO
Idomeneo, Rè di Creta
(Idomeneus, King of Crete)

Libretto by Giambattista Varesco
First performed: Munich, 1781
Three Acts

Cast in order of singing:

ILIA, A TROJAN PRINCESS, PRISONER TO THE CRETANS	*soprano*
IDAMANTES (Idamante), SON OF IDOMENEUS	*male soprano*
ELECTRA (Elettra), A GREEK PRINCESS, REFUGEE IN CRETE	*soprano*
ARBACES (Arbace), FRIEND OF IDAMANTES	*tenor*
IDOMENEUS (Idomeneo), KING OF CRETE	*tenor*
THE HIGH PRIEST OF NEPTUNE	*tenor*

Chorus of people, priests, soldiers and dancers
The scene is laid in ancient Crete

This is an 'old-fashioned' opera by the young Mozart using a classical plot (King Idomeneus, 'Idomeneo' in Italian, is mentioned in Homer and Virgil), rather stiff action and stilted language. The original cast had a castrato soprano as the youthful hero, Idamantes, best replaced today by a female voice. But the substitution of a tenor is acceptable if the version performed is that which Mozart himself revised for a concert performance in Vienna, using a tenor. The contrast in music between the two women who are rivals for the young man's love is very effective. The quartet in the third act was considered by Edward J. Dent 'perhaps the most beautiful ensemble ever composed for the stage', and the chorus of farewell in the preceding act has enjoyed fame even when the opera has remained unperformed. The two arias for Arbaces, a subordinate role, are usually omitted in the theatre so as to tauten the action and reduce the opera's excessive length.

*　*　*

ACT I: Ilia, a Trojan princess, gives vent to her torn feelings. The Cretans, to whom she is prisoner, are her enemies – but how can she hate them when she has fallen in love with Idamantes, the king's son? She fears he loves Electra. Idamantes enters and declares his admiration for her. The Cretan people and their Trojan prisoners sing together in praise of peace, for King Idomeneus's returning fleet has been sighted.

Electra, as a refugee from Greece, is outraged at the mercy shown to the Trojans, her people's enemies. But she is interrupted by Arbaces with the news that Idomeneus's ship has been wrecked. Electra rages: if the king dies, what can stop Idamantes from marrying her rival, Ilia?

Electra's aria of rage merges into the rage of a storm on a deserted beach, where the people implore the god's mercy for the shipwrecked sailors (who are heard in the distance). Eventually Idomeneus himself lands, dismisses his attendants and reveals that he vowed, if he were saved from the storm, to sacrifice to Neptune the first person he met.

The first person he meets is Idamantes, his son. They have not seen one another for many years and do not recognize each other: when he discovers who Idamantes is, Idomeneus turns away in horror, leaving his son alone to express his puzzlement. The people enter, rejoicing at the king's safety and honouring Neptune.

ACT II: Idomeneus discloses his terrible secret to his friend, Arbaces, who advises him to send Idamantes away to avoid his fate. Idomeneus decides to let Idamantes escort Electra back to Greece. Arbaces, after an aria, departs; Ilia enters and tells Idomeneus of her gratitude in finding a second homeland in Crete and a second father in him: 'Se il padre perdei' ('If I lost my father'). As she leaves, Idomeneus realizes that she loves his son: alas, it seems that Neptune will claim as victims not only Idamantes but Ilia and Idomeneus too. He sings of the disquiet in his heart: 'Fuor del mar ho un mar in seno'. ('Though saved from the sea I have a [stormy] sea in my breast').

Electra sings happily of the prospect of being accompanied by Idamantes. A march calls her to the harbour to embark, where a chorus bids her a gentle farewell: 'Placido è il mar, andiamo' ('Calm is the sea, let us depart'). As Idamantes and Electra take leave of Idomeneus, a fearful storm breaks and a monster arises from the sea, indicating the gods' anger. While the people flee in terror Idomeneus declares he is the guilty one.

ACT III: Ilia sings of her love for Idamantes: 'Zeffiretti lusinghieri' ('Playful breezes'). Idamantes enters; the two declare their love. Idomeneus and Electra enter. Idomeneus has still not told his son about his vow, and now simply bids him go and never return. Ilia is in despair and Electra furious and vengeful over Idamantes's impending departure. A quartet follows, begun by Idamantes: 'Andrò ramingo e solo' ('I shall go sadly all alone'); then there is an aria for Arbaces.

The sea monster has ravaged the city and killed thousands. At last, in the temple, the king discloses to the people the vow he made. To avert further disaster, the High Priest and the people call on him to fulfil it. King and priests utter a prayer to Neptune. A shout arises from outside: Idamantes has killed the monster. Now, having learnt about his father's vow, Idamantes presents himself for slaughter. Ilia wishes to take his place: But at the last moment Neptune's oracle intervenes, decreeing that Idomeneus is deposed, and Idamantes is to be king with Ilia as his bride. After expressing her fury, Electra leaves. Idomeneus presents to the people their new king and a chorus of rejoicing ends the opera.

★ ★ ★

Mozart wrote *Idomeneo* not long after his return from Paris. During his stay in the French capital a paper 'war' had been afoot between the supporters of Gluck's reform operas and those who preferred the traditional style, represented by Niccola Piccinni (1728–1800), one of those composers whose celebrity in his own time was not as now. Mozart – by instinct rather than conscious intention – steered a middle course in *Idomeneo*. Neither he, his singers nor his public wanted to break down, as Gluck was aiming to do, the conventional structure of recitatives and 'set-piece' arias. In this, and in his use of the chorus, Mozart followed Piccinni's example.

None the less, there is a debt to Gluck: in the great ritual invocation in the temple in Act III, and on the use of accompanied recitative for particularly dramatic passages. A good example is the moment where Idomeneus and Idamantes recognize one another (ex. 1). It must be remembered that Idomeneus – and the audience – realize the consequences of the situation but Idamantes does not. Idomeneus' exclamation 'Oh ye pitiless gods!' is thus greeted by his son with puzzlement: 'Do you join with me in lamenting my father's fate?' Only when Idomeneus lets fall the word 'figlio' (son) does Idamantes know that the father he has lost stands before him.

Ex. 1

The musical language of the opera is in general rather formal. But when, for special effect, Mozart breaks with this formality, powerful emotional stress results. Thus, notably, the phrase with which

Idamantes opens the great quartet in Act III is repeated towards the end; but instead of leading, as before, to an ensemble, it breaks off and the orchestra takes over, and concludes, the music: Idamantes is evidently overcome, and words fail him (ex. 2).

Ex. 2

To emphasize the solemnity of the utterance of the oracle, Mozart brings trombones into the score, as similarly in *Don Giovanni* and *Die Zanberflöte* – though it is doubtful whether they were in fact used in the original performances.

DIE ENTFÜHRUNG AUS DEM SERAIL
(The Abduction from the Harem)
Libretto by G. Stephanie, after a libretto by C. F. Bretzner

First performed: Vienna, 1782
Three Acts

Cast in order of singing or speaking:

BELMONTE, A SPANISH NOBLEMAN	*tenor*
OSMIN, OVERSEER OF THE PASHA'S HAREM	*bass*
PEDRILLO, SERVANT TO BELMONTE	*tenor*
THE PASHA SELIM	*speaking part*
CONSTANZE, A SPANISH NOBLEWOMAN	*soprano*
BLONDE, CONSTANZE'S ENGLISH MAID	*soprano*

Chorus of janissaries, Turkish women, etc.
The scene is laid in Turkey

A common British practice is to refer this opera as *The Seraglio*. This Italian term (in modern Italian spelt *serraglio*) is apparently taken from the Latin word for a door-bar in confusion with the Turkish word for a palace. The Italian term has long been used in English. But this is not an Italian opera: English reference to the work with the Italian article (*Il Seraglio*) have their origin in the fact that virtually all non-Italian operas (even *The Flying Dutchman*) were, from alleged convenience to singers, mounted in Italian in 19th-century London. *Die Entführung* is in fact a German opera with spoken dialogue, written for the company that had been specially established for such works by the Emperor Joseph II in Vienna.

It is a comedy about Europeans in a Turkish Pasha's harem, and its chief ingredients are conventional: a well-to-do hero and heroine who are serious characters, and the hero's manservant and the heroine's maidservant who are comic. The most memorable character, however, is none of these but the overseer of the harem, Osmin – a comic villain and one of the great comic characters of opera. But there is the musical appeal of one of the most famous of all coloratura arias (in which the heroine defies the threat of torture) to add in this opera to the appeal of the comedy, which includes a 'drunk' scene with appropriately rib-tickling music. An oddity of the work is that the Pasha (who in the end is magnanimous enough to let his captives go of his own free will) does not sing at all. There are other inconsistencies of style in the work, but Mozart's felicitous contribution outweights all defects.

★　★　★

ACT I: Finding himself outside a big country house, Belmonte wonders whether it belongs to the Pasha Selim and if he will find his lost love, Constanze, there. But he gets no satisfaction when he inquires of the Pasha's overseer, Osmin. Osmin persists in singing to himself – 'Wer ein Liebchen hat gefunden' ('He who has found a sweetheart') – and in taking no notice of his questioner. He discloses, however, that he hates Pedrillo, who is also in the Pasha's service. And when Belmonte leaves and Pedrillo appears, Osmin shows his hatred.

Osmin leaves. Belmonte returns, finds Pedrillo (his own former servant, now the Pasha's gardener), and learns that Constanze is still true to him. Belmonte decides to pose as an eminent visiting architect who could be useful to the Pasha. Before he leaves, he sings of his love: 'O wie ängstlich' (Oh, how anxious').

The Pasha enters, attended by his suite. He attempts to woo Constanze but she declares she loves another: 'Ach, ich liebte' ('Ah, I have loved'). Constanze leaves, the Pasha accepts the proffered services of Belmonte, and the enmity of Osmin towards Belmonte and Pedrillo is shown in a brisk trio.

ACT II: In the garden, Blonde (Constanze's maid) sings of her longing for a tender wooer, and in her duet with the coarse Osmin shows the cool disdain appropriate to an Englishwoman.

Constanze, after the Pasha has again attempted to woo her, bewails her sad fate and then voices her defiance: 'Martern aller Arten' ('Tortures of every kind').

A catchy song for Blonde, looking forward to her release, is followed by one in which Pedrillo sings of his approaching 'battle' – the battle being concerned with overcoming Osmin by making him drunk, despite the Prophet's injunction against liquor. This is accomplished in a rapid, brief drinking duet, 'Vivat Bacchus', and Osmin is led off. The four lovers are united, Belmonte greeting Constanze ecstatically, and then all join in a quartet in which the two men are ready to suspect the women of infidelity but are convincingly reprimanded (Pedrillo with a box on the ear from Blonde). The quartet is developed at length, to affirm the sentiments of love.

ACT III: It is midnight; Belmonte and Pedrillo are about to put their plan of escape into action. Pedrillo sings, as a signal to the women, the 'oriental' serenade 'In Mohrenland' ('In the Moors' land'). But Osmin, waking, interrupts the attempted abduction, refuses a bribe from Belmonte, arrests the four would–be escapers and rejoices: 'Ha! wie will ich triumphieren' ('Ha, how I shall triumph').

The Pasha, hearing who Belmonte really is, discloses that he himself was wronged by Belmonte's father. In revenge, all four captives shall be tortured. A duet of anguish for Belmonte and Constanze follows. But the Pasha, reappearing, announces that he despises Belmonte's father too much to follow his example and will set the captives free. All four join in giving thanks to the Pasha for his magnanimity; and the frustrated Osmin joins in too, with an empty repetition of the threats in his original song of hatred against Pedrillo (Act I). Osmin apart, their rejoicing is universal as the opera ends.

★ ★ ★

At the opening of the eighteenth century the percussion instruments characteristic of Turkish music began to invade European military music. From this came the employment of bass drum, cymbals and triangle in the modern orchestra – and Mozart employs them in the overture to *Die Entführung* precisely to convey oriental 'local colour'. This 'Janissary music', as music with this special percussion effect is called (from the Turkish military corps of Janissaries), recurs in the opera itself; and the male chorus of attendants on the Pasha are themselves described in the score as 'Janissaries'.

The serenade sung in the third act by Pedrillo (ex. 1) was presumably also intended by Mozart to have an oriental atmosphere; it has a curious modal scale (not in our modern major or minor keys) which sounds generally 'foreign' rather than specifically oriental to us. The serenade tells of a fair maiden imprisoned in a Moorish land.

Ex. 1 [Allegretto]

In Moh – ren – land ge – fan – gen war____ ein Mä – del hübsch und fein, sah roth und weiss, war schwarz von Haar, seufz' Tag und Nacht und wein – te gar, wollt' gern er – lö – set sein, ____ wollt' gern er – lö – set sein.

The two comic servants, Pedrillo and Blonde, seem to have a more approachable humanity in their music than their employers. Blonde is supposed to be an Englishwoman, cool and crafty – which means, in an English performance, that Osmin can directly address his audience when exclaiming: 'Oh, Englishmen, aren't you fools – you allow your womenfolk to do as they wish' (ex. 2).

Ex. 2

Belmonte and Contanze are personifications of the emotions supposed to be proper to heroes and heroines. Constanze indeed is allowed to take this to extremes in the most famous aria of the work, 'Martern aller Arten' ('Torture me and flay me'), in which she declares to the Pasha her determination to resist his advances, though torture and death may face her. This aria is on such an enormous scale, with contrasted sections and with sixty bars of instrumental introduction alone, that it seems to hold up the drama. It requires the full agility of a coloratura soprano (high notes, rapid runs, ornamentation) with more dramatic weight than most such singers can give. In fact, many of the songs are over-long.

The finale of the last act, with verses for different characters and a recurring refrain, is a *vaudeville* in the original and technical sense of that word.

LE NOZZE DI FIGARO
(The Marriage of Figaro)
Libretto by Lorenzo da Ponte, after the play by Beaumarchais

First performed: Vienna 1786
Four Acts

Cast in order of singing:

FIGARO, SERVANT TO COUNT ALMAVIVA	*baritone*
SUSANNA, MAID TO THE COUNTESS ALMAVIVA	*soprano*
DOCTOR BARTOLO	*bass*
MARCELLINA, FORMER HOUSEKEEPER OF DR BARTOLO	*soprano*
CHERUBINO, A YOUNG PAGE IN COUNT ALMAVIVA'S SERVICE	
	mezzo-soprano (or soprano)
COUNT ALMAVIVA	*baritone*
DON BASILIO, A TEACHER OF MUSIC	*tenor*
COUNTESS ALMAVIVA	*soprano*
ANTONIO, A GARDENER TO COUNT ALMAVIVA,	
AND UNCLE TO SUSANNA	*bass*
DON CURZIO, A LAWYER	*tenor*
BARBARINA, DAUGHTER OF ANTONIO	*soprano*

Chorus of villagers
The scene is laid in a castle and its grounds near Seville

Not a few music-lovers would call *Le nozze di Figaro* the greatest comic opera ever written, a spring of bubbling melody set to a sharp, fast-moving, witty plot. It is an opera about masters and servants and the complications in that relationship caused by sex. To the original audience it was an opera on a contemporary subject, with strong political undertones. It was based on a famous French play by an author then still living, Beaumarchais. The play was a sequel to another about the same character, *Il barbiere di Siviglia* ('The Barber of Seville'), which had already been set successfully as an opera – not yet by Rossini but by Giovanni Paisiello (1740–1816).

In *Il barbiere di Siviglia* (see page 121), Figaro is the barber and general factotum who outwits Rosina's stupid guardian Bartolo and smoothes the way for the marriage of Count Almaviva and Rosina. Now, in *Le nozze di Figaro*, Rosina has become the Countess and

Figaro is the Count's servant. He and the Countess's maid Susanna are betrothed.

The Count and Figaro are both jealous characters, Figaro justifiably so since he learns that the Count himself has designs on Susanna. The words of the libretto make pointed reference to 'the feudal right'. This alludes to the custom by which the lord of the manor, in compensation for the loss of one of his female serfs through marriage, was supposedly allowed to rob the girl of her virginity before the husband took possession. This custom, we learn, has recently been abolished on the Count's estates but, as Figaro puts it, the Count wishes to get back by consent from Susanna the right that he has given up by law.

The situation is complicated not only by the fact that Figaro is virile and self-willed enough to avenge any wrong done to Susanna, but also by the presence in the household of Cherubino, a page – that is, a young man of noble family sent to learn good manners. He is just at an age at which both the Countess and Susanna have to learn not to treat him as a pretty plaything any more. 'He' is sung in the opera by a mezzo-soprano or soprano.

The arias for Marcellina and Basilio in the final act are often omitted on stage as they are felt to hold up the action in providing the singers of minor roles with solos.

★　★　★

ACT I: Susanna is trying on a new hat. Figaro, who is to be married to her, is measuring out a room for a bed. But Susanna insists that this room will never do for their bedroom as it is far too near the Count's, and the Count is by no means to be trusted. Figaro vows, however, that if the Count wants to dance ('Se vuol ballare') then he shall dance to Figaro's tune. After Figaro's departure Bartolo, who was once outwitted by Figaro, comes in and shows his desire for vengeance. And if Bartolo is angry with Figaro, no less is Marcellina with Susanna, for she wishes to marry Figaro herself. The two women have a duet of mock courtesy: 'Via resti servita' ('Accept my deference'). Marcellina leaves.

Now enters Cherubino, the page. He declares his boyish passion for the Countess – but it is really a passion for all womankind, as his song shows: 'Non so più' ('I no longer know'). The Count's voice is heard and Cherubino (who should not be there at all) hides behind a chair. The Count suggests an assignation with Susanna, but then he has to hide himself when a voice is heard outside. It is that of Don

Basilio – a rascally *abbé* who is music master and organist in the Count's establishment, and general go-between for all manner of intrigue. So the Count is now hiding *behind* a chair and Cherubino *on* the chair, covered by a dress, while Basilio makes insinuations to Susanna about herself and the Count and about Cherubino's interest in the Countess.

The Count, enraged, reveals himself and declares that he is in any case going to get rid of Cherubino because of what happened the other day: he, the Count, was visiting a young lady called Barbarina, and happened to lift up a cloth from a table just in *this* way (and here the Count draws back the covering of the chair in the room where they are) and there was Cherubino hiding! And there, of course, Cherubino is now discovered hiding in exactly the same position. The Count is furious, particularly because Cherubino must have overheard everything (although Cherubino says he did his best not to listen).

The interchange is interrupted by the entry of Figaro with a group of peasants, who strew flowers before the Count: Figaro has come to ask the Count to join him and Susanna in marriage. The Count promises to do so, but puts him off till later, and now tells Cherubino that he must leave the castle and become an ensign in the Count's regiment. Figaro warns Cherubino that the hazardous military life which now awaits him must take the place of his amorous escapades: 'Non più andrai, farfallone amoroso' ('No longer shall you go like an amorous butterfly [from flower to flower]').

ACT II: The Countess, in her boudoir, laments that her husband no longer appears to love her: 'Porgi, amor, qualche ristoro' ('God of love, grant me some remedy'). Susanna enters and tells the Countess that the Count has designs on her (Susanna), and together they plan to outwit him. Cherubino enters and sings a song to the Countess which expresses his boyish love for her: 'Voi che sapete che cosa è amor' ('You who know what love is'). Susanna and the Countess plan to spite the Count by making an assignation with him in Susanna's name and then sending not Susanna but Cherubino in disguise. For this purpose they start to dress up Cherubino in women's clothes, having prudently locked the door first. But then the Count is heard outside. Cherubino rushes into an inner room and the Countess is in obvious confusion when she lets the Count enter. Meanwhile, Susanna has hidden in an alcove.

The Count's suspicions are aroused, but the Countess insists that in the inner room, which is now locked, is only her maid Susanna. The Count doubts her and says he will go and fetch tools to break the lock of the inner door, and insists on taking the Countess with him so that she cannot release any intruder. While Count and Countess are out of the room Susanna dashes out of the alcove in which she has been hiding, unlocks the inner door, and lets out Cherubino, who jumps down out of the window. Susanna then goes into the inner room and locks herself in it.

When the Count and Countess return, therefore, the room looks as if nothing has happened. The Countess, fearing that the Count will find Cherubino in the inner room, confesses to him and asks for pardon. Furious, and with his sword drawn, the Count opens the inner door – and out steps Susanna, to the surprise of the Countess no less than of the Count. Recovering herself, the Countess says that her 'confession' was a ruse to shame the Count and that, of course, it was only Susanna in the inner room all the time. It is now the Count's turn to beg pardon of the Countess.

Antonio, the gardener, who is also Susanna's uncle, comes in angry and half tipsy to complain that a man jumped down from the window and damaged his plants. Figaro, who has entered, says this was himself and sustains the part with difficulty when Antonio confronts him with a paper – it is the officer's commission which, in reality, Cherubino has dropped. The Count's suspicions are by no means allayed. Now he welcomes, as allies, Marcellina, Bartolo and Basilio who enter to put forward the case that Figaro is legally obliged to marry Marcellina in compensation for a debt which he is unable to repay. The complication is unresolved as the curtain falls.

ACT III: Susanna, still trying to mislead the Count, promises in a duet to meet him in the garden – though with some confusion between 'yes' and 'no' which arouses his suspicion. When she goes, the Count again becomes suspicious as he overhears her tell-tale words to Figaro. He vents his anger: 'Vedrò, mentr'io sospiro, felice il servo mio?' ('Shall I see my servant happy while I sigh?').

Now Marcellina, accompanied by Bartolo and the Count's lawyer, Don Curzio, confronts Figaro with his promise to marry her. Figaro prevaricates, saying he is of noble birth and cannot marry without the consent of his parents. In token of his noble birth he says that not only can he show them the fine garments in which he was found when an infant, but also a curious mark on his right arm. On seeing this mark Marcellina exclaims with excitement that Figaro is her long-lost son and, what is more, Bartolo is Figaro's father.

There follows a sextet of comic reconciliation. Even the Count is reduced to angry inaction. Figaro naturally enough embraces his new-found mother, Marcellina. When Susanna enters – having raised from the Countess money to pay the debt and release Figaro from Marcellina's claim – she misconstrues the embrace, goes straight up to Figaro and boxes him on the ear. Marcellina then takes the lead in explaining the new situation to Susanna, who repeats the words 'Sua madre? suo padre?' ('His mother? His father?') and insists that all should confirm them.

They leave, and the Countess enters. She remembers days of former happiness: where are they ('Dove sono')? Can she regain her husband's affection? She still hankers to punish him by a false assignation with Susanna in which he will find himself trapped, and instructs Susanna to write a letter to the Count accordingly: in their Letter Duet, Susanna repeats what the Countess dictates.

Village girls enter and pay tribute to the Countess; among them is Cherubino – who, however, is unmasked by Antonio and the Count. But when the Count threatens Cherubino, Barbarina reminds him of his promise to give her anything she wanted if . . . and Cherubino is spared.

Now Figaro announces that the ceremony and dancing are to begin, and two happy couples come to claim the Count's blessing – not only Figaro and Susanna, but also Marcellina and Bartolo, who have decided to get married. A crowd assembles to witness the ceremony. While a fandango is being danced Susanna slips a little note to the Count – the note she wrote at the Countess's dictation, making an assignation for that evening. Such is the Countess's plot, however, that when the Count turns up for his rendezvous he will find, not Susanna, nor Cherubino, whom it had originally been planned to send, but the Countess herself: Susanna and the Countess will have exchanged cloaks.

[In this act an alternative order of musical numbers is sometimes preferred, based on the conjecture that Mozart would have used a more logical sequence of events (as in the play) but was constrained because one singer in the original cast had to double two parts and would not have had time to change costumes.]

ACT IV: In the garden Figaro encounters Barbarina: the Count entrusted her with the errand of taking back to Susanna – as confirmation of their rendezvous – the pin that sealed her original note; but Barbarina has let it drop and is searching for it. Thus Figaro gathers that Susanna has a rendezvous with the Count, but does not discover that it is to be faked. Furious with his new wife – his unfaithful new wife, as he thinks – he invites Bartolo and Basilio to come along and witness her shameful meeting with the Count. Alone, he bids them beware of the unfaithfulness of women: 'Aprite un po'quegli occhi' ('Open your eyes a little').

As he retires, the Countess and Susanna enter, each disguised as the other. Susanna looks forward to the pleasures of love: 'Deh vieni, non tardar' ('O come, do not delay'). She knows that the jealous Figaro is watching her.

Now the complicated rendezvous begins, complicated further still by the fact that Cherubino is there too for a rendezvous with Barbarina. Cherubino sees the Countess, takes her for Susanna and attempts to kiss her. The Count steps in just at that moment and receives the kiss – but the Count's intended box on the ear for Cherubino goes to Figaro, who also intervenes just then. Now the Count starts to plead love to 'Susanna' (as he imagines – but really to the Countess, in Susanna's cloak). Figaro thinks he will pay the Count back and starts to disclose the 'plot' to the woman he imagines to be the Countess. It is, of course, Susanna; and when she forgets to disguise her voice Figaro spots who she is, and begins in fun to plead passionate love to her – which infuriates her, as she believes that Figaro thinks she is the Countess. Soon she realizes the truth, and they continue for the benefit of the Count, who now sees Figaro and the Countess apparently embracing. The Count prepares to denounce them both – but is astonished when the real Countess comes forth and shows that the figure in her cloak is Susanna.

It is the Count's turn once again to be humbled and to apologize to his wife, both for suspecting her and for his own misdemeanours. The Countess forgives him and the company gives itself up to revelry for the rest of the night.

★   ★   ★

Le nozze di Figaro, distinguished though it is for famous solo numbers, is also a marvellously conversational opera. The recitative is extensive, quick and complex: in the theatre an inability to grasp it must mean failure to follow the complicated plot. Moreover, at least three of the formal numbers have a conversational element worked with particular musical skill and particular dramatic effectiveness. One is the Letter Duet, in which Susanna takes down a love letter at the Countess's dictation, and then reads it back (ex. 1). It is a letter making an amorous rendezvous in words that hint obliquely at the real message.

Ex. I

Later comes the sextet in the third act in which it emerges that Figaro is the son of old Marcellina and of Bartolo, when the phrase 'his mother?', followed by 'his father?', passes from one character to another. And a little extra fun may occur because one of the participants, Don Curzio, the lawyer, is traditionally a stammerer; so it is 'm-m-mother' and 'f-f-father' when his turn comes.

But perhaps Mozart's greatest skill shows in the long, complicated finales to Acts II and IV, in which the orchestra seems to take its own part in the musical intrigue. At one particularly teasing point in the former, Figaro, confronted by the Count with a paper, is trying with all his wits to identify it: it is (as the Countess whispers to Susanna and Susanna whispers to Figaro) the officer's commission ('la patente del paggio') which Cherubino had dropped. Figaro's racking of his brains is virtually made audible in the repeated phrase of the orchestra (while, amid the talking of the others, Figaro himself is tongue-tied) (ex. 2).

Ex. 2

In the first part of the finale of Act IV Mozart uses a pointed change of key three times at crucial moments. The first is when the Countess (disguised as Susanna) realizes that the Count may discover her with the importunate Cherubino. The next is the point when Susanna, Figaro and the Count see her with him. Then (most tellingly of all) comes the point marked ★ in ex. 3: here the Count steps in and receives the kiss that Cherubino wants to give, 'Prendi intanto' ('Take this now') to the Countess, whom he takes for Susanna; and Figaro, at 'Vo' veder' ('I want to see') steps forward and receives the box on the ear intended by the Count for Cherubino.

Ex. 3

There is, we may suspect, one special orchestral joke. In Figaro's song warning men of women's infidelity, 'Aprite un po' quegli occhi', the reference to female deception is accompanied by a prominent figure on the horns – alluding to the well-known dramatic convention by which a pair of horns sprouting from a husband's head was a sign that he had been cuckolded. We quote Figaro's words: 'You all of you know!' (ex. 4).

Ex. 4

DON GIOVANNI
Il dissoluto punito, ossia Il Don Giovanni
(The Rake Punished, or Don Jaun)
Libretto by Lorenzo da Ponte

First performed: Prague, 1787
Two Acts

Cast in order of singing:

LEPORELLO, SERVANT TO DON GIOVANNI	*bass*
DONNA ANNA, BETROTHED TO DON OTTAVIO	*soprano*
DON GIOVANNI, A LICENTIOUS YOUNG NOBLEMAN	*baritone*
THE COMMENDATORE, FATHER OF DONNA ANNA	*bass*
DON OTTAVIO, FRIEND OF DON GIOVANNI	*tenor*
DONNA ELVIRA, A LADY OF BURGOS, DESERTED BY DON GIOVANNI	*soprano*
ZERLINA, A PEASANT GIRL, BETROTHED TO MASETTO	*soprano*
MASETTO, A PEASANT	*bass*

[The role of Donna Elvira's maid is silent.]

Chorus of peasants and invisible demons
The scene is laid in Seville

The French and Germans call this opera *Don Juan*; so, rightly, should we, for it provides a ready identification with the legendary hero, celebrated in many other works for the stage before Mozart's. (One was the English play of 1676, *The Libertine*, by Thomas Shadwell, for a revival of which Purcell wrote incidental music; another was an opera by Mozart's contemporary Gazzaniga, whose libretto by Bertati was freely drawn upon by Da Ponte in his libretto for Mozart.) However, *Don Giovanni* – Giovanni being simply the Italian form for Juan in Spanish or John in English – has become established in British usage, and the other characters have retained their Italian form too.

Mozart called the opera a *dramma giocoso*, meaning a sub-type of comic opera which admitted the presence of some 'serious' characters. In its treatment of moral issues *Don Giovanni* steps considerably beyond the traditional comic-opera framework, but the prevailing tone is comic and the entire action is presented in a comic context. When the 'great seducer' is eventually dragged down to hell by the statue of the man he killed, the remaining characters come on stage and warn the audience to learn from this to behave themselves! This they do in no solemn tones but in merry, scampering music of an absolutely 'comic opera' kind.

Don Giovanni is indeed an opera striking in both its dramatic force and its comic situations, and the characters are so memorably drawn as seemingly to have a life of their own outside the opera: Leporello (one of the great comic creations of musical drama) can be imagined in many other situations from what we know of him here. And the whole action is infused with music showing Mozart's genius at its height.

★　　★　　★

ACT I: The action opens outside Donna Anna's house. Don Giovanni is inside, masked and trying to seduce her. (He may perhaps have succeeded: interpretations of the opera vary on this point.) The first voice we hear is that of Leporello, Giovanni's servant, who is waiting outside and complaining at the drudgery of his life.

Giovanni appears from the house, with Anna holding on to him: she wants to identify her masked attacker. Her old father, referred to as the Commendatore (a title of honour with no special relevance to the action) comes out and insists on fighting Giovanni. In the ensuing duel the Commendatore is killed.

Giovanni and Leporello escape. Anna, attended by her betrothed, Don Ottavio, discovers her father's dead body; before they leave she makes Ottavio swear vengeance on the unknown attacker.

Giovanni and Leporello are in a street when a woman appears, singing about a lover who has deserted her. Giovanni decides she needs his 'consolation' – but then, addressing her, sees that she is Donna Elvira of Burgos whom he himself has deserted. He slips away and leaves Leporello to play the cruel trick of forcing Elvira to listen to a catalogue of Giovanni's international conquests:'Madamina, il catalogo'.

The scene changes to a nearby village. Two peasants, Masetto and Zerlina, are about to be married. Giovanni approaches, gives Leporello the task of hustling Masetto away and has no difficulty in exerting his aristocratic charm on Zerlina: 'Là ci darem la mano' ('There we will give each other our hands'). Giovanni is on the point of leading Zerlina away when Elvira steps in, sings an aria warning Zerlina, and guides her off.

Anna and Ottavio enter; in a quartet, Elvira tells them that Giovanni is a rogue, while he says that she is unbalanced. From Giovanni's voice Anna recognizes the masked attacker of the previous night. She announces her discovery to Ottavio: 'Or sai chi l'onore' ('You know now who attempted to rob me of my honour'). Alone, Ottavio sings 'Dalla sua pace' ('On her peace, mine depends').

Now Giovanni, alone, sings of his intention to invite the countryfolk to a party (the so-called Champagne Aria) and add to his list of conquests. Then he leaves. Masetto returns, offended with his flirtatious Zerlina. But Zerlina twists him round her little finger: 'Batti, batti' ('Beat me, beat me') and they are reconciled. Giovanni enters, but Masetto's wish for vengeance is sidetracked when all are invited to the party. Ottavio, Anna and Elvira, masked, plan to join the party uninvited and trap Giovanni there. The three utter a short but intense prayer: 'Protegga il giusto cielo' ('May Heaven's eternal justice').

At a party a minuet (for the gentry), a contre-danse (for the villagers) and a German dance (which Leporello insists Masetto shall dance with him) are heard together. Giovanni again makes an attempt on Zerlina's virtue and, when she screams, drags forward Leporello as the supposed villain. But he is confronted and denounced by Ottavio, Anna and Elvira, who have unmasked.

ACT II: For the moment, Giovanni's quarry has changed again: now it is a maid of Elvira's. He exchanges cloaks with Leporello for the purpose. After Giovanni has played another cruel trick on the passionate Elvira (luring her on to believe he still loves her, and sending her off with the disguised Leporello), he serenades the maid, with a mandolin: 'Deh vieni alla finestra' ('Pray come to your window').

Masetto arrives with friends to kill Giovanni. But Giovanni in Leporello's cloak pretends in the darkness to be Leporello; he sends Masetto's friends away and contrives to give Masetto himself a sound beating. Zerlina arrives and consoles Masetto: 'Vedrai carino' ('Come, my dear one').

Elvira and the disguised Leporello encounter Zerlina and Masetto, then Anna and Ottavio; thinking he is Giovanni, the four threaten him, but to their surprise Elvira defends him. Leporello is, however, forced to identify himself, in a sextet; then, with an aria, he manages to escape. Ottavio sings again of his love for Anna: 'Il mio tesoro' ('The one I treasure'); and Elvira yet again voices her sense of betrayal: 'Mi tradì quell'alma ingrata' ('That ungrateful one betrayed me').

In a cemetery, Giovanni and Leporello see a statue of the murdered Commendatore. The statue speaks, admonishing Giovanni, to Leporello's (but not Giovanni's) terror. Giovanni audaciously invites the statue to supper and the invitation is accepted.

To Ottavio, Anna excuses her delay in marrying him: 'Non mi dir' ('Tell me not that I am cruel').

Later, Giovanni is dining cheerily at home. His private band is playing and Leporello is waiting on him. (Properly, by the Italian words sung, Giovanni has female company; in most modern productions he dines alone.) Elvira comes in with another entreaty to him; but again it is vain. As she leaves she screams at something she has seen outside. So does Leporello when he goes to look. It is the statue of the Commendatore, approaching to fulfil the invitation to dine with Giovanni. It enters, speaks, and drags the still defiant Giovanni down to hell as flames arise and an invisible chorus of demons sings.

When the others enter, bent on vengeance, Leporello has to explain that they have been anticipated. Severally, they settle their affairs – Elvira will go to a convent, Anna will observe a year's mourning before marrying Ottavio, Zerlina and Masetto will go home to supper, Leporello will seek a new master. All, light-heartedly, tell the audience to learn a serious lesson from Giovanni's fate.

*   *   *

The part of Ottavio, the suitor of Anna, is dramatically weak; but through historical accident it included not one but two of the greatest arias Mozart ever wrote for tenor. For the first production in Prague

Mozart wrote the aria 'Il mio tesoro'. When the opera came to be staged in Vienna, in 1788, the leading tenor proved unable to sing this difficult song and an easier one (but not *very* easy!) was given to him: 'Dalla sua pace'. This, however, was placed by Mozart at a different point in the action. It rather holds up the drama; but, in most productions today, both arias are nevertheless given.

Also for the Vienna performance, Mozart wrote – at the insistence of the singer – a big solo aria for Elvira, 'Mi tradì quell'alma ingrata'. This again holds up the action; but, again, it is usually included. A third insertion demanded of Mozart by his Vienna cast, a rather foolish duet for Zerlina and Leporello, is not generally performed today (though it is found in some recordings). Of course, it would be quite reasonable for a modern production to stick entirely to the more concisely dramatic Prague score, at the acknowledged sacrifice of two superb musical items.

The orchestral score includes trombones. The trombone was primarily a church instrument in those days; to import it, therefore, was to bring in a special atmosphere of solemnity,★ just like the importation of the organ into *Faust* or *Die Meistersinger*. The trombones accompany the statue of the murdered man: they are heard only when the statue speaks on the stage – not even when, in the overture, the statue music is anticipated. There is an awesome moment when, in the cemetery, a lively conversation between Giovanni and Leporello on the subject of seduction is interrupted by the voice of the statue ('You will finish laughing before dawn comes') (ex. 1).

Ex. 1

★See also pages 65 and 95.

There is an even more unusual instrument than the trombone in the score of *Don Giovanni*: the mandolin. Giovanni uses it to accompany himself in the serenade to Elvira's maid (a character who never sings a word in the opera, though in the theatre we should see her face). One precedent for the use of the mandolin was in *Una casa rara* ('A rare thing') by Vicente Martìn y Soler (1754–1806), a Spanish composer of Italian operas. A song from this opera, and one song from *I due litiganti* ('The Two Litigants') by Giuseppe Sarti (1729–1802), are played by Giovanni's private band in the supper scene, who also play 'Non più andrai' (Figaro's martial farewell to Cherubino) from Act I of *Le nozze di Figaro* which Leporello greets with the observation: 'I know this tune rather too well!' The cheerful, easy-going music here is cleverly planned to set off the intensity of the scene which follows.

Mozart's high point of sheer musical skill, however, comes in the ballroom scene, when three small orchestras on the stage play three different tunes in different dance-rhythms which all fit astonishingly together. (In the score there is even provision for the musicians to tune up, using the open strings of the violin.)

A notable feature of the opera is the way in which Mozart provides distinctive music to portray the characters of the three women. The simple peasant girl, Zerlina, has essentially simple, tuneful music, like 'Batti, batti' (ex. 2), the song in which she wheedles her stupid but honest lover, Masetto. Anna's music, especially her Act I aria,

Ex. 2

'Or sai chi l'onore', shows her rather stiff nobility. In her determination to have revenge, she calls on the services of her accepted lover like a general commanding his troops (ex. 3). The personality of

Ex. 3

Elvira is more complex. Her temperament is passionate, her situation is tragic, but – in tune with the rather hard attitude of eighteenth-century society to a jilted woman – there is something slightly absurd about her. Mozart conveys this in the old-fashioned pseudo-Handelian idiom of 'Ah! fuggi il traditor!' ('Ah! fly from the traitor'), where she warns Zerlina of Giovanni, and, most of all, in the almost grotesque leaps in the melody of her opening song 'Ah, chi mi dice mai' ('Ah, where shall I find that cruel one'). In this she threatens to slaughter her seducer and tear out his heart (ex. 4).

Ex. 4

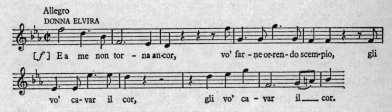

COSI FAN TUTTE
Così fan tutte, ossia La scuola degli amanti
(All Women do it, or The School for Lovers)
Libretto by Lorenzo da Ponte

First performed: Vienna, 1790
Two Acts

Cast in order of singing:

FERRANDO, AN OFFICER, IN LOVE WITH DORABELLA	*tenor*
GUGLIELMO, AN OFFICER, IN LOVE WITH FIORDILIGI	*baritone*
DON ALFONSO, AN ELDERLY PHILOSOPHER	*bass*
FIORDILIGI ⎫ SISTERS, YOUNG LADIES OF	*soprano*
DORABELLA ⎭ FERRARA	*mezzo-soprano*
DESPINA, THEIR MAID	*soprano*

Chorus of soldiers, townspeople, servants and musicians
The scene is laid in a village near Naples

'All women do it': that is, all women show fickleness in love. Such is
the idea of the opera. Literally the title is 'Thus do all *(feminine)*'.
Since the title-words have actually to be sung in the course of the
opera, in five syllables with an emphasis on the fourth, an English
version might be 'Just like a woman!'

Interpretations of the opera vary. Is it just a highly artificial frolic,
based on disguises of absurd improbability? Or is it a serious
commentary on human frailty, using the time-honoured device of
disguise as a means to propel the plot? Or is it a sophisticated mixture
of these, raised from what was intended as a frivolous piece into
something deeper by the power of Mozart's music? – for although
Mozart does parody the high-flown sentiment of operatic heroines
in the sisters' Act I arias, his score is never merely comic, and indeed
in the second act it is clear that he treats entirely seriously the
predicaments that his characters, male as well as female, have
brought upon themselves.

★   ★   ★

ACT I: In a café, Ferrando claims that Dorabella will always be
faithful to him. Guglielmo makes the same claim for Fiordiligi. But
Don Alfonso is an older man and says he knows better. The young

men are irritated and, challenged by Don Alfonso, agree to bet on their mistresses' honour against whatever scheme of temptation he may propose. The officers look forward to spending their winnings.

In a garden we discover two girls looking adoringly at miniature pictures of their lovers. Don Alfonso enters (this is the start of his scheme) with a pathetic song of bad tidings: Ferrando and Guglielmo, as officers, have been ordered away. Now they enter. In a quintet, led off by Guglielmo – 'Sento, o Dio' ('I feel my foot hesitating') – the four lovers express undying passion. A march is heard: the officers' troops enter, surrounded by townspeople. There are more tender farewells; with the girls asking their lovers to write daily (quintet: 'Di scrivermi ogni giorno') as Alfonso's laughter is heard in the background. The officers march off with their men, with Alfonso and the sisters wishing them a smooth journey ('Soave sia il vento').

In the girls' house, Despina, the girls' maid, enters, complaining of her work. She is incredulous when her mistresses give vent to extreme misery, expressed by Dorabella: 'Smanie implacabili' ('Implacable Fates'). To their protestations that they cannot live without their lovers, Despina advises them to take love lightly. The girls go off.

Alfonso enters; he determines to ask Despina's help and gives her some money. He introduces Ferrando and Guglielmo, now comically and extravagantly disguised as a pair of Albanian noblemen who have come to court the girls. Despina allows them to approach her mistresses. In a sextet, during which the girls react indignantly to the intrusion. Alfonso sings his part aside, unseen by the girls; then he enters, 'recognizes' the Albanians as old friends and commends them to the girls. But Fiordiligi, in an aria, says she will be 'firm as rock' ('Come scoglio'). Guglielmo presses his and Ferrando's claims in an aria, 'Non siate ritrosi' ('Do not be backward'), commending their fine noses and other masculine attractions. The girls leave in an attitude of disdain and the laughing suitors join in a trio with the still confident Alfonso.

Alone, and now serious, Ferrando sings of his continuing love: 'Un'aura amorosa' ('An aura of love'). Alfonso and Despina plan the next stage. Ferrando and Guglielmo enter and pretend, in the presence of the girls and Alfonso, to take poison and sink lifeless to the ground. Despina and Alfonso hurry away for the doctor. Meanwhile such pathetic devotion begins to have its effect on the girls, on which the 'dead' men (when the girls are not looking) comment amusedly.

Alfonso returns with the 'doctor' (Despina, disguised and spouting bogus Latin). Despina produces an outsize magnet, topically referred to as an invention of the celebrated Dr Mesmer, and waves it over the bodies. They 'wake' and shock the girls by demanding kisses as restorative. A long sextet ends the act.

ACT II: Despina further urges her mistresses to try a flirtation. Left alone, the girls decide they will do so after all. Dorabella chooses 'the dark one' (that is, Guglielmo) and Fiordiligi the other – each, in fact, choosing the other's lover.

In a garden Ferrando and Guglielmo have summoned musicians to sing and play for the girls, who enter with Alfonso. But the men are shy, or gauche (or pretend to be); so Despina and Alfonso, in a quartet with them, demonstrate the ritual of courtship.

Despina and Alfonso leave the four lovers alone. They start talking about the weather at first, then proceed to other topics. Ferrando leads Fiordiligi away. Guglielmo persuades Dorabella to give him as a keepsake the miniature she wears (it is Ferrando's portrait) and in return gives her a heart-shaped locket: 'Il core vi dono' ('This heart that I give you').

They leave, and Ferrando and Fiordiligi enter. He presses his case, but she still does not yield. Left alone she admits fonder feelings for the stranger but resists in the name of her duty to her absent lover: 'Per pietà, ben mio, perdona' ('For pity's sake, my love, forgive me'). The two men meet: Ferrando reports to Guglielmo this obstinacy of Fiordiligi's, but he has to be told that his Dorabella is weakening, and is shown the portrait with which she parted to Guglielmo. Guglielmo, with Fiordiligi still faithful, can afford to sing lightly of woman's inconstancy. But Ferrando asserts his continuing love even though he has been betrayed ('Tradito, schernito').

In the girls' apartment, Dorabella is cheerful. Fiordiligi decides that they must save their honour and leave the house dressed up in the soldiers' uniforms that their lovers have left. But Ferrando, still in disguise, comes in, renews his wooing – and eventually Fiordiligi yields. Alfonso, Ferrando and Guglielmo meet and sum it up: 'Così fan tutte'.

A room is lit for the party which is now to celebrate the approaching marriage of the girls and their 'Albanians'. Despina shows the servants and musicians their duties. Alfonso enters and leaves with

Despina. The four lovers (now, of course, each man paired off with the other's girl) sing an affectionate quartet with chorus – with some furious 'asides' from Guglielmo. Alfonso announces the arrival of the notary (Despina in disguise) with the marriage contract. But just as all are about to sign, the soldiers' chorus (as in Act I) is heard. The 'Albanians' go off to hide themselves and the 'real' Ferrando and Guglielmo enter in their own clothes. They find a marriage contract and spot the 'lawyer', who reveals himself to the astonished girls as Despina. The girls tremble as they admit that they were preparing a wedding. But the men surprise the girls by confessing the plot; and all ends happily with Alfonso the winner and the girls, chastened, reunited with their lovers.

★ ★ ★

Da Ponte's words mock the conventions of ever-faithful love. So does Mozart's music. In old-fashioned heroic style, Fiordiligi declares that she will stand firm as a rock 'against wind and tempest' (ex. 1). But of course a singer has the same opportunity to display her (or his) voice when a composer means his music ironically as when he means it seriously. This is a particular joy of this particularly sophisticated opera.

Ex. 1

Mozart three times makes notable use of recurrent themes. First, the overture (at the end of its slow introduction: ex. 2) presages the tune of the words 'Così fan tutte'. Second, when the masquerade is exposed, the two suitors make their own roles clear by quoting music from their and Despina's disguises. One of these is the

Ex. 2

nonsense of Dr Mesmer's magnet, previously heard when Despina was dressed as a doctor. Now the men do honour 'to the magnetic physician' (ex. 3). Note the exaggerated trill for the waving of the magnet in action. Third, the soldiers' chorus of the first act returns in the last.

Ex. 3

The opera is long, though in only two acts, and certain arias are sometimes cut. The action, be it noted, takes place within a single day – an old dramatic convention which here serves to emphasize the splendid artificiality of the comic tale.

DIE ZAUBERFLÖTE
(The Magic Flute)
Libretto by Emanuel Schikaneder

First performed: Vienna, 1791
Two Acts

Cast in order of singing:

TAMINO, A PRINCE	*tenor*
THREE LADIES, IN ATTENDANCE ON THE QUEEN OF NIGHT	*two sopranos, mezzo-soprano*
PAPAGENO, A BIRD-CATCHER	*baritone*
THE QUEEN OF NIGHT	*soprano*
MONOSTATOS, A MOOR, SARASTRO'S CAPTAIN OF THE GUARD	*tenor*

PAMINA, DAUGHTER OF THE QUEEN OF NIGHT   *soprano*
THREE BOYS OR SPIRITS   *boy singers, or two sopranos and mezzo-*
                                                 soprano
THE SPEAKER OF THE TEMPLE   *bass*
SARASTRO, HIGH PRIEST OF ISIS AND OSIRIS   *bass*
TWO PRIESTS OF THE TEMPLE   *tenor, bass*
PAPAGENA   *soprano*
TWO MEN IN ARMOUR   *tenor, bass*

Chorus of priests, onlookers, etc.
The scene is laid in ancient Egypt

Die Zauberflöte is like an English pantomime. That is, it takes the form of a popular entertainment with songs; it allowed a well-known comedian to gag (in this case Schikaneder, the actor-manager-librettist); it is highly moral, with personifications of good and evil on the stage; and in the use of transformations and other theatrical devices it suggests the workings of the supernatural in the middle of a tale about ordinary human beings.

Schikaneder and Mozart were both keen Freemasons at a time when Freemasonry was officially frowned upon in Austria as hostile to the Roman Catholic Church and even to the state itself. In laying the scene in ancient Egypt (where Freemasonry was believed to have its origins), in the rites of purification enacted in the opera in Sarastro's temple, and in some of the actual words of the libretto, Schikaneder and Mozart were obviously alluding to their brotherhood. Moreover, some of the actual music has Masonic significance. And if Sarastro stood for Enlightenment, then the wicked Queen of Night would seem to represent the Roman Catholic Church, or the late Empress Maria Theresa, who upheld the Church and proscribed the Freemasons.

It is part of the richness of *Die Zauberflöte* that its music ranges from the popular ditty (Papageno's first utterance) to a contrapuntal style suggesting Bach (the duet of the men in armour) and that it can be enjoyed on many levels, from sheer fooling to that which caused Bernard Shaw to say: 'I am highly susceptible to the force of all truly religious music, no matter to what church it belongs; but the music of my own church – for which I may be allowed, like other people, to have a partiality – is to be found in *Die Zauberflöte* and the Ninth Symphony'.

⋆   ⋆   ⋆

ACT I: Prince Tamino, trying to escape from a huge snake, falls unconscious. The three Ladies-in-Waiting to the Queen of Night enter, kill the snake, and leave. On recovering consciousness Tamino sees an odd-looking man approaching him: Papageno, the bird-catcher, covered with feathers as his trade demands. He introduces himself by singing a ditty in popular style, and playing his own panpipes. Papageno boasts to Tamino that it was he who killed the snake – for which lie he is punished by the Ladies-in-Waiting (who now re-enter) by having his mouth padlocked.

The Ladies show Tamino the miniature portrait of the Queen of Night's daughter, Pamina, with whom he at once falls in love: 'Dies Bildnis ist bezaubernd schön' ('This picture is wondrously fair'). When the Ladies tell him she is a prisoner of Sarastro, whom they represent to be evil, he resolves to rescue her. The Queen of Night herself appears and urges him on.

The quintet that follows, for the three Ladies, Tamino and Papageno, begins 'Hm, hm, hm, hm' – for Papageno, his mouth still padlocked, can only hum and not sing. But now the Ladies take off the padlock, give Tamino a magic flute to help him in his rescue, and give Papageno (who is to accompany and support Tamino) a magic chime of bells. They set off, and are told that three Boys or Spirits will show them the way.

The scene changes to a room in Sarastro's palace, where the imprisoned Pamina is importunately wooed by Monostatos, a Moor, Sarastro's captain of the guard. Papageno, who has somehow become separated from Tamino, bursts in – and Papageno and Monostatos have evidently an equally frightening effect on each other. Monostatos runs away. Papageno assures Pamina that she will be rescued soon by one who loves her, and in a duet she assures him that he, too, will find love: 'Bei Männern, welche Liebe fühlen' ('Among womankind who feel love's power').

Again the scene changes. The three Boys are seen leading Tamino to a temple with three doors. From within the first door a hidden voice bids Tamino 'Zurück!' ('Stand back'); similarly within the second door. But from the third door emerges the Speaker of the temple, whose utterance awakens in Tamino a desire for wisdom and a suspicion of the Queen of Night. A hidden chorus assures him that Pamina still lives. Tamino plays his flute and hears an answer from Papageno's panpipes. He hastens off in search of Papageno, who, with Pamina, rushes on in search of him – but they are caught by Monostatos. He and his band of slaves are about to arrest them when Papageno, at a touch of his magic bell-chime, stops them in their tracks and makes them dance.

Solemn music heralding Sarastro himself and his attendants is heard. Papageno asks Pamina what they should say to him when accused of attempted flight. 'The truth!' ('Die Wahrheit') says Pamina, in a solemn phrase. She confesses to Sarastro, who emphasizes that she is held captive in order to escape her mother's influence: woman's true destiny is to follow a man's guidance. Monostatos, who has now apprehended Tamino, brings him in. After a brief, rapt recognition between Tamino and Pamina, Monostatos tells Sarastro about his vigilance in thwarting an attempted abduction of Pamina and asks for his reward. But he has also made an attempt on Pamina's virtue, as she tells, and his reward is a beating. All others unite in Sarastro's praise.

ACT II: The priests enter to a solemn march. Sarastro announces that Tamino, before marrying Pamina, must prove himself worthy of admission to the Temple. The priests signify their accord on their trumpets. Sarastro prays for Tamino in his coming ordeal: 'O Isis und Osiris'.

Warned by two priests to keep silent and to pay no attention to women, Tamino and Papageno (who is to undergo an ordeal less arduous than Tamino's) find themselves confronted by the three Ladies-in-Waiting but ignore them. The first part of the ordeal is over.

The scene changes to where Pamina is sleeping. Monostatos is excitedly approaching her when Pamina's mother, the Queen of Night, appears, and gives her daughter a dagger with the instruction to kill Sarastro. Thus she will obtain 'hell's revenge' ('Der Hölle Rache').

The Queen of Night disappears. Monostatos re-enters, still with designs on Pamina, but Sarastro arrives and dismisses him. Pamina asks Sarastro not to take revenge on her mother. He answers that in these holy halls such thoughts would have no place ('In diesen heil'gen Hallen').

Tamino and Papageno now await the next stage of their ordeal. Papageno is confronted by an old crone who says she is his sweetheart Papagena (which he treats as a joke). The three Boys appear and bring Tamino his magic flute and Papageno his magic bells again. Pamina arrives and, when Tamino (as part of his ordeal) refuses to speak to her, gives way to utter grief: 'Ach, ich fühl's' ('Ah, I feel it').

Sarastro tells Tamino and Pamina to take their last farewell of each other. Papageno sighs for someone to love: 'Ein Mädchen oder Weibchen wünscht Papageno sich' ('A little maid, a little wife?'); the crone reappears, makes him swear to be true to her, and then reveals herself as young, beautiful and feathered like himself! But a priest prevents him from seizing her – for the present.

In a garden, the three Boys sing symbolically of the dawn. Pamina, distressed at Tamino's apparent desertion, contemplates taking her life, but is restrained by the Boys. Two Men in Armour, singing a solemn chorale, supervise the last stage of Tamino's initiation – ordeals by fire and water, in which he is joined by Pamina herself. The flute, which Tamino plays, leads them safely through.

Papageno, frustrated, comically contemplates suicide, but finally the Boys prompt him to try his magic bells again. He jingles them and finds his beautiful sweetheart at last. Their comic (yet ecstatic) stammering recognition provides a duet which starts: 'Pa-pa-pa-pa . . . [*forty-eight times!*] – geno!'

One more attempt to defeat Sarastro is made by the Queen of Night, her Ladies and Monostatos, who reappear in darkness. But they are driven away by the light: under Sarastro's benevolent guidance, Beauty and Wisdom shall be crowned for ever.

★　★　★

Papageno, as a bird-catcher, lures the birds by means of a set of panpipes, and Mozart writes a suitably light-hearted part for the instrument. Papageno sings in his first song of how the birds respond to his pipes' call and make him happy (ex. 1).

As equipment to see him through his ritual ordeal, Papageno is given a 'magic' set of bells, and these too enter the opera score: a bell-like instrument with a keyboard is needed (because of the way the music is written), not the usual orchestral glockenspiel played with small hammers held in the hand.

These, and other features of the score, are Mozart's counterpart to fooling. At the other extreme is the solemnity of the music associated with the Temple and with Enlightenment – not only with Sarastro but with the Speaker (or Orator, as this Priest is sometimes called) of the Temple.

This musical solemnity is first of all foreshadowed by the weighty chords at the opening bars of the overture. When the solemn chord-sequence returns in altered form in the middle of the overture, in many performances all the chords sound the same. They should not. The top note of the chord properly rises with each set of chords – a musical gesture full of meaning as is seen when the chords are repeated (supposedly played on the Priests' trumpets) in the temple at the opening of the second act (ex. 2). This chord-sequence, by the way, brings in the sound of trombones, instruments whose particular significance has been noted in our consideration of *Idomeneo* and *Don Giovanni*, pages 65 and 83.

Ex. 2

Another notable musical solemnity arises from the fact that the two Men in Armour, supervising part of the hero's ordeal, sing a Lutheran chorale – originally 'Ach Gott, vom Himmel sieh' darein' ('O God, from heaven look within'), now given new words referring to the path of the ordeal; Mozart perhaps got the idea from his brief study of some of Bach's works on a visit to Leipzig. The opera audience at Vienna (a Roman Catholic city) might not have recognized it, nor do most modern audiences today; but the peculiarly intense atmosphere of the music – the slow, measured melody sung in octaves by tenor and bass soloists, while contrapuntal phrases are uttered by the orchestra – is unmistakable, unique in this opera and all operas (ex. 3).

Ex. 3

The part of the Queen of Night is famous for its high notes and rapid pace: Josefa Hofer (Mozart's sister-in-law), for whom it was written, must have had a high F (above so-called 'top C') in her voice.

LA CLEMENZA DI TITO
(The Clemency of Titus)
Libretto by Pietro Metastasio and Caterino Mazzolà

First performed: Prague, 1791
Two Acts

Cast in order of singing:

SEXTUS (Sesto), FRIEND OF TITUS,
   IN LOVE WITH VITELLIA   *male mezzo-soprano*
VITELLIA, DAUGHTER OF THE LATE ROMAN EMPEROR *soprano*
ANNIUS (Annio), FRIEND OF SEXTUS,
   IN LOVE WITH SERVILIA   *soprano*
TITUS (Tito), ROMAN EMPEROR   *tenor*
SERVILIA, SISTER OF SEXTUS,
   IN LOVE WITH ANNIUS   *soprano*
PUBLIUS (Publio), COMMANDER OF THE PRAETORIAN
   GUARD   *bass*

Chorus of Romans
The scene is laid in Rome during the reign of Titus, AD 79–81

In the last months of his life, Mozart received a commission from Prague – a city where he had enjoyed great success with *Le nozze di Figaro* and *Don Giovanni* – for an opera on the coronation of the new Austro–Hungarian emperor as King of Bohemia. The libretto was specified: *La clemenza di Tito*, written by Metastasio in 1734 and since then set dozens of times by all the principal composers of *opera seria*. But the style was by now considered out of date, and for Mozart the text was heavily revised by Caterino Mazzolà, the court poet at Dresden. Mazzolà shortened the lengthy recitative, reduced the number of arias and provided some ensembles, including the Act I finale with chorus, and reduced the three acts to two.

La clemenza di Tito was one of Mozart's most admired operas in the decades after his death, but then faded in the public taste; writers on Mozart tended to dismiss it as composed in haste and in an antiquated form. Only recently has it been rehabilitated: though indeed formal and statuesque in some respects, these are attributes well suited to the subject, as too is the economical scoring – there is little here of the allusive, chattering woodwind of *Figaro* or *Così fan tutte*. The classical simplicity and nobility were noted by discerning contemporaries. The plot, typical in its dilemmas involving the rival claims of love and honour, is typical too in its glorification of benevolent rulers (fittingly for a coronation opera) – Leopold and his subjects could identify the new-crowned king with the generous and merciful emperor.

According to an early writer, Mozart wrote much of the opera in the coach between Vienna and Prague. He did in fact arrive in Prague little more than a week before the première, but probably much of the opera was written by then. It seems, however, that he left most of the arias – except those for Titus, whose role was taken by a singer he knew (the Ottavio in *Don Giovanni*) – to be composed after his arrival in Prague, when he would have heard the cast. As he was so pressed for time he left the recitatives to be written by an assistant, in all likelihood F. X. Süssmayr (famous for his completion of the *Requiem*).

★　★　★

ACT I: Vitellia, whose father had been dispossessed as Roman emperor by Titus's father, is furious to hear that Titus is considering taking a foreign wife, Berenice, thus passing over her own claims to be empress. She urges Sextus to proceed with a plot he has devised at her bidding to fire the Capitol and kill Titus; Sextus, who adores her, agrees, but both are in anguish. Annius enters with the news that Titus has despatched Berenice and is to choose a Roman wife, so Vitellia tells Sextus to delay the act. She leaves the two men alone and Annius reminds Sextus of his desire to marry Sextus's sister, Servilia; the two affirm their friendship.

In the forum, the Roman populace and envoys from the provinces assemble to greet Titus. Publius announces that the Senate has decided that a memorial should be built to the emperor, but Titus prefers the money to be spent on relieving distress after the eruption of Vesuvius. He is further acclaimed. All withdraw except Sextus and Annius, and, just as Sextus is to ask the imperial consent for Servilia's marriage to Annius, Titus tells them that his own choice has fallen on her. Sextus overcomes his confusion, Annius his dismay; and Annius is sent to tell Servilia that she is to be empress. Titus, unaware of their mixed feelings, expresses pleasure in the generosity he can offer. He and Sextus leave, and Servilia enters, to be told by Annius that they must exchange no more endearments: she is now to be his queen, and must forgive him his former love (duet: 'Ah perdona il primo affetto'), a love that for both of them remains strong.

In the gardens on Palatine hill, Titus is discussing affairs of state with Publius. Servilia arrives, to be greeted as 'empress'; but she begs him to pause, and (with Publius drawing aside) she confesses to him that her heart is Annius's – though if he so commands, she will be Titus's bride. Titus, a model of self-abnegation, expresses his pleasure at her frankness and at once yields her up. He departs; now Vitellia enters and ironically congratulates Servilia, who leaves, hinting that all is not yet decided. Vitellia is enraged at being passed over, and when Sextus enters she taunts him as a coward. He proclaims his readiness to go and secure her vengeance ('Parto, parto'), and hurries off. Now Publius and Annius arrive to tell Vitellia that she is Titus's chosen consort. She is horrified, for Sextus has gone and Titus is to be murdered; they take her confusion for the effects of great joy ('Vengo! aspettate! Sesto!' – 'I come! wait, Sextus!').

In the square before the Capitol, Sextus is in agonies over what he has done: for Vitellia (who does not even love him) he has traitorously agreed to murder his friend, the noble and just emperor, and already the Capitol is ablaze, showing that the conspiracy is under way. Annius arrives as Sextus enters the Capitol; Servilia and Publius soon follow, and then – as the distant, mournful cries of the people are heard, Vitellia. Sextus returns, thinking he has killed Titus; he is riven with shame. He tells them that Titus is dead and only Vitellia's silencing him prevents him from confessing the crime. All mourn the act of betrayal.

ACT II: Annius tells Sextus, in the imperial gardens, that Titus is not, after all, dead. Sextus admits his involvement in the conspiracy, and Annius advises him to return to Titus's side and prove his loyalty. As he departs Vitellia enters: Sextus's role has been discovered, she says, and he must flee from Rome. But it is too late, for Publius enters, with guards, and arrests Sextus – in the dark, thinking he was killing Titus, he had merely wounded one of the conspirators, Lentulus, who had now confessed. He bids farewell to the bitterly remorseful Vitellia as Publius impatiently waits to lead him to the Senate, where he is to be tried.

A crowd is assembled in a great hall to give thanks that Titus has been spared. Publius tries to lead Titus off to attend the public games, but the emperor is anxious to know the outcome of Sextus's trial. Publius comments on Titus's inability to believe in the falsehood of others. Annius comes to plead for Sextus, but Publius returns with the news that he has confessed his guilt and is to be thrown to the beasts; only Titus's signature is needed for the sentence to be carried out. Annius renews his pleas, then departs. Alone, Titus reflects on betrayal and friendship; should he sign the sentence of death? He resolves to summon Sextus to learn if there is some secret explanation of his conduct; the responsibilities of office

weigh heavily on him. Publius brings in Sextus, who is appalled at
the emperor's stern face ('Quello di Tito è il volto?'), just as Titus is
at Sextus's broken spirit. When Publius leaves, Titus begs Sextus to
reveal his secret; but Sextus – who must condemn Vitellia, empress-
elect, if he is to excuse himself – remains silent, and can only ask in
general terms for a mercy of which he knows he is unworthy,
begging the emperor to recall for a moment their former affection
('Deh, per questo istante solo'). He is taken away, and Publius
returns, eager to know what is decided; Titus says the decision is
made, and Publius expects the worst, although Titus now reflects,
before he leaves, on the virtues of magnanimity. Now Annius and
Servilia approach Vitellia, whose pleas, as empress-elect, Titus
could not ignore: Servilia begs her to intercede for her brother.
Vitellia, deeply disturbed, realizes now that she cannot let Sextus die
and, with that on her conscience, become Titus's wife; she bids
farewell to the garlands of flowers she had longed for ('Non più di
fiori vaghe catene').

Senators, patricians and plebeians are assembled in the amphitheatre, where Sextus is brought before Titus. Titus begins to
address him, but then Vitellia rushes in, throws herself at his feet,
and confesses that her ambition and jealousy led her to seduce Sextus
into his traitor's role. Titus forgives her, and Sextus and the other
conspirators; all sing in praise of his clemency.

★   ★   ★

An opera about honour and love in ancient Rome clearly demands a
musical style quite different from one about amorous intrigues in
contemporary Spain or Italy, so it is not to be wondered at that
Mozart set *La clemenza di Tito* in a manner entirely unlike that of his
Da Ponte operas. The serene, elevated style – even Mozart's contemporaries commented on its kinship with the German classical revival
of the late eighteenth century – is best seen in Titus's own arias,
though those for Sextus especially are charged with a good deal more
of emotion. But the most beautiful single number in the opera is the
sad little pledge of undying love between Annius and Servilia in Act
I, when they think they are to be parted; this melody was so popular
in the early nineteenth century that Shelley wrote verses to fit it, and
it was several times used as a hymn (ex. 1).

One of the outstanding moments of this opera is the ending of the
first-act finale. In contrast with the extended multi-section finales of
the Da Ponte operas, with their increasing tension and pace, this one,

Ex. 1
ANNIUS
Ah per - do - na il pri - mo af - fet - to que - sto ac - cen - te scon - si -

glia - to: col - pa fu del lab - bro u - sa - to a co - sì chia - mar - ti o -

- gnor, a co - sì chia - mar - ti o - gnor.

of more modest length, starts rapidly and at a high level of excitement, and ends slowly, on a sombre note, as all deplore the act of
treachery; the principals, on the stage, echo the words and the music
of the populace. Some of the credit for this inspired scene belongs
with Mazzolà, who inserted it into the original libretto of Metastasio; but the musical originality is remarkable (ex. 2).

Many of the arias in the opera are quite short; full–length ones are
generally reserved for the prima donna (Vitellia) and the primo
uomo (Sextus). Sextus has two extended arias; it is interesting to
note that in each the music goes slow-fast-faster, symbolizing,
especially in the first, his screwing up his courage and resolve. The
slow-fast aria was a standard form for a big, climactic outburst, and
here Mozart uses the device to powerful dramatic ends. He does so,

Ex. 2

too, for Vitellia's final aria in an analogous situation. For Sextus's
'Parto, parto' and this, 'Non più di fiori', Mozart supplied obbligato
parts – a rarity at this date – for clarinet and basset-horn (a clarinet-
like instrument of tenor pitch) respectively, composed for his friend
Anton Stadler, dedicatee of the clarinet concerto and quintet, who
was playing in the Prague orchestra; the interplay between Vitellia's
voice and the basset-horn (with its tones of 'watery melancholy', as
Bernard Shaw once said) gives a unique and fascinating colour to the
music (ex. 3).

Ex. 3

pur   a - vria   di   me   pie - tà

LUDWIG VAN BEETHOVEN

1770–1827

Mozart's greatest contemporary, Haydn, also wrote operas – mostly for the noble Esterházy family, to whom he was in service for much of his career. These operas, written in Italian or occasionally German, ranged from formal classical drama (one on the story of Orpheus and Eurydice) to light comedy of manners such as *La fedeltà premiata* ('Fidelity rewarded'). But in general Haydn lacked Mozart's sense of the theatre. His stage works were no models for the earnest young German composer who came to Vienna to study with Haydn and then made Vienna his home: Ludwig van Beethoven.

Nor was Beethoven satisfied with Mozart's ideas on opera. 'I could not compose operas like *Don Giovanni* or *Le nozze di Figaro*', he declared. 'They are repugnant to me. I could not have chosen such subjects. They are too frivolous for me!' The serious moral aspect of *Die Zauberflöte*, however, was another matter. Beethoven's one opera, *Fidelio*, was likewise an 'ethical' one. But its action, instead of being that of a fairy-tale, concerns real life. In having a rescue as its point of climax it is indebted to Cherubini's *Les deux journées*, 'The Two Days', known in English as *The Water Carrier*. Luigi Cherubini (1760–1842) was an Italian who lived in Paris from 1788: his French opera *Médée* ('Medea') has enjoyed modern revivals.

FIDELIO
Fidelio, oder die eheliche Liebe
(Fidelio, or Married Love)
Libretto by Josef Sonnleithner after a libretto by
J. N. Bouilly; revision by G. F. Treitschke

First performed: Vienna, 1805
Final revised version: Vienna, 1814
Two acts

Cast in order of singing:

JAQUINO, PORTER AT THE PRISON   *tenor*
MARZELLINE, ROCCO'S DAUGHTER   *soprano*
LEONORE, WIFE OF FLORESTAN, DISGUISED AS 'FIDELIO',
    A YOUTH   *soprano*
ROCCO, JAILER OF THE PRISON   *bass*
DON PIZARRO, GOVERNOR OF THE PRISON   *baritone*
FLORESTAN, A SPANISH NOBLEMAN   *tenor*
DON FERNANDO, MINISTER OF STATE   *bass*

Chorus of soldiers, prisoners and people
The scene is laid in a fortress near Seville

The urge which later led Beethoven to incorporate a setting of part of
Schiller's *Ode to Freedom* (camouflaged as an *Ode to Joy*) in the Ninth
Symphony also led him to write an opera which is really about
freedom. The contrast in *Fidelio* between the darkness of imprisonment – which is taken as unjust political imprisonment – and the
light of justice and liberty is both heard in the music and seen on the
stage. It is this ethical force in addition to the purely musical strength
and beauty of Beethoven's score that gives *Fidelio* its unique appeal
among the great operas.

Against the blackness of the villainous governor of the jail,
Pizarro, is set the character of the Minister of State: a brief role, but
one which must embody in performance the all-important idea of
light triumphant. The ethical tone is sustained by the fact that the
hero and heroine of the work are already married – a comparative
rarity in opera.

The story (of a woman who dresses in male clothes in order to
rescue her husband) is said to be a true one, happening within the
knowledge of J. N. Bouilly, a Frenchman who cast it originally as an
opera libretto for Pierre Gaveaux (1761–1825). Not only Gaveaux
made an opera of it but also the composers Simon Mayr (1763–1845)
and Ferdinando Paer (1771–1839).

Beethoven called the heroine by the German form 'Leonore'; the
name is often changed in English usage to 'Leonora', especially in the
concert hall (see below, page 110).

★   ★   ★

ACT I: In the lodgings of Rocco, the jailer, his daughter Marzelline
is being courted by Jaquino, the young porter of the prison. But she

does not care for him; her love is for the young man, known as Fidelio, who has been engaged as her father's assistant.

Rocco, her father, enters, and then Fidelio himself. But the 'young man' who has so taken Marzelline's fancy is really a woman in disguise. 'Fidelio' (the word, of course, suggesting *fidelity*) is the name which has been assumed by Leonore, wife of Florestan. Her aim in entering the prison's service is to find and rescue her husband, whom she suspects is languishing there, unjustly imprisoned. Even at the cost of seeming to accept Marzelline's devotion she cannot reveal her true identity.

Rocco, Marzelline, Leonore and Jaquino (who re-enters) now join in a quartet: 'Mir ist so wunderbar' ('To me it is so wonderful'). Jacquino leaves. Rocco points out in an aria that young people about to marry need money. A trio follows: Marzelline is now happy that Fidelio is her approved suitor, but Leonore thinks only of the rescue.

The scene changes. A military march announces the arrival of Pizarro, governor of the prison: it is he who has unjustly imprisoned Florestan. A message warns him that the Minister of State is coming on an inspection. He decides to have Florestan killed: 'Ha! welch' ein Augenblick!' ('Ha! what a moment!'). Bribing Rocco to dig the grave, he resolves to kill Florestan himself, and posts a trumpeter to sound a warning at the Minister's approach.

Leonore has overheard the plot. Alone, she delivers her feelings of love for her husband and loathing for Pizarro: 'Abscheulicher!' ('Monster!').

Now, on Leonore's intercession, the ordinary prisoners (not Florestan, in solitary confinement) are allowed out of their cells for a brief opportunity to breathe the open air. In the Prisoners' Chorus, they utter the word 'freedom' – but guardedly, as they remember that their every word is overheard. Leonore learns that she is to be given an opportunity to help dig the grave intended for a certain special prisoner. Meanwhile Pizarro is enraged that the prisoners have been allowed out, and is calmed only when Rocco remembers that it is the king's name-day and that this therefore is legitimate celebration.

But now the prisoners are sent back to their cells, their voices joining with the commands of Pizarro to Rocco and the private comments of Marzelline, Leonore and Jaquino.

ACT II: In the deepest dungeon, chained and in darkness, lies one man. It is Florestan. 'Gott, welch' Dunkel hier!' ('God, what darkness here!), he sings. His aria takes on the quality of hope when he sees, as in a vision, his 'angel, Leonore'. He sinks back and does not hear when Rocco and Leonore arrive to dig the grave in the cell itself. In dialogue interrupted by music we learn that Leonore cannot at first see the prisoner's face. But, having gained Rocco's permission to give the prisoner some food and drink, she becomes sure that it is Florestan indeed. Florestan, grateful for her human pity, still cannot recognize the jailer's young assistant as his own wife.

Now Pizarro, who has warned a trumpeter to sound the alarm should the Minister be seen approaching, enters and reveals himself to Florestan. He is about to kill Florestan when Fidelio throws herself in front of Florestan declaring that Pizarro must first kill Florestan's wife: 'Tödt erst sein Weib!' Her declaration of identity stuns both Pizarro and Florestan. Pizarro would now kill Leonore as well, but she produces a pistol – and suddenly a trumpet-call sounds: the Minister is at the gates. Guards enter with lights. Pizarro and Rocco go to meet him and a duet of 'joy beyond name' follows between the reunited Leonore and Florestan ('O namen-, namenlose Freude').

The scene changes. The Minister recognizes his friend Florestan, sends Pizarro away under arrest, and gives to Leonore the joyous task of unlocking Florestan's chains. Marzelline turns her affections back to Jaquino, and the chorus (now including onlookers as well as prisoners) salute the happy day and the strength of a wife's love.

★   ★   ★

The overture begins with a quick, arresting figure, as imperious as an upraised hand. This, the *'Fidelio* overture', is not the overture which Beethoven's first audience heard. They heard the overture which is now sometimes heard at concerts under the name of '*Leonora No. 2*': '*Leonora*' because that is the anglicized name of the heroine of the opera, the title of the original libretto and also the title under which Beethoven himself wanted the opera to be known (the theatre authorities decided otherwise), and '*No. 2*' because Beethoven was supposed to have composed and rejected an overture now known as '*Leonora No. 1*'.

At its first performance the opera was a failure. Originally in three acts, it was cut down to two for a performance in 1806, but this also was unsatisfactory. Beethoven wrote for the occasion another overture, now called '*Leonora No. 3*'. This is one of Beethoven's masterpieces, more an orchestral expression of the entire opera than a mere introduction to it. Next he wrote *Leonora No. 1*, probably in

1807, for a performance planned for Prague but abandoned. At the final revision of the opera (1814) he introduced a new and simpler overture, which we call the *Fidelio* overture.

Opera conductors, however, can be as vainglorious as any pima donna. Some of them *will* have their *Leonora No. 3*. In Victorian England this overture was sometimes inserted between the two acts. Then Mahler, as conductor at the Vienna Court Opera (1879–1907), established the practice of putting it in the middle of the last act, before the last scene – a practice followed by many other conductors (without Beethoven's authority, of course).

Other liberties have in recent decades been taken with *Fidelio* – the reversal of the order of the opening two numbers (this is a return to the first version of the opera); the omission of Rocco's song about money; and the curtailment of the choral part of the final scene. Such retouching is presumptuous; *Fidelio* has immensely moving theatrical power just as Beethoven left it.

A particularly audacious stroke, and a masterly one, is the quartet in the first act. This is a canon; here are four people expressing their different innermost feelings to the *same* melody in turn. Yet somehow the unity of mood embraces all. The melody is first sung by Marzelline: 'To me it is so wondrous, his heart inclines to me; he loves me, it is clear, I shall be lucky'); then – in the following stanza, from which we quote – it is sung by Leonore to new words ('How great the danger is! how weakly shines my hope! she loves me, it is clear, oh pain beyond name!'), while Marzelline puts her original words to a new melody (ex. 1).

Leonore's great aria in Act I harnesses the 'modernity' of Beethoven's language to an old-fashioned operatic 'scena' in three parts – introductory recitative, slow section, fast section. The slow section – to the words 'Come, hope, let the lost star's weary light not fade' takes the form of a sublime dialogue with three horns and strings (ex. 2, page 113).

Ex. 1

Ex. 2

The opera's great climax occurs when Leonore levels her pistol at Pizarro and suddenly (as she tells him 'One sound and you are dead!') the trumpet-call is heard off-stage (ex. 3). The suddenness is emphasized by a dramatic key-change (D major to B flat).

Ex. 3

CARL MARIA VON WEBER

1786–1826

The peculiar intensity of Beethoven's musical language left its stamp on the musicians who followed. But German opera, so far following the realistic, ethical (one might say 'political') path of *Fidelio*, turned mainly to the cultivation of the fantastic, the grotesque, the supernatural. This 'romanticism' is a feature of German literature no less than of German music of the period, and both are evident in the art of Carl Maria von Weber. His *Freischütz* remains the only German work between Beethoven and Wagner to have held the international stage.

Weber died prematurely, of tuberculosis, in London, having come for the first performance of his opera *Oberon* (1826). This was commissioned to an English libretto, which now needs thoroughly rewriting if the delightful music is to gain the currency it deserves.

DER FREISCHÜTZ
(The Marksman with Magic Bullets)
Libretto by Johann Friedrich Kind

First performed: Berlin, 1821
Three Acts

Cast in order of singing or speaking:

MAX, A YOUNG FORESTER, IN LOVE WITH AGATHE	*tenor*
KILIAN, A PEASANT	*bass*
CUNO, THE HEAD RANGER	*bass*
CASPAR, ANOTHER YOUNG FORESTER	*bass*
AENNCHEN, AGATHE'S COUSIN	*soprano*
AGATHE, CUNO'S DAUGHTER	*soprano*
THE DEMON ZAMIEL	*speaking part*

OTTOKAR, PRINCE OF THE REGION   *baritone*
A HERMIT   *bass*

The scene is laid in Bohemia shortly after the end of
the Seven Years War (1756–63)

Der Freischütz is one of the very few opera titles which cannot be
more or less straightforwardly translated. Literally it means 'The
free-shooter'; it might be paraphased 'The marksman with magic
bullets'. The casting of these magic bullets under the Devil's super-
vision, and the use thereafter made of them, forms one chief interest
in the opera; the other two are romantic love and conventional rustic
and hunting jollification. The music unites all three. Spoken
dialogue (usually shortened in performance) links the music. The
following synopsis makes the omissions which are customary in
modern performances.

The score has richness of melody (both solo and choral) and a
warmth of feeling which have kept it alive even in an age which
would never endure in a non-musical play such naïve representation
of the supernatural.

★   ★   ★

ACT I: Max, a forester, is derided because, at a shooting contest, he
has been beaten by Kilian, a peasant. Cuno, hereditary Head Ranger,
is worried too: his daughter, Agathe, is betrothed to Max. The very
next day, Max is due to demonstrate his marksmanship (and thus his
right to become Cuno's son-in-law and succeed him eventually)
before Prince Ottokar. But on this showing Max is unlikely to acquit
himself satisfactorily.

Alone, Max sings of his despair: 'Durch die Wälder' ('Through the
woods'). During this, unseen by Max, the figure of the demon
Zamiel makes a brief appearance. Now Max's fellow-forester,
Caspar, after a drinking-song, hands Max a gun and bids him fire at
an eagle high above – which falls dead at his feet. Caspar explains that
the shot was made with a magic bullet which always hits its mark,
and if Max will meet him in the Wolf's Glen at midnight they will
cast more such bullets, enabling Max to win tomorrow's contest.
Despite the stories of evil attached to the Wolf's Glen, Max consents.
Caspar, alone, exults. He has in fact sold himself to Zamiel and now
hopes to extend his own respite by substituting Max as Zamiel's
victim.

ACT II: In Agathe's room, her cousin Aennchen is hammering in a new nail for a picture that has fallen. Aennchen sings coquettishly, but Agathe is sad. Left alone, she sings of her love and her sense of anxiety: her song, at first a pious prayer ('Leise, leise' – 'Softly, softly'), becomes more impassioned as she sees her lover approach. Max enters, and Aennchen too returns. But Max soon declares he must leave them and go to the Wolf's Glen, and despite the girls' pleas he sets off.

The scene changes to the Wolf's Glen itself – with an owl, crows, a terrifying woodland landscape, a chorus of invisible spirits and Caspar, who is waiting for Max. At his bidding, Zamiel appears, but leaves before Max arrives. Despite ghostly warnings (one in the form of Max's mother, another in the form of Agathe) Max persists in his resolve. Together he and Caspar cast, by spells, the seven magic bullets, counting them. At each number some evil thing happens on the stage, and at the seventh, in place of a rotting tree, there stands Zamiel himself, reaching out his hand to grasp Max's own. Six bullets will hit as the marksman wishes; the seventh will do Zamiel's work.

ACT III: It is the day of the shooting trial and of the intended wedding. In her room, Agathe, in white bridal dress, is sad. After a song, alone, she tells Aennchen of a dream of ill omen. Aennchen pooh-poohs omens and then makes light of the matter, telling her 'Once my much-respected aunt had a dream' ('Einst träumte meiner sel'gen Base') – a tale involving a 'ghost' that turned out to be a dog. Agathe is not amused.

A chorus of bridesmaids arrives and Aennchen brings in a box which should contain a bridal bouquet. When the box is opened, however, there is a shock which cuts the bridesmaids' chorus short: it is a silver funeral wreath. A mistake in delivery, says Aennchen, but Agathe sees another bad omen. The bridesmaids' chorus, somewhat subdued, is resumed.

The scene changes to an open place. Prince Ottokar has been hunting and a chorus celebrates the sport as the huntsmen carouse. Max (who has evidently made three successful shots) is ordered by the prince to shoot at a white dove visible in a tree. 'Schiess nicht! ich bin die Taube!' ('Don't shoot, Max! I'm the dove!') says Agathe's voice; it seems too late, for her body falls and is picked up by a hermit who now appears. But she has only fainted. It is Caspar who has been hit; Zamiel (silent and unseen by anyone else) appears and claims him. Caspar dies.

Max relates the whole story. The prince sentences him to banish-
ment, but the hermit comes forward and bids the prince be merciful.
He relents. Max and Agathe may look forward to being married,
and all join in praise to heaven.

★   ★   ★

We have seen that Mozart, in several of his operas, quoted in the
overture from the music of the opera itself. In *Der Freischütz* the
overture is entirely built from melodies found in the opera.
Noteworthy are the extra two notes on the trombones (ex. 1, bar 5)
which give a sinister afterthought (which only just fails to sound
unintentionally comic) to the passionate melody with which Agathe
later greets her love to the words 'Himmel, nimm des Dankes
Zähren' ('Heaven, accept my thanks').

Ex. 1

But the real sinister element in *Der Freischütz* is in the music to the
Wolf's Glen – an unseen chorus, drum rolls, high woodwind shrieks
and *tremolo* on the strings. In the theatre it can still seem astonishingly
gripping as an accompaniment to the ever-increasing supernatural
storm.

Agathe's music is one of the peaks of German romantic expression
and Agathe herself stands musically between Leonore in *Fidelio* and
Senta in *Der fliegende Holländer*. A theme from her passionate first-act
aria is shown in ex. 1; her quieter aria in the final act (expressing her
belief in God's loving care), present 'even though a cloud covers the
sun', is equally characteristic – of herself and of Weber's style (ex. 2).

Ex. 2

Highly characteristic of German romantic opera too is the Huntsmen's Chorus. The convivial male choral society was an established
German institution for which a considerable repertory was provided
by Schubert, Schumann, Brahms and others, and the opera
admirably seizes on its special character in ex. 3 ('What pleasure
rivals the huntsman's?').

Ex. 3

GIOACCHINO ROSSINI

1792–1868

Stendhal, that witty champion of Rossini, wrote that he admittedly had his partiality as a critic but could still be good-natured: 'I have no craving actually to hang anyone, not even Herr Maria Weber, the composer of *Der Freischütz*.' Gioacchino Rossini and Carl Maria von Weber were, indeed, contemporaries – and opposites. Stendhal himself acutely pointed out the difference between the storm music in *Der Freischütz*, which musically conveys the evil atmosphere during the casting of the magic bullets, and the storm music in *Il barbiere di Siviglia* ('The Barber of Seville'), which just represents a storm.

Although *Le nozze di Figaro*, *Don Giovanni* and *Così fan tutte* were written in Italian, the tradition of Italian comic opera which had grown up in the eighteenth century is of a lighter kind than Mozart's. That tradition fully realizes itself in *Il matrimonio segreto* ('The Secret Marriage'; 1792) by Domenico Cimarosa (1749–1801). Ten years before *Il matrimonio segreto*, *Il barbiere di Siviglia* had already become operatically famous – not in Rossini's setting but in one by Giovanni Paisiello (1740–1816). Paisiello's version reigned internationally until superseded by Rossini's more vigorous score and has occasionally been revived in our own day.

Rossini worked substantially in three well-defined varieties of opera. First, comic opera, to which belonged *Il barbiere di Siviglia* and *La Cenèrentola* (both treated below), *L'italiana in Algeri* ('The Italian Girl in Algiers') and (in French) *Le Comte Ory* ('Count Ory'); second, old-fashioned Italian 'serious opera', Rossini's most famous example being *Semiramide* ('Semiramis'); thirdly, historical 'grand opera' of a distinctively French, nineteenth-century kind, exemplified in *Guillaume Tell* ('William Tell'; 1829). That work concluded Rossini's operatic activity, though he lived nearly forty years more.

IL BARBIERE DI SIVIGLIA
(The Barber of Seville)
Libretto by Cesare Sterbini, after Beaumarchais's play

First performed: Rome, 1816
Two Acts

Cast in order of singing:

FIORELLO, SERVANT TO ALMAVIVA	*bass*
COUNT ALMAVIVA, A YOUNG NOBLEMAN VISITING SEVILLE	*tenor*
FIGARO, BARBER AND FACTOTUM	*baritone*
ROSINA, A RICH WARD OF DR BARTOLO	*mezzo-soprano*
BARTOLO, A DOCTOR	*bass*
BERTA, AN ELDERLY MAID TO DR BARTOLO	*soprano*
AMBROGIO, SERVANT TO DR BARTOLO	*bass*
DON BASILIO, CLERIC AND MUSIC TEACHER	*bass*
A POLICE OFFICER	*baritone*

[The part of a notary is silent.]

Chorus (men only) of soldiers, police and musicians
The scene is laid in Seville

The French dramatist Beaumarchais (1733–99) wrote a cycle of three plays about Figaro. No well-known composer has set the third play as an opera. The first, however, *Il barbiere di Siviglia*, is the subject of Rossini's best-known opera; the second, *Le nozze di Figaro*, is the source of Mozart's. Thus Mozart's comes after Rossini's in time of action. The characters names mostly correspond.

Il barbiere di Siviglia has not the serious element of pathos notable in *Le nozze di Figaro*. Its music is the music of wit, coquetry, intrigue and excitement. The sparkle of the young Rosina, the comic nastiness of Basilio with his recipe for a successful slander, and the breezy bounce of the barber himself ('Figaro here, Figaro there') – Rossini characterizes all these with skill, verve and human insight. The score is always cut in stage performances, and the story as given below follows the action usually performed. The heroine's part was written for a mezzo-soprano; it has been grabbed by countless sopranos (who usually have to alter the notes considerably) but there is now a disposition to restore it to its proper voice.

In the Lesson Scene, prima donnas have sung songs of their own choice, even 'Home, Sweet Home' (composed long after the opera and ludicrously inappropriate to the situation). But Rossini, as a matter of fact, provided his own song for the Lesson Scene: 'Contro un cor che accende d'amore' ('Against a heart aflame with love'); and it is the new-fangled coloratura of this that Bartolo cries down in favour of good old-fashioned music of which he gives a comic example. This coloratura aria is introduced as coming from a new opera called 'The Useless Precaution'; so, too, is the piece of music which Rosina pretends to drop from the balcony in the opening scene. The subtitle 'or, The Useless Precaution' in fact belongs to *Il barbiere di Siviglia* itself.

★   ★   ★

ACT I: In a street by Bartolo's house a band of musicians is assembling under the direction of Fiorello, Count Almaviva's servant. To their accompaniment Almaviva sings a serenade 'Ecco ridente in cielo' ('See, smiling in the heavens') underneath Rosina's window in the house. The musicians make a noisy exit. The Count stands aside as Figaro enters: 'Largo al factotum della città' ('Make way for the factotum of the city'). He and Almaviva recognize each other and Figaro, having the position of visiting barber-factotum in Bartolo's house, agrees to help further Almaviva's plans.

Rosina, who appears on her balcony with Bartolo, drops a note into the street and asks Bartolo to go and retrieve it, saying it is the music of a song which she let fall by accident. Almaviva (for whom it was really intended) picks it up: in it Rosina asks to know his name. In a song (accompanied, properly, by himself on the guitar) he tells her it is Lindoro. (He does not wish to divulge his true rank.)

Stimulated by money from Almaviva, Figaro has the idea of introducing him into Bartolo's house as a drunken soldier demanding a billet. Figaro leaves Almaviva with a pattering description of how to find his shop 'with five wigs in the window'.

The scene changes to a room within Bartolo's house. In 'Una voce poco fa' ('A voice, a little while ago') Rosina shows her mettle; she can appear docile on the surface but will get her way. When she leaves, Bartolo tells Don Basilio – a cleric and scandal-monger as well as a music-master – that he has heard that Count Almaviva is in town and is pursuing her. Basilio advises spreading a scandal about him – and in his aria 'La calunnia' ('The slander') shows how a little rumour may grow and grow until it explodes like a thunderclap.

Figaro tells Rosina that 'Lindoro' is deeply in love with her and asks her to write a note to him. But she, the cunning creature, has prepared one already! Bartolo re-enters and warns Rosina not to try to deceive him. Then arrives the 'drunken soldier' (Almaviva in disguise), who cannot even pronounce Bartolo's name rightly. Rosina sees the game at once. Eventually Bartolo produces a document exempting him from billeting, but the 'soldier' brushes it aside and the comic disorder (now involving Basilio and Figaro too) increases.

Suddenly there is a knock. It is the police: they have come to investigate the noise. All except Almaviva try to catch the officer's ear simultaneously. The officer arrests Almaviva but, when Almaviva secretly identifies himself to him, releases and salutes him, to everyone's stupefaction. All in turn (Rosina first) join in an ensemble of perplexity – 'Fredda ed immobile' ('Cold and motionless') – in which the excitement gradually mounts.

ACT II: An unknown music-master enters the house and greets the surprised Dr Bartolo. Like Basilio, he is a cleric, and endlessly repeats his blessing: 'Pace e gioia sia con voi' ('Peace and joy be with you'). He declares that he is deputizing for Don Basilio, who is ill. It is Almaviva, in another disguise. To convince Bartolo he gives him the letter he had from Rosina, as if he had received it from someone else by means of intrigue. Rosina sings a song (this is the Lesson Scene) which enables her to come amorously near the 'teacher'. Bartolo comically demonstrates what his, old-fashioned idea of good music is. Figaro enters, with an appointment to shave Bartolo.

Basilio enters. All are disconcerted, but the lovers and Figaro tell him he really *is* ill. A purse slipped to him by Almaviva gives a firm hint to him and he goes, with endless repetition of 'Buona sera!' ('Good evening!'). Bartolo is shaved. The lovers, aided by Figaro, plan to elope at midnight.

Berta, the elderly maidservant, alone, sings pointedly about her employer wanting to marry his ward: 'Il vecchiotto cerca moglie' ('The old man wants a wife').

Bartolo confronts Rosina with her letter and insinuates that Figaro and the false 'music master' are conspiring to deliver her to another man – namely, Count Almaviva. The angry Rosina (not realizing that Almaviva and Lindoro are the same) discloses the plan for elopement and agrees to marry Bartolo.

The stage empties. There is a storm outside as Figaro and Almaviva enter. They explain matters to Rosina and disclose that

Lindoro is in fact Almaviva himself. A notary, procured by Bartolo
for his own marriage to Rosina, unites Rosina and Almaviva, with
Basilio (at pistol-point) and Figaro as witnesses. Bartolo, entering
with an officer and soldiers, orders the arrest of the miscreants – but
then, learning what has happened, realizes he is too late and accepts
the situation. A gay ensemble (backed by the soldiers as male chorus)
ends the opera.

★   ★   ★

Rossini makes *Il barbiere di Siviglia* a real play-in-music, with a
constantly developing plot, and at the same time he provides real
display-pieces for the singers. The barbier's own self-introducing
aria, with its rapid patter of 'Figaro here, Figaro there' is too
well-known to need quotation. Equally appropriate to situation and
personality is Don Basilio's Slander Song (with its musical illustration of how malicious rumour explodes on the victim's head 'like a
cannon-shot').

   When Rosina reveals herself to us at the beginning of the second
scene, the elaborated repetition of one of her phrases becomes a
musical demonstration of the cunning coquetry by which she will
twist her guardian round her little finger. She declares she will lay 'a
hundred traps' for him (ex. 1).

Ex. 1   Allegro moderato
        ROSINA

Rossini was thought in his day to be a very noisy composer. The
'Rossini *crescendo*' – a very long, gradual *crescendo* extending over a
whole ensemble with repeated sections – is indeed characteristic of
him, though he did not invent it. But it is a real dramatic device, and
never better used than in the finale of Act I of *Il barbiere di Siviglia*,
when it indicates a growing atmosphere of confusion and accusation. Shortly before this, with similar skill, Rossini uses the pace

and style of a patter-song not for one soloist but for six people addressing the officer of police simultaneously. It is often complained that in operatic ensembles one cannot hear different sets of words because they are all uttered together: this is exactly what happens here, but this time it is on purpose! The audience's reaction exactly corresponds to that of the bewildered officer. The repeated 'Si, signor' is tossed comically from one character to another in a section which begins with Bartolo's complaint at having been molested by 'this pest of a soldier' (ex. 2).

Ex. 2

The overture, by the way, was originally used by Rossini in an earlier opera altogether: so was the Count's serenade in Act I. In turn, an aria of the Count's in Act II (now usually omitted) was re-used as the heroine's final joyous strain 'Non più mesta' in *La Cenerentola*.

LA CENERENTOLA
(Cinderella)
Libretto by Jacopo Ferretti

First performed: Rome, 1817
Two Acts

Cast in order of singing:

CLORINDA } DAUGHTERS OF DON MAGNIFICO   *soprano*
TISBE   } AND HALF-SISTERS TO CINDERELLA   *mezzo-soprano*
ANGELINA (known as Cenerentola, i.e. Cinderella),
   STEP-DAUGHTER TO DON MAGNIFICO   *mezzo-soprano*
ALIDORO, TUTOR TO PRINCE RAMIRO   *bass*
DON MAGNIFICO, AN IMPROVERISHED NOBLEMAN   *bass*
RAMIRO, PRINCE OF SALERNO   *tenor*
DANDINI, THE PRINCE'S VALET   *baritone*

Chorus of ladies, gentleman and servants
of the prince's court
*The scene is laid in Don Magnifico's home
and a nearby palace*

Pathos and comedy, coloratura fireworks and witty patter are all in this operatic *Cinderella*, which the heroine concludes with one of Rossini's most celebrated vocal showpieces. It is no wonder that this opera has had a prominent place in the post-war theatrical revival of Rossini's work.

But the opera was heard in London as early as 1820, well before the pantomime version; indeed it seems to have contributed to the shaping of the pantomime. Yet so familiar is the latter that English-speaking audiences have now to be warned of the 'oddity' of the opera – namely, that there is no element of magic in its plot, Instead of a fairy godmother there is a plotting tutor, Alidoro, who pulls the strings and attends matter-of-factly to the details of Cinderella's going to the ball. Incidentally, Alidoro, after casting off his disguise as a beggar, is revealed 'in philosopher's clothing', according to the libretto. Anyone wishing to know the proper clothing for a philosopher has, therefore, only to see the opera.

To the baron, Cinderella's stepfather, Rossini gave two big

comic arias. In some modern English productions he has been allotted only the first of these, but it has been put in the place occupied by the second (that is, the opening of Act II). In the following synopsis the proper segment is observed. The part of the heroine, it will be noted, is for a mezzo-soprano, as in *Il barbiere di Siviglia* (and also *L'italiana in Algeri*). Her half-sisters are vain and silly; but they are not grotesque and are not called 'the Ugly Sisters'.

★　★　★

ACT I: While her half-sisters, Clorinda and Tisbe, are preening themselves, Cinderella is doing household tasks and singing her pathetic little song 'Una volta c'era un rè' ('Once there lived a king'). The entry of Alidoro, disguised as a beggar, shows up Cinderella's kindness and her half-sisters' lack of feeling. A group of courtiers enters with the announcement that Prince Ramiro will soon be here to bid Don Magnifico's daughters to a ball, where he will choose the fairest woman as his bride. Clorinda and Tisbe redouble their efforts to look attractive, each calling on Cinderella to bring her this and that.

The noise brings in Don Magnifico, angry at being wakened out of a dream. He tells it to Clorinda and Tisbe: though the dream involves his being turned into an ass he is sure it means that his daughters are to marry princes. Gleefully he anticipates dandling his royal grandchildren. Naturally, the news of the coming ball only strengthens his feeling.

Alidoro has persuaded Prince Ramiro to change identities with his valet, Dandini, and has advised him that a daughter of the baron will be the best bride for him. He arrives on a reconnaissance and is beguiled by the charms of the nervous girl who appears, and whom he takes to be a serving-maid: Cinderella. Her tender feeling are aroused too, and there follows a duet, 'Un soave non so che' ('O sweet something'). Don Magnifico re-enters fussily. Clorinda and Tisbe are still dressing themselves up when Dandini (masquerading as the prince himself) arrives, escorted by courtiers.

Dandini sings an affected song in stilted language and flowing musical phrases. He puts on a ridiculous 'grand manner' which mightily impresses Clorinda and Tisbe (who now enter) and their father. He extends 'his' invitation to the ball. Cinderella begs Don Magnifico to take her to the ball too – 'for just a half-hour, even for a quarter!' – but he rudely repulses her, and tries to justify himself to Dandini and Ramiro who have overheard.

Alidoro returns, this time as an official with a census-register, demanding to know where Don Magnifico's 'third daughter' is. Confused, Don Magnifico alleges that she died. There is a moment of doubt: in a quintet, each entering in turn, all present voice their suspicions of what is going on: 'Nel volto estatico' ('On [each] rapt face').

When all the others leave, Alidoro surprises Cinderella by telling her she *will* go to the ball, and he will take her. She can hardly believe him – is this just a play they are supposed to be acting? 'Yes, my daughter – all the world's a stage'. Alidoro's aria, which follows, is devoted to this theme. (An alternative aria, much grander, was later written by Rossini: it dwells on the mercy of Providence.)

The scene changes to Prince Ramiro's palace, where Dandini (still disguised as the prince) tells Don Magnifico that he will recognize his knowledge of wines by promoting him steward of his household. Then he pretends in his grand manner to plead love simultaneously to Clorinda and Tisbe, who have become jealous rivals of each other.

But, with Ramiro, Dandini tells him in a comically rapid patter-duet that he has found out both are boobies: 'Zitto, zitto, piano, piano' ('Quietly, quietly, softly, softly').

Again confronted with Clorinda and Tisbe, Dandini says he will marry one of them and give the other to his squire (pointing to the real prince). Both girls recoil in horror while Dandini and Ramiro enjoy the joke.

Alidoro enters with the announcement that a strange lady, veiled, has arrived. Clorinda and Tisbe feel agitated. The strange lady (Cinderella, of course) tells him that 'All is not gold that glitters' ('Sprezzo quei don che versa'). Dandini is delighted; Ramiro strangely moved. She unveils. Her beauty – and to Clorinda and Tisbe, her resemblance to Cinderella – are an astonishment.

Don Magnifico, who has been in the cellar, re-enters and does not know what to believe. All express doubt, confusion and excitement in a big ensemble.

ACT II: Dandini has himself fallen in love with Cinderella but she tells him she loves his squire. The 'squire' (that is, the real Prince Ramiro) overhears this and claims her. But she gives him a bracelet and then, telling him he must find its companion and so discover who she is, she leaves. Resuming his true identity, the prince summons his courtiers and declares he will go in search of her.

Dandini, piqued at having to resume his station, is interrupted by the baron, whom he leads further by the nose before revealing at last that he is not the prince but only a valet. The baron is furious.

Back in the baron's house, Cinderella is in her shabby clothes once more when her father and half-sisters return from the ball. A storm rages, and Alidoro contrives that the prince's coach shall break down outside the house and he shall ask for shelter. He does so, and recognizes Cinderella, who learns that her squire is really the prince. A big sextet of confusion follows – 'Questo è un nodo avvilupato' ('Here's an intricate knot'). Ramiro flings back in the faces of Clorinda and Tisbe their expressions of horror at the idea of marrying him (in Act I, when they thought him a courtier), and after another sextet he leaves with Cinderella. Clorinda and Tisbe face the problem of begging for pardon.

Back in the palace Cinderella, richly dressed, is welcomed as a princess. She forgives her step-father and his daughters and sings of her transformation: 'Nacqui all'affano, al pianto' ('Born to misery and weeping'). Then, in exultant style, supported by all present, she brings the story to an end: 'Non più mesta accanto al fuoco' ('No longer sad by the fireside').

★ ★ ★

The transformation from the household drudge to the princess is expressed in the distance from Cinderella's pathetic little opening air to the brilliant, joyous runs of her final one – that is, from her ditty 'Long ago there lived a king' (ex. 1) to the ecstasy when she dismisses her long suffering as only a vanished nightmare (ex. 2) – the latter using the entire range of the voice.

Ex. 1

The ensemble, steadily building up in volume and tension, and allowing one character at a time to break out into individually

Ex. 2

passionate expression, are a notable feature of the score. So is the use of the orchestra to add to the gaiety. In the dazzling patter-duet for Ramiro and Dandini (ex. 3), it is the violins that keep the rhythm and melody dancing along in short notes when the voice has an emphatic long one.

Ex. 3

GAETANO DONIZETTI

1797–1848

Among Rossini's lesser-known operas is one called *La donna del lago* ('The Lady of the Lake'), after Sir Walter Scott's poem. Scott's works inspired various other composers of the period (Byron is his only competitor among British authors after Shakespeare) and it is not surprising that Gaetano Donizetti's sixty-two operas include a now forgotten *Castello di Kenilworth* (after Scott's *Kenilworth*) and the celebrated *Lucia di Lammermoor* (after *The Bride of Lammermoor*).

Donizetti's audiences went to see the *latest* opera as modern theatre-goers seek the latest play. These audiences loved the sheer thrill of technically difficult singing, but reports of the time show that they were also emotionally moved by the characterization as conveyed in the voices. To a later generation, for whom Verdi's late works were still fresh and Puccini's were newly arrived, it was difficult to consider Donizetti's (or Bellini's) pretty warblings as adequate to the extremely dramatic scenes (of madness, betrayal, violence and so forth) which they had to represent at points of climax. Now that Verdi's and Puccini's conventions belong, with Donizetti's, to history, modern audiences have been re-attracted to Donizetti's serious works, especially when singers are available who can do justice to them. Donizetti's output also includes comic operas, for which he had a lively aptitude.

He followed the Italian tradition of using recitative (not speech), setting in relief the arias and ensembles. The climax of dramatic complexity is musically represented (again in a traditional way) by a big ensemble for all the characters at the end of the penultimate act. Besides those treated here, his operas include two celebrated treatments of British quasi-historical incident in *Anna Bolena* ('Ann Boleyn'; 1830), and *Maria Stuarda* ('Mary Stuart'; 1834), as well as *La fille du régiment* ('The Daughter of the Regiment'; 1840), one of his several operas in French.

L'ELISIR D'AMORE
(The Elixir of Love)
Libretto by Felice Romani

First performed: Milan, 1832
Two Acts

Cast in order of singing:

GIANNETTA, A COUNTRY GIRL	*soprano*
NEMORINO, A YOUNG FARM LABOURER	*tenor*
ADINA, A RICH YOUNG PROPRIETRESS OF A FARM	*soprano*
BELCORE, A SERGEANT	*baritone*
DULCAMARA, A QUACK DOCTOR	*bass*

Chorus of villagers and soldiers
The scene is laid in a Basque village

The 'elixir of love' is a bottle of wine which a quack doctor sells to a credulous country villager. We might from this expect uproarious comedy throughout. But this villager – who remains credulous, almost a simpleton – is the hero of the opera and moreover has a famous song which is genuinely (not mockingly) pathetic in appeal.

This balance between comedy and pathos is the distinguishing feature of the opera and shows a finely artistic judgement first of all from Felice Romani, the librettist. (He wrote not only this and other texts for Donizetti, but also those of the two Bellini operas treated in this book, and some for Rossini too; no hack writer, he enjoys an honourable position in Italian literature.) An equally judged balance between comic and serious elements was shown by Donizetti himself. The sophisticated city operagoers are allowed to laugh at the naiveties of country life – but not to laugh too hard.

The whole subject of the elixir is raised because the heroine, Adina, has been reading the story of Tristan and Isolde ('Tristano' and 'Isotta' in the Italian). In Adina's book Tristan used a love potion to win Isolde. Wagner saw the matter differently.

*   *   *

ACT I: The rich, beautiful Adina mocks at the bashful attempts of Nemorino to woo her and prefers to read aloud from her book about Tristan and Isolde. The villagers wish they had an elixir of love such as Tristan secured. Belcore, a sergeant at the head of a detachment, comes in and courts Adina, to Nemorino's despair.

A trumpet off-stage heralds the entrance of a gilded cart. In it stands Dr Dulcamara, a quack who eloquently proclaims his wares: 'Udite, o rustici' ('Attention, you country-folk'). The crowd is impressed. When Nemorino asks for 'the elixir that won Queen Isolde' Dulcamara says he has it. He hands Nemorino a bottle really containing Bordeaux wine, and declares he has never seen such a simpleton. They have a comic duet: 'Obligato' ('Much obliged').

Nemorino settles down to eat and drink. Happy that he will shortly win Adina by magic (the elixir is supposed to work after twenty-four hours) he sings to himself and does not bother Adina when she re-enters. Of course, this is just what stirs her interest in him.

Belcore receives a message that he and his detachment must leave. He asks Adina to marry him that very day, and she – to stimulate and pique Nemorino – appears to consent. Nemorino now becomes despairing again (after the elixir's twenty-four hours it will be too late!). He entreats Adina to postpone the wedding by a day; she refuses, and, while all others look forward in lively manner to the wedding celebrations, Nemorino feels hopeless.

ACT II: On Adina's farm the wedding feast has been prepared. After a merry chorus Dulcamara produces the latest piece of music, a 'barcarolle' from Venice about a beautiful poor girl who rejects the advances of a rich old senator. Dulcamara and Adina sing it, to the applause of the guests: 'Io son ricco, e tu sei bella' ('I have riches, you have beauty').

The crowd departs to watch the signing of the marriage contract, leaving Dulcamara to finish the food. Nemorino, who has been missing, comes in. Dulcamara offers him another bottle of 'elixir', to take instant effect this time. The sly Adina has postponed, after all, the signing of the contract, and Belcore re-enters. To gain money to pay for the new bottle, Nemorino enlists in Belcore's regiment, singing with him a duet, 'Venti scudi' ('Twenty florins').

Back in the village square, Giannetta tells the villagers a secret: Nemorino's uncle has died, leaving him (though he does not yet know it) now a rich man. The girls now pay Nemorino considerable attention – which he ascribes to the 'elixir'. Adina is touched when she learns that Nemorino has enlisted for her sake. Nemorino, delighted with his new popularity among the girls, leaves with the others. Adina learns from Dulcamara that he has sold Nemorino an 'elixir' –

but she says (and Dulcamara agrees!) that as a beautiful woman she owns a powerful elixir of her own.

Nemorino re-enters; he has observed a change in Adina's attitude towards him, and once again his love for her emerges: 'Una furtiva lagrima' ('A furtive tear'). Adina returns. She has bought Nemorino's discharge from the army, and hands him the papers. She declares her love for him, and she and Nemorino are united at last.

Belcore, returning with his soldiers, finds himself thrown over but consoles himself with the thought that the world is full of girls. Dulcamara does a brisk trade among the villagers with his evidently successful elixir – it brings not only love but money. The happy villagers give their enthusiastic thanks to Dulcamara as he leaves in his cart and the opera ends.

★ ★ ★

It is richness and range of melody, not of harmonic language or structural subtlety, that carries *L'elisir d'amore*. Sullivan must have learned a trick or two for his operettas from the duet 'I have riches, you have beauty' of which we may quote not the beginning but a catchy later fragment (ex. 1). Adina is here singing in the character of a humble Venetian girl and modestly rejects the honour of a Senator's love: notice the way the music exposes the clever internal rhyme (*onore, Senatore, amore*).

Ex. 1

Nemorina's famous pathetic song, 'Una furtiva lagrima', has an introduction surprisingly, and most effectively, using a solo bassoon. Later in the song, after expressing a wish to mingle his sighs with those of his beloved, Nemorino has a long note which breaks out into the word 'cielo' ('heaven'). At this very point (ex. 2) the music breaks out from the minor to the major key, with touching effect.

Ex 2

Larghetto
NEMORINO

i miei so-spir con — fon — de-re per po-co a su-oi so-

- spir   i pal - pi-ti, i pal - pi-ti sen-tir   con -

-fon - de-re i mi-ei co'suoi so-spir!   Cie-lo, si può mo-rir

LUCIA DI LAMMERMOOR
(Lucy of Lammermoor)
*Libretto by Salvatore Cammarano, after the
novel by Sir Walter Scott*

First performed: Naples, 1835
Three Acts

Cast in order of singing:

NORMAN (Normanno), AN OFFICER OF HENRY ASHTON'S
HOUSEHOLD   *tenor*
HENRY ASHTON (Enrico), LORD OF THE CASTLE OF
LAMMERMOOR   *baritone*
BIDE-THE-BENT (Raimondo), CHAPLAIN AT
LAMMERMOOR   *bass*
LUCY ASHTON (Lucia), HENRY'S SISTER   *soprano*
AILSIE (Alisa), HER COMPANION   *mezzo-soprano*
EDGAR (Edgardo), MASTER OF RAVENSWOOD, IN LOVE WITH
LUCY   *tenor*
ARTHUR BUCKLAW (Arturo)   *tenor*

Chorus of friends, relations and retainers
of the house of Lammermoor
*The scene is laid in Scotland towards the
end of the seventeenth century*

Emilia di Liverpool, the title of one of Donizetti's operas, must have sounded excitingly exotic to his Italian audiences: and *Lucia di Lammermoor*, in like manner, took these audiences to the life of a strange people living in feudal conflict in almost barbaric surroundings. Sir Walter Scott's novel was raided for a libretto by Cammarano (who later wrote *Il trovatore* and three other librettos for Verdi).

The names of characters were italianized by the librettist as Enrico, Lucia, *etc*. Scott's 'Bide-the-Bent' seems to have defeated translation and is made into 'Raimondo'. In our synopsis we return to the literary originals of the names; but the whole libretto of the opera is very free (or careless) with the original. Cammarano made Bucklaw and Henry both 'Lords', but they are not so in the original – nor does the form 'Lord Henry Ashton' make proper sense here. Nor, in the original, is there a 'Castle of Lammermoor': Lammermoor is only the region of Scotland in which the action takes place. Incidentally, in the novel Lucy does not murder her husband – she attempts to, but he recovers.

Musically there are two high points – the sextet (with chorus) in Act II, which is the opera's climax of dramatic complexity, and the Mad Scene in Act III, the point of greatest self-expression for the heroine. The opera very much 'belongs' to the heroine, and it is as a vehicle for the dramatic intensity and vocal suppleness of a Maria Callas or a Joan Sutherland that it has continued to be revived.

A scene of confrontation between Henry and Edgar at the beginning of Act II is omitted from most performances and from the ensuing synopsis.

★   ★   ★

ACT I: Henry Ashton, in conversation with his follower Norman, is agitated because his sister, Lucy, refused the marriage with Arthur Bucklaw which has been arranged for her and which would strengthen Henry's house. Henry has found that Lucy has secretly been meeting her lover, Edgar, whose inheritance Henry has usurped. A hunting-party returns with the news that Edgar is in the neighbourhood. Henry expresses his hatred for Edgar: 'Cruda, funesta smania' ('Cruel, fatal rage').

In a park by a fountain, Lucy is awaiting her love – with Ailsie, her companion, to keep watch. Lucy tells how she saw a spectre rising from the fountain: 'Regnava nel silenzio' ('[Night] reigned in the silence'); then she passes to rapturous anticipation of Edgar's coming: 'Quando, rapito in estasi' ('When, rapt in ecstasy') Edgar arrives

– but with the news that he must go at once to France, and they bid one another a loving farewell.

ACT II: Norman, conspiring with Henry, has intercepted the letters written by Edgar to Lucy and has written a forged one to the effect that Edgar is marrying someone else. In a duet, Henry gives the forged letters to Lucy. Festive music announces the arrival of Arthur Bucklaw, whom Henry intends Lucy to marry. Even in her grief over Edgar's 'unfaithfulness' she is still unwilling. The chaplain, Bide-the-Bent, to whom she turns for advice, tells her to resign herself to the marriage.

In a decked-out hall the company welcomes Arthur Bucklaw: 'Per te d'immenso giubilo' ('Through you comes immense joy'). Lucy, trembling and in misery, is induced to sign the marriage contract. Suddenly there is a commotion; Edgar has returned and confronts them all, and a sextet follows: 'Chi mi frena' ('Who restrains me?'). Bide-the-Bent stops Henry's men from attacking Edgar and himself shows Edgar the marriage contract which Lucy has signed. Edgar curses Lucy for her lack of trust and a further ensemble expresses the passionate feelings of all.

ACT III: The company is celebrating the marriage when Bide-the-Bent interrupts the revelry with awful news: Lucy has gone mad and killed her husband. Lucy herself, her wedding garment stained with blood, enters. In this, her Mad Scene, she imagines that she and Edgar are beside the fountain but that a spectre rises up between them; she imagines the marriage that was to have taken place between them: 'Alfin son tua' ('At last I am yours'). Finally she prays Edgar to shed a tear on her grave. She falls senseless.

By night, Edgar has come to the graveyard outside the castle. He prepares to die in a duel with Henry, thinking that Lucy has willingly married Arthur Bucklaw and is happy. The chorus enters to tell him she is dying; the castle bell tolls; Bide-the-Bent enters to announce that she is dead. Edgar is now overcome with grief and kills himself, thinking of her as he dies: 'Tu che a Dio spiegasti l'ali' ('Thou who heavenward art flying').

*   *   *

The sextet in Act II is remarkable for its building-up of tension. It is begun by Edgar and Henry (as the chief opponents) alone, afterwards joined by Lucy and then by Arthur Bucklaw, Bide-the-Bent and Ailsie, with the bystanders in chorus. Edgar, Henry and Lucy each have their moments of dominating the sextet. Ex. 1 shows one of Lucy's, as she sings 'Ah, I should like to weep and cannot; tears still desert me':

Ex. 1

The chorus, as is usual in such numbers, provides little more than an *oom-pah* marking of the rhythm. But in the welcome which they sing on Arthur's arrival they become musically and dramatically prominent. Here, as elsewhere, we may see Donizetti's technique as foreshadowing Verdi's.

Already in the first act, when she was waiting for Edgar, Lucy's florid, graceful music had displayed her character as romantic heroine. But it is the Mad Scene which gives the pathos and the coloratura another turn of the screw, so to speak. There is a poignant moment here when the orchestra, playing a melody from her love-duet with Edgar (Act I), suggests that she is recollecting that meeting; but now, terrified, she sees 'the fearful phantom' of her murdered husband rise to separate her lover from herself (ex. 2).

Ex. 2

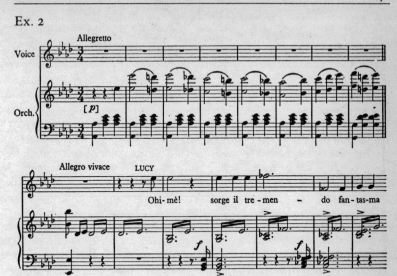

The companionship – or even rivalry – of voice and flute is a
feature of the scene. Ex. 3, for instance, shows voice and flute
rippling away together as Lucy sings of bliss for herself and her lover
in heaven. It may sometimes seem that this music speaks more of
prima donnas' showmanship than of madness; yet in the theatre a
great artist can even make us forget that we no longer think madness
a romantic state of mind.

Ex. 3

DON PASQUALE
Libretto by Giovanni Ruffini and the composer
First performed: Paris, 1843
Three Acts

Cast in order of singing:

DON PASQUALE, AN OLD BACHELOR	*bass*
DR MALATESTA, HIS FRIEND	*baritone*
ERNESTO, HIS NEPHEW	*tenor*
NORINA, A YOUNG WIDOW	*soprano*
A NOTARY	*baritone*

Chorus of merchants and servants
The scene is laid in Rome

For his last comic opera, and two from last of his total of seventy operas, Donizetti turned to a time-honoured plot – from the time of Pergolesi's *La serva padrona*, numerous comic operas had been written about elderly men who want to marry much younger women and who are frustrated in that by a combination of true love and their own silliness.

For many years the authorship of the text was uncertain; it was ascribed to Michele Accursi, but then it transpired that he laid claim to it only to protect its true author, Giovanni Ruffini, a Genoese revolutionary and a political exile in Paris. Donizetti's own involvement in the planning of the work entitles him to be reckoned part-author. He may well have expended more time on the text than than on the music: he claimed that the whole opera was composed in eleven days, though in fact it is known to have occupied him during more than two months. What is probably its most famous number, Ernesto's serenade 'Com'è gentil', is traditionally said to have been an afterthought, inserted between the final dress rehearsal and the first performance; but neither the autograph score nor the presence of its melody in the overture would seem to bear out the tradition.

★   ★   ★

ACT I: Don Pasquale, a wealthy old bachelor, has resolved to marry: this is mainly so that he can frustrate the expectations of his nephew Ernesto, who has irritated Pasquale with his wish to marry the lively, impecunious young widow, Norina. His friend Dr

Malatesta, pretending to assist in this scheme, has offered to find a suitable bride. Pasquale is eagerly awaiting his return; when he arrives, Malatesta tells of the innocent, docile creature he has found, 'beautiful as an angel' ('Bella siccome un angelo'), and what is more, she is his sister. Malatesta leaves and Pasquale expresses his delight at the prospect of family life: 'Ah, un foco insolito' ('An unaccustomed fire'). Now Ernesto enters. Challenged by his uncle as to his intentions, he makes it clear that nothing will sway him from his love of Norina; and he is astonished when told that if he marries her he must move out and fend for himself, for Pasquale himself now plans to marry. At first incredulous, Ernesto then sees the disappearance of his 'sweet and pure dream' ('Sogno soave e casto'), and is further taken aback to learn not only that Pasquale has consulted Malatesta (the likeliest person to dissuade him, he imagined) but that the proposed bride is Malatesta's sister.

The scene changes to Norina's house, where she is reading a romantic novel ('Quel guardo il cavaliere'); but she puts her book aside and expresses her confidence in her womanly wiles: 'So anch'io la virtù magica' ('I myself have the skills of magic'). A note is delivered from Ernesto, just as Malatesta arrives: she is distressed to learn that, because of his uncle's new plans, Ernesto is to leave Rome today. Malatesta reassures her, and explains his scheme: she, Norina, is to pass herself off as Malatesta's sister, fresh from the convent, to go through a mock marriage, and then to drive him to distraction. They discuss the plan with relish – Norina ready to try the impersonation ('Pronta io son') and Malatesta setting out at once to try 'the grand scheme' ('Vado, corro al gran cimento').

ACT II: Outside Pasquale's house, Ernesto, faced with the loss of home and bride, resolves to nurse his sorrow in a distant land ('Cercherò lontana terra').

In his house, Pasquale receives his friend Malatesta and Malatesta's 'sister' Sofronia (Norina in disguise). Norina, in their terzet, feigns fright at being alone with a man (while looking forward to the prospect of leading the old man a dance). He questions her about her tastes, which he learns are simple, frugal and thoroughly domestic. The marriage Pasquale decrees, must be immediate; and fortunately Malatesta thought to bring his notary along. He dictates the terms of the contract (quartet); and, just when another witness is needed, Ernesto happens to arrive. He is thunderstruck to discover Norina on the point of marrying Pasquale, but Malatesta manages to apprise him of the situation. No sooner is the contract signed and witnessed than the bride's manner begins to change. She refuses his proffered embrace, tells him to improve his manners, and says she wishes to be squired by a younger, less decrepit man – Ernesto will fit the bill nicely. Then she demands a coach and more servants (doubling the wages of the existing ones for good measure), then new furnishings. Pasquale explodes with fury – 'Son tradito' ('I am betrayed') – while Malatesta tries to calm him and the lovers express their affection and their amusement.

ACT III: Servants and merchants are bustling around, executing commands, to Pasquale's horror and alarm. Norina enters, dressed to go to the theatre, and not with her husband; 'Why this bustle?' asks Pasquale (duet: 'Signorina, in tanta fretta'). She provokes him into calling her a coquette, then slaps his face – though by now she is beginning to feel truly sorry for him. She leaves, dropping a note as she does: it is a pretended assignation with a lover for that very evening. Pasquale reads it and sends for Malatesta. After the servants have commented on the events of the day, Malatesta arrives, and learns of Pasquale's situation; he advises him of the best course of action – to allow the lovers to meet, expose them, and then take a justified revenge. The pleasure of anticipation is enough to bring Pasquale back to a happy mood.

In the garden, Ernesto serenades his beloved, and they sing of their love: 'Tornami a dir, che m'ami' ('Tell me again you love me'). Now Pasquale and Malatesta arrive, but Ernesto slips away and Norina denies everything. But Malatesta is happily alert, and devises a plausible way for Norina to call off the marriage, having first secured Pasquale's consent to Ernesto's. Ernesto is summoned; Pasquale is told that Sofronia is really Norina and after a brief outburst is reconciled to the situation; and they all draw the moral, with Malatesta leading off ('Bravo, Don Pasquale').

★　　★　　★

The opening scene of the opera introduces us to the bride Don Pasquale envisaged for himself, docile and home-loving; it is by musical means that Donizetti lets us know that Norina is very far from that person – not only does she read novels, she also, when she puts them down, shows just the kind of person she really is, knowing 'the magic virtue of a well-placed glance' (ex. 1). It would be a mistake, however, to think that the comical and the spirited are Donizetti's sole veins of invention in his *buffo* operas. Far from it. The most famous item in *Don Pasquale* is the haunting serenade on

Ex. 1

the second scene of Act III, where the soft voices of the chorus add atmosphere to Ernesto's line. And, just as we saw in *L'elisir d'amore*, the balance between the comic and the pathetic is finely held. Pasquale is not an evil man, deserving to be treated cruelly, but just a foolish one with illusions about himself. We are not just permitted but actually encouraged to feel sorry for him when his plans for his marriage end up, literally, with a slap in the face; the music slows to larghetto, slips into the minor mode, and a moment later Norina herself expresses her contrition with an unusually distant change of key adding force to her sentiment that 'the lesson is hard but necessary', while Malatesta says it only remains to 'go and stifle Don Pasquale' (ex. 2).

Still, in the end it is the high spirits and comedy that must prevail. These have several kinds of musical manifestation, among them a quite unusual chorus of servants, and some conventionally brilliant yet effective coloratura writing for Norina, which she throws off with such insouciance; but the one item that brings down every house, unfailingly, is the *buffo* duet in the second scene of the last act, where Malatesta is advising Pasquale; starting with a conspiratorial air, it ends in patter-song style, the orchestra reminding us of the

Ex. 2

tune while first Pasquale, then Malatesta, and finally both together
enunciate their words – 'you will see whether these coquettish tricks
and sighs will help you' – on a single repeated note as rapidly as their
tongues and lips will allow (ex. 3).

VINCENZO BELLINI

1801–35

Of the same type as Donizetti's operas were those of a composer four years younger, Vincenzo Bellini. In his last opera, *I puritani* ('The Puritans'), 1835, he not only showed a new adventurousness in harmony, but also set the recitative to be accompanied by the orchestra (not the piano, which had succeeded the harpsichord). This, a procedure occasionally followed by Gluck and certain of Bellini's more immediate predecessors, was designed to lessen the rigid differentiation in the audience's ear between recitative and aria. What, we may wonder, would Bellini's later works have been like if he had not died at thirty-three?

LA SONNAMBULA
(The Sleep-Walker)
Libretto by Felice Romani

First performed: Milan, 1831
Two Acts

Cast in order of singing:

LISA, KEEPER OF THE VILLAGE INN	*soprano*
ALESSIO, A YOUNG PEASANT, IN LOVE WITH LISA	*bass*
AMINA, A VILLAGE GIRL	*soprano*
TERESA, AMINA'S FOSTER-MOTHER	*mezzo-soprano*
A NOTARY	*baritone*
ELVINO, A YOUNG FARMER, ENGAGED TO AMINA	*tenor*
COUNT RODOLFO	*baritone*

Chorus of villagers
The scene is laid in Switzerland

The title gives away the element which imparts an unusual twist to the plot. Amina is caught in Count Rodolfo's bedroom at night, but is cleared of suspicion when it is shown that it was only somnambulism that led her there. (The age of Freud would have a different comment on this 'excuse', especially since certain undeveloped hints suggest the possibility that the Count is Amina's father.) Her actual sleep-walking is, by theatrical tradition, demonstrated by her perilous crossing of a rickety footbridge.

In the opera's kindly depiction of the simplicity of country-folk (they have not even heard of somnambulism until the Count explains) it is a kind of 'serious' complement to Donizetti's comic *L'elisir d'amore* – another tale of country simplicity from the pen of the same librettist. But *La sonnambula* lives most of all through the appeal of its melodies to coloratura sopranos and their fans.

★   ★   ★

ACT I: All the villagers rejoice at the forthcoming wedding of Amina and Elvino – all except Lisa, who keeps the inn. She, repulsing the advances of Alessio, who loves her, is jealous of Amina's good fortune. Amina sings of her joy: 'Come per me sereno' ('How serenely [the day dawns] for me!'). The notary arrives, preceding Elvino, and a betrothal duet follows: 'Prendi, l'anel ti dono'.

The sound of horses heralds the arrival of Count Rodolfo on an expedition. He decides to stay the night in the village, which evidently has associations for him: 'Vi ravviso, o luoghi ameni' ('I see you again, you pleasant places'). He pays rather too much attention to Amina for Elvino's liking. Led by Teresa, the villagers warn him of a local phantom. When they have gone, Elvino reproaches Amina for apparently flirting with the Count, but they are reconciled and sing a duet.

Rodolfo is conducted to his room by Lisa, who is not reluctant to flirt with him. Shortly afterwards Amina, in her nightdress, walks into the Count's room. He realizes that she is sleep-walking, hearing her speak of her coming marriage. The villagers and afterwards Elvino are brought in by the jealous Lisa; they put another construction on Amina's behaviour and her protests. There is a prolonged ensemble (for all the characters except the Count) begun by Amina's 'D'un pensiero' ('[I am not guilty] of a thought'). The combined expression of tension and doubt, during which Elvino breaks off the engagement, ends the act.

ACT II:The villagers are on their way to Count Rodolfo's castle, where they intend to beg him to establish Amina's innocence. They leave. Amina in her distress is comforted by her foster-mother Teresa, but Elvino spurns her. The villagers return to say the Count will be coming to testify for her. Unconvinced, Elvino takes back the ring he gave Amina. But, aside, he admits his feelings: 'Ah, perchè non posso odiarti?' ('Ah, why then can I not hate you?).

Nevertheless, he agrees to marry Lisa instead. Lisa rejects, once again, the pleas of Alessio, and rejoices at her new good fortune. While Elvino is about to arrange this new marriage, the Count attempts to dissuade him. He is adamant and disbelieves the Count's explanation about somnambulism, voiced in a quartet (for Lisa, Teresa, Elvino and the Count) and chorus.

Suddenly Amina herself is seen, again sleep-walking, on a dangerous ledge or bridge. The villagers watch, not daring to cry out and wake her – and hear her complaining in her sleep that, though innocent, she has lost Elvino. As Amina comes down, still sleep-walking and holding a bouquet formerly given her by Elvino, she sings of her unhappiness: 'Ah! non credea mirarti' ('Ah [you flower], I never thought to see you almost dead'). Elvino, agonized at his own lack of faith in her, interrupts and places the ring on her finger again. Amina wakes to a joyful chorus and sings of the happiness now restored to her and Elvino: 'Ah! non giunge' ('Ah! there never came [such happiness]'); the others (except Lisa, who has withdrawn) join in to end the opera.

★　　★　　★

Bellini's lyrical writing does not confine itself only to the heroine and her lover. An extract from the Count's aria in the first act (ex. 1) gives an idea of the warm expression of Bellini's solo music and of how, like Rossini and Donizetti, he often used the chorus merely to mark the beat. The Count is greeting those 'dear places' he is now revisiting after many years.

The big ensemble which ends the first act, consequent on the discovery of Amina in the Count's room, was the direct model (even as to key) for Sullivan's parody in *Trial by Jury*, 'A nice dilemma'. Amina leads it; then, when Elvino enters expressing his anguish at the situation, Amina follows him in canon and with words addressing him directly – 'Do not believe that I am guilty'. The effect is as if she were trying to enter his thoughts (ex. 2).

Ex. 1

Ex. 2

The heroine's vocal fireworks come chiefly at the end. The singer must emphasize the musical contrast between the tender, introspective strain sung while sleep-walking and the brilliant expression of joy. Here the excitement rises as the voice does when Amina sings of the earth transformed by her happiness into 'a heaven of love' (ex. 3).

Ex. 3

del - la - ter — ra in cui vi - via — - mo ci for-
- mia — mo un ciel d'a-mor, d'a — - mor, d'a — -
- mor d'a - mor.

NORMA
Libretto by Felice Romani

First performed: Milan, 1831
Two Acts

Cast in order of singing:

OROVESO, ARCH-DRUID	*bass*
POLLIONE, A ROMAN PRO-CONSUL	*tenor*
FLAVIO, HIS FRIEND	*tenor*
NORMA, A DRUID PRIESTESS, DAUGHTER OF OROVESO	*soprano*
ADALGISA, A YOUNGER PRIESTESS	*soprano*
CLOTILDA, ATTENDANT TO NORMA	*soprano*

Chorus of Druids, soldiers and people
The scene is laid in Gaul in Roman times

The conflict in a hero or heroine between love and duty is the mainspring of many operas. In this one, Norma's holy obligations as a Druid priestess are opposed to her love for the Roman pro-consul, Pollione, and involve her finally in suicide. An exotic background to the human struggle is provided by the setting in ancient Gaul. The point is emphasized when, before her great invocation to the moon – the 'Casta diva' 'Chaste Goddess' of the famous aria – Norma cuts off a spray of mistletoe with a sickle from the sacred oak. She is, by the way, no girlish heroine; her maturity and strength are contrasted with the inexperience of the younger priestess, Adalgisa. A performance which reverses the two is a perversion. Norma is a positive rather than a passive heroine, her acts of will influencing the plot: there is a power of characterization here, as well as a brilliance of vocal writing in the role which contributes to the opera's strength.

The names 'Pollione' and 'Flavio' are Italianizations of the Latin Pollio and Flavius.

★ ★ ★

ACT I: To the sacred oak come the people of Gaul in procession, followed by the Druids, who are addressed by Oroveso, their head. They pray for victory over the Romans and retire. The Roman officers, Pollione and Flavio, enter. Pollione, formerly in illicit love with Norma, chief Druid priestess, by whom he has two children, mentions that he now loves a younger priestess, Adalgisa. In an aria 'Meco all'altar di Venere' ('With me at the altar of Venus') he voices his foreboding of Norma's vengeance. In the distance the Druids' rites are heard.

Now the Romans retire as the Druids return to welcome Norma, who advances and speaks prophetically of Rome's coming fall. Then, cutting off the sacred mistletoe, Norma addresses the rising moon – 'Casta diva' ('Chaste Goddess') – supported by Oroveso and the chorus of people. Aside, she discloses her love for Pollione. All then leave.

Adalgisa enters and prays for the protection of her gods. Pollione reveals himself and woos her: Adalgisa is at first hesitant, but then admits that she returns his love.

Norma is at home with her children and reveals her sorely disturbed feelings. She bids Clotilda, her attendant, hide the children as the young Adalgisa approaches. There follows a duet for Adalgisa and Norma: 'Io fui così' ('I was the same'). Adalgisa's confession to Norma of her illicit love awakens Norma's sympathy: for she too broke her priestly vow of chastity. But then Norma asks Adalgisa who her lover is. 'Here he comes', Adalgisa replies, for Pollione approaches. Passions rise as the two women realize his deception. Finally the striking of the sacred shield is heard, in the distance, summoning Norma to inspire the people. The distant chorus of Druids add their voices to those of the three soloists.

ACT II: It is night. Norma holds a dagger and contemplates her sleeping children, whom, in her agony, she is tempted to kill. But she refrains, and sends Clotilda to bring Adalgisa. Norma presents the children to Adalgisa and bids her take them when she goes with Pollione to Rome, while Norma will die. Adalgisa begs Norma, instead, to live for the children's sake and says she will turn Pollione's affections back to Norma. The duet for the two women ends in passionate avowal together.

Within the Druids' forest, Oroveso and chorus show their hatred of the Romans but feel powerless until Norma advises them. At the temple, Norma hears from Clotilda that Adalgisa wishes to renew her vows as priestess but that Pollione has sworn to tear Adalgisa from the altar. Norma strikes the sacred shield three times and the Druids, entering to hear her, sing a chorus of war. Clotilda runs in with the announcement that a Roman attempting to enter has been caught. It is Pollione. Norma takes a dagger to kill the interloper but cannot strike the blow.

Norma takes Pollione aside. When he rejects her demand that he shall leave Adalgisa, she vows that Adalgisa shall be burnt as a priestess who has betrayed her vows. The people are told to prepare for a burning. But when Norma is asked to name the guilty priestess she replies 'I'. The people are incredulous, but Norma persists. When her children are brought in Norma asks Pollione to take care of them, but he stands aside.

Anguished, Norma's people prepare to sacrifice her. Much moved, Pollione goes with her to be sacrificed.

★　★　★

Among Bellini's melodies, with their smooth flow and long spans, Norma's invocation to the moon, 'Casta diva' (ex. 1), is perhaps the most famous of all. The duet of Norma and Adalgisa in Act II, after presenting the two women as opposed, finally shows them united in mutual feelings. Adalgisa begs Norma to have regard to her 'darling children', now kneeling before her and Norma feels her resolution weakening. This new unity between the women is naturally paralleled in the music (ex. 2).

Ex. 1

Ex. 2

But Norma herself is no mere mouthpiece for euphonious music. This is a genuinely dramatic part. The trio just before the end of Act II has been well said to foreshadow the end of Verdi's *Aida*. In her final duet with Pollione, Norma has to 'punch' out a simple melody (ex. 3) to make it carry a menacing text ('Already I am relishing your glances, through your grief and her death. I can at last – and I will – make you as unhappy as I am').

Ex. 3

The Druids are characterized as 'noble savages'. The exotic sound of a gong among the orchestral instruments, the solemnity of the off-stage choruses, and the striking of the sacred shield are musical evocations of this.

GIUSEPPE VERDI

1813–1901

'Viva Verdi' was the popular slogan when the composer went to Naples in 1858. It was a slogan with a hidden political meaning: 'Viva *V*ittorio *E*manuele *R*è *D*'*I*talia!' – a cheer (which could not be voiced openly in Naples under the Bourbons) for King Victor Emanuel of Piedmont, whom liberal opinion hoped to make king of a united Italy (as actually happened in 1861).

The identification of Verdi with liberal ideals was not just an acrostic. He was sympathetic to the liberal cause (which, in the nineteenth-century Italian context, meant the anti-clerical as well as anti-despotic cause) and eventually accepted nomination as a deputy in the parliament of the new Italy, though he was not active in politics. Moreover many of his operas made biting social or political comment and ran into trouble with censorship (see *Rigoletto* and *Un ballo in maschera*, below); and even in a work like *Aida*, the casting of the priests as an intolerant and vindictive force behind the throne would not have been considered accidental in Verdi's Italy. In the early *Nabucco* (short for Nabucodnosor. i.e. Nebuchadnezzar, 1842) the celebrated chorus of exiled Hebrews was heard as a patriotic lament of contemporary Italians in political exile. So was the chorus of Scottish exiles in *Macbeth*.

Verdi was not, in fact, writing a kind of refined diversion for an international audience of canary-fanciers. He was writing a kind of romantic drama intended to appeal – in its melodies, its plots and its stagecraft – to the Italy of Cavour (one of Verdi's great heroes), Garibaldi and Manzoni (the patriot novelist in whose memory Verdi wrote his Requiem). It is the achievement of Verdi's genius to have lifted this type of drama beyond the circumstances of its creation.

Love duets, bold and catchy choruses, brilliant arias for soprano and heroic ones for tenor – these are the traditional ingredients for Italian opera, and Verdi started off with them. But as he progressed, he came to place less stress on such individual numbers, each complete and rounded off and ready to be followed by applause. Instead he developed a greater continuity of drama-through-music, prominently using the device of musical recall (reintroducing a theme when the drama recalls some person or situation previously encountered). Verdi's last two operas, *Otello* and *Falstaff*, depend much more on their total sweep, less on their individual songs and choruses, than do the earlier works.

Apart from works mentioned above and those discussed in the following pages, some of Verdi's other operas such as *I Lombardi* (1843) and *Ernani* (1844) are occasionally revived.

MACBETH
Libretto by Francesco Maria Piave, after Shakespeare

First performed: Florence, 1847
(revised version) Paris, 1865
Four Acts

Cast in order of singing:

MACBETH, A GENERAL	baritone
BANQUO, A GENERAL	bass
LADY MACBETH	soprano
SERVANT TO MACBETH	baritone
MACDUFF, A NOBLEMAN	tenor
MALCOLM, SON OF DUNCAN	tenor
LADY-IN-WAITING	mezzo-soprano
	baritone
THREE APPARITIONS	soprano
	soprano
DOCTOR	bass

[The roles of Fleance, son of Banquo, and Duncan, King of Scotland, are silent.]

Chorus of witches, attendants, nobles, soldiers
The scene is laid in Scotland in the mid-eleventh century

The first product of Verdi's lifelong love of Shakespeare was *Macbeth*. He took great trouble over it, and particularly over its staging, even demanding that the singers served the poet primarily, the composer only second; for the sake of dramatic verisimilitude he even deprecated the beauty of voice and appearance of the proposed soprano, as Lady Macbeth ought to be ugly and evil, with a hard, dark voice. He had never before – this was his tenth opera – set a text of such power; it was understandable that he decided to plan the libretto himself, and indeed he drafted it out in prose before handing it over to Piave.

The first version of the opera dates from 1847; he was to write five more operas after *Macbeth* before *Rigoletto*, his earliest opera that remains firmly in the established repertory. In 1865, with such works as *Un ballo in maschera* and *La forza del destino* behind him, he returned to it, for a Paris revival, and made several changes; it is the later version that is generally performed today, for although it has some discrepancies in style it does contain some fine music that it would be foolish to forgo. Lady Macbeth's Act II aria, 'La luce langue', was written for the later version, as was the duet ending Act III; Verdi also rewrote the exiles' chorus in Act IV, and recast the ending, a short death scene for Macbeth being replaced by a battle depiction and a celebratory chorus (some productions seek the best of both worlds and include the rejected material along with the new). And he touched up details here and there throughout the opera.

★ ★ ★

ACT I: On a 'blasted heath', Macbeth and Banquo are walking, having been victorious against an army of invaders. They encounter a group of witches, who utter enigmatic prophecies, addressing Macbeth by titles to which he had no expectation, among them King of Scotland; then Banquo is told he will be the sire of kings. The witches disappear; then messengers arrive from King Duncan and tell Macbeth that he has been granted the rights and title of Thane of Cawdor – just as the witches had predicted. The men reflect on the situation: 'Due vaticini compiuti or sono' ('Two truths are told').

In Macbeth's castle, Lady Macbeth is reading a letter from her husband telling her of the witches. She knows that he has only to murder Duncan for the most important of the prophecies to be fulfilled, and hopes he will not balk at that: 'Vieni, t'affretta' ('Hie thee hither'); a servant announces the king's impending visit, and she realizes that the deed must be done that night ('Or tutti sorgete, ministri infernali' – 'Come, you spirits that tend on mortal thoughts'). Macbeth arrives; they quickly agree. Now the king and his retinue enter, are received, and depart for their rooms. Macbeth, alone, contemplates: 'Mi si affaccia un pugnal?' ('Is this a dagger which I see before me?'). He goes to murder the king, and emerges, appalled at what he has done, by the blood on his hands, by his inability to add 'Amen' to the muttered prayer of the drowsing attendants. He has brought out the dagger, and must return and smear blood on the attendants; but he cannot bring himself to do so, and Lady Macbeth does.

Knocks are heard at the door: Banquo and Macduff have arrived to meet and travel on with Duncan. Macduff goes to the king's room, while Banquo meditates on the wailings and other portents of the night. The murder is revealed, and Macduff arouses the household who foregather and express their horror at the terrible deed.

ACT II: Macbeth and his wife are alone in the castle. They remark that Duncan's death may be blamed on his son, Malcolm, who has fled to England; but that to make the kingship of his line secure Macbeth must now frustrate the prophecy and kill Banquo, and that he will attend to this this very night. He departs, and Lady Macbeth expresses her powerful ambition ('La luce langue' – 'The light fades').

In the park, some distance from the castle, Macbeth's assassins wait for Banquo and his son ('Sparve il sol'). They conceal themselves; then Banquo and Fleance arrive, and Banquo comments on the dark, sinister night ('Come dal ciel precipita'). As they move on towards the castle, the assassins emerge: Banquo is struck down, but he dispatches his son, who flees his pursuer.

In the great hall of the castle, a banquet is laid. Macbeth and his lady receive the guests. Lady Macbeth sings a toast. One of the assassins enters and reports to Macbeth that Banquo is dead but Fleance has escaped. Macbeth expresses to the company his regret at Banquo's absence, and moves towards his empty chair; but then he starts back in horror as he sees the ghost of the murdered man. The guests (who do not see the ghost) are astonished and alarmed at his terror. Lady Macbeth tries to calm him and to reassure the guests, and renews the toast. Then again Macbeth recoils in horror as he sees the ghost, and this time there can be no covering up; the guests, sensing his guilt, withdraw.

ACT III: In a dark cave, the witches are conducting their rituals around a cauldron. Macbeth enters and demands to be told his fate. The witches summon up apparitions: first Macbeth is told to beware of Macduff, then to be bloody, bold and resolute, for he cannot be harmed by man born of woman, and third, that he will not be vanquished until Birnam Wood comes to Dunsinane. Now he asks to know if Banquo's line shall reign. and the witches call up a silent procession of future kings – all in the likeness of Banquo (who himself appears eighth and last). The witches disappear, and Lady Macbeth comes; her presence reassures Macbeth and they assert their determination to triumph over Macduff and Banquo's son. They sing of death and vengeance: 'Ora di morte e di vendetta'.

ACT IV: Close by the English border, a group of unhappy exiles are bemoaning the fate of their oppressed country ('Patria oppressa!'). Among them is Macduff, mourning the deaths of his family at Macbeth's hands ('Ah, la paterna mano'). Now Malcolm arrives, at the head of an army of English soldiers; he instructs them to cut branches from the nearby wood to camouflage their advance on Dunsinane. They move off to liberate Scotland: 'La patria tradita piangendo ne invita!' ('The betrayed country, weeping, calls on us').

In the hall of Macbeth's castle, a doctor and a Lady-in-Waiting watch anxiously; the Lady-in-Waiting has heard the queen's words the last two nights as she has walked in her sleep. Now Lady Macbeth enters, sleep-walking ('Una macchia è qui tuttora!' – 'Out, damned spot'); her complicity in the murders is unmistakable.

In another part of the castle, Macbeth expresses his rage at his situation: deserted by his friends, about to be attacked by the English. He still derives confidence from the witches' prophecies, although the tributes of respect and love will never be paid to him ('Pietà, rispetto, amore'). News comes that his wife is dead, and then that Birnam Wood seems to be approaching. He and his men move off to do battle. In the fighting, Macbeth meets Macduff and assures him he cannot be slain by man born of woman; but Macduff, 'from his mother's womb untimely ripped', prevails, and Macbeth falls dead. The conquerors sing a hymn of victory.

★ ★ ★

Macbeth, understandably, did not quickly establish itself with English-speaking audiences, who were used to Shakespeare's words in their original form and without music – and, moreover, were apt to find the occasional jollity and the band-music element of early Verdi alien to the gloomy northern atmosphere of the play. Yet there is a certain crude power about this score that marvellously parallels Shakespeare's, and Verdi was certainly equipped to give life to the horrific and eerie ambience and the intense emotions of the original.

Ex. 1

It is music like the traditional conspirators' chorus, sung by the assassins waiting for Banquo, that may seem to strike a false note (ex. 1: they call on night to cover their deeds). Yet the gulf between this and the greatest scene in the opera – by general acknowledgement – is, in terms of musical style, small. Verdi wrote the sleep-walking scene in the original 1847 version, and indeed modelled it on the established 'mad scene' with which sopranos like Donizetti's Lucy had long been inspiring awe and pity with the most fanciful vocal pyrotechnics. In that sense Verdi is relatively restrained, and his concentration on an accompaniment rich in sinister overtones and a relatively simple vocal line proves brilliantly effective without any suspicion of merely cheap effect. Thus Lady Macbeth looks in horror at 'A spot . . . still there!' on her hand (ex. 2). Nevertheless, the greater depth and subtlety of the older Verdi's technique is very much evident in some of the music he suppled for the 1865 Paris revival, especially the Act I aria for Lady Macbeth ('La luce langue'), though not perhaps the ballet music for the witches that he inserted to accommodate Parisian taste. Perhaps the most remarkable and the boldest of his changes occurs in the final scenes, where not only did he delete Macbeth's soliloquy and death on stage but chose to represent the battle: 'You will be amused to learn that I have written a fugue for the battle – I, who hate everything that smacks of theory . . . in this case fugue is permissible: its chase of subjects and countersubjects and its dissonances and confusion serve well to suggest a battle' (ex. 3).

Ex. 2

Ex. 3

RIGOLETTO
Libretto by Francesco Maria Piave, after Victor Hugo

First performed: Venice, 1851
Three Acts

Cast in order of singing:

THE DUKE OF MANTUA	*tenor*
BORSA, A COURTIER	*tenor*
COUNTESS CEPRANO	*mezzo-soprano*
MARULLO, A COURTIER	*baritone*
RIGOLETTO, THE DUKE'S JESTER, A HUNCHBACK	*baritone*
COUNT CEPRANO, A NOBLEMAN OF MANTUA	*bass*
COUNT MONTERONE, A NOBLEMAN OF MANTUA	*baritone*
SPARAFUCILE, A PROFESSIONAL ASSASSIN	*bass*
GILDA, RIGOLETTO'S DAUGHTER	*soprano*
GIOVANNA, HER ATTENDANT	*mezzo-soprano*
A PAGE	*mezzo-soprano*
AN USHER	*baritone*
MADDALENA, SPARAFUCILE'S SISTER	*mezzo-soprano*

Chorus of courtiers, servants, etc.
The scene is laid in Mantua in the sixteenth century

Rigoletto is an opera to stir the moral passions. It is this quality that
helps to make the opera a persistent favourite – apart from the sheer
musical gifts of Verdi that have made 'La donna è mobile' and the
major-key theme of the quartet among the best-known tunes in the
world. The hero of the opera is a hunchback jester who is made the
cruel sport of an idle court. But the hunchback's vengeance is
terribly turned back on himself. A dramatic force is made of the
curse laid on the jester – *The Curse* was the opera's originally

intended title. (It may seem curious that, in this later operas too, the 'progressive' Verdi attached such dramatic validity to the superstition of cursing.)

The opera's implied attack on court life, doubtless appealing to Verdi himself and his original audiences, brought composer and librettist into conflict with the censor at Venice (at that time under Austrian imperial rule) who banned the original libretto as enshrining 'revolting immorality and obscene triviality'; however, after some changes of names, the plot was eventually accepted.

★   ★   ★

ACT I: To music from a band back-stage (light music suitable for a merry gathering), the curtain rises to show the Duke's palace. In conversation with Borsa the Duke mentions the latest girl he has his eye on, whose name he does not know. He shows his devil-may-care attitude towards women: 'Questa o quella' ('This one or that one?') The band strikes up a minuet in which the Duke dances with Countess Ceprano, whom he has also been pursuing.

Marullo brings the courtiers a surprising discovery: their ugly hunchback jester, Rigoletto, keeps a mistress. Now Rigoletto himself enters and mocks Ceprano, whom his master is openingly attempting to cuckold. There is a big ensemble, mainly of revelry, but Ceprano is planning vengeance. Suddenly Monterone, a nobleman whose daughter the Duke has seduced, pushes his way in; the Duke allows Rigoletto to mock Monterone, then orders the old man's arrest. Monterone curses Rigoletto – and continues to do so as he is led out. For the others, the revelry continues.

A change of scene shows Rigoletto returning home as the evening darkens, Monterone's curse still preying on his mind. He is accosted by an assassin, Sparafucile, who offers his services and explains his methods. Rigoletto says he has no use for him – at present. As Sparafucile leaves, Rigoletto thinks of his own pitiful state. He, too, is a hireling – like an assassin, except that he uses his mocking tongue instead of a dagger: 'Pari siamo' ('We are equals').

Entering his home, he is greeted by Gilda. She is his daughter, not (as Marullo has told the courtiers) his mistress. They have been here three months, but he has kept her locked up, and he now emphasizes that she must never go out except to church. He tells her of her dead mother, showing a grief which Gilda tries to comfort. He sternly warns her attendant, Giovanna, to guard her well.

Unseen, outside, the Duke has arrived. Gilda is the new girl he was pursuing, and only now does he realize that she is Rigoletto's daughter. When Rigoletto, hearing some noise outside, opens the gate, the Duke slips into the garden, throws a bribe to Giovanna and conceals himself. Before leaving the house again Rigoletto sings in an impassioned duet with Gilda and again warns Giovanna to guard her. Gilda now confides to Giovanna that she has been attracted by a youth she saw in church. It is the Duke, who now shows himself and professes his love; together they sing 'E il sol dell'anima' ('The sun of our life is love'). He declares that he is a student, by name Gualtier Maldè. Outside, unknown to both, the courtiers are gathering; Ceprano's and Borsa's voices are heard. They are planning to abduct Rigoletto's 'mistress'. After a passionate farewell to Gilda, the Duke leaves.

Gilda, alone, echoes the words 'Gualtier Maldè', delighting in that dear name ('Caro nome'). The words 'Gualtier Maldè' die away on her lips as she enters the house by an outside stairway; the conspirators can see her over the wall, and marvel at her beauty. It is now dark. Rigoletto is accosted by the conspiring noblemen who pretend to him that they are going to abduct Ceprano's wife. Rigoletto joins them. Under pretence of masking him they blindfold him. There is a softly excited chorus of conspiracy as they make the blindfold dupe hold a ladder against the wall of his own house and abduct Gilda before Rigoletto discovers – as he now does, too late – that his eyes are bandaged. He rushes into the house and finds her gone. In anguish he recalls Monterone's curse 'Ah! la maledizione!'.

ACT II: Back in the palace the Duke is disconsolate because, on returning to Rigoletto's house, he could not find Gilda. (The abduction had been made without his knowledge.) He sings with genuine passion of Gilda: 'Parmi veder le lagrime' ('I think I see her tears'). Then the courtiers enter and tell him that they have abducted and brought to the palace Rigoletto's 'mistress'. The Duke realizes it is Gilda and goes off to 'console' her.

Enter Rigoletto, arrayed as jester but in anguish. The appearance of a page discloses that the Duke is 'busy'. Rigoletto's anguish bursts out: 'I'll have my daughter!'. The word 'daughter' stuns the courtiers, whom Rigoletto now denounces: 'Cortigiani, vil razza' ('Courtiers, you vile tribe') – his fury then softening into a plea to have Gilda restored to him. She rushes in. Rigoletto orders the courtiers out. Gilda tells her story: 'Tutte le feste al tempio' ('Every Sunday, at church'); Rigoletto consoles her. Just then Monterone is led, under guard, across the scene. Seeing Rigoletto, Monterone declares that his curse was evidently in vain. But Rigoletto now plans revenge on the Duke both for his own sake and for Monterone's. In the duet 'Sì, vendetta' ('Yes, revenge') Gilda pleads with her father for mercy on the Duke but he refuses.

ACT III: Sparafucile keeps an inn where his sister Maddalena acts as a decoy for robbery or murder. The Duke, inside, is observed from outside by Rigoletto and Gilda (who has been brought by her father to see the kind of man the Duke really is). The Duke gives voice to his guiding rule: 'La donna è mobile' ('Woman is fickle'). Sparafucile comes out of the house and asks Rigoletto – on whose instructions he has evidently lured the Duke there – for further orders. A quartet follows: inside the house the Duke is light-heartedly pleading love to Maddalena (who affects to resist him, but is charmed), while Gilda and Rigoletto look on from outside.

Rigoletto, thinking that the town will be unsafe for them when he has accomplished the deed he has in mind, instructs Gilda to go home, put on boy's clothing and leave for Verona. She departs unwillingly. Rigoletto arranges payment with Sparafucile for killing the Duke – whose body is to be sewn up in a sack – and says he will return at midnight. A storm rises as Maddalena shows the Duke the way to the upper room for the night. She descends to the lower room and pleads with her brother not to kill the young man ('He's an Apollo') and to murder Rigoletto instead – a suggestion Sparafucile indignantly repudiates as unworthy of a honest assassin under contract to his client. But he agrees to substitute for the Duke any other male victim who may present himself before midnight. Gilda, now in boy's clothes, has returned and stands outside; she knocks, deciding to sacrifice herself for the Duke, and enters. What happens in the house amid the storm and darkness is left to the imagination.

The storm ceases. Rigoletto enters as midnight strikes; he receives from Sparafucile a sack with a body in it and goes exultantly to throw it in the river. Suddenly from the house a voice is heard – the Duke's voice, with his unmistakable song, 'La donne è mobile'. The horrified Rigoletto opens the sack and in it discovers Gilda, not quite dead. She asks forgiveness for disobeying him, and dies. With a cry from Rigoletto – who recalls Monterone's curse – the opera ends.

★   ★   ★

The musical drama in *Rigoletto* is much more closely integrated than in the older (Donizetti-Bellini) kind of Italian opera. Instead of a formal overture there is the orchestral pronouncement of the 'curse'

Ex. 1

theme which appears throughout the opera (ex. 1). And just as the orchestra thus becomes a voice, so the chorus become instruments: in the storm scene they sing wordlessly for purely atmospheric effect. The element of display in the vocal parts, while sufficient for the characters to be musically conveyed, is subordinated to drama. Gilda disappears into her room at her father's house with her lover's supposed name of 'Gualtier Maldè' on her lips, and the name fades out on a dreamy trill. Ex. 2 shows what Verdi wrote. (We omit the subdued chorus of those who are about to abduct her.) The prima donna who puts it up to top E (an octave above what Verdi wrote) is impertinently thinking of herself, not of Gilda.

Ex. 2

The tune in which the Duke sings of woman's fickleness 'La donna è mobile' is marvellously catchy – and its catchiness is itself part of the drama: a few bars must serve to identify both the tune and its singer at the moment of climax when Rigoletto is bearing on his shoulders the sack supposedly containing the Duke's body.

Verdi does not need a solo to establish every character: Maddalena has none, but her concerted music defines her as clearly as anyone else on the stage. The high point of the opera is no solo at all but the quartet where even Maddalena's laughing – she says, but only half-truly, that she does not believe the Duke's pretensions of love – is woven into the texture at the same time as the Duke light-heartedly woos her. Meanwhile Gilda pours out her anguish in a long phrase which is paralleled in her father's vocal line (note Verdi's way of conveying sympathy between characters) (ex. 3).

Ex.3

IL TROVATORE
(The Troubadour)
Libretto by Salvatore Cammarano

First performed: Rome, 1853
Four Acts

Cast in order of singing:

FERRANDO, CAPTAIN OF THE GUARD TO THE COUNT OF
  LUNA   *bass*
INEZ, CONFIDENTIAL MAID TO LEONORA   *soprano*
LEONORA, A LADY-IN-WAITING AT THE COURT OF
  ARAGON   *soprano*

THE COUNT OF LUNA, A YOUNG NOBLEMAN,
  IN LOVE WITH LEONORA   *baritone*
MANRICO, A TROUBADOUR, REPUTED SON OF AZUCENA   *tenor*
AZUCENA, A GIPSY   *mezzo-soprano*
A GIPSY   *baritone*
A MESSENGER   *baritone*
RUIZ, A SOLDIER IN MANRICO'S SERVICE   *tenor*

Chorus of followers of the Count and of Manrico, soldiers,
nuns and gipsies
The scene is laid in Spain in the fifteenth century

Il trovatore lives by its stream of memorable melodies. The Miserere, the Anvil Chorus, the Soldiers' Chorus, Manrico's 'Di quella pira', Luna's 'Il balen', Azucena's 'Stride la vampa', the duet 'Ai nostri monti' – all these would inevitably be in a short-list of the most popular of all operatic tunes, tunes heard repeatedly with delight in thousands of drawing-rooms and bandstands. But the opera was also intended to be exciting dramatically, with its scenes of gipsy life and of abduction from a convent. This is romantic opera, in which the characters display their romantic aspects as a means of moving the drama forward: the soldiers, even in private, still sing about the splendours and glory of fighting.

The plot is complicated, and far-fetched in an old-fashioned way: we are to believe that, before the opera opened, the gipsy Azucena, raving, 'hurled into the flames her own child, instead of the young Count (thus preserving, with an almost supernatural instinct for opera, the baby that was destined to grow up into a tenor with a voice high enough to sing "Di quella pira")'. We quote this from one of the classics of operatic literature* – though we must spoil the fun a little by adding that the high C's with which tenors insist on preening themselves in this aria are not Verdi's at all, but an interpolation.

It is further demanded that the Troubadour, instead of flying off to the rescue of his mother for whom the stake is already burning, shall stay and sing of his intentions for two verses of that very song (an extreme example of a 'contradiction' implicit in opera and mocked by Gilbert and Sullivan). The second verse is therefore often cut in performance.

*Kobbé's Complete Opera Book (1919, with later revisions).

Much of the story happens *between* the acts and before the opera begins, as indeed is explained in Ferrando's opening narration. Performances in Italian before English-speaking audiences, who fail to follow this narration and subsequent explanatory passages, have given the opera the reputation of being much more absurd than it really is.

*   *   *

ACT I: The curtain rises on a guard-room. Ferrando, captain of the guard, reminds his men that their master, the Count, loves Leonora and wishes to track down a mysterious troubadour in whose serenading of her he detects a rival. Ferrando also tells about the gipsy Azucena's misdeed of many years ago: when her mother was being burned at the stake, Azucena threw a baby (the present Count's abducted young brother, as all believe) into the flames.

The scene changes to the garden. Leonora confesses to her attendant Inez that she loves the unknown knight who comes to serenade her. She expresses her ardent feelings: 'Di tale amor che dirsi mai può' ('What can be said of such a love?'). The Count, who loves (but is not loved by) Leonora, enters the garden, when the sound of a harp discloses the presence of the serenader. It is the troubadour, Manrico, who now woos Leonora in song. A trio follows for Leonora, Manrico and (unseen at first, then fiercely denouncing the lovers) the Count. The two men face each other in anger as the curtain falls.

ACT II: We see Manrico again – in the gipsies' camp. The mysterious troubadour is thus revealed as a gipsy, the son (as he supposes) of Azucena. After the gipsies' opening Anvil Chorus, as they begin their day's work, Azucena sings of the harrowing sight she witnessed when they burnt her mother: 'Stride la vampa' ('The blaze is harsh'). After the others have left, she explains in a further song that she was ready to avenge her mother by throwing the present Count's abducted infant brother into the flames but instead, distracted, threw in her own son.

Then who is Manrico, if not her son? He himself tells her of meeting the Count in battle and being prevented by some mysterious feeling from killing him. Now a message arrives telling him that Leonora believing him dead is to enter a convent that evening. After a duet with Azucena reflecting his agitation, he leaves.

Outside the convent the Count, attended by Ferrando, sings of his love for Leonora: 'Il balen del suo sorriso' ('The lightning of her smile'). He plans to abduct her before she takes the vow. He and his followers retire and comment, unseen by the nuns who now approach in procession. Leonora, attended by Inez, is ready to enter the convent building, but the Count and his men step forward to abduct her. Suddenly Manrico appears, attended by Ruiz and other followers. Leonora can hardly believe her senses. Her voice rises above the big ensemble which expresses the agitation of all. Manrico's forces prevail and he leads Leonora away.

ACT III: The soldiers of the Count, who is now laying siege to the castle to which Manrico has taken Leonora, are in camp. Led by Ferrando they sing of the coming assault in the Soldiers' Chorus. Ferrando brings the Count news that an old gipsy has been apprehended. It is Azucena, whom the Count and Ferrando interrogate and recognize; not only is she held responsible for the baby-killing of long ago but she declares herself the mother of their enemy, Manrico. She is condemned to the stake.

In the besieged castle Manrico sings to Leonora of his love: 'Ah sì, ben mio' ('Ah yes, my love, I am yours'). They are about to be married and an organ from the chapel of the castle is heard. Ruiz enters with the message that Azucena has been captured by the enemy. Manrico sings of his determination to leave the castle (and his bride) to save his mother: 'Di quella pira' ('That funeral pyre's flames burn through me'); Leonora, Ruiz and a chorus of Manrico's soldiers join in. He leaves hastily.

ACT IV: Manrico's effort has failed. He and Azucena lie in a prison-tower of the Count's. But unknown to him, at night, Leonora is outside with Ruiz. She sings of her love: 'D'amor sull'ali rosee' ('Born on the roseate wings'). In the distance, a choir is heard chanting the Miserere for an approaching death, over which are heard the lamenting of Manrico and the forebodings of Leonora. The Count enters. Leonora accosts him and eventually offers to marry him if he will free Manrico (she plans to take poison herself): 'Mira, d'acerba lagrime' ('See, the bitter tears'). He accepts the offer jubilantly.

Inside the tower Azucena is delirious and Manrico tries to soothe her with a promise to take her away: 'Ai nostri monti' ('To our mountains'). Leonora enters to tell Manrico he is free but he, saying that he guesses the terms, repels her. She then explains that she has taken poison, and dies in Manrico's arms. The Count comes in and finds himself tricked. Manrico is taken outside for execution. Azucena informs the Count he has executed his own brother, and exultantly declares that her mother has been, after all, avenged.

★ ★ ★

Italian opera in Verdi's day was meant to provide 'hit tunes', and Verdi did not fail. Not to be missed is the essentially popular, downright, strongly rhythmic nature of the Anvil Chorus ('Who brightens the gipsy-man's days?') (ex. 1).

Ex. 1

Even in the numbers expressing the soloists' private thoughts of anguish or desire, Verdi manages to keep the melodies in immediately memorable form, with here and there an ornament that adds an emphasis – like a sigh or an indrawn breath – to emotion, as in ex. 2. This is Manrico's despairing utterance ('Ah, death, you

Ex. 2

come slowly') when he and his mother are imprisoned and when the mood has been set by the chanted Miserere. The continuation sums up Verdi's power of ensemble. In the first bar Manrico dominates, with his high A flat as he cries 'Do not forget me!' to Leonora (far away, as he thinks). But she is hidden outside his prison and hears him: 'I forget you?' she cries in the third bar, her voice now rising to dominate the music. At the same bar the orchestra begins a 'drumming' rhythm characteristic of Verdi's expression of moments of fatality; and meanwhile the death-warning of the Miserere continues (ex. 3).

Ex. 3

LA TRAVIATA
(The Woman Gone Astray)
Libretto by Francesco Maria Piave, after the play
'La dame aux camélias' by Alexandre Dumas the younger

First performed: Venice, 1853
Three Acts

Cast in order of singing:

VIOLETTA VALÉRY, A COURTESAN	*soprano*
FLORA BERVOIX, HER FRIEND	*mezzo-soprano*
BARON DOUPHOL, SUITOR TO VIOLETTA	*baritone*
GRENVIL, A DOCTOR	*bass*
MARQUIS D'OBIGNY	*bass*
VISCOUNT GASTONE DE LETORIÈRES	*tenor*
ALFREDO GERMONT, IN LOVE WITH VIOLETTA	*tenor*
ANNINA, MAID TO VIOLETTA	*soprano*
JOSEPH, SERVANT AT THE COUNTRY HOUSE	*tenor*
GIORGIO GERMONT, ALFREDO'S FATHER	*baritone*
A MESSENGER	*baritone*

Chorus of party guests, street revellers, etc.
The scene is laid in and near Paris

'The death of Violetta is of a grand realistic effect, and has drawn many a tear from many fair eyes.' So says the introduction to an edition of the score published for English readers during Verdi's lifetime. This is, indeed, an opera meant to affect the audience by its true-to-life nature: the way the street-noises from the carnival burst into the dying heroine's bedroom is an example. With this dramatic method Verdi drew as strong a set of principal characters as any opera knows. Soprano, tenor and baritone have constantly changing personal relationships – and from the light-hearted drinking-song (Brindisi) of the first act to the heroine's final farewell Verdi gives each change its own memorable music.

La traviata was originally set (like the play on which it is based) in the audience's own time. It was, however, a failure at its first performance and later was put back into the period of Louis XIV. Today there is every reason for restoring it to Verdi's own period. There would indeed be a case for presenting it now as a modern-dress drama (that is, set in our own time), were it not that the situation of the central character – a woman not accepted in 'society' but ready to sacrifice herself so that her lover's sister may make a 'good' marriage – could hardly seem even remotely plausible today.

Dumas' names for the two leading characters were Marguerite and Armand; Verdi's librettist italianized them as Violetta and Alfredo.

★   ★   ★

ACT I: The rise of the curtain discloses the well-to-do house of Violetta, a courtesan. (Not a prostitute, selling her favours casually and privately; a courtesan of Violetta's type was a woman who lived a regular social life, attaching herself to one man at a time in an 'underworld' which was frequented by men of fashion but which was nòt officially recognized by respectable married society.)

A party is in progress to which Violetta welcomes Flora and her other friends. Among them is Baron Douphol, an old admirer of hers. Gastone, another friend, enters and brings with him Alfredo, introducing him to Violetta as one who has long admired her. Beneath her merry manner she is touched. When Alfredo, called on by the other guests, leads a drinking song or Brindisi, 'Libiamo, libiamo ne' lieti calici' ('Let's drink, let's drink from the goblets of joy'). Violetta rises and sings the second stanza; the chorus of guests joins in festively.

Dance-music is heard from an adjoining room. As the guests are about to go to dance, Violetta is seized with coughing. She asks her guests to proceed to the dance, but, as she looks in a mirror and sees how pale she is, she finds that one guest has stayed with her. It is Alfredo, who declares that he has loved her from afar for a year. Gastone calls from the other room, and Violetta dismisses Alfredo tenderly.

The other guests return and take their leave. Alone, Violetta reflects on Alfredo: 'È strano' ('How curious'), and then, 'Ah! fors' è lui' ('Ah, perhaps he is the one'). She seems to see a new, purer life in what Alfredo offers to her. But finally (for she is no more than half persuaded that such a new life would be possible) she declares – 'Sempre libera' ('Ever free') – that she can only pursue the merry round of social pleasures.

ACT II: But Alfredo has evidently won her over. He and Violetta have now settled in a country villa not far from Paris. Alfredo, alone, sings of his new happy existence: 'De' miei bollenti spiriti' ('My turbulent spirits'). But when Annina, Violetta's servant, comes in, he learns that she has been in Paris on Violetta's instructions, selling off her mistress's possessions, in order to pay for the idyllic life they have been living. Alfredo is ashamed and embarrassed and immediately leaves for Paris to attend to their finances.

Violetta enters and receives a letter from Flora inviting her to a dance that evening. She is expecting a caller on business, but there enters Giorgio Germont. As Alfredo's father, he comes to denounce Violetta, first of all for squandering his son's money – but discovers that, after all, it is Violetta who has had to sell her possessions. Then he asks her for a sacrifice on behalf of his daughter, 'Pura siccome un angelo' ('Pure as an angel'). His daughter, he explains, faces the breaking of her engagement because of Alfredo's 'disgrace'. He asks Violetta to leave Alfredo but not to tell him why. At first she refuses, but eventually she sadly consents, asking Germont only that she should tell his daughter that someone made such a sacrifice: 'Dite alla giovine' ('Tell your daughter'). Violetta writes a note telling Alfredo that she has left him – without explanation, so that he will think her false to him. Germont has been more and more moved by Violetta's nobility of spirit and he embraces her as a father. He leaves.

Violetta rings the bell and is about to give Annina the note for Alfredo when Alfredo himself enters. Passionately she asks Alfredo to love her as she loves him: 'Amami, Alfredo'. She leaves. He does not understand what is happening until a messenger gives him a letter. It is Violetta's, saying she has left him. In anguish, he sees his father enter. Germont attempts to console his son and proposes to take him home to the sea and sun of Provence ('Di Provenza, il mar, il suol'). But Alfredo already suspects that Violetta has gone to Douphol, her old admirer. Seeing the letter which Violetta received from Flora he resolves to go to the party, meet Violetta there, and take his revenge.

The scene now changes to Flora's party. Some of the guests enter dressed up as Spanish fortune-telling gipsies, others as matadors, with appropriate music. Suddenly Alfredo enters and joins a group of card-players. Violetta enters, on Baron Douphol's arm. Alfredo, who is winning at cards, makes insulting remarks which can only be taken to refer ro Violetta. Tension rises between him and the baron and a duel seems imminent.

Left alone with Alfredo, Violetta asks him to leave for his safety's sake. Alfredo's fury only rises, reaching a climax when she says (to avoid telling him the truth) that she loves the baron. He calls in the other guests, insults Violetta, and tells them to witness (flinging a purse at Violetta) that he has now paid his debts in full. While the other guests show their indignation at Alfredo's behaviour, Giorgio Germont enters and denounces his son's conduct. In the final ensemble the miserable Violetta is heard affirming that she loves Alfredo still.

ACT III: Violetta, separated from Alfredo, is living alone with the devoted Annina; she is ill with consumption and they have hardly any money left. She is in bed when, early in the morning, the doctor comes to see her. He reassures her, but tells Annina that Violetta has really only a few hours to live. Annina leaves and Violetta re-reads a letter she has received from Giorgio Germont, revealing that he has told Alfredo of Violetta's sacrifice and that Alfredo is coming to beg her forgiveness. As she reads she hears (in the orchestra) a strain from the melody Alfredo sang when he first declared himself to her – the strain she had taken up in her song at the end of the first act. She feels her illness, and laments the fair hopes of the past ('Addio, del passato bei sogni ridenti')*.

From outside her window the carnival revellers are heard in the street. Annina returns and admits a visitor: Alfredo. All bitterness is forgotten as the lovers embrace. He speaks of taking her away from Paris ('Parigi, o cara, noi lasceremo'). But after the exhilaration Violetta feels weak and has to send Annina for the doctor. She realizes that she is going to die. Giorgio Germont enters. Violetta gives Alfredo a medallion, asking him to give it to the girl he eventually marries. Annina has returned with the doctor and all join in as Violetta utters her plea to Alfredo.

Suddenly her agitation leaves her. Reliving the joyful first moments of their love, Violetta dies.

★   ★   ★

All Verdi's dramatic insight and human sympathy are poured into the delineation of Violetta and her relationship with the other characters. The contrast between the 'brilliant' but hard life of Parisian parties and the idyll of the country retreat is paralleled by the contrast within Violetta's music – between her song at the end of Act I (very remarkably, Verdi does not end the act with Violetta as transformed by Alfredo but with Violetta still the courtesan) and the

*'Literally, 'Farewell, fair smiling dreams of the past'. The common shortening to 'Addio del passato' as if that could mean 'Farewell to the past' is misleading. It is in this aria that Violetta refers to herself as 'traviata', a woman gone astray.

tenderness of her final 'Farewell' song. Particularly subtle is the musical expression of her responses to Alfredo. As soon as he has struck up the drinking-song in the first act, Violetta feels drawn to sing the second stanza to the company herself. Then, when he has made his suit to her and left, it is his musical phrase and his very words she takes over in her own aria (ex. 1). This recurs twice (as

Ex. 1

though returning in Violetta's memory) as she lies dying in the final scene. Similarly, in this scene Violetta is drawn to repeat the words and melody used by Alfredo (ex. 2) when he spoke of taking her away from Paris.

Ex. 2

This particular section of music corresponds in fact to the slow section of the old-fashioned operatic aria divided into a slow, pathetic opening and a more brilliant concluding part. Verdi, like other composers before him, modified the convention for the sake of dramatic realism. After the slow section there is an agitated interruption, when Annina is sent again for the doctor. Only after that is the quick concluding part allowed to follow: 'Oh God, to die so young, I am punished too much' (ex. 3). Here, in fact, Verdi unites the psychological strength of slow-followed-by-fast music with the dramatic strength of 'realistic' interruption.

Ex. 3

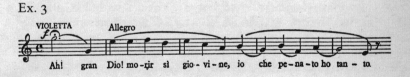

As remarkable as the portrayal of the lovers is that of Giorgio Germont who – unlike almost all such 'baritone father' parts – undergoes a real development of character. Violetta softens even him. His music is noble in the conventional operatic sense, but never heavy or blustering. Even his self-righteousness is transformed into tenderness (ex. 4).

Ex. 4

SIMON BOCCANEGRA
Libretto by Francesco Maria Piave, after a play by
Antonio Garcia Gutierrez; revised version
with alterations by Arrigo Boito

First performed: Venice, 1857
(Revised version: Milan, 1881)
Prologue and Three Acts

Cast in order of singing:

PAOLO ALBIANI, A GOLDSMITH, LEADER OF THE PLEBEIAN PARTY IN GENOA, LATER A FAVOURITE ASSOCIATE OF BOCCANEGRA AS DOGE	*baritone*
PIETRO, A GENOESE CITIZEN, LATER A COURTIER OF BOCCANEGRA AS DOGE	*baritone*
SIMON BOCCANEGRA, CORSAIR IN THE SERVICE OF THE GENOESE REPUBLIC, LATER THE DOGE	*baritone*
JACOPO FIESCO, A GENOESE NOBLEMAN, LATER GOING UNDER THE NAME OF ANDREA	*bass*
AMELIA [MARIA], DAUGHTER OF SIMON BOCCANEGRA GOING UNDER THE SURNAME GRIMALDI	*soprano*

GABRIELE ADORNO, A GENOESE OF NOBLE FAMILY   *tenor*
AMELIA'S MAID   *soprano*
CAPTAIN OF THE ARCHERS   *tenor*

Chorus of sailors, people, soldiers, servants to Fiesco,
the Doge's courtiers, senators, etc.
The scene is laid in and near Genoa, in the fourteenth century

Simon Boccanegra was a historical doge (ruler) of Genoa in the fourteenth century. He was a plebeian (that is, he was not of noble birth) and was poisoned – facts which were incorporated into Gutierrez's Spanish drama and into the opera which Verdi based on it. There is, as often with Verdi, a strong intermingling of political and personal passions in such a way as to provide strong emotional situations – a villain forced to pronounce a curse on himself, a father recognizing his long-lost daughter, a deathbed forgiveness and so on. It adds up to a forceful drama: and if the score has not the memorable melodies of Verdi's earlier operas it has power and psychological truth.

But the opera was originally (1857) a failure and Verdi not only got Arrigo Boito to revise the over-complicated libretto (the great Council Scene is entirely Boito's addition) but himself made many additions and alterations, both small and great. (Boito as an original librettist we shall consider under *Otello*, page 216, and *Falstaff*, page 222.) The result is still dramatically rather complex and 'difficult' (especially the twenty-five-year gap between the Prologue and Act I); but individual scenes and episodes are powerful.

Both forms of the name, Simon/Simone, are sung in the course of the opera.

★ ★ ★

PROLOGUE: In Genoa, in a square showing the church of San Lorenzo and the Fiesco Palace, Paolo, leader of the plebeian party, is discussing with Pietro the forthcoming choice of a Doge. It is night. Paolo suggests Simon Boccanegra, who has lately restored Genoa's maritime glory by driving the African pirates from the seas. On promise of a suitable reward, Pietro guarantees popular support.

Pietro leaves and Boccanegra enters. At first he is unwilling to accept nomination; but Paolo tempts him with the observation that as Doge he could no longer be refused the hand of the girl he loves – Maria Fiesco, who had already borne him a child and is now held prisoner by her father (the present Doge) in the Fiesco Palace. He agrees to accept nomination. As Boccanegra leaves, a crowd of workmen and sailors enters, led by Pietro. He and Paolo counsel them to support Boccanegra. Paolo angrily points to the palace where Maria is incarcerated: 'L'atra magion vedete' ('Do you see the sombre mansion?').

As they move off, Fiesco emerges from the palace. His daughter Maria has just died and he expresses his own sorrow: 'Il lacerato spirito del mesto genitor' ('A sad father's lacerated soul'). Sounds of mourning for Maria's death are heard from the palace as he sings.

Boccanegra enters, hoping that he may soon be united with Maria. Fiesco angrily reproaches him, refusing to forgive him even when he offers to pay for his seduction with his life. But Fiesco is prepared to forgive Boccanegra if he will yield up the child Maria bore him. Boccanegra explains that this is impossible, as the child has vanished. Coldly, Fiesco turns away, refusing to hear Boccanegra's plea for reconciliation. Boccanegra knocks at the door of the palace, demanding to see Maria; he finds within only silence and gloom, and discovers that she is dead. As he comes out, horror-struck, voices in the distance are proclaiming him as the new Doge. Paolo and Pietro come to tell him of his election, the news of which dismays Fiesco. Crowds acclaim Boccanegra and bells ring out in his honour.

ACT I: Twenty-five years have elapsed. Simon Boccanegra is still Doge; Fiesco, now using the name 'Andrea', is conspiring against him.

At dawn, in the garden of the Grimaldi Palace outside Genoa, a young woman is admiring the beautiful scene: 'Come in quest'ora brune sorridon gli astri e il mare' ('How the stars and the sea shine in this hour of darkness'). It is Boccanegra's illegitimate daughter, the child who 'vanished' in the Prologue. Unaware of her parentage, she knows herself as a foundling who now goes under the name of Amelia Grimaldi. She regards Andrea (actually her grandfather) as merely her guardian. Her lover, Gabriele, approaches. She warns him that his and Andrea's political intrigues against the present Doge may lead to trouble. Amelia's maid enters, announcing a messenger from the Doge. It is Pietro, who asks Amelia to receive Boccanegra himself. When Pietro has left, Amelia explains to Gabriele that Boccanegra wishes her to wed Paolo; she, of course, wants to marry Gabriele, and asks him to hurry and find Andrea and obtain his consent to their speedy marriage.

Amelia goes into the palace. As Gabriele is about to depart he meets Fiesco, who tells him that Amelia is not a Grimaldi; in infancy she was substituted for a child of Count Grimaldi, in order to save the family fortunes from confiscation by the Doge (two Grimaldi brothers are in political exile). Fiesco blesses Gabriele and consents to their marriage.

The sound of trumpets introduces Boccanegra, and Fiesco and Gabriele (as the Doge's enemies) leave hastily. Paolo and others are with Boccanegra, but he sends them away. Amelia tells him that she has a lover and does not wish to marry the rapacious Paolo (who seeks the Grimaldi fortunes). Boccanegra has decided to pardon the exiled Grimaldis (whom he supposes to be her brothers) but she now explains that she is not a Grimaldi by birth but an orphan. It becomes clear to Boccanegra from what she says that she is in fact his long-lost daughter, by name Maria, and this is confirmed when they compare pictures of her mother. They rejoice in the discovery: 'Figlia, a tal nome io palpito' ('Daughter! I sigh at that name').

As Amelia leaves, Paolo enters. Boccanegra, before he goes, tells Paolo to abandon any hopes of marrying her, but Paolo refuses to accept the decision and arranges with Pietro for her abduction.

The scene changes to the council chamber, where Boccanegra, as Doge, presides over an assembly comprising twelve patricians, twelve plebeians (including Paolo) and various officers. He tries unsuccessfully to persuade the council to agree to peace with Venice. In the distance the shouts of an angry mob are heard; Boccanegra sees from a window that Gabriele and another man are being attacked. Paolo is about to flee, but Boccanegra orders the doors to be guarded. The people are calling 'Morte ai patrizi' ('Death to the nobles'), to the alarm of the twelve patrician councillors, and even 'Death to the Doge'. Boccanegra sends out a herald to say that he awaits the people. They are quickly pacified, but they enter the chamber demanding the blood of Gabriele. It emerges that Gabriele has killed a certain Lorenzino, who abducted Amelia; and now Gabriele, believing that Lorenzino acted on Boccanegra's instructions, attempts to attack Boccanegra himself.

Suddenly Amelia enters and throws herself between the two men. She tells the true story of her abduction. She thinks she knows the man responsible, staring pointedly at Paolo. A fight nearly breaks out between the two sides of the assembly and Boccanegra steps angrily between them: 'Plebe! Patrizi!' ('Plebeians! Nobles!'). An elaborate ensemble follows.

Gabriele yields his sword to Boccanegra, who says he must be a prisoner for one night, till the plot is unravelled. Then Boccanegra calls forcefully on Paolo. He demands that he, as an officer of state, should join in cursing the man who perpetrated these evil doings. Paolo forces himself to pronounce the curse ('Sia maledetto') then shrinks in terror ('Orrore, orror!') of what he has done. All assembled join in the curse and Paolo attempts to flee.

ACT II: In a room of the Doge's palace, Paolo (now determined to revenge himself on Boccanegra) pours poison into the Doge's goblet. Gabriele and Fiesco, who are prisoners in another room, are brought in. He tells Fiesco that he (Paolo) will support Fiesco against the Doge if he may himself marry Amelia. Fiesco rejects such dishonourable terms and leaves. He then plants into the mind of the credulous Gabriele the idea that Amelia, whom Gabriele loves, is Boccanegra's mistress. Paolo leaves and Gabriele expresses his furious jealousy: 'Sento avvampar nell'anima urente gelosia' ('I feel raging jealousy burn in my soul').

Amelia enters. She is now living privately as Boccanegra's daughter – not, of course, as his mistress – but when Gabriele accuses her she can only assure him that she is faithful to him, and says she cannot yet tell him of her relationship with Boccanegra. As Boccanegra approaches, Gabriele, determining to murder him, hides on the balcony. Seeing Amelia weeping, Boccanegra asks what is wrong; she discloses that she loves Gabriele – to Boccanegra's great distress, for Gabriele and his family, the Adornos, have been plotting against him. As she departs he considers whether he can pardon Gabriele. He drinks of the poisoned wine and falls asleep, dreaming of Amelia. The poison will take its effect, but slowly.

Gabriele enters to find his enemy asleep. He is on the point of stabbing Boccanegra (partly to avenge his own father's death at Boccanegra's hands) when Amelia enters and stops him. Boccanegra wakes and bids him strike, and eventually tells him that by robbing him of his daughter Gabriele has more than avenged his father's death. Gabriele, seeing the situation, is full of remorse, begging Amelia for forgiveness ('Perdon, perdon, Amelia'); Boccanegra prays for the city's peace, and Amelia begs that the spirit of her dead mother may soften her father's heart.

From outside a warlike crowd is heard approaching: a patrician revolt has started, aimed at overthrowing Boccanegra. Boccanegra tells Gabriele to go and join his friends, but he now refuses to fight against Boccanegra and agrees to bear a message of peace to the clamouring rebels. In return, Boccanegra awards him Amelia's hand.

ACT III: The scene is a great hall in the palace. The revolt has been quickly put down, and from outside the people's joyous shouts can be heard. The Captain of the Archers returns his sword to Fiesco, who is now freed. On his way out Fiesco meets Paolo being brought in under guard: he had escaped to join the rebel cause but now, recaptured, is under sentence of death. Paolo tells Fiesco that he has poisoned Boccanegra. Distant voices are heard intoning a wedding-hymn for Gabriele and Amelia – whom Paolo once again, to Fiesco's fury, calls 'Boccanegra's mistress'.

Paolo is led off to execution and Fiesco conceals himself. From a balcony, a trumpeter calls the people to silence and the Captain announces that the Doge wishes the jubilation to cease as it is offensive to the dead. Alone, Boccanegra enters, unsteadily, feeling ill as the poison begins to take effect. He looks forward, apostrophizing the element that brought him his glory. Fiesco steps forward and foretells Boccanegra's doom. Boccanegra recognizes the voice as that of Fiesco, long since assumed dead; he tells his old enemy who Amelia is, and the two men are at last reconciled. Sadly Fiesco tells Boccanegra that he has been poisoned.

Amelia and Gabriele enter, with their wedding procession. Boccanegra tells them who 'Andrea' is – Fiesco, father of Maria (who died before Boccanegra could marry her), and thus Amelia's grandfather. Their joy at the marriage and reunion is tempered by the realization that Boccanegra is approaching death. Boccanegra blesses them. In an ensemble he begs her to come close to him and she prays that he may be spared, while Gabriele and Fiesco, in different ways, bewail the ephemeral nature of human happiness and the courtiers express their grief.

As he dies, Boccanegra gathers the senators around him and in a failing voice decrees that Gabriele shall be his successor. Fiesco, from the balcony, tells the people that Gabriele Adorno is their Doge. They call for Boccanegra: he is dead, Fiesco tells them. They pray for him as the curtain falls.

★   ★   ★

The father–daughter relationship dominates *Simon Boccanegra*. In the prologue Fiesco laments for his daughter Maria who has been seduced by Boccanegra and has died: 'Il lacerato spirito'. He begins in the minor key; when he changes to the major (with more

consoling thoughts of God's pardon) the offstage chorus of
mourners insists on the minor-key sadness (ex. 1).

Ex. 1

In Act I there is the dramatic scene of recognition between
Boccanegra and Amelia, when the words 'padre' and 'figlia' ('father'
and 'daughter') are many times repeated. Finally, after Amelia has
gone off-stage and her father's gaze is lovingly following her, the
orchestra plays the melody they have just been singing, and we hear
the tender words once again (ex. 2).

In contrast with these two 'private' scenes is the great 'public'
drama of the council chamber in which Boccanegra forces Paolo to
pronounce a curse on an unnamed traitor (in reality, Paolo himself).
Preceding it is a long utterance by Boccanegra showing his suspicion
of Paolo: musically the expression is shared by the orchestra, with
explosive figures displaying the force behind the singer's monotone.

Ex. 2

His words mean: 'You have authority in all that touches the people: on your good faith rests the honour of this city; today I need your help' (ex. 3).

Ex. 3

BOCCANEGRA
(con tremenda maestà e con violenza sempre più formidabile)

In te ri-sie – de l'au-ster-o drit-to po-po-lar.

sempre col canto

a tempo

È ac-col – to l'o-no-re cit – ta-din nel-la tua fe – de;

col canto

bra – mo l'au-si – lio tuo

a tempo

UN BALLO IN MASCHERA
(A Masked Ball)
Libretto by Antonio Somma, after Eugène Scribe

First performed: Rome, 1859
Three Acts

Cast in order of singing:

OSCAR, A PAGE	soprano
GUSTAVUS III, KING OF SWEDEN	
[Riccardo, Governor of Boston]*	tenor
CAPTAIN ANCKARSTROEM, GUSTAVUS' SECRETARY	
[Renato]	baritone
ARMFELT, MINISTER OF JUSTICE [A Judge]	tenor
MAM'ZELLE ARVIDSON, A FORTUNE-TELLER	
[Ulrica, a negro fortune-teller]	contralto
CRISTIAN, A SAILOR [Silvano]	bass
A SERVANT	tenor
AMELIA, WIFE OF ANCKARSTROEM	soprano
COUNT RIBBING AND COUNT HORN [Samuele, Tomaso],	
ENEMIES OF GUSTAVUS	basses

Chorus of deputies, officals, sailors, guards, people,
conspriators, servants, masked dancers
*The scene is laid in and near Stockholm at the end of
the eighteenth century*

Here are *two* famous soprano roles (tragic heroine and skittish page-boy); strong male solo roles; fine choruses; and sharp dramatic situations. And yet *A Masked Ball* is not quite as popular as some other Verdi operas preceding and following it. Part, at least, of the trouble arises from non-musical circumstances surrounding its creation. We must start with an event 21 years before the composer's birth, when on 16 March 1792 King Gustavus III of Sweden was killed by a shot during a masked ball in the court opera house at Stockholm. The French dramatist Scribe wrote a libretto on this subject for an opera by Auber (1782–1871), which was produced in 1833. On this libretto, Somma's libretto for Verdi – originally to have been entitled simply *Gustavo III* – was based. But in an Italy where revolutionary movements were being repressed with difficulty, an opera depicting the assassination of a king was frowned on by censorship; and the first performance, in Rome, was permitted only on condition of transferring the action to Boston, Mass., in seventeenth-century America under British rule. Only an English governor, not a king, would then have to be shown as the assassin's victim!

*For explanation, see below.

The ridiculousness of the action in its American setting has long
been felt and in many opera-houses the action has been restored to
Sweden. The names of the characters are therefore given here in their
original Swedish forms, but with Verdi's 'American' (Italianized)
names shown in the cast-list in square brackets, since performances
on gramophone records still trundle along in the old groove.

★   ★   ★

ACT I: In the hall of his palace, King Gustavus is about to give an
audience: courtiers are singing his praises, and the mutterings of
conspirators (among them Count Ribbing and Count Horn) can also
be heard. Oscar, the page-boy, announces the approach of the king,
who receives various petitions. He glances over a list of visitors
invited to a masked ball, and sees with delight that Amelia (the wife
of his secretary, Anckarstroem) will be there: secretly, Gustavus
loves her. Aside, he shows his feelings: 'La rivedrò in estasi' ('In
ecstasy I shall see her'). The courtiers depart and Oscar brings in
Anckarstroem.

Anckarstroem tells the king of a plot against him. Gustavus does
not take it seriously, but even though now 'Life smiles on you' ('Alla
vita che t'arride') Anckarstroem bids him do so. Oscar announces
the Minister of Justice, who brings for his signature an order to
banish Mlle Arvidson, a fortune-teller. Gustavus asks the opinion of
Oscar, whose plea on the fortune-teller's behalf – She turns her ashen
brow ('Volta la terrea fronte') – arouses Gustavus' interest. When the
courtiers (and conspirators) return, the king tells them that he will go
in disguise to test the woman's powers: all sing with pleasure of the
prospect.

The scene changes to Mlle Arvidson's hut, where a few women
and boys listen to her solemn invocation of the powers of darkness,
during which Gustavus enters, dressed as a fisherman. A sailor,
Cristian, comes to have his fortune told: Mlle Arvidson predicts
promotion, and Gustavus ensures the truth of her prediction by
writing out a commission and slipping it unseen into Cristian's
pocket, which the sailor soon discovers, to his pleasure. A servant of
Amelia's comes, asking for a private audience for his mistress. Mlle
Arvidson dismisses the crowd but Gustavus manages to hide.

Amelia comes in and tells Mlle Arvidson that she loves Gustavus
(he overhears this with delight) but wishes to exorcise this guilty
love. The fortune-teller informs her of a special herb, which will
serve the purpose if gathered at the gallowsfoot by night. In a trio,

Amelia prays for strength, Mlle Arvidson tells her not to fear, and the concealed Gustavus sings of his love.

As Amelia departs, the courtiers and Oscar arrive. The king steps forward and, pretending to be an ordinary fisherman, asks Mlle Arvidson to tell his fortune: 'Di' tu se fedele' ('Say, have I been loyal'). His hand is that of a nobleman, she says; she asks him not to press her to tell his fate. He and the assembled courtiers insist that she should complete the prophecy. She does: he will soon die, and by a friend's hand. All are horrified except Gustavus himself, who does not take it seriously. His murderer, she goes on to predict, will be the next man to shake his hand. The courtiers all decline to do so. Then Anckarstroem enters; the king immediately grasps him by the hand. Gustavus then tells Mlle Arvidson who he is, and Cristian summons the people to join with the courtiers in singing to him, with only the voices of the conspirators dissenting, and those of Mlle Arvidson and Anckarstroem singing with foreboding of the future.

ACT II: At midnight, near the gallows outside the city, Amelia is seeking the magic herb: 'Ma dall'arido stelo divulsa' ('When the leaf is torn from the arid stem'). Suddenly Gustavus enters. She tries to send him away, but their love proves too strong. They are interrupted by Anckarstroem, who comes to warn the king that the conspirators are around, intending to kill him. The men exchange cloaks, and Gustavus makes Anckarstroem swear to escort Amelia (heavily veiled and unrecognized by her husband) back to the city without inquiring who she is.

Gustavus goes off and the conspirators, led by Ribbing and Horn, approach. They are frustrated to discover that it is Anckarstroem, not the king, whom they had seen with the lady. Despite Anckarstroem's protests, they strip off her veil – and he is horrified to find that it is his own wife; Ribbing and the conspirators, however, are amused. To take revenge on the king, Anckarstroem resolves to join the conspiracy, and summons Ribbing and Horn to visit him next day.

ACT III: The next day, Anckarstroem and his wife are at home. He is determined to kill her for her faithlessness. She pleads her innocence and begs for a final favour – 'Morrò, ma prima in grazia' ('I shall die, but first grant me a favour') – to be allowed to see their small son. He agrees, and she goes out. He addresses an accusation to the portrait of Gustavus that hangs on the wall ('Eri tu' – 'It was you') and decides to spare her.

Ribbing and Horn arrive. Anckarstroem says he will join their plot and the three swear to avenge themselves on Gustavus. They draw lots to decide who shall strike the fatal blow. The names are placed in an urn and just as one is to be picked Amelia enters to say that Oscar has come. Before they admit him, Anckarstroem compels his uncomprehending wife to pick a piece of paper from the urn. The one she selects bears her husband's name, to his great satisfaction. Again the three men swear vengeance and Amelia begins to understand that they plan to murder Gustavus.

Oscar enters with the invitations to Gustavus' masked ball. Anckarstroem accepts, realizing that this will provide his ideal opportunity. All join in a quintet, Oscar looking forward to the evening's delights, while Amelia expresses her fears and the others their intention of taking advantage of the chance to kill Gustavus.

The scene changes to Gustavus' palace. The king is alone, writing out an order appointing Anckarstroem Governor of Finland, where he will take Amelia: he has thus honourably decided to renounce his illicit love. Dance music is heard in the distance. Oscar brings in a letter: it is a warning that an attempt will be made on Gustavus' life. But he will not be so cowardly as to stay away, and proceeds with preparations.

The court opera house has been turned into a ballroom, and the masked ball is now in progress. The three conspirators confer, wondering whether the king has arrived. Anckarstroem meets Oscar and tries to find out Gustavus' disguise for the ball, but Oscar declines to say: 'Saper vorreste' ('Should you wish to know'). Again Anckarstroem presses Oscar, saying that he has important matters to discuss with the king; this time the page gives way.

As a waltz strikes up, Gustavus and Amelia meet, and she tells him to fly from the murderers. He fails at first to recognize her in her disguise: when he does, they sing together as the dance proceeds. She again begs him to go. He tells her that she will be leaving for Finland with her husband. As they bid one another farewell, Ancharstroem comes and stabs the king.

Amelia and Oscar call for help; Anckarstroem is seized and the crowd call for vengeance. Before he dies, Gustavus assures Anckarstroem of his wife's purity, and orders that he should be spared. Anckarstroem repents his action and, mourned by all, Gustavus dies.

⋆　　⋆　　⋆

This is a powerful opera into which – especially when the work is given in its historically correct setting – the chorus enters with considerable dramatic point, both as the common people who support the king and (men only) as the conspirators who (in Act II) come to assassinate the king and are amused to have surprised their 'enemy' Anckarstroem taking his own wife, veiled, for a midnight walk. The private confrontation of husband and wife next day produces two of the opera's outstanding arias: first for Amelia (ex. 1), when she believes her husband will kill her, but prays to see her

Ex. 1

young son first, and then for Anckarstroem (ex. 2), who addresses the king's portrait and delivers an accusation of the king himself: 'It was you that laid the stain of dishonour'. Note the characteristic 'hammering' accompaniment. Later, Anckarstroem's utterance softens as he laments his lost days of love.

Ex. 2

The opera also has Verdi's most celebrated page part, that of Oscar, with two arias for a brilliant light soprano voice – in Act I, describing the fascination of the fortune-teller, and in the final scene, when the page's skittish refusal to divulge the king's disguise is dramatically ironic because we know (as the page does not) of the deadly reason why the conspirators are so anxious for him to divulge it. The page replies: 'Oscar knows it, but will not tell!' (ex. 3).

Ex. 3

LA FORZA DEL DESTINO
(The Force of Destiny)
Libretto by Francesco Maria Piave, after a Spanish play by the Duke of Rivas

First performed: St Petersburg, 1862
Four Acts

Cast in order of singing:

THE MARQUIS OF CALATRAVA	*bass*
LEONORA, HIS DAUGHTER	*soprano*
CURRA, HER MAID	*mezzo-soprano*
DON ALVARO, LEONORA'S SUITOR	*tenor*
AN OFFICIAL	*bass*
DON CARLO DE VARGAS, LEONORA'S BROTHER	*baritone*
TRABUCO, A MULETEER AND PEDLAR	*tenor*
PREZIOSILLA, A GIPSY GIRL	*mezzo-soprano*
BROTHER MELITONE, A FRANCISCAN MONK	*baritone*
THE FATHER GUARDIAN OF A FRANCISCAN MONASTERY	*bass*
TWO SENTRIES	*tenor, baritone*
A MILITARY SURGEON	*baritone*

Chorus of muleteers, Spanish and Italian peasants, Spanish
and Italian soldiers, camp-followers, beggars
*The scene is laid in Spain and Italy about the
mid-eighteenth century*

Elopement, duels, a woman dressed as a man, gay military music,
the chanting of monks . . . Such a list of trusted operatic ingredients
made a rich store for Verdi, but (in the event) a rather confused one.
Indeed, the anglicized title *The Force of Destiny* could be more aptly
replaced by *The Force of Coincidence*, for a series of mere chances runs
through this opera and diminishes its dramatic credibility, making it
little more than a chain of unprompted tableaux. Moreover, *La forza
del destino* rests on a series of social conventions a good deal more
remote from us even than those underlying *La traviata*. Carlo (Verdi
Italianized the Spanish 'Carlos') is justified in killing his sister
because she dishonoured the family name in eloping with a lover
who killed their father (although accidentally); and Carlo is not,
operatically, a 'bad' character.

But the character of Leonora, at least, comes over as a fully
sympathetic one; and as an equally sympathetic background we have
the consoling figures of the Father Guardian and the serenely chanting Franciscan friars. Among these friars is the heavily humorous
Brother Melitone: in his music he is often held to anticipate Falstaff,
but because his big scene (the mock-sermon) is based on purposefully bad Italian puns and the crowd's reaction to him, he can

hardly make quite the effect that Verdi intended unless the audience follows his every word.

★   ★   ★

ACT I: The marquis is bidding goodnight to his daughter in her room at his castle in Seville. He notices her troubled mood, which he attributes to the fact that he has separated her from her suitor (Don Alvaro, whom he regards as unworthy). When he goes she and her maid, Curra, talk of the plans for her elopement, that very night, with Alvaro; she is sorrowful at deceiving her father and leaving her home, singing sadly at the prospect 'Me pellegrina ed orfano' ('As wanderer and orphan').

Alvaro arrives. Overcoming her hesitation, Leonora is on the point of leaving with him when footsteps are heard and her father appears with servants. He angrily orders Alvaro's arrest. Yielding himself, Alvaro throws his pistol at the marquis's feet, but it explodes and the marquis is mortally wounded. As he dies he curses his daughter, who leaves with Alvaro.

ACT II: In an inn at the Spanish mountain village of Hornachuelos, the people are singing and dancing. The clients led by an official sit down to the meal ('A cena!') and a 'student' – in reality the marquis's son Don Carlo, disguised and seeking his sister and her lover – says grace. Leonora arrives – alone, disguised and in male clothes – and realizes who the student is. The student starts to question a muleteer, Trabuco, about his travelling companion (he arrived with Leonora), but before he replies the gipsy Preziosilla enters. She sings a gay patriotic song, echoed by the whole company: 'Al son del tamburo' ('At the sound of the drum'). It is momentarily interrupted by Carlo, who asks her to tell his fortune: she predicts tragedy, and adds that she can see he is not really a student.

A group of pilgrims is heard approaching: the assembled company joins them in prayer, Leonora praying that she may escape from her vengeful brother. She goes into an inner room. The student then starts questioning Trabuco and the official about the young stranger; Trabuco evades the questions and retires to bed. Next Carlo tries to go upstairs to find the stranger, but the official refuses to let him and asks him who he is himself. Carlo answers that he is Pereda, a student ('Son Pereda'), looking for a friend called Vargas. The singing and dancing are resumed until all go to bed. Leonora has evidently escaped safely.

The scene changes to the gateway of Hornachuelos monastery. It is bright moonlight and will soon be dawn. Here we rediscover Leonora, still dressed as a man, still a fugitive, and now exhausted. She prays to the Virgin for forgiveness: 'Madre, Madre, pietosa Vergine'. From within she hears the friars chanting. The door-keeper, Brother Melitone, at first hesitates to call the Father Guardian, but eventually does so. The Father Guardian sends Melitone away and hears her story. During their long scene together, she tells him who she is (he has heard about her from another priest) and he exhorts her to prayer and repentance; he suggests that she should enter a convent, but she protests imploringly ('Un chiostro? un chiostro? no') and asks to be allowed the use of a hermit's cave near the monastery. He agrees, then calls Melitone and tells him to gather the friars together, and she thanks God for his mercy.

In the monastery chapel, the Father Guardian tells the friars that the cave is to be occupied. Anyone disturbing the hermit (whose sex, of course, is undisclosed), or trying to find who it is, is accursed ('Maledizion!'). All pray to 'the Virgin of the angels' ('la Vergine degli angeli') to extend her protection to the hermit.

ACT III: At night, in a wood near Velletri in Italy, some soldiers are playing cards. Their officer is Alvaro who under a false name has joined the Spanish Army in Italy fighting against the Austrians. He ruminates on his unhappiness and on Leonora, whom he believes dead: 'O, tu che in seno', A cry for help is heard; Alvaro rushes off and comes back with Carlo (also now an officer in the Spanish army) whom he has saved from attempted assassination. The two men, who have not met before, exchange names (both false) and swear eternal friendship.

An alarm is sounded and they go off to fight. There is a rapid change of scene. A surgeon and some orderlies watch the battle, in which Alvaro leads his men to victory but is wounded. He is carried in: Carlo, complimenting Alvaro on his bravery, says he will be given the Order of Calatrava (that name, his family name, alarms Alvaro). Then Alvaro asks Carlo to carry out his last wish, to destroy unopened a packet of papers: 'Solenne in quest'ora' ('Solemnly in this hour').

Left alone, Carlo wonders whether his new friend, who was disturbed at mention of the name Calatrava, could be his father's murderer. He struggles with his conscience as to whether he should open the papers: 'Urna fatale del mio destino' ('Fateful urn of my destiny'). In Carlo's valise he finds a small box without a seal; in it is a portrait of Leonora, confirming his suspicions. He is glad to learn from the surgeon that Alvaro has been saved by the surgeon ('Ah! egli è salvo!') so that he himself can kill his enemy.

The scene changes to an encampment. A patrol passes. Alvaro is alone, in pensive mood, when Carlo enters. He tells Alvaro who he is and demands a duel. Alvaro is unwilling, pleading that it was fate, not he, that killed the marquis, and he affirms real friendship for Carlo. But Carlo (incidentally revealing that Leonora is not dead, as Alvaro thought) deliberately provokes Alvaro and the two men fight. The patrol, re-entering, separates them. Alvaro, saddened, resolves to retire to a monastery.

The scene changes to the main army camp. First, soldiers and female camp-followers (*vivandières*) sing gaily, with Preziosilla offering to tell fortunes; then, after various toasts, the pedlar Trabuco enters, buying booty and selling trinkets; next, a few poor peasants enter, with children, begging for bread ('Pan, pan per carità'); then a group of homesick boy-recruits arrives, soon to be cheered by the camp-followers and Preziosilla. She leads the company in singing and dancing a tarantella. They are interrupted by Melitone, who delivers a mock-solemn sermon, full of puns ('You prefer bottles to battles!'): eventually he is hustled off by the two groups of soldiers, Italian and Spanish. Another song from Preziosilla ('Rataplan', imitating drums), with chorus, cheers the company.

ACT IV: The scene moves back to Spain, some time later. Outside the monastery at Hornachuelos, beggars are demanding charity and Melitone is distributing food to them. The Father Guardian is also present. It becomes clear that they much prefer a certain Father Raffaello to Melitone, to the latter's irritation. The Father Guardian reproaches Melitone for his impatience and mentions the virtue and self-denial of Father Raffaello – who is in fact Alvaro.

The bell at the gate rings and the Father Guardian sends Melitone to open it. Don Carlo is there: he has at last traced Alvaro, and asks Melitone to call him. While he waits he reaffirms his resolve to kill Alvaro, and he challenges him when he comes. Feeling no animosity and wanting only to be left in peace as a monk, Alvaro is unwilling to fight: 'Le minaccie, i fieri accenti' ('Your threats, your proud speech'). Carlo, however, repeatedly taunts him – finally striking his face. Alvaro, who so far has restrained himself, can do so no longer: they run off to fight.

The scene changes to Leonora's lonely hermitage. She is praying – 'Pace, pace, mio Dio' ('Peace, peace, O Lord') – that God may send a speedy end to her suffering. Sounds are heard nearby and she retires into her cavern: then Carlo and Alvaro approach, fighting. Carlo, mortally wounded, calls for a priest, and Alvaro, approaching the cell, calls on the 'hermit' to come. Leonora rings her bell to summon aid and then, coming out, recognizes Alvaro as her lover. In despair, he tells her what has happened, and that her brother lies dying. She rushes off to Carlo. A scream is heard: Carlo has summoned up sufficient strength to strike his 'guilty' sister a mortal blow. Supported by the Father Guardian, she returns to Alvaro, who furiously curses the forces that govern their destiny. In a trio, Leonora and the Father Guardian admonish him. As she dies, Leonora looks forward to a heavenly reunion with Alvaro.

★ ★ ★

La forza del destino starts with a full-scale overture, more often heard at concerts than any other of Verdi's. The opening three hammer-like blows, repeated, constitute a 'fate' motive, which is followed by an agitated theme (in a minor key) from Leonora's scene in Act II outside the monastery gate; later comes Leonora's great major-key prayer from the scene in Act II in which the heroine has arrived at the monastery gate. But the three-note 'destiny' theme, though it recurs in the course of the overture, does not do so in the actual opera: it is not, therefore, a leading-motive in Wagner's sense.

We may quote from the 'prayer' theme as it occures in the scene itself, to the words 'Do not abandon me, O God!' (ex. 1): it is one of

Ex. 1

Verdi's most memorable (and most characteristic) tunes, with a vocal line whose rise and fall seem to portray in turn the strength and weakness of the human spirit. Equally famous is the duet (ex. 2) in which Alvaro, who thinks he is dying, asks Carlo to do him a service. Carlo consents: 'I swear it, I swear it'.

Ex. 2

The part of Preziosilla, a gipsy camp-follower, calls for a brilliant mezzo-soprano. She has nothing to do with the basic plot; her music is very effectively designed to throw a lively element into the sombre story. Her 'Rataplan' with chorus is accompanied only by two side-drums on the stage (ex. 3).

Ex. 3

The use of the word 'Rataplan' for this purpose was not new; it became popular in Donizetti's *La fille du régiment*. The operetta *Cox and Box* (music by Sullivan, words by F. C. Burnand) made fun of this usage in 1867, a few months before *La forza del destino* was first staged in London.

DON CARLOS
Libretto by François-Joseph Méry and Camille du Locle, after Schiller's play

First performed: Paris, 1867
Five Acts

Cast in order of singing:

DON CARLOS, INFANTA OF S PAIN	tenor
THIBAUT, PAGE TO ELISABETH	soprano
ELISABETH DE VALOIS, DAUGHTER OF THE KING OF FRANCE	soprano
A MONK	bass
RODRIGO, MARQUIS OF POSA	baritone
PRINCESS EBOLI	mezzo-soprano
PHILIP II, KING OF SPAIN	bass
A HERALD	tenor
A VOICE FROM HEAVEN	soprano
THE COUNT OF LERMA	tenor
THE GRAND INQUISITOR, A BLIND NONAGENARIAN	bass

Chorus of huntsmen, courtiers, monks, soldiers,
deputies, people, etc.
The scene is laid in France and Spain, about 1560

Two famous soliloquies – of a king recognizing that his young wife does not love him, and of a woman cursing her own beauty – are among the features of *Don Carlos* which show Verdi's dramatic power at its height. Public and private passions run strong in this opera, which requires bold spectacle as well as highly individual characterization.

Don Carlos is a political drama on the familiar theme of 'liberty versus tyranny'. Schiller's play presented Don Carlos, son of Philip

II of Spain, as a heroic and virtuous young liberal (apparently without historical justification); and his rivalry with his father, both in politics and in love, forms the subject of the play and of Verdi's opera. In Schiller's play the Inquisitor's power compels the king, at the very end, to hand his son over to him; in the opera as written, Carlos is saved from this fate by being spirited away in the nick of time by the ghost of his royal grandfather. (At Sadler's Wells, 1951, Schiller's more strongly dramatic, non-supernatural ending was used.)

Don Carlos was written in French for the Paris Opéra: it was in the long, five-act form, with ballet, which had become established at that house. In 1884 it was given in Milan as *Don Carlo*, to an Italian translation by Antonio Ghislanzoni, in a version which jettisoned not only the ballet but the whole first act. This means the loss of a love-duet not only fine in itself but providing a musical phrase purposefully used in later scenes. Modern practice is to restore the first act whatever other incidental cuts may be made; indeed a few productions have gone further and restored some ten minutes of music at the start of the opera which Verdi himself cut out before the première. The synopsis below follows this scheme whilst omitting the ballet-episode and one or two other minor episodes in the drama; but it does include the final scene of Act IV, which is sometimes omitted. Since performances not in English are still encountered more often in Italian than in French, lines quoted are given in their Italian form. In the four-act version Carlos's aria from the first act is inserted – with different words, 'Io l'ho perduto' ('Ah, I have lost her!') – in Act II as indicated.

Verdi's original French or Spanish names are kept for the personages mentioned, except for Philip II and Charles V, Spanish emperors always referred to as such in English history books.

★　★　★

ACT I: In France, in the forest of Fontainebleau, a hunt is in progress. Princess Elisabeth and her page Thibaut, separated from the other riders, disappear to look for them. Don Carlos, son of King Philip of Spain, is to marry Elisabeth and, alone, sings of his joy. She, however, has never met him; and now, when she reappears, he introduces himself merely as one of the Spanish envoy's staff. But he shows her what he declares to be a portrait of Don Carlos, which she recognizes as himself. They confess their mutual love.

But then Thibaut, who has left them alone, returns with the

message that the king, Carlos's father, intends to marry her himself. Her grief contrasts with the jubilant chorus of courtiers who are heard approaching to greet her on the prospect of becoming a queen.

[By the point of time at which the next act begins – or at which the four-act version of the opera begins – this has taken place: Elisabeth is married to King Philip.]

ACT II: In the cloister of the Yuste monastery in Madrid, near the tomb of Charles V, the chanting of monks, led by one of their number, is heard; they are mourning their late monarch. As the sun rises, the monks depart and Don Carlos enters. (In the four-act version of the opera he sings here of his loss of Elisabeth.) His conversation with a monk discloses that the ghost of Carlos's grandfather, the Emperor Charles V – or perhaps the Emperor himself, not in fact dead – is sometimes seen in the monastery.

Rodrigo, Don Carlos's life-long friend, enters, newly arrived from the Spanish province of Flanders. He is troubled by Carlos's anguish and asks its cause. Carlos explains that he loves his father's wife; Rodrigo advises him to leave Madrid, to obtain his father's permission to go to Flanders and show his worth by helping the oppressed populace there. They swear eternal friendship and ask God for strength to fight for freedom: 'Dio, che nell'alma infondere' ('God who has implanted in our souls'). Philip and his wife enter; he kneels for a moment at the tomb, and they pass on without speaking. The monks resume their chanting, and Don Carlos, though momentarily disturbed on seeing Elisabeth, resumes singing with Rodrigo of their friendship.

The scene changes to a garden, where ladies of the court are passing the time. First the page Thibaut joins them, then Princess Eboli, who sings a Moorish song – the Song of the Veil (Canzone del velo) – assisted by Thibaut and the assembled ladies. The queen enters and a moment later Thibaut announces Rodrigo, newly returned from Paris. He presents to the queen a letter from her mother, and also slips another note into her hand.

While Rodrigo and Eboli talk of the news from fashionable Paris, she reads the note: it is from Carlos, asking if he may see her, and Rodrigo adds his own voice to the request. She consents. When Carlos enters the others all withdraw. At first he asks her to persuade the king to make him Governor of Flanders, but when she admits that her love for him is still strong he loses his self-control and addresses her passionately. She draws away, asking if he means to kill his father and marry her, and he rushes off distracted.

Thibaut announces the king, who, angry at finding his wife alone, peremptorily dismisses from his service the lady who should have been waiting on her. She bursts into tears and Elisabeth consoles her: 'Non pianger, mia compagna' ('Do not weep, my companion'). Rodrigo and the attendant ladies and gentlemen commiserate, and even Philip, who nurses suspicions over his wife's fidelity, is almost moved into believing in her sincerity.

Rodrigo is left alone with Philip, who asks if he has any favour to request. He asks his harsh king to alleviate the wretched state of affairs in Flanders, where the Protestants are being persecuted; but Philip, unmoved, only warns Rodrigo to beware of the Grand Inquisitor. In a flood of confidence, he tells Rodrigo of his suspicions of the queen and his son, asking him to watch her carefully. But it is with a final warning of the Inquisition that Philip at last dismisses Rodrigo.

ACT III: Don Carlos has received an anonymous note (which he presumes is from the queen) making an assignation. To fulfil it, he now waits in the queen's garden at midnight. A veiled woman enters and Carlos sings of his love. Suddenly he realizes that it is not Elisabeth but Princess Eboli to whom he has poured out his heart. She in fact loves him, but quickly guesses that his words were intended for another – the queen. Rodrigo arrives and tries to smooth over the situation, but Eboli is furiously jealous and warns them that she is determined to exact revenge. As she goes, Carlos and Rodrigo pledge their mutual faith, and Carlos entrusts to Rodrigo some vital secret papers – correspondence with the revolutionary leaders in Flanders.

In a square in front of the cathedral, a funeral pyre is prepared for an auto-da-fé. Crowds sing in honour of the king. Monks singing a funeral chant bring forward the prisoners condemned by the Inquisition; then the crowds resume jubilantly as a procession of courtiers, deputies and pages, and including Elisabeth and Rodrigo, draws up before the cathedral. A herald announces the opening of the cathedral doors, disclosing the king; the people prostrate themselves.

Don Carlos leads in six Flemish deputies, who fall in supplication before the king. They make a moving plea for mercy for their people, but it is rejected out of hand by Philip and the monks, although the crowd are sympathetic. Eventually, Carlos steps forward and asks to be appointed ruler of Flanders, so that he may prove his worthiness to become king. Philip rejects his request: he will not give his son power which may be used against himself. Swearing to help the suffering people of Flanders, Carlos draws his sword – an outrage before the king. Despite Philip's call to disarm Carlos, no one steps forward to do it. Then Rodrigo does so; Carlos, astonished, yields his weapon to him, and the king creates Rodrigo a duke in recognition of his service.

The people resume their praises of the king and the monks resume their chant of death. A voice from heaven proclaims future joy for those so cruelly dealt with on earth. The funeral pyre is lit, and all but the condemned deputies sing to the glory of God.

ACT IV: Philip, alone in his apartments, meditates sadly: 'Ella giammai m'amò' ('She never loved me'; the French original has a different sense: 'She no longer loves me'). The Count of Lerma brings in the aged Grand Inquisitor. Philip asks what punishment should be administered to Carlos, and the Grand Inquisitor advises death, countering Philip's scruples by pointing out that God sacrificed *his* own son. Then the Inquisitor demands that Philip turn Rodrigo over to the Inquisition on the grounds that he is plotting against king and Church. Philip resists, but, before he departs, the Inquisitor warns that even the king himself is not above the Inquisition.

Elisabeth enters. Her casket of jewels has been stolen, and she demands justice. Philip produces the casket, ordering her to open it. She refuses: he opens it himself and confronts her with Carlos's portrait which is inside. She faints when he angrily rejects her explanation that she had been betrothed to Carlos. Rodrigo and Princess Eboli come when he calls for help. Now he regrets his hasty conduct, and Eboli, who had given him the casket, regrets her betrayal of the Queen. In a quartet, each expresses his reaction to the stituation; then, after the men have departed, Eboli begs Elisabeth's forgiveness for her betrayal. She discloses that she herself loves Carlos and has been seduced by the king. Elisabeth orders her to leave the court, either in exile or to enter a convent; left alone, Eboli curses her 'fatal gift' of beauty ('O don fatale'), but vows to help rescue Carlos from his threatened punishment.

Carlos, in an underground prison, is visited by Rodrigo who explains that Carlos's papers have been found in his possession and that he is being hunted by the Inquisition. At that very moment an assassin, under the orders of the Inquisition, enters and shoots him. As he dies he tells Carlos that the queen will meet him the next day, and charges him to bring freedom to Spain and Flanders: 'O Carlo, ascolta' ('O Carlos, listen').

The king, with grandees in attendance, comes to restore his sword to Carlos, but the son denounces his father for complicity in Rodrigo's murder. Outside, an angry crowd is clamouring in support of Carlos. The grandees are afraid, but Philip demands that the doors be opened. Eboli, in disguise, bids Carlos escape. The Inquisitor appears and orders the tumultuous crowd to kneel in homage before God's chosen king. Overawed, they do so, and beg Philip for mercy.

ACT V: Elisabeth, in profoundly sorrowful mood, is alone in the cloisters of Yuste, kneeling before the tomb of the Emperor Charles V, whom she invokes: 'Tu che le vanità' ('You who know the vanities of earth'). She bids her joys a sad farewell, and recalls the happy days of her youth in France. Carlos arrives and they sing a duet, in which they acknowledge that their love can be fulfilled only in heaven.

King Philip enters with the Grand Inquisitor and guards. As the guards move to seize the lovers, the tomb of Charles V opens and a figure in a monk's robes emerges and, to the terrified astonishment of all, takes Carlos away.

★   ★   ★

Musically the opera is remarkable for its mezzo-soprano and bass solo parts, rather than the (usually more prominent) tenor and soprano. Princess Eboli – sharing with Amneris in *Aida* the claim to be considered the most compelling of Verdi's mezzo-soprano roles – has the famous aria in which, remorseful, she curses her 'fatal gift' of beauty ('O don fatale'). Here Verdi starts in 4/4 time with a rhythm of ordinary crotchets and quavers (ex. 1) which later gives way to the urgency of triplets and, at the end, after climbing to a testing high note, hammers out strict quavers again (ex. 2).

Ex. 1

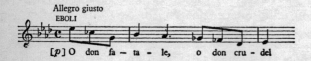

Ex. 2

King Philip may be accounted Verdi's greatest bass part, and his duologue with the blind Grand Inquisitor (two basses, but the king weak in character by comparison with the strength of the Inquisitor) is unique. The measured, pacing orchestral accompaniment is that which served to introduce the Inquisitor just previously. Philip asks whether he should condemn his son to exile or death – and would the Church absolve him if he did? The Inquisitor's firm reply is: 'The peace of your dominions is worth a rebel's dying' (ex. 3). This is the 'conversational' musical style of the mature Verdi, dramatically fulfilling the purpose of recitative in older opera.

Ex. 3

ma–no?

[*mf*] La pa – ce dell'im – pe –ro   i di val d'un ri – bel – le.

mf   *f*

AIDA

Libretto by Antonio Ghislanzoni, from a French prose
text by Camille du Locle and A. E. Mariette

First performed: Cairo, 1871
Four Acts

Cast in order of singing:

RAMFIS, HIGH PRIEST OF EGYPT	*bass*
RADAMES, CAPTAIN OF THE EGYPTIAN GUARD	*tenor*
AMNERIS, DAUGHTER OF THE KING OF EGYPT	*mezzo-soprano*
AIDA, SLAVE OF AMNERIS AND DAUGHTER OF	
AMONASRO	*soprano*
THE KING OF EGYPT	*bass*
A MESSENGER	*tenor*
HIGH PRIESTESS	*soprano*
AMONASRO, KING OF ETHIOPIA	*baritone*

Chorus of priests and priestesses, soldiers, Ethiopian
prisoners and slaves, Egyptians
The action is laid in Memphis and Thebes
at the time of the Pharaohs

Italian opera began its conquest of the whole world of music in the
eighteenth century and consolidated it in the nineteenth. In November 1869 an Italian theatre was opened in Cairo, and *Aida* was
commissioned for it by the Khedive (ruler) of Egypt and produced
there two years later. (The original plan had been for an opera to

celebrate the opening of the Suez Canal in 1869.) The plot had been provided by the French Egyptologist Mariette (known as Mariette Bey, for he had received that title from the Egyptian government); the libretto was written in French prose by Camille du Locle and put into Italian verse by Ghislanzoni, with a good deal of direct intervention by the composer himself.

Verdi's *Aida* turned out to be one of the most universally popular of all operas. It has tremendous spectacle, intermingles personal and political plots, and has its major conflict between soprano and mezzo-soprano – features which relate it to *Don Carlos*. In both works, too, the priests are the villains. But musically and dramatically *Aida* is the more compelling, and only in the dances does it show traces of being constrained by superficial theatrical needs. Solos and ensembles of deep personal passion are set off by massive choral effects and great orchestral splendour.

★   ★   ★

ACT I: The curtain rises on a hall in the royal palace at Memphis, with temples and pyramids visible in the background. The high priest, Ramfis, tells Radames that the Ethiopians have invaded Egypt, and that the goddess Isis will declare who is to lead the Egyptian armies. Hoping to be chosen leader, Radames dreams of returning, after a victorious campaign, to Memphis and to Aida, whom he loves. He sings of her: 'Celeste Aida'. Aida, a captive Ethiopian, is a domestic slave to Amneris, the daughter of the Egyptian king. Amneris enters and, seeing his elation, suspects that his ardour is not merely for military glory. Her fears – for she is in love with him herself – are reinforced on Aida's entry. In the ensuing trio she detects the strong feeling between Aida and Radames.

The king then enters, in procession, with Ramfis and various officers. A messenger tells of the devastation of the Egyptian countryside and the threat to the capital, Thebes, from the Ethiopian armies under their king, Amonasro. At mention of this name, Aida exlaims 'Mio padre!' ('My father!') – but her exclamation is unheard by the Egyptians, who do not know of her royal birth. The king proclaims that Isis has chosen Radames to command the Egyptian armies. Led by the king, the assembled Egyptians sing a battle chorus, and Amneris exhorts Radames to return victorious: 'Ritorna vincitor!'. Left alone, Aida echoes the words with tragic irony; she is torn between loyalty to her father, her country and her people on the one hand, and her love of Radames on the other.

The scene changes to the Temple of Phtha (a god equated in the Italian text with Vulcan, Roman god of fire and the working of metals), where the high priestess, Ramfis and the assembled priests and priestesses present Radames with consecrated arms.

ACT II: Radames has been victorious; and Amneris in her apartment is being attired for the triumphal feast in celebration of the victory. Her Moorish slaves dance for her. Soon Aida enters, and Amneris resolves to find out whether her jealous suspicions are justified. At first she treats Aida with feigned kindness. Then she tells her that Radames has been killed in battle, leading Aida to reveal her love for him. Then Amneris scornfully tells her that he is in fact alive – and how dare a mere slave presume to rival the Egyptian princess herself in love! The women's duet is joined by the battle song heard previously (sung in the distance by the returning warriors). Then Aida, left alone, implores the gods' pity: 'Numi, pietà!'.

The scene changes to the outside of a temple near Thebes. The king arrives in state. After a chorus of praise and thanksgiving to Isis and the king, a Grand March opens a resplendent procession including soldiers, dancing girls, chariots, banners and idols. At the height of the ceremony Radames enters. The king greets him, orders Amneris to place the victor's crown on his head, and tells Radames that he may ask any boon.

Next the Ethiopian captives arrive, including Amonasro, whom Aida at once recognizes and embraces, with a cry of 'Mio padre!' ('My father!'). The Egyptians hear this, but he tells Aida not to disclose to them his real identity. Amonasro tells the Egyptians that the Ethiopian king is dead, and pleads for the lives of the prisoners and slaves; his plea is supported by the Egyptian people and by Radames (who claims this as the boon earlier offered him by the king). The priests and Amneris oppose the plea, but the king consents, retaining as hostages (at Ramfis's insistence) Aida and her father. The king awards Amneris's hand to Radames, to her great delight but to the distress of Aida and Radames himself. The final ensemble expresses the jubilation of the people and the diverse reactions of the individual characters.

ACT III: From a temple of Isis, by the Nile, priests and priestesses are heard chanting. Ramfis enters with Amneris, leading her to the temple to pray for the goddess's blessing on her marriage, which is to take place the next day. Aida arrives for an assignation with Radames, and sings of her sadness at the prospect of never seeing her beloved homeland again: 'O cieli azzurri' ('O azure skies'). Suddenly

Amonasro appears: he tells her that she could return to her home safely if only she could find out from Radames what route the attacking Egyptian armies were planning to take. At first she recoils from the idea, but in face of her father's bitter contempt and his threatened curses she ultimately agrees.

Amonasro hides as Radames enters. With womanly wiles Aida overcomes his scruples and persuades him to fly with her to Ethiopia. As they depart she pauses to ask him by which route they can avoid the army; he tells her that the army will go through the Gorge of Napata. At that moment Amonasro; having overheard the vital information, steps forward and reveals himself as the Ethiopian king. Radames can hardly comprehend that he has been led into betraying his country. As Aida and Amonasro try to lead him away, Amneris, Ramfis and their guards emerge from the temple; they have witnessed Radames's disclosure and come to arrest him. Amonasro attempts to kill Amneris, but Radames steps between them, and bids Aida and her father flee while he yields himself to Ramfis.

ACT IV: Amneris is alone in a room in the palace, close to Radames's prison and above the hall of justice where his fate is being decided. She sends for Radames and offers to intercede on his behalf and save his life, on condition that he swears never to see Aida again. He steadfastly refuses and Amneris, proud and despairing, lets him go to face judgment. In increasing distress she overhears his trial, taking place offstage. He offers no answer to the charges of Ramfis and the priests; he is condemned three times as a traitor ('traditor!') and is sentenced to be buried alive. The priests emerge and in an impassioned outburst Amneris curses them for their bloodthirsty cruelty.

The final scene is a double one – the Temple of Phtha above, a crypt below. As the scene opens, the crypt is being sealed as a living tomb for Radames, who is within. He discovers that Aida had previously concealed herself in the crypt. While, from the distance, the priests and priestesses chant the praises of their god, and Amneris in bitter isolation prays for Radames's eternal peace, Aida sinks into his arms and dies.

★   ★   ★

Aida, Radames, Amneris: it is perhaps the most powerful 'triangle' of love in opera, with each character superbly delineated in music. Radames establishes himself at the start with his aria 'Celeste Aida',

Ex. 1

with its long sweeping lines which test a tenor's abilities (ex. 1). It
ends with an ascent from F to high B flat which Verdi marked
'*pianissimo*, dying away' – an effect beyond most tenors, who sing it
very loudly instead (and contrive to be applauded for doing so). The
scene when Amneris uncovers Aida's love for Radames enshrines a
double dramatic contrast – not only between the two women's
attitudes, but between their 'private' scene and the festive air of
victory outside. The chorus off-stage shouts its cry of death to the
invader, while before us Amneris threatens vengeance on Aida and
Aida humbly asks pity from the gods (ex. 2).

Ex. 2

Amneris, the 'villain' in her actions towards Aida, is herself
trapped when she tries (repenting at last) to make the priests show
mercy to Radames. It is a strong dramatic moment, of an almost
classical dramatic irony, and Verdi puts into it his most intense
writing for mezzo-soprano against the relentless unison of the
chorus of priests. The role of Amonasro is also one of great power.

The Grand March is famous, with its sudden key-change (ex. 3,
second bar) but it is at its most effective when producers observe (as

Ex. 3

they generally do not) the remark in the score that it represents one
group of trumpeters moving away in procession and a new group
coming in.

For an oriental subject a composer is faced with the question of
whether to include 'oriental' musical effects. Verdi, in the scene in
Phtha's temple, created an admirable stylization using the regular
rhythms of 'western' solemnity in the harp accompaniment and
unusual 'oriental' melodic intervals in the high priestess's solo as she
invokes the deity (ex. 4).

Ex. 4

OTELLO
(Othello)
Libretto by Arrigo Boito, after the play by Shakespeare

First performed: Milan, 1887
Four Acts

Cast in order of singing:

MONTANO, OTHELLO'S PREDECESSOR AS GOVERNOR OF CYPRUS	bass
CASSIO, OTHELLO'S LIEUTENANT	tenor
RODERIGO, A VENETIAN GENTLEMAN	tenor
IAGO, OTHELLO'S ENSIGN	baritone
OTHELLO, A MOOR, GENERAL IN THE VENETIAN ARMY AND GOVERNOR OF CYPRUS	tenor
DESDEMONA, OTHELLO'S WIFE	soprano
EMILIA, IAGO'S WIFE AND COMPANION TO DESDEMONA	mezzo-soprano
A HERALD	bass
LODOVICO, VENETIAN AMBASSADOR	bass

Chorus of soldiers and sailors, ladies, gentlemen and children
The action is laid at a seaport in Cyprus,
at the end of the fifteenth century

The librettos of Verdi's last two operas were written by Arrigo Boito (1842–1918). who was himself a composer of standing. His opera *Mefistofele*, a failure on its first performance in 1868, has since achieved a modest place in the world's opera houses. As a librettist his standing is even higher: *Otello* and *Falstaff* are sometimes reckoned the best texts ever written for Italian opera. Certainly they are marvellous abridgements of the original plays. Perhaps the most striking solo in *Otello*, curiously enough, is not from Shakespeare's pen at all: Iago's Creed, 'Credo in un Dio crudel' ('I believe in a cruel God'), which is a creation of Boito's own.

In *Otello* and *Falstaff* the 'static' element of formally separate numbers is almost banished; the onward development of the drama takes precedence. There is no grandeur of spectacle (or parallel grandeur of choruses) comparable with that of say, *Aida*. But the role of Othello, immensely heavy and difficult for the tenor, and the hardly less difficult role of Iago give the opera an exciting virtuoso element on top of its dramatic tension.

In the following synopsis we have restored Shakespeare's spelling of his hero; in Italian he drops his 'h'. 'Desdemona' is accented in Italian on the second syllable, not the third; and Iago (in Italian also spelt Jago) is pronounced strictly in two syllables, Yah–go.

* ★ ★ ★

ACT I: A crowd at the quayside, near the castle which is the Governor's residence, is waiting to greet Othello on his return from the wars. There is a violent storm at sea and the crowd are fearful for the safety of his ship, which Montano and Cassio identify. Iago and Roderigo watch too as the storm abates and the ship makes harbour. Othello steps on to the quay, briefly tells the crowd to rejoice ('Esultate!') since the Turks have been defeated, and goes into the castle. After a short chorus of jubilation, it emerges that Roderigo loves Othello's wife, Desdemona, and that Iago hates Othello and is jealous of Cassio, whom Othello has promoted above him.

The people light a fire, singing and dancing around it. Then while the officers are taking their ease, Iago starts a drinking song, makes Cassio gradually drunk, and engineers a · quarrel. Provoked by Roderigo, Cassio draws his sword and in the ensuing brawl Montano is hurt. Meanwhile Iago has sent Roderigo for Othello, who soon exercises his authority, making the men lower their swords ('Abbasso le spade!') and dismissing Cassio from his service. Thus the first part of Iago's plot – to discredit Cassio – has succeeded.

Desdemona followed Othello out when he came to stop the brawl but she does not speak till the others are gone and she and Othello are left alone. They sing of their love and of their happy memories of the past: 'Già nella notte densa' ('Now in dense night'). As their love-duet ends they return to Othello's castle.

ACT II: In a hall of the castle, Iago pretends that he wishes to help Cassio regain Othello's favour: he advises him to ask Desdemona, who has great sway over her husband, to intercede on his behalf. As Cassio walks off into the garden, Iago (alone) reveals that it is part of his plot to sow suspicions in Othello's mind about Desdemona and Cassio. He sings his creed: 'Credo in un Dio crudel che m'ha creato simile a se' ('I believe in a cruel God, who has made me in his image').

Iago watches Cassio and Desdemona in conversation, and, when Othello approaches, mutters, as if to himself, 'Ciò m'accora' ('This worries me'), for Othello to overhear. Then he subtly arouses

Othello's jealousy, while pretending to warn him against 'the green-eyed monster'.

A chorus of sailors, women and children serenades Desdemona, who is now in the garden. Witnessing the scene, Othello's doubts of her innocence are shaken; but his suspicions well up again when she asks him to forgive Cassio. His gruff manner leads her to think him unwell, and she moves to place her handkerchief to his forehead. He throws it down roughly. It is picked up by Emilia, who has been attending Desdemona; she yields it to Iago at his request, with some foreboding.

The two women leave. Othello gives way to jealous doubts, and says an anguished farewell to his former peace of mind: 'Ora e per sempre addio' ('Now and for ever farewell'). He demands of Iago positive proof of Desdemona's faithlessness. Accordingly Iago relates how, one night recently ('Era la notte'), Cassio talked in his sleep as if making love to Desdemona. He goes on to ask Othello whether Desdemona has a certain spotted handkerchief ('fazzoletto'); Othello says she has one of this description, his own first gift to her; and Iago states that such a one is in Cassio's possession (in fact it is now in Iago's own pocket). For Othello this is the final confirmation of her guilt, and the two men, kneeling, swear vengeance: 'Sì, pel ciel marmoreo giuro!' ('Yes, I swear by yonder marble heaven').

ACT III: In the great hall of the castle, a herald announces to Othello that messengers from Venice will shortly arrive. As Desdemona approaches, Iago warns Othello to be watchful, and then leaves him. His conversation with her is calm, with a touch of irony; but when she again asks him to forgive Cassio he does not answer, only asking to see the handkerchief. She says it is at home, and renews her pleas. He answers by accusing her of infidelity, which she strenuously denies. Othello thrusts her away, calling her a strumpet ('cortigiana'). Alone he shows his anguish: 'Dio, mi potevi scagliar' ('God, you might have hurled me').

Iago returns, with Cassio following; Othello conceals himself before Cassio enters. As the two talk, Iago drawing Cassio on the subject of his amorous conquests, Othello tries to overhear, but Iago takes care that he only catches remarks that could apply to Desdemona. Othello expresses his feelings to himself as he sees Cassio produce Desdemona's handkerchief, which Iago had previously had placed in his room.

Trumpet calls announce the arrival of the messengers, headed by

Lodovico. Before they arrive, Othello asks Iago to obtain poison to kill Desdemona. Iago advises strangling, and offers his own services for the killing of Cassio. In return for this advice Othello appoints him his lieutenant. The crowd welcomes Othello, and Lodovico enters to hand the message to him.

Still seething with jealousy, and almost striking Desdemona (to the scandal of Lodovico and the others), Othello reads the message aloud. He himself is to be recalled to Venice, and Cassio is to be his successor as governor of Cyprus. In fury, he throws Desdemona to the ground. She pleads with him pathetically, and in a prolonged ensemble all express their reactions to the situation, with Iago secretly jubilant. At the climax, Othello furiously curses his wife. Left alone with Iago, his imagination runs wild and he faints. As the crowd, outside, shout their praises of Othello, the 'Lion of Venice', Iago looks down contemptuously on his inert form: 'Ecco il leone!' ('See here the lion').

ACT IV: In her bedroom, Desdemona talks sadly with Emilia. Remembering a poor serving-maid of her mother's called Barbara, forsaken by her lover, she sits before the glass and sings Barbara's song – the Willow Song, with its refrain, 'Salce, salce' ('Willow, willow'). As Emilia leaves, Desdemona, full of foreboding, bids her a passionate farewell. Alone, she kneels in prayer 'Ave Maria', and when she finishes she lies down on the bed.

Othello enters, places his scimitar on the table, looks at her sleeping form, blows out the candle, advances to the bed, draws aside the curtains and gazes at her, then kisses her three times. She stirs. He asks if she has prayed for forgiveness for her sins, and once more accuses her of loving Cassio. She again repeatedly denies it; he tells her that nothing can save her, refuses her a moment for prayer, and stifles her with a pillow.

Emilia enters to tell Othello that Cassio has been attacked by Roderigo but has killed him. With horror, she finds Desdemona dying. She calls for help, and Iago, Cassio, Lodovico and others arrive. Iago's cunning plot is exposed by Emilia and he runs out, pursued by soldiers: then Othello, realizing and repenting his monstrous injustice to Desdemona, stabs himself, kisses her again, and falls dead.

★ ★ ★

Towards the end of the love-duet concluding the first act comes a memorable recurring phrase as Othello kisses Desdemona with the

words 'A kiss!' (ex. I). This is poignantly recalled when Othello
kisses his sleeping wife just before he kills her, and again when he
kisses her dead body, after having realized the truth and stabbed
himself, at the very end of the opera. But this remains a special effect:
the opera is not built on such 'recollections'.

Ex. I

The characterization of the three leading personages is strong.
Othello is a 'heroic' tenor (it is a role whose arduousness even within
the Italian style makes it particularly difficult to cast). Iago's sinister
power is conveyed by the striking *fortissimo* octaves in the orchestra
before he delivers his Creed; and, equally sinister, the orchestral trills
as he begins (ex. 2).

Ex. 2

Note the treatment of the 'octaves' theme as it becomes softer towards the end of the creed, sinking to 'La morte è il nulla' ('And death's a nothing').

Desemona's two great set pieces follow one another in the final act: the Willow Song and the Ave Maria (not the traditional Ave Maria in Latin, by the way). It is preceded by a mysterious orchestral chord-sequence and itself opens on a monotone while the chord-sequence continues. The Italian declamation is exact, a literal translation being: 'Hail to thee, Mary, full of grace, be elect among married and virgin women; let the fruit be blessed (O thou blessed one!) of thy maternal loins, Jesus' (ex. 3). Here is the musical language of Verdi's final period at its richest.

Ex. 3

FALSTAFF
Libretto by Arrigo Boito, after Shakespeare

First performed: Milan, 1893
Three Acts

Cast in order of singing:

DR CAIUS	tenor
SIR JOHN FALSTAFF	baritone
BARDOLPH, FOLLOWER OF FALSTAFF	tenor
PISTOL, FOLLOWER OF FALSTAFF	bass
MISTRESS FORD (Alice)	soprano
MISTRESS PAGE(Meg)	mezzo-soprano
MISTRESS QUICKLY	mezzo-soprano
NANNETTA, DAUGHTER OF FORD, IN LOVE WITH FENTON	soprano
FENTON	tenor
FORD	baritone

Chorus of townspeople, servants, etc.
The scene is laid in Windsor in the time of Henry IV

After an unparalleled succession of tragic operas, Verdi finished his operatic career with a comedy. It has a thread of intriguing musical cross-references and a great richness of musical resource, as well as subtle delineation of character. It has enchanting love-music, too; but it is the delineation of Falstaff himself and the web of conspiracy round him that gives the opera its chief celebrity.

Boito, having provided one masterly Shakespearean libretto for Verdi in *Otello*, showed equal mastery in this adaptation of *The Merry Wives of Windsor* (he also drew on *King Henry IV, Part 1*, for Falstaff's 'Honour Monologue'). Shakespeare's plot, too complex as it stands for operatic treatment, is cleverly shortened by the 'telescoping' of certain incidents and by making the young girl in love with Fenton the daughter of Ford, not – as in *The Merry Wives of Windsor*, and Nicolai's opera of the same title (1849) – the daughter of Page. Page himself does not appear. The Italian name, Nannetta, is retained in the following synopsis, but Bardolph has been reconstituted from the Italianized Bardolfo, and so forth. Dr Caius, in Shakespeare a French physician whose foreign speech is made fun of, is in the opera a silly (but not foreign) pedant, past his youth; and Mistress Quickly is introduced in her own right, not as Dr Caius's servant – she is a confidant of Mistress Ford and Mistress Page but not quite their equal.

*   *   *

ACT I: Falstaff is drinking in the Garter Inn; Bardolph (recognizable by his big red nose) and Pistol are in attendance. Dr Caius enters and brushes past the protesting Bardolph, complaining that Falstaff has broken into his house and beaten his servants, and that Bardolph and Pistol made him drunk and robbed him. Falstaff does not deny it, but tells him to keep more sober company – to which Pistol and Bardolph, hustling Caius out, reply 'Amen'.

Falstaff has no money left to pay the innkeeper's bill. He determines to carry on an amorous intrigue with two merry wives of Windsor, Alice Ford and Meg Page, whom he thinks have looked on him favourably, and asks Bardolph and Pistol to take them letters arranging assignations. They decline to act the pandar and he entrusts the letters to his page, haranguing Bardolph and Pistol for their new-found scruples: 'Che è dunque l'onore? una parola' ('What is honour? A word').

In the garden of Ford's house, Meg Page, Alice Ford, Mistress Quickly and Nannetta are together. Comparing notes, Mistress Page and Mistress Ford find that they have received identical love-letters from Falstaff, differing only in the names Alice and Meg. They are amused and slightly indignant about their elderly, corpulent admirer (Alice reads out Falstaff's extravagant phrases in a caricatured voice) and resolve to make a fool of him.

The women, keeping together, retire into the background as Ford enters, followed by four men agitatedly talking to him – Caius, telling him what a rogue Falstaff is; Bardolph and Pistol (chased out by Falstaff) trying to warn him of Falstaff's designs on his wife; and Fenton, Nannetta's suitor. Eventually the women leave and Bardolph tells Ford that Falstaff has already sent a letter of assignation. The men leave too.

Fenton and Nannetta steal some hurried kisses and sing a love duet, which is momentarily interrupted when the three women return, planning to send Mistress Quickly as a messenger to Falstaff. Finally Fenton joins the men when they return, still discussing plans to deal with the errant knight. A little later the two groups, men and women, again congregate on opposite sides of the stage; only

Fenton, singing in large rapturous phrases, is out of the conspiratorial chatter. The men go off first; then the women complete the hatching of their plot, repeat the caricature of Falstaff's extravagant literary phrases and go off laughing.

ACT II: Back in the Garter Inn, Bardolph and Pistol (now in Ford's pay) present themselves to Falstaff and feign penitence at having angered him earlier. When Bardolph and Pistol have gone, Mistress Quickly enters, with an exaggerated curtsey and greeting ('Reverenza!'); she delivers affectionate messages from both ladies and tells Falstaff that Alice Ford would welcome a visit between two and three o'clock, when her husband will be out. (Unfortunately, she adds, Meg Page's husband is rarely away!')

No sooner has Falstaff paid her for her trouble and congratulated himself on his good fortune than Bardolph announces another caller, by name 'Fontana' (in Shakespeare, Brook). This is Ford himself, who, in order to find out how things stand between his wife and Falstaff, has come under the pretext of asking for help in pressing his own suit with Mistress Ford. So far, he says, he has failed: offering Falstaff a purse of gold, he asks if the knight could first assail her virtue so as to ease his path. With pleasure, says Falstaff: he himself has an assignation with her between two and three that afternoon, when her jealous fool of a husband will be out. Left alone for a moment, Ford bursts out with rage against his apparent faithless wife and Falstaff: 'È sogno? o realtà?' ('Is it a dream? or reality?'). Sir John returns, dressed up to the nines for his intended seduction, and the two go off together ceremoniously.

In a room in Ford's house, Alice, Meg and (aside) Nannetta are waiting. Mistress Quickly gives a lively account of her interview with Falstaff, with imitations of his words and manner. She tells them that he will be coming in a few minutes' time, between two and three. Nannetta does not join in the others' laughter; she tearfully tells them that she is sad as her father intends her to marry not her beloved Fenton but old Dr Caius. The other ladies tell her not to worry – they will arrange something. Meanwhile, they set about preparing the scene (with such 'props' as a laundry basket and a screen) for Falstaff's arrival. First Alice, then Meg and Nannetta, sing of the 'merry wives of Windsor' ('gaie comari di Windsor').

With the others in hiding, Alice plays the lute to herself as she awaits her visitor. He arrives, sings a refrain to her lute, and then converses with her. Falstaff boasts that love is a vocation for him and sings of his merry youth: 'Quando ero paggio' ('When I was a page to the Duke of Norfolk'). Suddenly Mistress Quickly comes in, to say that Meg urgently needs to speak to Alice; so Falstaff is hurried behind a screen and Meg warns Alice that her husband is approaching.

Ford strides up angrily, with Caius and Fenton, Bardolph and Pistol; he accuses his wife and sets about searching the house – emptying the dirty linen from the laundry basket to see if anyone is hidden there before he goes. The agitated Falstaff emerges from behind the screen to find only Meg, tells her he loves her alone and begs her to save him. She and Mistress Quickly stuff him into the basket and fill it with dirty clothes again. Fenton and Nannetta enter together and, seeing the screen, retire behind it. The other men return, Ford and Caius still ranting angrily and looking in cupboards and up chimneys.

In a moment of silence, a kiss is heard from behind the screen. While Meg and Mistress Quickly hush the suffocating Falstaff in his basket, Ford gives instructions to his assembled servants for the unmasking of his wife and Falstaff – behind the screen, as he supposes. After a step-by-step advance in comic style. Ford throws down the screen, and is scarcely less enraged to find his daughter and her lover than he would have been to find his wife and hers. He strides off to renew the search. Alice summons servants to throw the basket of dirty laundry out of the window and laughingly shows Ford and the other men, who have returned, the magnificent spectacle of Falstaff in the Thames outside. A great outburst of laughter from all ends the act.

ACT III: Outside the Garter Inn, Falstaff is not unnaturally in dampened spirits as he grumbles to the landlord. But he perks up: 'Va, vecchio John' ('Go on, old John'). Mistress Quickly enters – with her 'Reverenza!' again – bearing apologies from Alice; at first Falstaff will not listen, but he eventually calms down and, watched from a distance by the concealed Ford, Alice, Meg, Nannetta, Caius and Fenton, he reads out a note from Alice suggesting an assignation at Herne's Oak in Windsor Forest, to which he should come disguised as the fabled 'black huntsman' ('cacciator nero').

Mistress Quickly and Falstaff depart, while Ford and the others discuss plans for the night's revels at Herne's Oak. Alice announces that Nannetta shall be Queen of the Fairies (Regina della Fate), clad in white. As they go off, Ford tells Caius he will make him his son-in-law at the revels: Caius is to come dressed as a monk. Mistress Quickly overhears this, and the women determine to circumvent it. As they go off their voices are heard in the distance. Night begins to fall.

The scene changes to Herne's Oak, by moonlight. Fenton is the first there and is soon joined by Nannetta, Alice, Meg and Mistress Quickly in their various disguises. They bring monk's robes for Fenton, to his mystification, and all hide. As the clock strikes midnight Falstaff arrives, costumed as requested, in nervous mood. Alice emerges and Falstaff starts to plead love to her. She mentions that Meg is nearby. Suddenly there is a terrified scream from Meg, shouting that witches are coming; Alice, as if frightened, runs off.

Falstaff is utterly petrified by the fairies, elves and other spirits (in fact Alice's friends, later with Bardolph and Pistol, Ford and Caius) who suddenly appear. They are led by Nannetta, who sings the fairies' song: 'Sul fil d'un soffio etesio' ('On the thread of a breeze'). They set about Falstaff, rolling him round, pinching him ('Pizzica, pizzica!'), and he is scared out of his wits. Eventually he recognizes Bardolph (by his big red nose), fulminates against him, and asks for respite.

While Mistress Quickly sends Bardolph away to don a new disguise (a white veil), Ford goes up to Falstaff, asking him 'Il cornuto chi è?' ('Which of us wears the horns?'). Falstaff begins to address him as Fontana, but Alice interrupts to introduce him as . . . her husband. Then Mistress Quickly identifies herself to him too, singing the same phrase as on their previous encounters. Falstaff takes it all in good part.

Ford then suggests the formal betrothal of a loving couple, Dr Caius (a man in monk's disguise steps forward) and the fairy queen; Alice proposes the addition of another pair of lovers, both masked. As the couples unmask it is seen that Caius has pledged his troth with Bardolph! – and Fenton with Nannetta, to the astonishment of Ford (not to mention that of Caius himself). 'Lo scornato chi è?' ('Which of us is the dupe?'), Falstaff asks Ford merrily. All three – Falstaff, Ford and Caius – answers Alice, and she begs Ford to forgive the young lovers. He quickly does so, and led by Falstaff, the proceedings are brought to a hilarious close: 'Tutto nel mondo è burla' ('Everything in this world is a jest').

*　*　*

The music of the young lovers (ex. 1) is ardently romantic, fitting for language that speaks of kisses and of love which renews itself like the moon (a quotation from the fourteenth-century poet, Boccaccio).

Ex. I

Note that the orchestral tune at bar 6 is the one sung just a moment
previously by the lovers.

Memorable too is the exaggerated greeting of Mistress Quickly to
Falstaff (ex. 2). Both these are among the phrases which later recur
prominently. Falstaff's own role is marvellously varied – phlegmatic

Ex. 2

Ex. 3

to Caius, angry to Bardolph and Pistol, amorous to Alice. To her he boasts of how nimble a page he used to be (ex. 3).

And it is Falstaff who leads the final ensemble of jollity – a fugue, incidentally (ex. 4). The whole orchestra seems to join in the laughter. With this ebullient ensemble, Verdi wrote the last pages of his last opera.

Ex. 4

RICHARD WAGNER

1813–83

We turn now to a composer who was born in the same year as Verdi
and who, with him, dominates opera in the nineteenth century:
Richard Wagner. From *Der fliegende Holländer* ('The Flying Dutchman', produced in 1843) to *Parsifal* (1882), he produced a succession
of works for the stage unmatched in their influence on the international development of opera in particular and music in general. We
need not be concerned here with Wagner's earlier operas, *Die Feen*
('The Fairies', composed in 1833 but not staged till after the composer's death), *Das Liebesverbot* ('The Ban on Love', based on
Shakespeare's *Measure for Measure*), produced in 1836, and the huge
'grand opera' *Rienzi* (based on Bulwer-Lytton's once celebrated
novel), produced in 1842.

As a conductor himself, Wagner knew the operas of his own time
well, including those of Weber, with their evocation of the romantically supernatural, and those of Meyerbeer, in which the drama
served to display vocal set pieces. But his own aim was to portray the
human soul with a new force, a force he detected in Beethoven's
Ninth Symphony. By fitting a symphonic finale with words Beethoven had attached concreteness to a 'pure' musical form. Wagner
wished his operas similarly to be 'music fertilized by poetry', not
merely poetry set to music.

Already, as we have seen, composers were increasingly tending to
intersperse their operas with recurring musical themes, the recurrence serving a dramatic point. But these recurrences hitherto took
place only at special, selected moments of the score. Wagner, from
Tristan und Isolde on, aimed to make such themes the actual stuff
from which his musical fabric was woven. The themes do not each
simply represent a mere personage (as Prokofiev in *Peter and the Wolf*
has a tune for the cat, a tune for the duck and so on): they may
represent an emotion, a destiny, an aspect of character, or something
equally abstract. What they represent is to be *deduced* from their

dramatic use in the opera: Wagner wrote the music, not the labels for the themes.

Through the use of these themes Wagner writes music which is, in intention, symphonic – and the symphonic argument almost (but not quite) eliminates the division of an act into separate numbers.

In the three works preceding *Tristan und Isolde* Wagner still laid out his score in separate numbers, and still made only a limited, non-symphonic (though considerable) use of recurring themes. Moreover, the orchestra part may still be described as an accompaniment.

Wagner's recurring themes, each bearing a dramatic meaning are usually called by the name 'leading-motive'—an anglicization of the German *Leitmotiv* (plural *Leitmotive*).

DER FLIEGENDE HOLLÄNDER
(The Flying Dutchman)
Libretto by the composer, after a story by Heinrich Heine

First performed: Dresden, 1843
Three Acts

Cast in order of singing:

DALAND, CAPTAIN OF A NORWEGIAN SHIP	*bass*
STEERSMAN ON DALAND'S SHIP	*tenor*
THE DUTCHMAN, A SEA-CAPTAIN	*baritone*
MARY, SENTA'S OLD NURSE	*contralto*
SENTA, DALAND'S DAUGHTER	*soprano*
ERIK, A HUNTSMAN, BETROTHED TO SENTA	*tenor*

Chorus of Norwegian sailors, Dutch sailors and
Norwegian girls
*The scene is laid in a Norwegian fishing village
in the eighteenth century*

Wagner was his own librettist – and, unlike many composers, a good one. He wrote *Der fliegende Holländer* originally as a one-act libretto, and offered it to the director of the Paris Opera hoping for a commission to complete the music. Instead, the director offered the libretto to other composers and paid Wagner five hundred francs for it – a sum much needed by the almost penniless young German musician, who had been obliged to leave his conductor's post in Riga secretly to escape his creditors. The five hundred francs gave Wagner the leisure to convert *Der fliegende Holländer* into a full-length work of his own.

Its story is a strong one – of a man supernaturally doomed to sail the seas until he can earn redemption. The supernatural element links it with the operatic world of Weber; the element of man's redemption through womanly love points to Wagner's later works. The music here is striking in its evocation of sea, storm and superstition (first of all in the overture) – and no less striking for its sheer tunefulness, as in Senta's Ballad, the Spinning Chorus and other numbers.

★ ★ ★

ACT I: The stormy overture sets the atmosphere for the opening scene, in which we see a Norwegian ship just anchored, after a violent tempest, in rough seas off the Norwegian coast. Daland, the captain, finds that they are not far from the port where they were intending to put in. Leaving a steersman on watch, he and the sailors go below for some much-needed rest. The steersman tries to keep awake, singing a ballad 'Mit Gewitter und Sturm' ('Through tempest and storm'), but eventually succumbs to sleep.

A ghostly ship, with blood-red sails and black masts, approaches. She puts in alongside the other ship, momentarily disturbing the steersman, and in silence the spectral crew make fast. Its captain, the legendary 'Flying Dutchman', comes ashore and sings of the terrible curse upon him. Once, rounding the Cape of Good Hope in a storm, he invoked the Devil's aid, and consequently his fate is to sail unceasingly until the Day of Judgment unless he can find a woman 'faithful unto death'. His is allowed to search for her every seven years, and that time has now come. The crew echo his bitter complaint.

Daland comes on the deck of his own ship and rouses his steersman, who signals the other ship. In reply there is only an eerie silence. Then Daland sees the Dutchman himself. The two captains talk: the Dutchman tells Daland of his wanderings, asking for his friendship and for shelter at Daland's home (which is nearby), and offering a magnificent casket of jewels in return. The Dutchman ascertains that Daland has a daughter and begs to be allowed to make her his wife ('Sie sei mein Weib'); to which Daland, though mystified, willingly consents. In a duet, Daland rejoices at the prospect of great riches and the Dutchman at the prospect of finding peace at last. Meanwhile the storm has passed and the steersman reports a favourable south wind ('Süd-wind!'); Daland and his sailors weigh anchor and set sail for their home port, the Dutchman promising to follow as soon as his crew have rested. The Norwegian sailors sing joyfully as their ship moves off.

ACT II: In a room in Daland's house, Senta's friends and Mary, Senta's old nurse, are singing as they sit at their spinning-wheels (Spinning Chorus). Only Senta, Daland's daughter, does not spin: she is preoccupied with a picture hanging on the wall, depicting the Flying Dutchman. Mary reprimands her for her idleness and the others tease her for her interest in the Dutchman when she has a suitor (Erik, the huntsman). Senta asks Mary to tell the tale of the Dutchman, but the old woman refuses, so Senta herself sings of the curse and the hoped-for redemption (Senta's Ballad).

The other girls join in. Finally Senta is seized with the sudden idea that she could be the one to save the doomed Dutchman, to the horror of all – including Erik, who arrives and has overheard her. He mentions that Daland's ship is arriving, to the delight of all the girls, who are excited at the prospect of seeing their menfolk. Mary reminds them of the domestic preparations now to be made.

The girls and Mary go off, leaving Erik and Senta alone. In a duet he begs her to promise to remain faithful to him, but she only wishes to go, to meet her father. She tells Erik of her compassion for the Dutchman: he is deeply troubled and relates to her a dream he has had in which he saw her father lead the Dutchman to her, and saw them embrace and go off together. (She adds an occasional detail, 'identifying' the dream from the picture.) She is now convinced that it is her fate to save the Dutchman, and Erik rushes off in despair.

Alone, Senta gently sings the refrain of her ballad: then the door opens and she sees her father, with the Dutchman himself, standing there. Her eyes remain riveted on the Dutchman as her father greets her. Daland is disconcerted when she does not run to embrace him as usual; then he praises the guest, asking her to receive him kindly and to consider accepting him as her husband. The Dutchman and Senta remain contemplating one another, in silence: Daland, puzzled and none too pleased by their apparent coldness, goes out, leaving them alone.

Senta and the Dutchman, both as if entranced, can hardly believe the fulfilment of their dreams. Their mutual love becomes clear to them both: 'Wie aus der Ferne' ('As if from afar'). When Daland returns he is delighted to find that she has accepted the visitor as her husband-to-be and that he can announce her betrothal at the forth-coming feast.

ACT III: In a bay, overlooked by Daland's house, the two ships are seen – the Dutchman's shrouded by a ghostly stillness, the Nor-wegian one full of light as the sailors sing and dance lustily: 'Steuer-mann, lass' die Wacht' ('Steersman, leave the watch'). The Norwegian women arrive with food and drink. They go to take some to the silent Dutch ship (the Norwegian steersman attributes their silence to their thirst) but there is no response to the women's calls, which they repeat, louder and louder. Eventually they become afraid, especially when the Norwegian sailors jokingly suggest that the ship resembles that of the legendary Flying Dutchman.

When the Norwegian sailors have eaten and drunk they move towards the Dutch ship. Suddenly a sinister dark blue flame is seen on board: the spectral crew come to life, singing a wild chorus, as the wind whistles and the sea rises round their ship. The Norwegian sailors, mystified and frightened, resume their song. Eventually, suspecting evil, they make the sign of the cross and go below, to the eerie laughter of the Dutchman's crew.

Calm returns just as Senta emerges from the house, followed by the agitated Erik, who reproaches her for her behaviour towards him. He begs her to remember her pledge to him of eternal love – which she recollects with terror. He reminds her of her solemn promises. The Dutchman steps forward (Erik recognizes him as the man in his dream): he has overheard their conversation and believes Senta untrue to him. He immediately determines to put to sea once more. As the Dutchman rebukes her for her supposed infidelity, she begs him to stay, while Erik pleads with her to leave the Dutchman to depart.

Before he leaves, he starts telling her who he is: she answers that she already knows and intends to save him from the terrible curse. In front of Daland, the Norwegian sailors and the girls (who have hurried out), he proclaims his identity as the dreaded Flying Dutch-man. Meanwhile, his crew make preparation to put to sea; he steps on board and they depart. Senta rushes to the edge of a cliff and calls to him, then throws herself into the sea. As she does so, the ship is sucked down into a whirlpool: in the sunset, the forms of Senta and the Flying Dutchman are seen rising heavenward from the sinking wreck.

★   ★   ★

The storm-tossed Dutchman is portrayed in the opening bars (beneath a string tremolo, omitted in ex. 1) and a little later the redeeming Senta is portrayed (ex. 2).

Ex. 1

Ex. 2

These two principal motives persist throughout the opera; they both appear (the Dutchman's motive transformed to a peaceful guise) in the very last moments. Senta's theme is first heard vocally in her Ballad (Act I). The overture thus represents (in minature and in anticipation) what is going to happen; and like the opera itself it ends quietly. The fact that the Dutchman's theme is used both for the appearance of the actual man (Act I) and for the telling of his legend (by Senta in Act II) musically establishes that this *is* the man of the legend: a point which may seem obvious but which in fact illustrates a basic operatic method of communication.

It is notable that the Dutchman's theme is made up of quite 'ordinary' components of rhythm and of melody (two notes only, D and A!); but Wagner stamps his own originality on it. In *Der fliegende Holländer* we also sense the more daring harmonic touch which Wagner fully developed in his later works. The Norwegian sailors hail the Dutch ship (in Act III) in a carefree C major; in place of a human answer there comes, after an ominous pause, an 'otherworldly', musically unexpected chord (on the horns and bassoon) in the remote key of C sharp minor (ex. 3).

Ex. 3

The sequence is shortly repeated twice more, at a different pitch and
with slightly different music for the Norwegians, but always with
the bleak unrelated minor chord (higher each time) to express the
supernatural mystery of the Dutch vessel.

TANNHÄUSER
Libretto by the composer

First produced: Dresden, 1845
Three Acts

Cast in order of singing:

VENUS, GODDESS OF LOVE		*soprano*
TANNHÄUSER, MINSTREL AND KNIGHT		*tenor*
A SHEPHERD BOY		*soprano*
HERMANN, LANDGRAVE OF THURINGIA		*bass*
WALTHER VON DER VOGELWEIDE		*tenor*
BITEROLF		*bass*
WOLFRAM VON ESCHENBACH	MINSTREL KNIGHTS	*baritone*
HEINRICH DER SCHREIBER		*tenor*
REINMAR VON ZWETER		*bass*
ELISABETH, NIECE OF THE LANDGRAVE		*soprano*
PAGES		*two trebles, two altos*

Chorus of sirens, pilgrims, Thuringian nobles, knights
and their ladies
*The scene is laid in Thuringia at the beginning of the
thirteenth century*

Like *Der fliegende Holländer*, *Tannhäuser* has memorable tunes, several of them foreshadowed in the overture which is so well known. Like *Der fliegende Holländer* again, it is concerned with redemption – but this time with the conflict of good and bad represented by the roles of the two principal sopranos, who never confront each other on the stage.

Tannhäuser himself was an actual thirteenth-century minstrel ('minnesinger'), some of whose verse survives. Perhaps because of a 'Song of Repentance' attributed to him, in the sixteenth century his name became linked with the legend of the Venusberg – the hill within which Venus was supposed still to hold her court and to destroy the souls of men who fall into her hands. In his opera, Wagner linked this legend with a contest of song which actually took place in 1210 at the Wartburg, a castle in Thuringia (central Germany).

Dramatically, this yields the theme of sacred versus profane love (to which Wagner returned in *Parsifal*), as well as a contest of song with its obvious operatic opportunities (to which the composer returned in *Die Meistersinger*) – all against a background of medieval courtly life which exercised a strong attraction for 'romantic' writers and composers of Wagner's day. In the opera, Christian love triumphs over pagan sensuality, but in the older traditional legend Tannhäuser is *not* redeemed and returns to the Venusberg.

Wagner completed *Tannhäuser* in 1845, and later that year it had its first performance – in Dresden, where he held a resident conductor's post. But when the opportunity came to present the work in Paris, in 1861, Wagner was no longer the Wagner of 1845: he had by now written *Tristan und Isolde*, and accordingly he felt he needed to modify the score of Act I of *Tannhäuser*. In the new version, now known as 'the Paris version' of the score, there are three major changes. The overture does not bring back the opening Pilgrims' Chorus and does not come to a formal close, but merges into the opening music of the Venusberg. The music to the dances in the Venusberg, depicting pagan ecstasy, is expanded* with detailed scenic indications to match (for example, 'Numerous sleeping Cupids are huddled together in a confused tangle like children who, tired after play, have fallen asleep'). Venus's plea to Tannhäuser to stay with her is rewritten with greater subtlety of expression – Venus is less shrewish, more meditative.

*In concerts this is known as the Bacchanal or the Venusberg Music.

These modifications do not affect the actual outline of the opera; and the Paris version has not universally banished the earlier (and musically more homogeneous) one from theatrical performances.

★ ★ ★

ACT I: The opening scene is set within the Venusberg, where the profane rites of love are celebrated to appropriate music. Tannhäuser is resting his head on Vénus's lap. He is feeling discontent with the indolent, abandoned life he has led for the past year, and tells Venus so; but she soothes him and asks him to sing to her, which he does: 'Dir töne Lob' ('Praise resound to thee'). But he is determined to leave her, despite her repeated seductive pleadings. Eventually she dismisses him, with proud anger, telling him that he can have no hopes of salvation. His hope rests in the Virgin, he replies; Venus and the Venusberg disappear at the mention of her name.

The scene changes suddenly to a valley near the Wartburg, where Tannhäuser finds himself. A shepherd boy is playing on his pipe and singing, and a group of chanting pilgrims moves past. The shepherd wishes them Godspeed; then Tannhäuser, deeply moved, falls to his knees and raises his voice in fervent prayer. As the pilgrims finally disappear, the sounds of approaching huntsmen are heard. It is the Landgrave (ruler) of Thuringia with his minstrel knights.

The Landgrave and the knights Walther and Biterolf do not at first recognize Tannhäuser; then another knight, Wolfram, realizes who the stranger is. Wolfram, Walther and Biterolf in turn welcome him. Reinmar and Schreiber join in the greeting, which the Landgrave takes up: they all beg him to return to their company, but Tannhäuser feels that he cannot go back to the past after his transgressions. Only when Wolfram mentions the Landgrave's niece Elisabeth, and tells Tannhäuser that she loves him (a self-sacrificing disclosure, for Wolfram loves her himself), does he agree to return. They all sing joyfully at the prospect of reunion.

ACT II: Elisabeth, alone in the Minstrels' Hall, sings happily of Tannhäuser's return: 'Dich, teure Halle' ('To you, O hall of song') – Elisabeth's Greeting. Tannhäuser, led in by Wolfram, throws himself at her feet; she is confused. When she asks about his long absence, he answers vaguely: then the two sing a long love duet, while Wolfram, in the background, comments briefly on the hopelessness of his own passion for Elisabeth.

Tannhäuser and Wolfram go and the Landgrave enters, greeting his niece. Flourishes of trumpets announce the arrival of the guests for a contest of the minstrel knights. As the nobles and their ladies enter, to the strains of a choral march – 'Freudig begrüssen wir' ('Joyfully we greet') – they are greeted by the Landgrave and Elisabeth: then they raise their voices in praise of song and in praise of the Landgrave. Next the minstrels enter. The Landgrave rises and addresses them, telling them that Love is to be the theme of the song-contest about to take place.

The nobles seat themselves while pages collect slips of paper bearing the minstrels' names, one of which Elisabeth draws from a cup. The first contestant, the pages announce, is Wolfram. He duly rises and, with harp accompaniment, sings a simple, restrained song about the purity of love, hinting at Elisabeth as the source of his inspiration. The assembled company express their approbation. Tannhäuser comments briefly on the more passionate nature of love; then the second contestant, Walther, sings like Wolfram of love's purity.

Now Tannhäuser rises impatiently and startles his audience by singing of the sensual delights of love and its fulfilment. Angrily, Biterolf challenges him to fight, to the approval of the nobles and the other minstrels, who are only more angered by Tannhäuser's answer. The Landgrave and Wolfram restore peace, but no sooner has Wolfram finished than Tannhäuser, carried away, sings his song of impassioned praise to Venus (which was heard in Act I).

All now are scandalized: the ladies rush out in alarm and the minstrels and nobles close on Tannhäuser with their swords drawn, calling curses upon him. But Elisabeth stands in front of Tannhäuser to protect him, and passionately pleads with them to spare him and grant him an opportunity of salvation. In a long ensemble, the outraged company agree to spare him in view of Elisabeth's intercession, though they still consider him accursed, while she continues pleading and Tannhäuser prays to God for forgiveness.

The Landgrave steps forward and pronounces his verdict. Tannhäuser's only prospect of salvation lies in his joining a second party of pilgrims, on the point of departure for Rome, and seeking absolution from the Pope. All echo his words, threatening Tannhäuser with death if he does not go. The chanting of the pilgrims is heard in the distance, and with a cry of 'Nach Rom!' ('To Rome') Tannhäuser rushes off to join them.

ACT III: Elisabeth is seen kneeling before a shrine in the valley by the Wartburg, praying for the absent Tannhäuser's redemption and return. Wolfram watches her, reflecting on her love. The song of the pilgrims, returning at last, is heard. Elisabeth and Wolfram, watching as the pilgrims pass by, see that Tannhäuser is not among them.

Elisabeth kneels again in prayer: 'Allmächt'ge Jungfrau' ('All powerful Virgin'). When she finishes, she moves off, declining Wolfram's offer to accompany her. As night falls, he sings to the accompaniment of his harp, comparing Elisabeth with the bright evening star: 'O du mein holder Abendstern' ('Oh thou, my fair star of eve').

As he finishes, a weary, ragged pilgrim enters. It is Tannhäuser: he is seeking the path to Venusberg. At first he mistrusts Wolfram, whom he takes as his enemy, but Wolfram's kindness moves him. He tells Wolfram of the ordeals he subjected himself to on his pilgrimage, and how he approached the Pope, who had forgiven thousands that day. He was met with a stern refusal: it was as impossible that he should be absolved as that the Pope's barren staff should flower. So now, he explains, he is turning to Venus once more.

As he calls on Venus, visions of her appear and her voice is heard. Wolfram tries to hold Tannhäuser back as she calls to him: as he struggles, Wolfram mentions Elisabeth's name. Tannhäuser, rapt, repeats it – and at this moment voices are heard: Elisabeth has died and her funeral cortege is approaching, attended by the Landgrave, nobles and minstrels. The pagan visions disappear as Venus calls 'Mir verloren' ('Lost to me!'). Wolfram, telling Tannhäuser that he is absolved as a result of Elisabeth's intercession, signs them to halt and guides Tannhäuser to her bier; he falls beside it and dies. As the new day breaks, the second group of pilgrims arrives, exalted by the news they bear: the Pope's staff has miraculously burst into flower. Tannhäuser is indeed saved. All raise their voices in praise of God.

* * *

Wagner 'tells the story' of the opera in advance in the overture, which is built from motives of the opera – but the 'story-telling' is more obvious in the earlier (Dresden, not Paris) version when the Pilgrims' Chorus, which opened the overture softly, returns to close it loudly: Christianity has triumphed.

Tannhäuser, as a minstrel, apostrophizes Venus in Act I to the accompaniment of his harp and with words beginning (literally) 'Thanks be to thy grace!' (ex. 1). This is the air which in English is often called 'O gracious fair', and which recurs – to Tannhäuser's disgrace – in the contest in Act II. Venus herself is musically

Ex. 1

characterized by all the allurements of the Venusberg music as well
as by her own sensuous appeal to Tannhäuser (note its free, 'airy'
declamation of the words 'Beloved, come!' with no insistent beat
below: ex. 2).

Ex. 2

Elisabeth is characterized with equal clarity. Her great moment of
self-revelation (Elisabeth's Greeting to the hall of song in Act II) has
such distinctive phrases as this, as she speaks of the pride in her
bosom in recalling Tannhäuser's former triumphs (ex. 3).

Ex. 3

The climax of Tannhäuser's part comes in what is often called (in
clumsy, mock-German English) the Rome Narration – that is, his
account in Act III of his pilgrimage to Rome and his bitter dis-
appointment. As an orchestral counterpoint to Tannhäuser's words
about the day breaking in Rome to the sound of bells, we hear a
theme which has already been stated in the prelude to the act,

anticipating the narration (ex. 4). The theme signifies Christian salvation, and Wagner carries it over into *Lohengrin* and *Parsifal* where it is usually called the Grail Motive – on which see page 286.

Ex. 4

Thirty-seven distinct motives have been identified and labelled (according to the emotions or situations they represent) in *Tann-häuser*. Wagner had already advanced considerably towards the total penetration of the drama by recurring motives which is found in his later works.

LOHENGRIN
Libretto by the composer

First performed: Weimar, 1850
Three Acts

Cast in order of singing:

A HERALD	bass
KING HENRY I OF GERMANY	bass
FRIEDRICH VON TELRAMUND, A NOBLE OF BRABANT	bass
ELSA, DAUGHTER OF THE LATE DUKE OF BRABANT	soprano
LOHENGRIN, KNIGHT OF THE GRAIL	tenor
ORTRUD, A SORCERESS, WIFE OF TELRAMUND	mezzo-soprano
FOUR NOBLES	two tenors, two basses
FOUR PAGES	two sopranos, two altos

[The role of Gottfried, Elsa's brother, is silent.]

Chorus of Saxon and Brabantian nobles and retainers,
ladies, pages, etc.
*The scene is laid in Antwerp in the first half of
the tenth century*

The romantic, picturesque and dramatic appeal of medieval Christianity furnished Wagner, after *Tannhäuser*, with *Lohengrin*. The opera's famous Bridal Chorus is the one piece of Wagner known to those who do not know Wagner. The first conductor of the opera was Liszt who, as conductor at the court of Weimar (central Germany), was a keen champion of the most vital new music of his day. For the production of *Lohengrin* at his theatre, he spared no expense and sent out to buy a bass clarinet – a recently invented instrument which Wagner's score calls for.

According to medieval legend, the Holy Grail is 'the platter used by our Saviour at the Last Supper, in which Joseph of Arimathea received the Saviour's blood at the cross . . . Sometimes, the Grail or Sangreal has been erroneously supposed to be the cup or chalice used at the Last Supper' (*Oxford English Dictionary*). Wagner appears to have held this 'erroneous' view. The legendary Knights of the Holy Grail had the Grail in their possession.

With this legendary element Wagner links the historical German king, Henry I ('the Fowler'; ?876–936), who made war on the Hungarians and who, in the opera, is supposed to be visiting Antwerp to raise an army to fight the Hungarian invader. It was only in the twelfth century that Brabant became a Duchy, carrying with it the marquisate of Antwerp; Wagner mistakenly (or deliberately?) antedates the dukedom.

* * *

ACT I: By the banks of the Scheldt, near Antwerp, a herald calls the people of Brabant to arms. They respond gladly. King Henry explains that before going to war in defence of his kingdom against the Hungarian barbarians, he wishes to resolve the disunion evident in Brabant itself. He calls on Telramund, who is present with his wife Ortrud, to give an account of the dispute.

Telramund tells the king that he was left in charge of the late duke's children when the duke died. One day the son, Gottfried, disappeared when alone with his sister, Elsa; Telramund now accuses Elsa of having killed her brother so as to have the dukedom for herself. Consequently he resigned his previous claim to her hand, marrying Ortrud instead, through whose noble descent he now claims to be ruler of Brabant. The assembled nobles and the king are horrified by his accusation. The king sends for Elsa, determined to find out the truth and pass judgement.

Elsa comes. She can give no clear answer to the king's questions, but she relates a dream, to everyone's mystification, in which a knight in shining armour appeared as her champion: 'Oft in trüben Tagen' ('Once in dreary days'). Telramund presses his case further, and the king and Brabantines are inclined to believe him. The king rules that the matter shall be decided by combat between Telramund and any man who will act as Elsa's champion.

At the king's command the herald, with a flourish of trumpets, calls upon such a man to step forth. Twice the proclamation is read out, but no one comes. Then, as Elsa and the attendant ladies kneel in prayer, the crowd is astonished to see a swan ('Ein Schwann!') appear on the river, drawing a boat in which there is a knight in silver armour. All greet him (except Telramund and Ortrud): he bids farewell to the swan and steps on to the shore. He asks Elsa if he may act as her champion, but imposes the condition that she must never ask him his name or his origin. With absolute trust, she agrees and they pledge mutual love.

Lohengrin (for it is he) steps forward and challenges Telramund, whose friends advise him to withdraw. The herald announces the combat and all call on God to see that justice prevails. The two men fight: Lohengrin defeats Telramund but spares his life. All applaud his success and Elsa expresses her joy; the only dissident voices are those of Ortrud and Telramund.

ACT II: On the cathedral steps at night, Telramund and Ortrud are musing on their defeat. Sounds of revelry are heard from the palace. Telramund blames his disgrace on the evil machinations of his wife, who is a sorceress. She tells him that the power of the victorious knight can be overcome only if Elsa can be induced to ask about his name and origins, or if he should be wounded. They determine to seek vengeance.

Elsa appears on the balcony of the Kemenate (the women's dwelling), singing of her happiness. Ortrud sends Telramund away and calls to Elsa, bemoaning her own fate – but while Elsa is on her way down (and thus out of earshot), Ortrud exults in the prospect of revenge. Elsa enters and tells Ortrud she forgives her and promises to try to restore her and Telramund to favour; in their duet, Ortrud cunningly sows in Elsa's mind the seeds of doubt about her champion.

They go off and Telramund enters, concealing himself when, as dawn breaks, trumpeters sound the reveille and a summons to the people. The nobles and retainers arrive. A herald announces that Telramund is banished and that the mysterious knight (Lohengrin) shall marry Elsa, become Guardian of Brabant and lead the Brabantians in war. The royal decrees are acclaimed. Four disaffected nobles, Telramund's friends, are displeased at the prospect of following Lohengrin, and Telramund, defying the decree, reveals himself to them. They conceal him.

Four pages announce the arrival of Elsa and a train of ladies. As she is about to enter the cathedral Ortrud intervenes, saying angrily that Elsa occupies her (Ortrud's) rightful place. She taunts Elsa for not knowing her lover's name. Elsa, astonished, replies that she has entire trust in him, but Ortrud continues to assert that he is a traitor. Lohengrin arrives with the king and comforts Elsa, but now Telramund boldly presents himself. At first all refuse to listen, but Telramund demands of Lohengrin that he disclose his identity, for otherwise he may be suspected of having his origins in evil magic.

Lohengrin contemptuously refuses to answer. Only Elsa can compel him to speak, he says – and he sees that she is deeply troubled. In an ensemble, Ortrud and Telramund rejoice in her doubts, Elsa expresses her wish to know Lohengrin's secret, he prays to heaven to shield her and the king and people reaffirm their confidence. Telramund speaks for a moment to Elsa against Lohengrin, but Lohengrin draws her away and all enter the cathedral.

ACT III: The scene shows the bridal chamber. To the strains of the wedding march, Elsa is led in by the ladies and Lohengrin by the king and nobles, and the couple are soon left alone together. They sing tenderly of their love: but when Lohengrin calls Elsa by her name she is sad at not being able to answer with his, and asks if she may know it. He begs her not to ask, but she presses him more and more impetuously – saying she foresees the day when the swan will come again and Lohengrin will leave her.

At the climax of her demand, the door is flung open and Telramund enters with his four friends. With a single blow, Lohengrin kills him, and the four nobles kneel before Lohengrin. He tells Elsa that their happiness is over, and summons ladies to lead her into the king's presence, where he will disclose his identity to all.

The scene changes to the banks of the Scheldt, where the king and nobles assemble. It is early morning and they are preparing to march off to war. The four nobles enter bearing Telramund's body, followed by Elsa, in mournful mood, and a train of ladies. Finally Lohengrin enters. He tells the king, to everyone's consternation, that he cannot lead the campaign, and that Elsa has broken the vow she made and has demanded to know his name and origins.

He now discloses his secret: he is a knight of the Holy Grail, by name Lohengrin, son of Parsifal; and now that his secret is known his power has departed and he must return. He reproaches Elsa, who is crushed by the realization of what she had brought upon them. In despair, she begs him not to leave her, and the king and people add their voices to her plea. But Lohengrin cannot stay. He predicts a glorious victory for the German armies: then the swan appears, drawing an empty boat. He greets it: 'Mein lieber Schwann' ('My dear swan'); then he embraces Elsa in a final farewell, handing her sword, horn and ring to give to her brother Gottfried if he should return.

Suddenly Ortrud steps forward in apparent triumph. She tells Elsa that she had transformed Gottfried into a swan, the swan who now serves Lohengrin; if Lohengrin had been able to stay he would have been able to restore him to human form, but now the opportunity is gone. Lohengrin sinks to his knees in prayer. In response, a white dove appears over his boat, the swan sinks and re-emerges as Gottfried, to Ortrud's rage. The Brabantians bow before Gottfried, who will now rule them. The dove draws the boat away, Lohengrin in it. As Elsa sees him go she falls lifeless into her brother's arms.

*   *   *

Lohengrin is an opera of patriotism and spectacle (the two often go together in the theatre). Wagner asks for twelve trumpets on the stage in the opening and final scenes, as well as those in the orchestra, and in the final scene the noblemen are also supposed to arrive on horseback. Musically, however, it is distinguished not by 'big' effects but for its evocation of intimate, lyrical feeling. The overture opens with a suggestion of high, ethereal mystery (the 'divine' mission of Lohengrin: ex. 1) – and towards the end of the overture a theme (ex. 2) rings out from trumpets and trombones to signify the triumph not of Lohengrin's earthly love, but of that divine mission, the mission of the knights of the Holy Grail to which Lohengrin belongs. The kinship of this to themes used in *Tannhäuser* (ex. 4) and *Parsifal* (ex. 1) will be noted.

Ex. 1

Ex. 2

When in the first scene Elsa tells of her dream of a knight coming to her rescue it is the 'ethereal' theme which is given to the orchestra, and Lohengrin on his arrival sings his thanks to his swan to a phrase which evokes this theme. Naturally, the return of the swan in the final act brings a return of the same music.

When Lohengrin first approaches Elsa and declares his love for her he adds a warning not to ask his name (ex. 3); this is usually called the 'Motive of Warning' (or we might retitle it 'Ban on Inquiry' – Wagner's actual musical motives are more precise than any names for them can be). It recurs prominently – with that bass clarinet which Liszt's orchestra had to buy! – when Ortrud tempts Elsa to put the forbidden question to Lohengrin.

Ex. 3

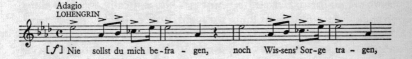

TRISTAN UND ISOLDE
Libretto by the composer

First performed: Munich, 1865
Three Acts

Cast in order of singing:

A SAILOR	*tenor*
ISOLDE, AN IRISH PRINCESS	*soprano*
BRANGÄNE, HER ATTENDANT	*soprano*
KURWENAL, TRISTAN'S SQUIRE	*baritone*
TRISTAN, A CORNISH KNIGHT, NEPHEW OF KING MARKE	*tenor*
MELOT, A COURTIER	*tenor*
KING MARKE OF CORNWALL	*bass*
A SHEPHERD	*tenor*
A STEERSMAN	*baritone*

Chorus of sailors, knights, attendants, etc.
The scene is laid on a ship near Cornwall,
in Cornwall and in Brittany, in legendary times

This is a long opera about love and about almost nothing else: sexual passion is expressed with the full force of Wagner's newly enlarged musical language and the full splendour of his newly enlarged orchestra.

Tristan und Isolde is, moreover, the first of Wagner's new-style operas (he preferred the word 'music-dramas') in which a symphonic texture, an interplay of leading-motives and a use of 'endless melody' (Wagner's term) replace the old operatic style, and in which there are no formal ensemble numbers. Dramatically, Wagner clung to the domain of legend, but characteristically altered the old story. In the original, Tristan and Isolde's love is purely the result of sorcery – that is, of the magic potion. In Wagner, their mutual love is present from the beginning, and the potion only 'fixes' it and makes it dominant.

★   ★   ★

ACT I: A young sailor is heard singing on board the ship on which Isolde, with her attendant Brangäne, is being carried from Ireland, laterly conquered, to be the bride of the ageing King Marke of

Cornwall. His voice arouses Isolde, who in conversation with Brangäne vents her angry grief at her fate. When Isolde asks for air ('Luft!'), Brangäne draws aside the curtains, and a further part of the ship is seen: Tristan, the king's nephew (who had been charged to bring Isolde back), and his squire Kurwenal are there with the sailors.

The voice of the young sailor is again heard. Isolde gazes contemptuously at Tristan; then she orders Brangäne to summon him. Kurwenal warns Tristan of Brangäne's approach. Tristan is unwilling to go to Isolde and Kurwenal, rather insolently, makes his excuses – that Tristan owes no allegiance to an Irishwoman. Tristan is embarrassed, especially when Kurwenal sings loudly (echoed by the crew) as Brangäne goes.

Isolde, alone with Brangäne, is enraged by Tristan's refusal to come. She tells Brangäne how Tristan, wounded in a fight in which he had killed her betrothed, came to her, under the false name of Tantris, and how she overcame her desire for revenge and nursed him back to strength. And now she, Ireland's princess, has to submit to the indignity of being conveyed by the man whose life she saved to be the bride of his elderly monarch. She curses him angrily.

Brangäne tries to comfort her by pointing out that Tristan is bringing her to be a queen. She does not perceive the true cause for Isolde's grief and humiliation – her love for Tristan: when Isolde mentions love, Brangäne thinks she refers to her future husband, and says that the magic potions of Isolde's mother can be used to keep his love alive and strong. Thoughts of such potions lead Isolde to the idea of poisoning herself and Tristan.

Shouts are heard from the sailors: the ship is nearing land. Kurwenal comes to call the women, but Isolde tells him that she will not consent to be led ashore by Tristan unless he first comes to seek her forgiveness. When Kurwenal goes Isolde tells Brangäne to prepare poisoned drinks for herself and Tristan. Brangäne, horrified, protests vehemently. Kurwenal announces Tristan and retires. Isolde reminds Tristan of the past and how she saved his life when he had killed her betrothed. He offers her his sword so that she can take revenge, but instead she suggests that they drink to the end of their strife. She signs to Brangäne to prepare the draught. In the distance, the sailors' voices are heard.

Isolde hands him the drink, still taunting him bitterly. As he takes it he realizes she means to poison them both, and he – in love with her as he is, but having hitherto concealed a love which he knows cannot be fulfilled – drinks willingly. But Brangäne has substituted a love-potion for the poison. They are both instantly overwhelmed by their longing and fall into each other's arms. As the sailors greet King Marke, Brangäne realizes the consequences of what she had done. Tristan and Isolde sing passionately, unaware of what is happening. Brangäne calls to them as the ship reaches land, to shouts from the crew, and Kurwenal tells Tristan that Marke is coming to greet his bride. Brangäne confesses to Isolde that she gave them a love-potion. As the ship berths and people clamber on board, Isolde faints on Tristan's breast.

ACT II: From a garden outside King Marke's castle, overlooked by Isolde's room, sounds of a hunt are heard. It is night, and Isolde, with Brangäne, impatiently awaits Tristan. As the sound of horns fades, Isolde prepares to give Tristan the signal. But Brangäne suspects treachery from a courtier, Melot (who organized the hunting party), and begs her not to be reckless. Isolde sends Brangäne to where she can keep watch, while she signals to Tristan by extinguishing the torch burning on the castle wall.

Tristan arrives. In their prolonged duet, they explore their love; they denounce the day (which keeps them apart) and welcome the night. Passionate strains lead to the quieter ecstasy of 'O sink hiernieder, Nacht der Liebe' ('O sink upon us, night of love'). As they embrace, the voice of the watchful Brangäne is heard for a moment in warning. Later, as night is succeeded by day, Brangäne warns them again.

Suddenly Kurwenal enters, calling to Tristan to save himself. At the same time the courtiers, led by Melot and King Marke, arrive, and Brangäne comes from her watching-place. The lovers are discovered. Melot asks Marke if he now thinks his warnings justified. Marke, in a long soliloquy, shows his bitter grief at the faithlessness of his long-trusted friend and nephew.

Tristan asks Isolde if she would follow him to the gloomy land to which he must go. She says that she would. In fury, Melot draws his sword to challenge Tristan; Tristan charges him with duplicity and is about to fight, but then lowers his guard, allowing Melot to wound him. He sinks into Kurwenal's arms and Isolde flings herself on to his breast.

ACT III: Tristan, gravely wounded, has withdrawn to his father's castle in Brittany. A shepherd plays a melancholy strain on his pipe and inquires from the faithful Kurwenal about the health of Tristan, who is sleeping on a couch which has been placed under a lime tree.

Tristan stirs and, bewildered, asks Kurwenal where he is: he can remember little except of Isolde, for whom he expresses his great longing. To his delight, Kurwenal promises to have Isolde brought to him.

Tristan expresses his warmth of feeling towards Kurwenal, and excitedly contemplates Isolde's coming. But – as the shepherd's pipe is heard, still on its former strain – no ship is within sight, and he lapses into melancholy. He goes over the past, then becomes agitated again as he remembers the love-potion. Eventually he falls back, unconscious, but soon revives, still thinking of Isolde's coming and growing agitated once more.

At long last the shepherd's pipe gives out a livelier melody and Kurwenal tells Tristan that it is indeed Isolde's ship. With mounting excitement Tristan, with Kurwenal, watches the ship approach. He sends Kurwenal to being Isolde. As he waits, Tristan, almost frenzied, tears the bandage from his wound. Isolde enters and he falls into her arms; in a few moments he is dead. After trying to revive him she falls upon his body.

The shepherd comes to tell Kurwenal that a second ship has arrived. Kurwenal, seeing King Marke and Melot, orders his men to prepare to defend the castle, despite the entry of the steersman saying that defence is useless. Brangäne's voice is heard from below, asking for admittance, then Melot's. Kurwenal attacks Melot and kills him, shouts defiance to Marke and fights with Marke's men; he is wounded and dies, falling at Tristan's feet. Meanwhile Brangäne has entered, climbing over a wall, and is relieved to find Isolde still living. Marke had come with only peaceful intentions (Brangäne had told him about the potions), and is sad and dismayed to find Tristan dead. Isolde, hardly aware of what is happening, raptly sings her lament over Tristan's body: 'Mild und leise' ('Mild and gently'). At the end she sinks lifeless into Brangäne's arms, over Tristan's body, and Marke silently invokes a benediction over the dead lovers.

*　　*　　*

There are no more famous bars in the history of music than those (ex. 1) which open the prelude of *Tristan und Işolde*: while the historic novelty of the harmony, and the novelty of beginning an opera in this way, may not now concern us, the theme is still arresting in itself and for what Wagner does with it. This is the chief love-motive of the opera and can be melodically separated into two phrases, as quoted in ex. 1, which have been respectively called 'Avowal' and

Ex. 1

'Desire' (this at any rate seems more plausible than an alternative allocation of the first to Tristan and the second to Isolde). Very shortly follows a motive related to this (ex. 2) usually called the 'motive of the Love Glance'.

Ex. 2

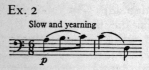

The love–duet in Act II prominently quotes and 'develops' the first of these. Then, at the height of ecstasy, Tristan suggests that this is how they should die, never parting, and his melody (ex. 3) announces a new theme, that of Love-as-Death (Liebestod). In the last act when Tristan is dead and Isolde, over his body, is herself looking forward to death, it is this that she sings to the words beginning 'Mild und leise'. Hence the word 'Liebestod' has been applied – by Liszt first of all, not by Wagner – to the final pages of the work, accompanying Isolde's death. (It is frequently joined to the end of the prelude in concert preformances, often with the voice-part taken over by the orchestra.)

Ex. 3

Tristan and Isolde's love-music is by intention concretely erotic: its chromatic sensuousness is tellingly contrasted with the diatonic 'upright', extraverted music of Kurwenal and the sailors in Act I.

The music which the shepherd in Act III plays on his pipe is of a kind never heard before, with its strange intervals and repetitions (ex. 4). The pipe is simulated in the orchestra by an English horn when a quicker tune is reached (Isolde's ship is sighted at last!);

certain performances have substituted a powerful Hungarian single-reed instrument, the tárogató.

Ex. 4

DIE MEISTERSINGER
VON NÜRNBERG
(The Mastersingers of Nuremberg)
Libretto by the composer

First performed: Munich, 1868
Three Acts

Cast in order of singing:

WALTHER VON STOLZING, A YOUNG FRANCONIAN KNIGHT		tenor
EVA, DAUGHTER TO POGNER		soprano
MAGDALENE, EVA'S MAID		mezzo-soprano
DAVID, APPRENTICE TO HANS SACHS		tenor
VEIT POGNER, A GOLDSMITH		bass
SIXTUS BECKMESSER, TOWN CLERK		bass
HANS SACHS, A COBBLER		bass
KUNZ VOGELGESANG, A FURRIER		tenor
KONRAD NACHTIGALL, A TINSMITH		bass
FRITZ KOTHNER, A BAKER	MASTERSINGERS	bass
HERMANN ORTEL, A SOAP–BOILER		bass
BALTHASAR ZORN, A PEWTERER		tenor
AUGUSTIN MOSER, A TAILOR		tenor
ULRICH EISSLINGER, A GROCER		tenor
HANS FOLTZ, A COPPERSMITH		bass
HANS SCHWARZ, A STOCKING–WEAVER		bass
A NIGHTWATCHMAN		bass

Chorus of apprentices, burghers, girls, etc.
The scene is laid in Nuremberg in the mid-sixteenth century

Die Meistersinger (or 'The Mastersingers', as the title is usually abbreviated) is Wagner's only comic opera – and a most successful one, with real comedy backed by the lyric inspiration of the Prize Song and the springing vigour of the various choruses. It is an opera about the triumph of real, living art over false academic art, and Wagner saw the victory of the young knight Walther as representing his own victory over crabbed criticism. Such criticism is represented in the opera by the character of Beckmesser whom, in the original form of the libretto, Wagner named Hans Lick. No wonder that Eduard Hanslick, the bitterly anti-Wagnerian Viennese music critic, walked out of a private reading of the libretto!

Hans Sachs, the central character among the Mastersingers, was a historical personage (1494–1576), a shoemaker and poet. The chorus of acclamation to Sachs in Act III of the opera ('Wach' auf') is in fact a setting of words by the real Sachs. The Mastersingers were, historically, a middle-class type of minstrel as distinct from the aristocratic minstrels (Minnesingers) whom Wagner had already celebrated in *Tannhäuser*. The opera is not without its patriotic appeal: at the end, the triumphant Walther is ready to turn his back on the Mastersingers who originally spurned him, but is persuaded to join them when Sachs puts forward the claim of 'holy German art'.

* * *

ACT I: At a service in the church of St Catherine, at Nuremberg, the final hymn is being sung. The young knight Walther von Stolzing, a visitor to the town, is watching Eva, the daughter of Pogner the goldsmith. As the service ends he approaches her; she contrives to send her maid, Magdalene, away momentarily and he asks if she is betrothed. Magdalene, overhearing as she returns, explains that Eva's hand is to be the prize in a song contest to be held by the Mastersingers the next day. Walther does not fully understand. But presently David (an apprentice, betrothed to Magdalene) comes, with other apprentices, to prepare the scene for a preliminary song trial; and, after Eva and Magdalene have gone, he explains to Walther some of the complexities of the rules of song.

The apprentices, their preparations complete, retire to the back as Pogner enters, with Beckmesser, who is not only town clerk but also himself an aspirant to Eva's hand. Walther greets Pogner, saying he wishes to become a Mastersinger; Pogner welcomes him and introduces him to the other Masters as they enter. Finally Sachs arrives and Kothner call the roll. When this is done Pogner addresses the Masters – 'Nun hört' ('Now hear!') – announcing that the victor in the next day's contest may claim the hand of Eva, as long as she is willing to accept him. The Masters and apprentices are excited by this and a discussion ensues, Beckmesser demanding strict adherence to the rules of song while Sachs would permit a freer style.

Pogner introduces Walther as a candidate for membership of the guild. In answer to their questions he says, in his song 'Am stillen Herd' ('By silent hearth'), that his teacher was Walther von der Vogelweide, an ancient Minnesinger, and that he studied 'in nature'. The Masters are unimpressed, but he is allowed to proceed with a song. Beckmesser is appointed Marker (to count the faults in his song) and retires into the Marker's box with a slate and chalk. Kothner tells Walther some of the rules and Beckmesser calls to him to begin. He sings a song of love: 'So rief der Lenz' ('So cried the spring'). As he sings, noisy scratchings are heard from the marker's box, and before he has finished Beckmesser emerges, his slate completely covered with chalk marks (he has realized that Walther is a rival for Eva's hand and is at pains to discredit him).

The other Masters agree that the song was not in accord with the rules and that Walther should be rejected, but Sachs speaks up for Walther, saying that although his song does not conform to the Masters' rules it is different in kind and demands new rules of its own. He also mentions that Beckmesser is not as disinterested as a marker must be. Beckmesser replies that the cobbler should stick to his last. Sachs tells Walther to continue singing. As he does so, Beckmesser angrily shows his catalogue of faults to the other Masters, who agree that Walther is not qualified to be a Mastersinger (and so cannot enter the contest). The apprentices and David join in the general hubbub. As he finishes, Walther proudly goes off and the meeting breaks up in disorder, Sachs remaining deep in thought as the others disperse.

ACT II: That evening, the apprentices sing of the morrow, St John's Day ('Johannistag'), as, in the street, they close their masters' shutters. Magdalene comes and learns from David that Walther has failed. The other apprentices are teasing David about Magdalene when Sachs arrives and takes him into the workshop. Pogner and Eva enter, and sit talking on a bench. Before Eva follows her father indoors she learns from Magdalene of Walther's failure.

Sachs emerges from his shop, sends David off and settles down to work out of doors under an elder tree, singing of its scent ('Was duftet doch der Flieder') – the 'Fliedermonolog'. Eva comes to seek his advice. Sachs, a widower, is deeply fond of her himself, though he realizes not only that he is far too old but also, by her reaction to his apparently slighting reference to Walther, that she really loves the young knight. As Sachs goes indoors, Eva joins Magdalene, who tells her that Beckmesser is coming to serenade her and who tries to lead her indoors. Eva asks Magdalene to take her place at the window, and as Walther arrives she goes to his side. He declares his love for her and tells her of his contempt for the Masters and their rules. They arrange to elope and she goes indoors.

The nightwatchman, sounding his horn, comes past. Sachs has overheard their plan to elope and considers it unwise, so he arranges his light to shine on the street so that they would be seen. Eva comes out in Magdalene's clothes and at that moment Beckmesser arrives, with his lute. Walther and Eva conceal themselves as he prepares to sing his serenade. But before Beckmesser begins Sachs starts a noisy cobbling song. Angrily Beckmesser tries to silence him, especially when he sees a woman (Magdalene, whom he takes for Eva) at the window. Sachs continues tormenting him and Beckmesser gets more and more irritated.

Eventually they agree that Sachs shall act as marker during Beckmesser's serenade, being allowed to sound one hammer-stroke on the shoes for each fault in the singing. Beckmesser's grotesque, misaccentuated serenade brings forth blow after blow from Sachs's hammer, to Beckmesser's fury. He sings louder and louder, bringing all the neighbours to their windows. David sees him serenading Magdalene, whom he recognizes, and comes down with a cudgel and gives him a good beating. Neighbours and others are aroused and a general brawl breaks out. In the confusion Walther and Eva try to escape, but Sachs seizes Walther and hands the false Magdalene (really Eva) over to Pogner, who is standing anxiously in his doorway, and pulls Walther into his shop. The nightwatchman's horn is heard and the crowd quickly disperses. When the nightwatchman appears all is peaceful again.

ACT III: Sachs is in his workshop, reading. David enters, in some trepidation after the previous night's doings, but finds his master in benevolent mood. It is St John's Day (Midsummer Day) which, David realizes with a start, must be his master's name-day [Hans=Johannes=John]. When he goes, Sachs ruminates on human folly: 'Wahn! Wahn!' ('Mad! Mad!') – the 'Wahnmonolog'. Walther, who has been staying overnight at Sachs's house, comes in. He tells Sachs of a song revealed to him in a dream and eventually sings it to him: 'Morgenlich leuchtend' ('Shining in morning light'). Sachs, impressed, writes down the words of the two stanzas Walther sings. They go off to prepare themselves for the contest of song.

A moment later Beckmesser enters the shop, looking somewhat the worse for his drubbing the previous night. He notices the manuscript in Sachs's handwriting on the table and, seeing Sachs coming, quickly pockets it. In their ensuing conversation Beckmesser accuses Sachs of trying to discredit him because he is intending to compete himself, producing the song as evidence. Sachs assures him that he is not, saying that he may keep the song and sing it if he wishes to, promising, in answer to Beckmesser's request, that he will not claim its authorship for himself.

Beckmesser departs and Eva enters, on the pretext of an uncomfortable shoe. Walther comes in and the lovers stare raptly at one another. While Sachs repairs Eva's shoe, Walther bursts into song (producing spontaneously the third, final verse required to give his song complete musical form). In profound gratitude and emotion, Eva falls weeping on Sachs's breast. He passes her to Walther and talks of the sad life of a cobbler. Eva says that she would happily have chosen Sachs as her husband if she were not so much in love with Walther. Magdalene and David come in and Sachs promotes David (with the customary box on the ear) from apprentice to journeyman ('Geselle'). Then all, led by Eva, join in a quintet of happiness: 'Selig, wie die Sonne' ('Blessed as the sun').

As horns and trumpets ring out festively, the scene changes to a meadow outside Nuremberg. Large crowds are gathering, the various guilds of the city marching ceremoniously in with banners flying. The apprentices, festively attired, guide people to their places. The tailors sing a story of Nuremberg which involves comic choral imitation of a goat. There is lively dancing from the journeymen, the apprentices (with them David) and girls. The gathering is completed by the majestic entry of the Mastersingers themselves, heralded by trumpets. Pogner leads in Eva, who is attended by Magdalene and other maidens.

The apprentices call for silence and Sachs step forward, to be acclaimed by the people to a traditional salutation ('Wach' auf!'). With some emotion, he announces the terms of the contest. Pogner thanks him. Meanwhile Beckmesser has vainly been trying to memorize the words of the pirated song. (The music was not written down; he must compose his own.) He is the first contestant and Kothner calls on him to sing. He clambers up on to the rostrum, almost falling as he does so, and looking so ludicrous that the crowd begins to titter. Rather uneasily, he plays some chords on his lute and starts. His melody is ridiculously ugly and he confuses Walther's words so hopelessly that they emerge as completely absurd. The Masters and people are astonished. Eventually Beckmesser, having provoked everyone's ridicule, rounds on Sachs, saying that he was the writer of the song. The Masters and people are shocked and demand an explanation. Sachs say that he could not write so fine a song himself and he calls on its true composer.

Walther bows to the Masters and steps forward. As he sings his song – the Prize Song – all are struck with its beauty. Though Walther was debarred from the Mastersingers' guild, he is plainly the victor. When he finishes, Eva crowns him with the victor's wreath and they kneel before Pogner, who blesses them. He is about to invest Walther as a Master, but Walther proudly declines. Sachs, however, in an address on the glory of German art, persuades him to accept. Walther accepts the honour from Sachs himself, while Eva takes the wreath from Walther's brow and places it on Sachs's. The people echo Sachs's words and pay him homage.

★   ★   ★

The recurring musical motives in *Die Meistersinger* are used with great subtlety – great dramatic subtlety, that is, apart from the musical skill with which so many are combined successively and contrapuntally in the overture.

Hardly has the curtain gone up when, after the first line of the congregational hymn, we hear ex. 1 in the orchestra: Walther is in church to snatch an opportunity of speaking to Eva, and this melody anticipates the Prize Song which Eva's beauty later inspires in Walther and which, in its turn, wins him Eva as his bride.

Ex. 1

There is even a reference by means of motive to Wagner's own *Tristan und Isolde* – in Act III (after Beckmesser has left Sachs's room). Sachs as a widower might well have been a suitor for Eva's hand; but he tells Eva that he well knows the story of Tristan and Isolde and does not wish to have the role of King Marke!

Beckmesser's role has rare comedy in music, especially in the scene of his serenade to the disguised Magdalene, whom he takes for Eva. In this serenade, with its absurdly 'decorative' lute accompaniment (sometimes played in the theatre on a harp with newspaper between the strings), each false accent committed by Beckmesser is marked by a blow of Sachs's hammer. For instance, the accent should fall on the first syllable of 'schönes' and 'Fräulein' but does not (ex. 2). We may wonder indeed how Beckmesser ever came to be made a Mastersinger in the first place!

Ex. 2

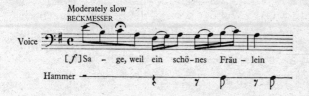

The lute serves also to emphasize the period atmosphere of the opera, as does the Nightwatchman's song and the hymn which opens the first act. In a further deliberate gesture, Wagner also founded two of his principal leading-motives on two old tunes reproduced in a seventeenth-century book. One of these old tunes (ex. 3) became the march of the Mastersingers (ex. 3b). We encounter this in full in the overture and again in the final scene – both times in C major, the key which significantly also begins and ends the opera. In this key too we encounter Walther's Prize Song, both when it is 'composed' (Act II) and when it is delivered (Act III); and nothing is more magical in it than the orchestral chord of C major which precedes it. The special lay-out and tone-colour of this chord gives it the distinctiveness of a leading-motive in itself.

Ex. 3

(a)   [17th Century]

(b)   [WAGNER: In march time]

DER RING DES NIBELUNGEN

The Nibelung's Ring

In 1848 Wagner completed a libretto for an opera to be called *The Death of Siegfried*. He later decided that three other operas should precede it in performance, dealing with earlier events in the same story. He completed and published the librettos of all four in 1853 and in the same year began working on the music. He finished the last opera in 1874, and the first performance of the complete cycle of four was given in 1876 in the opening season of the new Festival Theatre at Bayreuth (Bavaria) – a theatre built to Wagner's own specification. The first two operas of the cycle had already been given separately at Munich.

The cycle itself Wagner named *Der Ring des Nibelungen*, or *The Nibelung's Ring*. (Only *one* Nibelung in the title, be it noted: it is Alberich.) He described it as 'a theatre festival play for three days and a preliminary evening'. The individual operas are named *Das Rheingold* ('The Rhinegold'), *Die Walküre* ('The Valkyrie'), *Siegfried* and *Götterdämmerung** ('Twilight of the Gods'); the last of these corresponding to the original conception of *The Death of Siegfried*.

The basic material of the story was taken by Wagner from the old legend – which appears in German form as an epic poem, the Nibelunglied, and in Scandinavian form in prose, the Volsunga Saga (not identical with the other in detail). Apart from the now standardized English forms Valkyrie and Valhalla (both from the Scandinavian source) Wagner's own German forms of proper names are used, as is customary, in the following pages. The Nibelungs are a race of dwarfs; the story also deals with gods, men and giants.

Theatrically *The Ring* is opera's colossus. The sheer musical planning involved would compel admiration; but we must add to this an amazing psychological skill in the shaping of the actual themes. The use of myth, though far from new in opera, was

---

*Not '*Die* Götterdämmerung'.

intended to give a special and symbolic universality to the drama – a universality that was seized upon in the style of production associated with the Bayreuth Festival in the 1950s and 1960s. It is this universality that has led to commentators' numerous attempts to interpret *The Ring* in various ways: Jungians, for example, have seen it as a study of the human psyche, and several writers (notably Bernard Shaw) have seen it as a socialist, or specifically Marxist, view of society – a line that has been followed by several stage producers in the 1970s and 1980s. Any attempt to particularize the work, however, is liable to diminish it.

Wagner made opera not only bigger but more solemn. It was Bayreuth which established the modern convention that the auditorium is darkened during the performance and that late-comers to opera are prevented from taking their seats in mid-act. Opera as an after-dinner diversion is not consistent with a performance of *Das Rheingold*, in one unbroken act lasting more than two-and-a-half hours.

A continuous development of leading-motives goes right through all the four operas of *The Ring*. In the following pages, therefore, we first of all tell the story itself as it runs through all four, and then discuss some of the musical aspects of the complete work.

DAS RHEINGOLD
(The Rhinegold)
Part I of 'The Ring'
Libretto by the composer

First performed: Munich, 1869
One Act

Cast in order of singing:

WOGLINDE	RHINEMAIDENS	*soprano*
WELLGUNDE		*soprano*
FLOSSHILDE		*mezzo-soprano*
ALBERICH, A NIBELUNG		*bass-baritone*
FRICKA, WIFE OF WOTAN AND GODDESS OF		
MARRIAGE		*mezzo-soprano*
WOTAN, RULER OF THE GODS		*bass-baritone*

FREIA, SISTER OF FRICKA AND GODDESS OF LOVE
  AND SPRING   *soprano*
FASOLT ⎫   ⎧ *bass-baritone*
               GIANTS
FAFNER ⎭   ⎨   *bass*
FROH, GOD OF JOY AND YOUTH   *tenor*
DONNER, GOD OF THUNDER   *bass-baritone*
LOGE, GOD OF FIRE AND CUNNING   *tenor*
MIME, A NIBELUNG, ALBERICH'S BROTHER   *tenor*
ERDA, GODDESS OF EARTH AND WISDOM   *mezzo-soprano*

The scene is laid in the Rhine, on a mountain above
the Rhine and in the underground caverns of
Nibelheim, in legendary times

In the waters of the Rhine, the three Rhinemaidens, Woglinde,
Wellgunde and Flosshilde, are playing. Their task is to guard the
river's treasure, the Rhinegold. The grotesque dwarf Alberich
comes and watches; entranced by their beauty, he longs to possess
one of them. All three in turn tease him cruelly. As he angrily
pursues them, his eye is caught by the gleam of the Rhinegold as the
rays of the sun illumine it. They tell him of its magic – of how the
man who fashions a ring from it can, if he renounces love, become
supremely powerful and ruler of the world. As the maidens idly
play, Alberich, angry and frustrated, clambers up towards the gold
and tears it away from its rock, to the consternation of the
Rhinemaidens – uttering the required renunciation, 'So verfluch ich
die Liebe!' ('Thus I curse Love!).

The waves and rocks disappear into darkness: in their place there
appears a splendid castle on a mountain height, with the Rhine
visible far below. It is the newly built home of the gods. Outside it
Wotan, ruler of the gods, and his wife Fricka are sleeping. Fricka
awakens Wotan and he contemplates the great castle: 'Vollendet das
ewige Werk' ('The eternal work is finished'). She chides him for the
promise he made to its builders, the giants Fasolt and Fafner, to give
them her sister Freia as their reward. Freia herself enters, asking to be
protected from the giants. Wotan is relying on help from Loge, god
of fire and cunning, to extricate him from his promise.

The giants come and Fasolt demands their reward. Wotan tem-
porizes. In response to Freia's call for help, two more gods, Froh and
Donner, enter. Donner threatens the giants with his hammer while
Froh embraces Freia. Then Loge arrives. He admits, to Wotan's

anger, that he has found no alternative payment to suggest; but he goes on (deliberately tempting the giants) to tell of the theft by Alberich of the Rhinegold, mentioning that the Rhinemaidens have asked Wotan to help them recover it.

The giants, listening, begin to covet the gold as an alternative to Freia. But Wotan, wishing to have the gold himself, refuses. The giants seize Freia and bear her off as a pledge, giving Wotan until the evening to decide.

Loge watches them depart and turns back to the gods. He is surprised to see them looking aged and weary. Freia, goddess of youth, has left them. Aroused from his lethargy, Wotan decides to go to Nibelheim (the land of the Nibelungs) with Loge. The scene changes as they descend deep into the earth, and the clanging of anvils is heard as they reach Nibelheim.

In an underground cavern in Nibelheim Alberich, who now possesses a Ring formed from the gold, is berating his brother Mime. Mime has just forged from the gold a magic helmet, the Tarnhelm, which allows its wearer to take on any form or become invisible. Alberich puts it on, becomes invisible, beats his brother and goes off, revelling in his possession of the gold and its power. Wotan and Loge arrive and try unsuccessfully to console Mime. Alberich returns, driving before him more Nibelungs, carrying gold and silver trinkets which they pile up. He brutally sends them back to work, Mime among them.

To Wotan and Loge, Alberich boasts of his power and his cunning and talks of his intention to conquer the gods. Loge cleverly leads the dwarf on, and Wotan manages to overcome his anger as he sees Loge's plan working. In response to Loge's inquiry as to how he can protect himself, Alberich tells how he can transform himself, with the Tarnhelm, into different forms. Loge pretends to doubt him, so he changes first into a dragon, then into a toad – whereupon Wotan puts his foot on him. Loge seizes the Tarnhelm. As Alberich returns to human shape they bind him and take him off as their prisoner.

We are now transported back to the mountain heights where the gods' new castle stands, shrouded in mist. As ransom for Alberich's freedom, Wotan and Loge demand the Rhinegold. Angrily and grudgingly, he agrees. They untie him, as the Nibelungs bring the treasures and pile them up at his command. He asks to be released, but first Loge demands the Tarnhelm, then Wotan the Ring. Defiantly, Alberich refuses to part with the Ring and finally Wotan has to tear it from his finger. Contorted with rage, he curses the Ring and all who shall possess it ('Verflucht sei dieser Ring!') before he departs.

The mist clears as Donner, Froh and Fricka enter, and a few moments later Fasolt and Fafner bring in Freia. They refuse to hand her over until the ransom is paid, and Fasolt is so sorry to part with her that he insists that the amount of gold be sufficient to hide her. Wotan agrees, and Loge and Froh pile up the hoard. Fricka and Donner are much grieved at Freia's humiliation. To conceal her hair, visible at the top, the Tarnhelm is added, and, finally, when a crevice in the great pile discloses her eyes, the giants demand the Ring. When Wotan refuses, Fasolt angrily seizes Freia and makes as if to go. All press Wotan to give way. Then Erda, goddess of the earth, wisdom and destiny, appears, and solemnly warns him to part with the cursed Ring.

Wotan ponders deeply. Eventually he decides to give up the Ring, and summons Freia to him ('Zu mir, Freia!'); she is freed, and embraces the other gods joyfully. The giants start sharing out the gold. Fafner demands that he should have the larger share, as it was Fasolt who was particularly willing to resign all the gold for Freia. When it comes to the Ring itself, the two fight and Fasolt is killed. The curse laid on the Ring is already working.

Fafner goes off: Loge ironically congratulates Wotan on having parted with the Ring. As Wotan, deeply troubled, determines to consult Erda, Fricka bids him enter their castle with her. Swinging his hammer, Donner now calls forth a mighty thunderstorm ('Heda, hedo!'); then the clouds disperse, and Donner and Froh are seen at the foot of a dazzling, radiant rainbow bridge stretching across the valley to the castle. After being seized with a new, grand idea, Wotan greets the castle, names it Valhalla (Walhall) and leads Fricka across the rainbow bridge, followed by Froh, Freia and Donner, while Loge stands by and watches them with wry detachment. From below, the mournful singing of the robbed Rhinemaidens is heard, to Wotan's irritation: his triumph on entering Valhalla is marred by his realization of the wrong that he, as well as Alberich, has committed.

DIE WALKÜRE
(The Valkyrie)
Part II of 'The Ring'
Libretto by the composer

First performed: Munich, 1870
Three Acts

Cast in order of singing:

SIEGMUND }	THE WÄLSUNGS, TWIN BROTHER AND SISTER, CHILDREN OF WOTAN	{ tenor
SIEGLINDE }	BY A MORTAL WOMAN	{ soprano
HUNDING, HUSBAND OF SIEGLINDE		bass
WOTAN, RULER OF THE GODS		bass-baritone
BRÜNNHILDE, A VALKYRIE, DAUGHTER OF WOTAN AND THE GODDESS ERDA		soprano
FRICKA, WIFE OF WOTAN AND GODDESS OF MARRIAGE		mezzo-soprano

GERHILDE		
HELMWIGE		
WALTRAUTE		
SCHWERTLEITE	VALKYRIES, DAUGHTERS OF WOTAN AND ERDA, SISTERS OF BRÜNNHILDE	sopranos and mezzo-sopranos
ORTLINDE		
SIEGRUNE		
GRIMGERDE		
ROSSWEISSE		

The scene is laid in Hunding's hut, a rocky place, and at the summit of a mountain, in legendary times

Since the events of *Das Rheingold*, Wotan, in union with Erda, has fathered nine warrior-maidens, the Valkyries, whose task is to bring fallen heroes to Valhalla where they can form an army for the gods' defence. Wotan's favourite among these is Brünnhilde. Disguised as a mortal, 'Wälse', he has also fathered twin brother and sister, Siegmund and Sieglinde (known as the Wälsungs), on a mortal mother, in the hope that, as a hero and an independent agent, Siegmund may fulfil Wotan's will using means that the god himself cannot, and thus right the wrongs that have been done.

★   ★   ★

ACT I: The scene is a forest hut, enclosing the stem of a huge ash tree, belonging to Hunding and his wife Sieglinde. During a storm, Siegmund enters the hut, exhausted and in flight from his enemies, the Neidings. Finding it empty, he lies down to rest. Sieglinde enters. She sees the stranger and brings him water, pressing him to accept shelter until Hunding returns. The two are strongly drawn to one another.

Hunding enters. Suspicious at finding a stranger in his hut, and noting his resemblance to Sieglinde, he asks his name and story. Siegmund says his name is Wehwalt ('Woeful'), son of Wolfe: he tells his story – of the loss of his mother and twin sister, the pursuit of his father and himself by their enemies, and of his fight to save a woman from a marriage she abhorred, a fight in which he lost his weapons. Hunding realizes that this man is an enemy of his race. He tells Siegmund he may stay overnight but the next morning they must meet in combat. He sends Sieglinde off to the other room, but before she goes she looks meaningfully at a particular spot in the ash tree's trunk. Then Hunding follows her.

Alone in the subdued firelight, Siegmund muses on his position, defenceless in his enemy's home, and in love with his enemy's wife. He recalls his father's promise to provide a sword when he needs it. A shaft of light from the dying embers illuminates the point on the ash stem that Sieglinde had indicated.

As it becomes completely dark, Sieglinde, in night clothes, enters. She has drugged Hunding and comes to warn Siegmund to escape. She relates the story of her wedding-feast, where she sat in sadness as Hunding's kinsmen celebrated, and an old man clad in grey came in and plunged a sword deep into the ash tree; many strong men had tried, without success, to withdraw it. Both Siegmund and she realize that he is the man for whom it was intended. The two feel themselves irresistibly drawn together: they embrace passionately. The door flies open, disclosing the beauty of the night, and Siegmund sings of love and spring: 'Winterstürme wichen dem Wonnemond' ('Winter storms give way to May'); she responds passionately: 'Du bist der Lenz' ('You are the Spring'). He tells her that his father's name was really Wälse, and he is a Wälsung: they know now that they are brother and sister, and she gives him his true name, Siegmund ('Victory'). He pulls forth the sword, to Sieglinde's delight, calling it Nothung ('Needful'). With renewed ecstasy the lovers again embrace.

ACT II: Siegmund has taken Sieglinde away with him and Hunding is in pursuit. Wotan, wishing to protect Siegmund as his son (and as an instrument in his larger plan), has summoned Brünnhilde to the wild, rocky place where he stands. He tells her to support Siegmund against Hunding. She sounds her war-cry ('Ho-jo-to-ho!'), warns Wotan of Fricka's approach, and goes off.

Fricka arrives, in a chariot drawn by two rams. As goddess of marriage, she demands of Wotan that Siegmund be punished by being duly killed by Hunding; the gods must not lend their assent to adultery and incest. Painfully and reluctantly Wotan realizes that he must submit to Fricka's will, even though it means the sacrifice of his long-nurtured plan. He finally gives his oath that Siegmund will die: 'Nimm den Eid'.

Brünnhilde's war-cry as she returns has already been heard. Now, as Fricka leaves, she enters. She is distressed to see her father so unhappy. He tells her the story of Alberich and the Ring, of Erda's prediction of the gods' downfall and the gods' struggle to avert it – through the Valkyries (who will being an army of heroes to Valhalla) and through Wotan's own half-godly children. But now Siegmund has to die, to satisfy Fricka. In bitter despair, he realizes the inevitability of the gods' downfall. Brünnhilde, appalled, remonstrates with him and begs that Siegmund be allowed to win, as Wotan had at first ordered. Angrily, he insists that Brünnhilde ensure Hunding's victory.

Both go off. Shortly Siegmund and Sieglinde enter, in flight; Siegmund is trying to calm the agitated Sieglinde, now full of remorse. In her fevered imagination, she hears the distant sound of horns – she believes that Hunding and his kinsmen, with hounds, are in hot pursuit, and visualizes Siegmund's death at their hands. She faints, and Brünnhilde enters.

Brünnhilde now tells Siegmund what is ordained: he will die in his fight with Hunding, and she invites him to accompany her to Valhalla to take his place among the dead heroes. He questions her: can he bring Sieglinde with him? She says he cannot; and he accordingly tells her he will not go to Valhalla. She offers to protect Sieglinde and their unborn child after his death, but rather than leave her defenceless he will kill her. He draws his sword; Brünnhilde, much moved, stops him, saying that she will after all ensure his victory.

Brünnhilde departs. Siegmund bids farewell to the sleeping Sieglinde and goes off to meet Hunding in battle. As she stirs in her sleep, a thunderstorm breaks. In the lightning flashes, Hunding and Siegmund can be seen as they seek one another, shouting their defiance. Soon they meet and fight. Brünnhilde is seen protecting Siegmund with her shield. As Siegmund is about to strike Hunding down, Wotan himself appears, in a red glow: Siegmund's sword shatters on Wotan's spear, and Hunding kills his defenceless enemy. Brünnhilde lifts Sieglinde on to her horse and bears her off, gathering up the fragments of the sword. Wotan sadly contemplates Siegmund's body, and, at a wave of his hand, Hunding falls dead. Then, vowing to punish Brünnhilde's disobedience, Wotan disappears.

ACT III: The 'Ride of the Valkyries' is heard. The Valkyries have been carrying the bodies of heroes to Valhalla on their horses, and now they gradually assemble on a mountain peak. They comment that Brünnhilde is missing. Eventually she comes – supporting Sieglinde. They are horrified to learn of her defiance of Wotan's command and are unwilling to help her conceal Sieglinde from their father.

Sieglinde revives and tells them that she does not wish to live, but rallies when she is told that she is to bear Siegmund's child. Brünnhilde sends her eastward, to the forests – Wotan is unlikely to go there, since in that region are the Ring and the rest of the Rhine's treasure, protected by Fafner in his shape as a dragon. Before Sieglinde goes, Brünnhilde gives her the fragments of Siegmund's sword, telling her that her unborn son is to be a great hero, to be called Siegfried; he must re-forge the sword, and will be universally victorious.

Wotan arrives, in a fierce storm. The eight Valkyries at first shield Brünnhilde, but she steps forward when he calls on her. In furious rage, he pronounces his sentence. She was his favourite, he says, but she has turned against him. He rejects her completely: she is no longer to be a Valkyrie but an ordinary mortal, to lie in sleep until a man shall awaken her and take her as his wife. The Valkyries, appalled at his severity, beg for leniency, but he refuses to give way and dismisses them, warning them not to help her.

The Valkyries ride off and Brünnhilde is left alone with her father. She begs him to be merciful, pleading that she carried out his true wishes in defending the Wälsung, despite his later command. She tells him of her meeting with Siegmund and mentions the child that Sieglinde is to bear. Wotan remains unmoved and repeats his sentence.

Brünnhilde falls on her knees before him and asks that some great difficulty be placed before anyone wishing to awaken her, so that only a hero dares to venture there. Deeply affected, he agrees to encircle her with fire. They embrace and bid each other a solemn and profoundly loving farewell. He kisses her godhead away, and she sinks into a deep sleep. He closes the visor of her helmet and covers her with her shield. Then he describes a circle round her with his spear, calling on Loge, the god of fire. The ring of fire appears. Wotan proclaims that no one who fears his (Wotan's) spear shall penetrate the fire. With a sorrowful look back at Brünnhilde, Wotan disappears through the flames.

SIEGFRIED
Part III of 'The Ring'
Libretto by the composer

First performed: Bayreuth, 1876
Three Acts

Cast in order of singing:

MIME, A NIBELUNG, BROTHER OF ALBERICH	*tenor*
SIEGFRIED, SON OF SIEGMUND AND SIEGLINDE	*tenor*
THE WANDERER (WOTAN, RULER OF THE GODS, DISGUISED)	*bass-baritone*
ALBERICH, A NIBELUNG	*bass-baritone*
FAFNER, A GIANT, NOW IN THE FORM OF A DRAGON	*bass*
THE VOICE OF A WOODBIRD	*soprano*
ERDA, GODDESS OF EARTH AND WISDOM	*mezzo-soprano*
BRÜNNHILDE, FORMERLY A VALKYRIE	*soprano*

The scene is laid in a forest and on a mountain, in legendary times

In the time that has elapsed since the action of *Die Walküre*, Sieglinde has died in giving birth to Siegfried. The dwarf, Mime, brought up Siegfried in the knowledge that Siegfried would be able to kill Fafner, who obtained possession of the Ring and, using the Tarnhelm, has assumed the form of a dragon, the better to guard it. Mime plans that he will thereupon kill Siegfried and obtain the Ring and the treasure which Fafner now holds.

★　★　★

ACT I: The opening scene takes place in Mime's cavern, where the dwarf is at work forging a sword. No ordinary sword, he reflects, will do for Siegfried, who simply breaks them like toys; only his father's sword, Nothung, will suffice, and Mime is unable to repair the fragments of it which Siegfried's dying mother left behind.

Siegfried enters, driving a bear (to Mime's terror), which he soon despatches back into the forest. Mime hands Siegfried his newest sword, which Siegfried tries and promptly breaks, expressing his contempt for Mime's work. Mime chides him for his ingratitude, and reminds Siegfried of how he has cared for him. Siegfried only expresses his arrogant loathing of the dwarf.

Siegfried now demands to know who his mother and father were. Mime at first says he is both father and mother to Siegfried; then, when Siegfried threatens to strangle him if he does not reveal the truth, tells him of Sieglinde and shows Siegfried the fragments of Nothung. Siegfried orders Mime to make a new sword from it, so that he can go away properly armed, and never return to see Mime again. He goes out, leaving Mime to prepare the sword.

Mime tries unsuccessfully to forge the sword. A Wanderer enters (Wotan, in disguise). He asks for hospitality, which Mime is unwilling to grant. The Wanderer asks Mime to test his wits with three riddles, with his head as forfeit if he fails to answer correctly. Mime, instead of probing the Wanderer's wisdom, merely asks who inhabits the underground caverns, the earth's surface, and the heights: the Wanderer tells him – the Nibelungs, the giants and the gods. Then he asks Mime to answer three riddles in return, on the same conditions. In fear and trembling, Mime answers the first two – he identifies Wotan's beloved race as the Wälsungs and the sword as Nothung – but he cannot answer the third, about who will repair the sword. The Wanderer tells him: only one who does not know fear can mend the sword – and to him the Wanderer will leave the forfeit of Mime's head.

The Wanderer goes off – forbearing to claim Mime's life, saying that the 'fearless' one will take it – and a few moments later Siegfried returns, to find Mime hiding. Mime tells him what the Wanderer said and tries to explain, but Siegfried cannot understand: he does not know what 'fear' means. He impatiently decides to remake the sword himself; as he does so, Mime expresses his intention of guiding Siegfried to Fafner (the dragon), then poisoning Siegfried when he has killed Fafner and taken the Ring. Siegfried sings his forging song – 'Nothung! Nothung!' – and eventually finishes his hammering. Finally, to Mime's alarm, with one mighty blow of the refashioned sword he splits the anvil in two.

ACT II: In the wood, outside the cavern which is Fafner's lair, Alberich is keeping watch at night. The Wanderer arrives: Alberich quickly recognizes him as Wotan and treats him with angry contempt, boasting of how, when Fafner dies, he (Alberich) will regain the Ring and conquer Valhalla. The Wanderer tells him that a young hero, ignorant of the Ring and the treasure, will soon come and kill Fafner. He wakens Fafner and both tell him of the boy's coming. Wotan goes off and Alberich continues his watch.

As morning dawns, Siegfried and Mime arrive – Mime has promised to teach Siegfried what fear is by showing him the dragon. Siegfried is dissatisfied with the lesson and sends Mime off. He sits there musing for a while on Mime and on his mother, then, during an interlude (the 'Forest Murmurs'), listens with growing enchantment to the sounds of the forest and the songs of the birds. He tries vainly to imitate the birdsong on a reed, then lifts his horn and sounds a long call. This rouses Fafner, the dragon. Siegfried defies him. They fight and Siegfried kills Fafner, who before dying warns him against Mime.

As Siegfried removes his sword, he is scalded by the dragon's blood and automatically puts his hand to his mouth. This gives him the power to understand birdsong, and he hears the voice of a woodbird tell of the hoard of treasure, including the Tarnhelm and Ring, within the cave. As he goes into the cave, Mime and Alberich arrive, quarrelling about the treasure. They hide as Siegfried, with the Tarnhelm and Ring, comes out. Again he hears the bird's voice, this time warning him of Mime's treachery. Mime approaches Siegfried thinking to entrap him. But the dragon's blood enables Siegfried to hear what Mime *thinks*, not what he intends to say. Thus Mime reveals that the drink he now offers Siegfried is poison. Siegfried kills him.

Siegfried now sinks down to rest and thought. He calls again on the bird. This time he is told that a bride, Brünnhilde, awaits him and at present is sleeping on a rock within a circle of fire. In answer to his excited questioning, the bird says that she can be awakened by a man who knows no fear. Siegfried realizes that he is the man, and the bird leads him away towards Brünnhilde. He bears the Tarnhelm and the Ring.

ACT III: At night, in a wild, rocky place, the Wanderer (Wotan) summons the earth-goddess Erda (here also called the Wala), who appears from a deep chasm. She suggests that he consult the Norns (Fates), but he presses her to answer his query – how can the wheel of destiny be halted, and the fall of the gods be averted? Erda mentions Brünnhilde, her child and Wotan's; Wotan recalls her disobedience and punishment. Erda wants only to return to sleep, but Wotan will not let her go. He tells her that he is now resigned to the gods' downfall, and has bequeathed the world to Siegfried who, feeling no greed and happy in love, is immune from the Ring's curse: Siegfried will awaken Brünnhilde and they will redeem the world. He dismisses Erda, who returns underground.

As day dawns, the Wanderer sees Siegfried approaching, led by the bird's voice. He asks Siegfried various questions, about Mime, Fafner, the sword, and how he came to seek the woman encircled by fire. The answers please him. But Siegfried grows impatient with the 'old man' and speaks insolently to him, which annoys Wotan. Eventually, in irritation, Wotan bars the way with his spear. In the gathering darkness, he points up the mountain towards the glow of the fire, telling Siegfried he will be unable to pass through the flames. Both become angrier, and when Wotan says that his spear earlier broke the sword when Siegfried's father wielded it, Siegfried is all the more determined. At a single blow, Siegfried shatters Wotan's spear; defeated, Wotan gathers the fragments and retires.

Siegfried continues on his way up the mountain, and the fire grows increasingly bright. Fearless, he sounds his horn and plunges into the flames. Soon the flames disappear, for Siegfried has passed through them. Brünnhilde is seen sleeping, in her armour, covered by her shield, wearing her helmet, with her weapons by her. Her horse too is sleeping there. Siegfried is astonished and at first thinks that the 'warrior' is a man. He loosens the helmet and armour, cutting the iron with his sword. When he realizes it is a woman he is still more amazed and bewildered – he does not know whom to summon for help, and calls on his mother. He thinks the strange emotions and desires he feels are the mysterious 'fear', about which he has heard so much.

He calls on the woman to wake, bends over her and kisses her. Slowly Brünnhilde awakens from her long sleep. She hails the sun and light, and is enraptured when she realizes that it is Siegfried who has awakened her. Now Brünnhilde feels many conflicting emotions – joy at awakening, love of Siegfried, nostalgic regret at the loss of her identity as a warrior, shame and even anger at the coming loss of her maidenhood. She even asks him to leave her, untouched: but

finally she is aroused by his intense ardour, and they embrace
passionately.

GÖTTERDÄMMERUNG
(Twilight of the Gods)
Part IV of 'The Ring'
Libretto by the composer

First performed: Bayreuth, 1876
Prologue and Three Acts

Cast in order of singing:

THE THREE NORNS (fates)   *contralto, mezzo-soprano, soprano*
BRÜNNHILDE   *soprano*
SIEGFRIED   *tenor*
GUNTHER, LORD OF THE GIBICHUNGS   *baritone*
HAGEN, SON OF ALBERICH AND HALF-BROTHER TO
  GUNTHER   *bass*
GUTRUNE, GUNTHER'S SISTER   *soprano*
WALTRAUTE, A VALKYRIE   *mezzo-soprano*
ALBERICH, A NIBELUNG   *bass-baritone*
WOGLINDE ⎫   *soprano*
WELLGUNDE ⎬ RHINEMAIDENS   *soprano*
FLOSSHILDE ⎭   *mezzo-soprano*

Chorus of Gibich vassals and female attendants
*The scene is laid on a rocky mountain, in the Gibichung
castle by the Rhine and in a wood by the Rhine,
in legendary times*

PROLOGUE: At night, by the rock on which Brünnhilde slept, the
three Norns are weaving the rope of Fate. They sing of the crum-
bling of Wotan's power, of Loge and of Alberich and the Rhinegold;
but at that point the rope frays and then breaks. The Norns, in terror,
gather up the pieces of rope and descend for ever into the earth.
   The sun begins to rise and Brünnhilde and Siegfried enter from a
cave. They sing of their love. But Siegfried must go in quest of
further heroic adventure. As a token of love he gives her the Ring
and in return she gives him her horse, Grane. She watches him
depart, listening to the sound of his horn fading away in the distance.

She is still encircled by the flames – now her defence against any man but Siegfried.

[An orchestral interlude (known as 'Siegfried's Journey down the Rhine') links the Prologue to the next scene.]

ACT I: In the castle of the Gibichungs, on the Rhine, live the half-brothers Hagen (Alberich's son) and Gunther, with Gunther's sister Gutrune. They talk of their plans to enhance the Gibichungs' fame. Hagen suggests that Gunther should marry Brünnhilde and Gutrune marry Siegfried. Much cunning will be necessary to arrange this, he says, as only Siegfried can penetrate the flames surrounding Brünnhilde; he suggests that a love-potion be administered to Siegfried by Gutrune so that he should forget Brünnhilde.

In the distance Siegfried's horn is heard. Soon he arrives and is welcomed into the castle hall. The three men talk of the Nibelung's hoard, Siegfried mentioning that he has the Tarnhelm and has given the Ring to a woman. Gutrune, who had gone out, returns with a drinking horn which she gives to Siegfried. He drinks to Brünnhilde; but in doing so (the drink contains a love-potion) he conceives a violent passion for Gutrune. She retires again, and Siegfried asks Gunther if he has a wife. He say he has not, for he wishes only to marry Brünnhilde, who is unattainable as he cannot pass the wall of firë: Siegfried's memory momentarily stirs, but his love for Brünnhilde is forgotten as, in exchange for the promise of Gutrune's hand, he offers to help Gunther win her. With a solemn ceremony of blood sacrament, they swear eternal brotherhood. Then they go off, in a boat on the Rhine, to bring back Brünnhilde. Gutrune watches them go, delighted that she is to be Siegfried's wife. Hagen too watches, contemplating the prospect of obtaining the Ring, which he, as Alberich's son, thinks of as his heritage.

The scene changes to the rocky mountain (as in the Prologue) where Brünnhilde is fondly contemplating Siegfried's Ring. She is excited to hear the voice of her sister, Waltraute, and greets her affectionately, telling her of her great joy in Siegfried's love. But this means nothing to Waltraute who, desperate with anxiety over the terrible decline in Wotan's power, has come to ask Brünnhilde to give her the Ring so that it can be returned to the Rhine, thereby allaying the curse on the gods and the world. But to Brünnhilde the Ring is the symbol of Siegfried's love. She sends her sister away empty-handed.

Darkness falls and the flames round the mountain glow more vividly. Brünnhilde hears Siegfried's horn call and prepares to greet him, but is horrified to see a different man approaching. It is in fact Siegfried, but he is wearing the Tarnhelm and has assumed Gunther's form. He identifies himself as a Gibichung, by name Gunther, and commands her to follow him. She refuses, invoking the Ring's protection; but it is powerless (she has not renounced love), and in a struggle he wrenches it from her finger. Her spirit is now broken. He drives her into the cave, calling on his sword to stand between them during the night, in token of his faith to his blood-brother.

ACT II: By night, outside the Gibichungs' Hall, Alberich appears to the sleeping Hagen. He urges his son to act with cunning so as to defeat their enemies, telling him to help complete the overthrow of the declining gods and to obtain the Ring from Siegfried.

As day dawns, Alberich disappears; soon Siegfried arrives and tells Hagen of his success. Hagen calls Gutrune, who questions Siegfried about events on the mountain and greets him as her betrothed. They enter the hall together to prepare for the wedding.

Hagen places a cowhorn to his lips, summoning the Gibich vassals to come at once and bring their weapons. They arrive in force, anticipating danger. But Hagen tells them that the occasion is a wedding party for Gunther and his bride; sacrifices must be made to Froh, Donner and Fricka, and then all can drink and make merry. A boat bearing Gunther and Brünnhilde draws up and the vassals sing in welcome.

Gunther presents his reluctant bride to his people and greets Siegfried, who comes from the hall with Gutrune. Brünnhilde sees Siegfried and almost faints. She is bewildered at his failure to recognize her; then bursts out angrily on seeing the Ring (taken from her by Gunther, she imagines) on Siegfried's hand. Gunther is unable to explain this; Brünnhilde then accuses Siegfried, who says he obtained the Ring when he killed the dragon. Now Hagen intervenes, saying that Siegfried must have won it by guile, and Brünnhilde, in terrible anguish, charges Siegfried with betraying her. But he, his memory of his love for Brünnhilde completely blotted out by the potion, denies it – his sword, he says, separated them during their night on the mountain. Gunther, Gutrune and the people are much disturbed.

Siegfried, placing his hand on the point of Hagen's spear, takes a solemn oath on the truth of his story: 'Helle Wehr! Heilige Waffe!' ('Bright defence! Holy weapon!'); and Brünnhilde, with a like invocation, dedicates the spear to his destruction. The bystanders call the gods as witness. Siegfried nonchalantly advises Gunther to send Brünnhilde to where she can rest, then, taking Gutrune by the arm, calls on the men to follow him in to the wedding feast.

Brünnhilde, Hagen and Gunther remain. Brünnhilde bewails her terrible dilemma, with its conflict of love and hate. Hagen approaches and offers to help her. Eventually Brünnhilde discloses that Siegfried's one vulnerable spot, unprotected by her spells at his birth, is his back. Hagen turns to the crushed Gunther, telling him that only Siegfried's death can purge his shame. Brünnhilde willingly agrees, and all three determine that he shall die. Hagen suggests that the deed be done during a hunting party the next day. The bridal procession emerges from the hall and Gunther and Brünnhilde join it.

ACT III: Near where Siegfried and others are out hunting, the three Rhinemaidens are seen swimming in the river where it passes through a woody and rocky valley. They are lamenting the loss of their gold. Siegfried, separated from the rest of the hunters, comes upon them. The Rhinemaidens talk to him teasingly and ask if he will give them his Ring. He at first refuses, then later offers it to them. They tell him to keep it, saying that its curse will soon be fulfilled on him. Their threats leave him all the more determined to keep the Ring, and they swim off.

Hagen, Gunther and other hunters arrive, and a meal is prepared. Hagen asks Siegfried what game he has won: none, he tells them, but he met some 'water birds' who predicted his death. The three men drink, then Hagen asks Siegfried about his understanding of bird-song. In reply, Siegfried tells the story of the sword, his killing of Fafner and his contact with the dragon's blood, his understanding of the birds, his taking of the Tarnhelm and Ring and his killing of Mime. After drinking further from a horn into which Hagen has squeezed the juice of a herb, to revive his memory, he resumes, and begins to recall how he passed through the fire and aroused Brünn-hilde. Gunther, astonished, begins to comprehend Siegfried's rela-tionship to Brünnhilde before he arrived at the Gibichungs' castle.

Some ravens, portents of death, fly over. Hagen draws Siegfried's attention to them and as he turns to watch them Hagen plunges his spear into Siegfried's back. Hagen walks slowly off as Gunther and the vassals, horrified, kneel at Siegfried's side. As he lies dying, he recollects his awakening of Brünnhilde and their love. Night falls: Gunther commands the vassals to lift up Siegfried's body and convey it to its funeral. The procession moves off slowly and solemnly in the moonlight, to a Funeral March.

Mists rise from the Rhine, obscuring the scene: when they clear we find ourselves once more in the Gibichungs' Hall. Here Gutrune is alone, waiting anxiously for Siegfried to return. Hagen soon comes, and tells her to her intense grief that he has been killed by a boar. His body is borne in and she falls upon it. Gutrune blames her brother, but Gunther tells her that Hagen was responsible. He defiantly admits it, claiming that he was justified: then he goes on to demand the Ring. Gunther denies his claim and the two fight; despite the intervention of his vassals, Gunther is killed. Hagen advances to take the Ring off Siegfried's hand; but suddenly the hand raises itself menacingly.

Now Brünnhilde enters, having understood all. As Siegfried's rightful wife, she demands vengeance. Gutrune angrily blames her for what has occurred, but Brünnhilde soon silences her. Brünnhilde orders a great funeral pyre to be prepared for Siegfried. As the men build it and the women decorate it with flowers, she recalls his nobility and purity. Ordering Siegfried's body to be taken to the pyre, she draws the Ring from his finger and places it on her own. With a firebrand in her hand, she sends two ravens (Wotan's messengers) to tell Wotan what has happened and to bid Loge to the burning of Valhalla. She lights the pyre and, mounting Grane, she rides into the flames to join Siegfried.

The flames burn more fiercely. As they threaten to burn the hall itself, the Rhine overflows and quenches them. The three Rhinemaidens are in its waves. Hagen, still coveting the Ring, leaps forward into the flood: he is seized by two of the Rhinemaidens and drawn away beneath the waters while the third joyously holds aloft the Ring. As the three swim merrily, playing with the Ring, the Rhine waters subside, and in the distance a glow of fire appears in the sky. The hall of Valhalla, with the gods all assembled, is seen consumed by flames.

★   ★   ★

Expositors of *The Ring* have identified more than a hundred motives. We confine ourselves here to showing the kinds of way in which a few of them are used. Certain motives identify *things*. Ex. 1a, heard in the opening scene of *Das Rheingold*, is one of those that represent the gold itself, or a particular aspect of it; ex. 1b, from the music accompanying Mime's complaints about the forging of the gold in Nibelheim under Alberich's dominion (the rhythm of the forging is heard in the bass), shows the same figure put to new purposes, and the sourness of the harmonic twists applied to it is unmistakable in its symbolic significance. And its links with the motive of a falling semitone, much heard in *Siegfried* and sometimes called the 'slavery motive', carries rich implications about the gold and its true meaning.

Ex. 1

In other cases, musical meaning is extended from a thing to what that thing stands for. When the giants are bickering with the gods over the payment for Valhalla, Wotan quells the quarrel by uttering the command 'Halt, wild one! Nothing through force!' and by brandishing his spear (ex. 2). Wotan's spear stands for the sanctity of contract and oath; so this motive is also heard, during *Götterdämmerung*, when Siegfried takes an oath of blood-brotherhood with Gunther. Siegfried does this only after having been deceived by Gutrune's love-potion: but an oath remains an oath, so the 'spear motive' recurs.

Ex. 2

The meaning of the first example was doubly identified – on the stage (we *see* the Rhinegold glinting at this point) and by the word 'Rheingold!'. But the 'spear motive' on its first full appearance is not identified by words, nor is it sung: it is enunciated by trombones. It is none the less identified because we see the spear as Wotan brandishes it, and we learn from Wotan's own conduct to associate his spear with 'contract'. Thus the motive has meaning also in the swearing of blood-brotherhood in *Götterdämmerung*.

Motives may be musically related because their meanings are related. Loge the god of fire enters to ex. 3. The flickering semi-quavers representing 'fire' reappear in the 'Magic Fire' music to which, in *Die Walküre*, Wotan lays Brünnhilde to sleep. First they retain their agitated character: then they are lulled into more restful harmony as the 'sleep motive' (*x*) and another motive representing 'destiny' or 'inevitability' (*y*) are combined with them (ex. 4).

Ex. 3

Ex. 4

Sometimes the significance of a motive is deliberately not made clear at first. At the end of *Das Rheingold*, when Wotan – just before leading Fricka into Valhalla – is seized with a grand idea, we hear a trumpet (ex. 5). Only in *Die Walküre* do we identify this with 'the sword' – the sword Wotan places in the hands of the Wälsung race he has begotten, and which (in *Siegfried*) shatters even Wotan's own spear.

Ex. 5

Similarly, at the end of *Die Walküre*, after encircling Brünnhilde with magic fire, Wotan sings that only one who knows no fear shall break through it; and his stirring melody, in Wagner's typical fashion, only half-coincides with the actual motive which the trombone is busy announcing (ex. 6). This theme is discovered (in *Siegfried*) to represent Siegfried himself, who *is* fearless.

Ex. 6

The 'heroine' of *The Ring* is Brünnhilde, even though she does not appear in Wagner's 'preliminary evening' (*Das Rheingold*). We first meet her as a Valkyrie, when she shares the characteristic music of the other Valkyries and utters her war-cry in a famous (and, to the singer, extremely difficult) melody against a tumultuous orchestral accompaniment (ex. 7). When in *Siegfried* she awakens from her

Ex. 7

magic sleep, now all woman and no longer a Valkyrie, her music is changed. Her themes are new (but a subdued snatch of the Valkyrie motive, above, comes through in a reminiscence). At first Brünnhilde is ashamed and distressed before Siegfried; then a new motive arrises which we might call 'Love's Content', to the words 'Eternal was I, eternal am I' (ex. 8). It is a theme familiar from Wagner's separate concert piece, the *Siegfried Idyll*. Its mood is never struck again in the relationship of Siegfried and Brünnhilde. The theme does not recur in *Götterdämmerung*: the non-recurrence of a motive is as significant as its recurrence.

Ex. 8

PARSIFAL
Libretto by the composer

First performed: Bayreuth, 1882
Three Acts

Cast in order of singing:

GURNEMANZ, A VETERAN KNIGHT OF THE GRAIL	*bass*
A KNIGHT OF THE GRAIL	*bass*
TWO ESQUIRES ATTENDANT ON THE KNIGHTS OF THE GRAIL	*soprano, alto*
A KNIGHT OF THE GRAIL	*tenor*
KUNDRY, A SORCERESS	*soprano*
AMFORTAS, RULER OF THE KNIGHTS OF THE GRAIL	*baritone*
THIRD AND FOURTH ESQUIRES	*two tenors*
PARSIFAL, A YOUTH OF UNKNOWN ORIGIN	*tenor*
TITUREL, FATHER OF AMFORTAS AND FORMER RULER OF THE KNIGHTS OF THE GRAIL	*bass*
A CELESTIAL VOICE	*alto*
KLINGSOR, A MAGICIAN	*bass*
SIX FLOWER-MAIDENS	*sopranos*

Chorus of knights, esquires, youths, flower-maidens
The scene is laid in Spain in the tenth century

We have noted how Lohengrin finally reveals his identity by refer-
ring to 'my father Parsifal'. The legend of Parsifal (also spelt
Parzival) was set down in the thirteenth century by Wolfram von
Eschenbach (a minstrel whom Wagner brought into *Tannhäuser*).
There is a connection with yet a third of Wagner's operas: Wagner
originally planned to have Parsifal, in his quest for the Holy Grail,

come as a pilgrim to where the dying Tristan lies in the third act of *Tristan und Isolde*. (As Robert L. Jacobs says in his book on Wagner: 'Tristan renounces life for the sake of passion – Parsifal renounces passion for the sake of eternal life'.) Parsifal is the 'Percival' of Malory's *Morte d'Arther* and Tennyson's *Idylls of the King*.

Thus, after the heathen legend of *The Ring*, Wagner turned to the Christian legend of the Grail for his last opera. He called *Parsifal 'ein Bühnenweihfestspiel'*, perhaps best translated 'a sacred festival drama'; and something like a Holy Communion is enacted on the stage. Consequently the request is often made of audiences to abstain from applause. This may be logically indefensible (the make-believe rite is not the real rite) but it is the culmination of Wagner's own tendency to make the theatre into a temple. The atmosphere of mystic exaltation is remarkably conveyed in this music.

'Monsalvat' (Mont Salvagge) in Spain is here named as the site of the stronghold of the knights of the Holy Grail, to whose company the 'guileless fool' Parsifal is admitted. Part of Spain at this period was under Arab rule; in that part Wagner places the castle of the knights' antagonist, Klingsor. As to the Grail, see page 243: Wagner uses the word in its erroneous sense of a chalice from the Last Supper, supposing that in the same chalice Christ's blood was collected from the cross.

★　★　★

ACT I: Reveille sounds in a forest in the domain of the knights of the Holy Grail. Gurnemanz, an aged knight of the Grail, calls his two esquires to prayer, then sets them to work preparing for the arrival of the king of the knights, Amfortas, who is coming to bathe in the nearby lake. Two knights come, one telling him that Amfortas's wound is more painful than ever. The mysterious heathen sorceress Kundry, in a wild, dishevelled state, enters with a phial of balsam for Amfortas, which she gives to Gurnemanz; then she flings herself wearily to the ground.

Amfortas is borne in on a litter, with a train of knights and esquires. He talks with a knight, mentioning the prediction that a 'guileless fool, made wise by pity' ('Durch Mitleid wissend . . . der reine Thor') will bring him relief. Gurnemanz hands him the phial from Kundry, whom Amfortas thanks before he goes off. Four esquires talk with Gurnemanz, who tells how the holy Spear and the Grail (the spear which wounded Christ and the cup used at the Last Supper) were delivered to Titurel, who founded a band of knights to guard them and eventually handed them on to his son, Amfortas.

We learn that Klingsor, a knight who on account of his transgressions had been refused admittance to the brotherhood, magically created a garden of seductive women to tempt the Knights of the Grail. Amfortas succumbed to the charms of one of them, and while he was with her Klingsor stole the Spear and wounded Amfortas's side with it. His wound can never heal, nor the Spear be recovered, except through the agency of 'the guileless fool, made wise through pity'. The esquires repeat Gurnemanz's words.

At that moment a wounded swan flies across the lake – to the horror of the knights and esquires, for animal life is sacred in the domain of the Grail. The swan was shot by a young man, who is brought forward; he is deeply contrite. It is Parsifal: but, to Gurnemanz's question he cannot even declare his name and origins. After the esquires have taken away the body of the swan, Kundry, who is still present, discloses that Parsifal's father was slain in battle and he was brought up in innocence by his mother, who is now dead (Parsifal is filled with wild rage at this).

Gurnemanz leads Parsifal away and, as the scene changes, they reappear in the great hall of the knights. Bells are heard and knights, esquires and youths are assembling for a sacred feast. Voices are heard from a dome aloft. The aged Titurel bids his son, Amfortas, uncover the Grail. Amfortas, with his burden of guilt and pain, can receive no comfort from the Grail and asks that it be left unrevealed ('Nein! lasst ihn unenthüllt!'). But eventually at Titurel's command the crystal cup is uncovered: it glows in the darkness, and Amfortas consecrates with it the bread and wine which are distributed to the knights who sing in praise of its holy powers of regeneration. The knights and others move off, with Amfortas, whose agony is renewed. Parsifal, who has watched in silence, clutches his own heart and slightly shakes his head. Gurnemanz, irritated at what seems Parsifal's dumb stupidity, sends him off. But from above the words ring out: 'Made wise by pity, the guileless fool . . .'

ACT II: In his magic castle, Klingsor anticipates the coming of Parsifal to his domain and resolves to trap him by magical means. He summons Kundry from a deep slumber (she is half in his power, half drawn to the knights) and orders her to seduce Parsifal. She is unwilling, but has to agree. Klingsor sounds a horn to alert his company of defenders against the attack led by Parsifal.

The tower with Klingsor and Kundry disappears and a magic garden, full of beautiful maidens, appears in its place. Parsifal, who has routed Klingsor's warriors, enters. The maidens reproach Parsifal for killing their friends, but their anger changes to gaiety as he approaches and talks with them. They deck themselves in flowers and dance around him, competing for his attention and love. He is about to leave when Kundry, transformed into a beautiful woman, calls to him, and the flower-maidens go off.

Kundry tells Parsifal the story of his mother, who died of grief when he went away; then she tries to console his sorrow with a passionate kiss. As she kisses him, he remembers Amfortas and the wound he received from the Spear. Momentarily he feels Amfortas's pain himself. Kundry is disconcerted as Parsifal, almost in a trance, recalls the sight of the Grail.

As she approaches him again, he realizes what is happening and repulses her. She tries to persuade him to save her, telling him of the terrible curse that has lain upon her since she once reviled Christ himself. Parsifal tells her he can save her, but not in the way she wishes. Becoming more and more frenzied, she begs him to spend one hour in her arms, but he continues to repulse her. Enraged, she curses him and calls Klingsor, who appears on the castle walls overlooking the garden and hurls the sacred Spear at Parsifal. Miraculously, it remains suspended over his head: he grasps it and makes the sign of the cross, whereupon the castle falls in ruins and the magic garden withers and becomes an arid desert. As Parsifal goes off with the Spear he calls to Kundry that she knows where to find him.

ACT III: It is some years later. The aged Gurnemanz is outside his hermit's hut, where he finds Kundry, dressed as a penitent, half-dead in a thicket. He revives her. Her former wildness is gone and she starts to act like a servant to him. She goes into the hut as a man approaches. It is Parsifal, clad in black armour. Gurnemanz does not recognize him, but says that no man must come armed into the domain of the Grail, especially on Good Friday. Parsifal removes his armour and Gurnemanz sees that he was the foolish boy who killed the swan.

Parsifal tells Gurnemanz that owing to a curse (Kundry's) he has hitherto been unable to find his way back, but now he brings the holy Spear. Gurnemanz is thankful, for the knights are in a piteous state: Amfortas refuses to show the Grail, and as a result of that deprivation Titurel has just died. Parsifal is deeply grieved. Kundry and Gurnemanz bathe Parsifal's feet and sprinkle water on his head; he says he is to be their king, as Titurel's true successor, and

Gurnemanz anoints him. Then Parsifal baptizes Kundry. He and
Gurnemanz gaze with wonderment on the beautiful scene of the
Good Friday morning. Bells are heard in the distance: it is midday
and Gurnemanz must lead Parsifal, as king, to the knights. They go
off, Parsifal bearing the Spear and wearing the mantle of a knight of
the Grail.

The scene changes to the great hall of the Grail. Two processions
are seen, one with Amfortas and the Grail, the other with Titurel's
coffin. The knights express their woe as the coffin is set down before
the altar and Titurel's body is uncovered; the weary Amfortas adds
his voice, praying to be released by death. They press him to reveal
the Grail, but he refuses animatedly: he is dying, he says, and does
not want to be revived. Instead he begs them to kill him.

At that moment Parsifal enters. He holds the Spear to Amfortas's
wound, which heals instantly. Amfortas is absolved, he tells the
knights, but he, Parsifal, is now their king. All stare, enraptured, at
the Spear; then Parsifal commands that the Grail be shown. As
before, it glows. Voices are heard from above. As Parsifal silently
blesses the assembled company with the Grail, a white dove hovers
above his head. All kneel before him, and Kundry, her curse
removed, sinks lifeless to the ground.

★   ★   ★

The prelude introduces three of the work's prominent motives. First
is heard the 'motive of sacrament', which we shall meet when
Amfortas (in the second scene of Act I) answers Titurel's request to
have the Grail shown.

Then, after a pause, the Prelude goes on to announce two motives
in succession (ex. 1). In this (*a*) is the motive of the Grail, which we
shall meet when Gurnemanz first mentions the Grail to Parsifal and
Parsifal ignorantly asks '*Who* is the Grail?'. Following it, (*b*) is the
motive of Faith, which will first be sung by the boys' voices issuing
from above in the second scene of Act I.

Ex. 1

But the motive which prophesies the coming of Parsifal himself is
not heard in the Prelude. It is sung by Gurnemanz ('With knowledge

gained through pity, the guileless fool') in the opening scene, and
repeated by the esquires (ex. 2).

Ex. 2

In the last act, after Parsifal has baptized Kundry, a motive which
has already been hinted at comes to the fore. It is the Good Friday
Spell motive (ex. 3). (The Good Friday Music as played in orchestral
concerts includes the passage preceding this, as well as the music of
the Spell itself: all, of course, minus the voices.)

Ex. 3

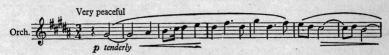

HECTOR BERLIOZ

1803–69

Rossini (to revert for a moment to page 120) conquered not merely Italy but the whole world of European music. In 1823, after visiting London, he took up a musical director's position in Paris – the capital which was then attracting young, enterprising musical geniuses from everywhere, among them Chopin, Liszt and a German known as Giacomo Meyerbeer (1791–1864), whose career reached its climax with the opera *Les Huguenots* (Paris, 1836). It is a pre-eminent example of French 'grand opera' – in five acts, historical in setting, spectacular in action, making full use of chorus and ballet.

Of native French operas of this period, however, none has lasted securely into today's repertory. We may just mention the work of two composers. Great success was won by Daniel Auber (1782–1871) with *La muette de Portici* ('The Dumb Girl of Portici'), otherwise *Masaniello* (1828), and with *Fra Diavolo* (1830). Fromental Halévy (1799–1862) created in *La Juive* ('The Jewess'; 1835) a French 'grand opera' of Meyerbeer's type, which enjoyed many revivals, principally because of its tenor role.

Unlike these composers, Hector Berlioz was never in his life a successful composer for the theatre, but today his repute in the general world of music has compelled a reconsideration of his operatic work. He was led to opera both by his musical bent and by his literary enthusiasm. For him, opera at its highest was a means of experiencing psychological dramatic truth: Gluck and Beethoven were his gods. His opera *Benvenuto Cellini* (Paris, 1838) enshrines his idea of the artist as a kind of romantic hero, and in this respect has been called an anticipation of Wagner's *Die Meistersinger*. Berlioz's enthusiasm for Shakespeare led him to write an operatic version of *Much Ado About Nothing* which he called *Béatrice et Bénédict* (which, in English, ought to be *Beatrice and Benedick*, reproducing Shakespeare's spelling of the hero's name). It was produced in 1862 – not in France, but in Germany, where Liszt (as court musical director at

Weimar) had already conducted *Benvenuto Cellini*. Between these two operas Berlioz composed *Les troyens* ('The Trojans'), completing it in 1858. Paris mounted only the second part, *Les troyens à Carthage*, in 1863, but the first part was not given until 1890 when the whole work was produced at Karlsruhe (in Germany, again!)

None of Berlioz's operas, in fact, has become standard in the world's opera houses at any period from that day to this. But all, today, are thought worthy of the occasional revival. If *Benvenuto Cellini* is dramatically stiff, and if *Beatrice and Benedick* dauntingly asks opera-singers to speak Shakespeare as well as to sing Berlioz, in *Les troyens* music and drama are splendidly unified.

LES TROYENS
(The Trojans)
Libretto by the composer, after Virgil

First performed complete: Karlsruhe, 1890
Five Acts (see below)

Cast in order of singing:

A TROJAN SOLDIER	*baritone*
CASSANDRA, DAUGHTER OF PRIAM	*soprano*
CHOROEBUS, BETROTHED TO CASSANDRA	*baritone*
AENEAS, A TROJAN WARRIOR	*tenor*
HELENUS, SON OF PRIAM	*tenor*
ASCANIUS, SON OF AENEAS	*soprano*
HECUBA, WIFE OF PRIAM	*mezzo-soprano*
PANTHEUS, A TROJAN PRIEST	*bass*
PRIAM, KING OF TROY	*bass*
THE GHOST OF HECTOR	*bass*
POLYXENA, DAUGHTER OF PRIAM	*soprano*
A GREEK CHIEFTAIN	*bass*
DIDO, QUEEN OF CARTHAGE	*soprano*
ANNA, SISTER OF DIDO	*mezzo-soprano*
IOPAS, A CARTHAGINIAN POET	*tenor*
NARBAL, MINISTER OF DIDO	*bass*
MERCURY	*bass*
HYLAS, A YOUNG TROJAN SOLDIER	*tenor*

[The parts of Andromache and Astyanax (Hector's widow and infant son) are silent.]

Chorus of Trojans, Greeks, Carthaginians, spirits, nymphs, etc. *The scene is laid in Troy at the end of its siege by the Greeks, and then in Carthage*

Berlioz's gift for tender expression as well as for musical excitement is shown in *Les troyens*. Its huge, fresco-like score still permits fine shading of personal detail. The opera was dedicated by Berlioz 'divo Vergilio' (to the divine Virgil). The Roman poet had been a passion of Berlioz's since his boyhood, and he tells of having been moved to tears on hearing of Aeneas's desertion of Dido. He based his own libretto for *Les troyens* on the original Latin (*Aeneid*, Books II, IV). Note the title of the work. The innumerable eighteenth-century operas on classical subjects nearly all took their titles from the name of a particular hero or heroine: Berlioz instead depicts the story of a nation, the Trojans. The first part is dominated by Cassandra, who dies at the end of it, the second by Dido and Aeneas.

The two parts (*La prise de Troie* and *Les troyens à Carthage*) were issued at the original publisher's insistence as separate entities, divided into three and four acts respectively. But Berlioz had intended the whole work to be given in a single evening, in five acts, to take about 4½ hours including intervals. This five-act division has been followed here.

The Royal Hunt and Storm, which (usually with the small vocal cries omitted) is so well known in the concert-hall, was placed by Berlioz at the end of Act III; here, as in modern productions generally, it is placed at the end of Act IV. The Trojan March, also familiar in concerts, reproduces the music to which the Greeks' wooden horse is dragged inside the city by the unsuspecting Trojans.

★   ★   ★

Part I: *La prise de Troie*

ACT I: On the plain of Troy, a Trojan soldier shows some people the grave of the Greek captain, Achilles. It appears that the Greeks have abandoned the siege of Troy – but left a giant wooden horse behind: the people go to view it, outside the city walls. Cassandra enters and, with her gift of prophecy, foretells the city's doom: her lover Choroebus tries to banish her fears, but in vain.

In front of the Citadel (outside the city proper), the Trojan people give thanks for their deliverance from the Greeks. Andromache, Hector's widow, and her infant son Astyanax enter in the mourning colour of white but speak no word; Cassandra foretells yet more sorrow. Aeneas suddenly enters with dread news: the priest Laocoon, suspecting an ambush in the wooden horse, had thrown a javelin at it, whereupon two sea-serpents had arisen and devoured him. The people are appalled at the portent. King Priam orders the horse to be brought within the city walls.

Cassandra is left alone. In agitation she sings of the impending destruction of the city. The sound of the people joyously dragging in the wooden horse comes nearer. Suddenly the joyous music stops – an ominous clash of arms has been heard within the horse – but then is resumed. The procession with the horse passes. Cassandra is left alone.

ACT II: Aeneas is asleep in his bedroom; his young son Ascanius, having heard a noise of fighting, runs in terrified, then leaves. The ghost of Hector appears; Aeneas wakes and recognizes him. The ghost bids Aeneas flee from Troy and found a new empire. The priest Pantheus, wounded, enters with the news that the horse contained a Greek ambush and that Priam is dead. Ascanius and Choroebus, entering, add to the tidings. Aeneas and the others rush off to fight.

In the temple of Cybele (the goddess Vesta), the Trojan priestesses and other women, including King Priam's daughter Polyxena, are praying in terror. Cassandra, as chief priestess, rushes in. She tells the others that Aeneas and his men will escape and will found a new Troy; that Choroebus is dead; and that only death can save the women from violation by the triumphant Greeks.

The majority of the women, taking up their lyres, sing heroically and prepare to kill themselves; a smaller group are afraid and are driven out by the others. A Greek chieftain and his soldiers are astonished at the sight of the defiant women. Cassandra stabs herself and hands the dagger to Polyxena; the other women follow their example.

Part 2: *Les troyens à Carthage*

ACT III: Dido and her people, who came to this region seven years ago as refugees from Tyre (and so are sometimes referred to in the text as 'Tyrian'), are holding a festival to celebrate their progress in building the new city of Carthage. The people sing and then greet their queen on her entry: 'Gloire, gloire à Didon!'. With her sister Anna and her minister Narbal at her side, Dido addresses the people and tells them that Iarbas, the Numidian king, threatens invasion in order to force her to marriage. The people swear to defend her against him. After a ceremony in honour of the construction of the city, they leave.

Dido is left alone with Anna, who wishes that Dido would remarry and Carthage acquire a king. Dido swears she must be faithful to the ring she wears, a gift from her dead husband, but (aside) confesses that Anna's plan is attractive to her. Iopas, a poet, enters to tell her that a fleet of foreign sailors has been driven on to their shores; Dido sends him to bring them and, while waiting, expresses a strange apprehension. The foreigners are brought in: they are the Trojans. Aeneas, their leader, is disguised. His young son Ascanius presents Dido with ceremonial gifts, supported by Pantheus.

Narbal rushes in with news that the Numidians have invaded; Aeneas throws off his disguise and promises to lead the defence of Dido's realm, leaving Ascanius to her care. The Carthaginians rally to him and prepare to fight.

ACT IV: Aeneas has been victorious. Anna is in conversation with Narbal, who expresses anxiety because Dido is neglecting all else for Aeneas's company – the very thing which delights Anna.

Dido and Aeneas enter with Ascanius, Iopas and attendants. A ballet (with chorus of made-up 'Nubian' words) is performed for them. At Dido's command, Iopas sings. Then Aeneas relates to Dido the fate of Andromache, mentioning that Andromache has now wed the son of the man who slew her first husband, Hector. In that case, Dido thinks, may she herself not think of remarriage? Absently she allows Ascanius to remove her former husband's ring from her finger. Dido and Aeneas hail the beautiful evening, with Anna, Iopas, Ascanius, Narbal and Pantheus: 'Tout n'est que paix et charme' ('There is nothing but peace and delight'). Then, left alone, they declare their love: 'Par une telle nuit' ('On such a night as this' – the text is modelled on the famous lines in *The Merchant of Venice*). As they depart together they receive a fateful warning: Mercury appears and reminds Aeneas of his appointed destiny, the foundation of a great city in Italy: 'Italie!'

[Symphonic entr'acte: Royal Hunt and Storm.] In a forest, naiads swim and a storm is heard; Dido dressed as Diana enters with Aeneas dressed as a warrior, and they take shelter in a cave. Their ecstasy together is portrayed in the music and visually symbolized by lightning. Fauns and other creatures dance and cry out the fateful message, 'Italie!'

ACT V: The harbour at Carthage is seen, with the Trojan encampment nearby. A young sailor on board one of the Trojan ships sings with nostalgia of his homeland; the two sentries comment on his song. Pantheus and other Trojan chiefs enter, having been told by Aeneas to prepare to sail. (A ghostly cry of 'Italie!' is again heard.) The two sentries are annoyed at having to sail: life has been easy at Carthage. They retire as Aeneas comes. He soliloquizes: 'Inutiles regrets' ('Useless regrets'); he is torn between Dido's love and the gods' command. The ghosts of Priam, Choroebus, Hector and Cassandra appear and reinforce the command. Aeneas stirs up the Trojans asleep in their tents.

Dido enters precipitately and begs Aeneas to stay. The sound of the Trojan March (first heard when the wooden horse was being dragged into Troy, now a rallying-tune for the Trojan force) recalls him to duty. Dido, heart-broken, leaves; Aeneas, escorted by his men, embarks.

In a room in her palace, Dido is in agony at Aeneas's desertion. To Anna, Narbal and Iopas (who enters to announce that the Trojan fleet has sailed) she proclaims her fury. But when they have left, her bitterness turns inward in an intense, tragic soliloquy: 'Je vais mourir' ('I shall die').

On a terrace overlooking the sea a funeral pyre has been lit. The priests of Pluto pray for infernal aid; Anna and Narbal solemnly curse Aeneas. Dido throws into the fire her own veil and a toga which belonged to Aeneas; prophetically, she is inspired to utter the name of the man who will one day avenge Carthage – Hannibal. Then she stabs herself. The people lament. In another prophetic inspiration Dido sees a vision of her people's coming enemy, Rome. She dies. The people vow the vengeance of Carthage on the Rome that is to be.

★   ★   ★

Les troyens contains some of Berlioz's greatest music: it also contains it in a truly dramatic framework. The brassy pride of the Trojan march, first heard in procession as the Trojans pull the wooden horse within their walls (ex. 1), comes again at the very end of the work to indicate that, for all Dido's hope and her people's curses, it is Rome (the successor to Troy) which will triumph over Carthage.

This is in Berlioz's heroic manner, and so is the strain to which

Ex. 1

Dido is hailed by her courtiers (Act III, Scene 1) and which – as
Edward J. Dent pointed out—may have been based by Berlioz, who
had visited England, on *God save the Queen* (ex. 2). Likewise couched
in this heroic manner is the tremendous chorus to which Cassandra
and the other Trojan women immolate themselves before the eyes of
the astonished Greeks.

Ex. 2

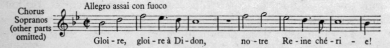

No less remarkable is the more intimate music – the two great
soliloquies in Act V (for Aeneas in Scene 1, for Dido in Scene 2) and
the nocturne-duet for them both ('O night of rapture and ecstasy
unending') (ex. 3):

Ex. 3

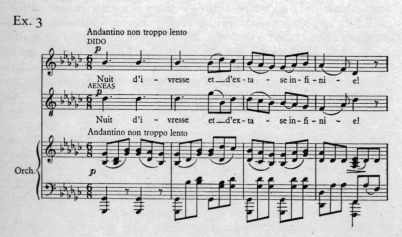

– a number which may be compared with the equally ravishing one
for Hero and Ursula (two women this time) in *Beatrice and Benedick*.

One of the peculiar and fascinating features of Berlioz's music is
the irregularity of its rhythmic patterns. Note the strange, haunting
refrain of the young sailor's song in Act V, Scene I ('Rock me gently,
on thy majestic bosom, o mighty sea!', ex. 4).

Ex. 4

CHARLES FRANÇOIS GOUNOD

1818–93

Berlioz wrote a *Damnation of Faust* for the concert-hall which has occasionally been staged as an opera; but *Faust* in opera belongs to Gounod. It was the greatest single success of a composer who was enormously successful and enormously prolific. Since the Second World War the position of *Faust* in the international public repertory has significantly declined, much as the position of Rossini, Donizetti and Bellini has risen; yet it remains much loved in spite of superior sneers. Gounod's *Roméo et Juliette* (1867; after Shakespeare), formerly often given, is now something of a rarity; *Mireille* (1864), a romance set in Provence, is still given in French theatres and has enjoyed revivals as a curiosity elswhere.

FAUST
Libretto by Jules Barbier and Michel Carré,
after the play by Goethe

First performed: Paris, 1850
Five Acts

Cast in order of singing:

FAUST, A LEARNED DOCTOR	*tenor*
MEPHISTOPHELES	*baritone*
WAGNER, A STUDENT	*bass*
VALENTIN, A SOLDIER, MARGUERITE'S BROTHER	*baritone*
SIEBEL, A VILLAGE YOUTH, IN LOVE WITH MARGUERITE	*mezzo-soprano*
MARGUERITE	*soprano*
MARTHE, MARGUERITE'S NEIGHBOUR	*mezzo-soprano*

Chorus of students, soldiers, villagers, angels, demons,
legendary figures, etc.
The scene is laid in Germany in the sixteenth century

The first part of Goethe's drama *Faust* was finished in 1808, the
second not till 1831. It had great influence on the romantic composers of the nineteenth century (among them Schumann, Wagner,
Liszt and Boito – see page 216) and Gounod's *Faust* is founded on it,
or rather on that part concerned with Gretchen, known in the
opera as Marguerite.

Originally the opera was an 'opéra-comique' in the French sense
– that is, using spoken dialogue (the term does not necessarily
imply 'comic' opera). But later Gounod arranged it for the Paris
Opéra, where recitative had to replace speech: and this has become
its standard form. It was also for the Opéra that Gounod added the
long ballet in Act V (often cut, in part or altogether, today). For the
first London production in 1863 Gounod wrote Valentin's air,
known in the lamentable standard English version as 'Even bravest
heart may swell', to a tune which he had used in the prelude to the
opera.

A word about Mephistopheles – a classic role for baritone as
Faust is for tenor and Marguerite for soprano. Mephistopheles is
not a pantomime demon with green eye-shadow and so forth. He
expressly describes his own first appearance to Faust (we translate
literally):

Here I am! Why are you surprised?
Am I not as you imagined me? –
Sword at my side, feather in my hat,
A full purse and a rich cloak over my shoulder –
In a word, a proper gentleman!

* * *

ACT I: Old Dr Faust is alone in his study, disillusioned and weary
of life. He is contemplating suicide when he hears in the distance
the happy voices of young people. Faust takes up their injunction to
prayer, as the voices fade away, but then bursts out bitterly, cursing his learning, his prayers and his patience, and calling on the
powers of darkness.

To his astonishment, Mephistopheles appears. He identifies himself, then asks Faust what he wants – is it gold, honour, power? 'Je

veux la jeunesse!' ('I want youth'), Faust replies. When Faust hesitates before signing away his soul, Mephistopheles summons up a
vision of a young and beautiful girl, Marguerite, promising her to
Faust, who hesitates no longer. Faust is suddenly transformed into
an eager youth, and the two sing of pleasures in store.

ACT II: A gay crowd is gathered at a 'Kermesse' (festival fair-
ground). The chorus 'Vin ou bière' ('Wine or beer') introduces, in
turn, the voices of students (led by Wagner, one of their number),
soldiers, older citizens, girls and matrons, and men. Valentin,
Marguerite's brother, sings of his regrets at going to war and leaving
his sister unprotected – 'Avant de quitter ces lieux' ('Before leaving
these parts') – though her young admirer Siebel has promised to look
after her.

Wagner has just embarked on a song when Mephistopheles enters
and interrupts, asking if he may sing instead. He sings a profane
song: 'Le veau d'or' ('The calf of gold'). Valentin and Wagner invite
him to drink, but before doing so he tells Valentin's and Siebel's
fortunes – gloomy, foreboding ones; Siebel will find that flowers
fade at his touch. Mephistopheles then draws wine by sorcery from
the barrel forming the inn-sign, and proposes Marguerite's health,
to Valentin's annoyance: Valentin draws his sword, but finds himself powerless to use it. The men, recognizing the powers of evil,
form the sign of the cross with their swords, and Mephistopheles,
angry and impotent, recoils.

The crowd leaves and Faust enters. Seeing Mephistopheles, he
asks him if he may meet Marguerite. Mephistopheles tells him that
the waltz which now begins will bring her. Young people re-enter,
dancing in high spirits, and the older people follow them. Siebel,
longing only for Marguerite, refuses to dance. When Marguerite
enters, Siebel's approach to her is foiled by Mephistopheles, and
Faust proffers his arm. She politely declines, but has evidently been
impressed. She leaves. Mephistopheles and Faust depart to plan the
next steps, and the dance goes on in rousing fashion.

ACT III: Siebel is alone in Marguerite's garden, singing of his love
for her. He picks a flower, which withers in his hand (as Mephistopheles had predicted); but the next flower, picked after he has
dipped his fingers in holy water, stays alive. He leaves.

Faust and Mephistopheles enter and Siebel returns with a nosegay
for Marguerite; to outshine it, Mephistopheles goes to fetch a casket
of jewels. Meanwhile, Faust sings the romance 'Salut! demeure
chaste et pure' ('Greeting, pure and chaste dwelling'). Mephis-

topheles returns with the jewels. Faust overcomes his scruples; Mephistopheles places the jewels where Marguerite will see them, and they leave.

Marguerite enters. She is thinking about the charming man (Faust) who spoke to her. Sitting at her spinning wheel, she sings an old ballad about the King of Thule, interrupting it from time to time with thoughts of the stranger. As she enters the house she sees Siebel's flowers, then the casket of jewels. She opens it and is astonished to see its contents: she cannot resist bedecking herself in them, and sings with delight: 'Oh, je ris de me voir' ('Oh, I laugh to see myself': the Jewel Song).

Marthe, an older neighbour of Marguerite, enters and admires Marguerite in her finery. Mephistopheles comes to tell Marthe that her husband has been killed, to her distress (which is short-lived). In a quartet Faust converses with Marguerite while Mephistopheles makes himself pleasant to Marthe. Soon Mephistopheles draws her away so as to leave Faust and Marguerite alone. By now they are both in love, and as evening falls they sing tenderly together. Faust bids Marguerite goodnight, arranging to meet her in the morning, and leaves; but Mephistopheles stops him and draws his attention to her window, where she is singing rapturously of her love. Mephistopheles's mocking laughter is heard as Faust climbs through the window to embrace her passionately.

ACT IV: Marguerite has borne Faust's child but has been deserted by him. She is in her room, spinning; her wretchedness contrasts with the gay snatch of song heard from the street. Siebel offers his love but she still hopes for Faust's return.

A scene in a church follows. Marguerite is praying for forgiveness, but Mephistopheles and the distant voices of demons intervene: he tells her that it is too late for repentance and that her soul is his. The voices of a choir in the church, with organ, proclaim the coming Day of Judgment. She prays all the more fervently but the voice of Mephistopheles pursues her.

The scene changes to the street, with the church on one side and Marguerite's house on the other. A march is heard. The soldiers, Valentin among them, are returning from war and sing a rousing chorus: 'Gloire immortelle' ('Undying glory'). It is momentarily interrupted as Valentin greets Siebel. When it is finished Siebel begs Valentin to forgive his sister. Valentin – puzzled, for he has not heard of what has happened – rushes into the house. Mephistopheles, arriving with Faust (who, against Mephistopheles's advice, still wants to see Marguerite), sings a cynical serenade to his own guitar accompaniment.

Valentin angrily emerges from the house, having learnt about Marguerite, and challenges one of them to a duel. After a trio (during which Valentin throws away his medallion of the Madonna, given to him by Marguerite, whom he now rejects), Valentin and Faust fight. With Mephistopheles's supernatural aid, Faust triumphs. As Valentin lies dying, Marthe and other people come to help him, and Marguerite throws herself over his body. But despite pleas from onlookers and from Siebel to forgive her, Valentin curses her angrily.

(The three scenes in this act are sometimes played in the order Street–Room–Church.)

ACT V: A chorus of will-o'-the-wisps leads off the infernal Walpurgis Night celebrations in the Harz Mountains. Faust is conducted there by Mephistopheles, who presides over the revels, in which many legendary and historical characters appear (in a ballet). A drinking-duet for Faust and Mephistopheles is interrupted when Faust sees a vision of Marguerite with blood round her neck as though from the blow of an axe. Faust orders Mephistopheles to take him to see Marguerite again.

She is by now in prison, having been condemned to death for the murder of her child during a fit of madness. Mephistopheles leads Faust to her cell, to effect her escape, and leaves them alone together. They sing of their happiness at being reunited. But her deranged mind wanders – recalling their meeting at the Kermesse and their evening in the garden – and Faust cannot persuade her to leave with him, for she is now content to die. Mephistopheles returns to hurry them before they are all discovered.

She prays to heaven for salvation while Faust presses her to fly with him and Mephistopheles tries to persuade Faust to leave, even without her. At its climax she makes the meaningful gesture of pushing Faust away. 'Jugée!' ('Damned!'), says Mephistopheles, exultantly; but a chorus of angels contradicts him with : 'Sauvée!' ('Saved!'). Her soul is borne away. Faust sinks to his knees and (to quote the stage direction) 'Mephistopheles is half bent back under the luminous sword of the Archangel'. A choral outburst – the Easter hymn of Christ's resurrection – ends the opera.

★   ★   ★

No opera has produced more 'hit tunes' – we use the words without a hint of being patronizing – than *Faust*. The Fair Scene, the Soldiers' Chorus, 'Avant de quitter' (Valentin's farewell); the Choral Waltz in Act II; Siebel's song when bringing his bouquet for Marguerite, Faust's 'Salut! demeure', Marguerite's Jewel Song, Marguerite and Faust's love-duet, the tune of the final trio, several of the tunes from the ballet music – all these came down from the opera stage to conquer the 19th-century public in song-albums, piano selections, arrangements for bands and orchestras of all kinds. Today *Faust* sounds (to borrow the old joke about *Hamlet*) 'full of quotations', and the very familiarity of the music may make us overlook its inventiveness. Take for example the musical delineation of the different groups of participants in the Choral Waltz ex. 1 ('Like the gentle breeze'). The orchestral tune (which is the main one, the chorus accompanying) starts off in such a way that it could be notated in 2/4 time.

Ex. 1

Another melody from this waltz recurs later in the opera – when Marguerite, in prison and half delirious, begins to recall in Faust's presence the scene where they first met. Note the dramatic aptness: Marguerite, her thoughts turning inwards in concentration, can manage only a single note (in fact she keeps that single note for thirty-two bars of music) and it is on the orchestra that the reminiscence steals in; moreover, it does so with a modulation (from F to D)

which is simple but which exactly hits off the change of 'plane' between the present and the memory of the past (ex. 2).

Ex. 2

Marguerite's words as the vision appears to her are 'But wait! . . . Here is the street . . .' The introspective aspect of Marguerite's character makes an admirable foil to the brilliance of the Jewel Song – and there, again subtly, the brilliance is never overdone: Marguerite still manages to be her innocent, unspoilt self, suddenly swept off her feet.

The final trio has one of the most powerful strokes in opera, the repetition of a melody at a higher pitch to screw up the excitement. (Verdi did it later in the trumpet tune of the Triumphant March in *Aida*.) Marguerite, asking the angels to transport her to heaven, leads off in G (ex. 3). Note the harp accompaniment: its 'celestial' connotations are obvious, just as are the connotations of the organ in the church scene.

Faust asks her to fly with him; her prayer gets more intense by being pushed into A; Mephistopheles adds his plea but Marguerite now pushes the tune up to B. And even this is not the end; the angelic interruption of 'Sauvée' (harps again!) leads to the key of C major, the actual chord being struck when the Easter hymn of the resurrection (organ again!) begins. This is musical language absolutely wedded to the dramatic action.

Ex. 3

JACQUES OFFENBACH

1819–80

Among the many musicians attracted to Paris from other countries
(see page 288) was Jacques Offenbach (born Jakob Eberst, in Col-
ogne; his family came from Offenbach), who in 1833 came to study
the cello at the Paris Conservatory and became, from the 1850s, the
leading composer of French operettas. He turned out nearly a
hundred of these (including *Orpheus in the Underworld*, first version
1858; *La belle Hélène*, 1864; and *La vie parisienne*, 1866), but wrote
only one serious opera and did not quite finish it nor live to see it
performed. It is a masterpiece and – with its peculiar dramatic
intermingling of reality and fantasy – a work like no other in the
opera repertory: *Les contes d'Hoffmann*.

LES CONTES D'HOFFMANN
(The Tales of Hoffmann)
Libretto by Jules Barbier and Michel Carré, after a play
of their own based on stories of E. T. A. Hoffmann

First performed: Paris, 1881
Prologue, Three Acts and Epilogue

Cast in order of singing or speaking:

Prologue and Epilogue

COUNCILLOR LINDORF	*baritone*
ANDREAS, SERVANT OF STELLA	*tenor*
LUTHER, KEEPER OF A BEER-CELLAR	*bass*
HERMANN ⎫	*baritone*
NATHANIEL ⎬ STUDENTS	*tenor*
HOFFMANN, A POET	*tenor*

NICKLAUS, HIS FRIEND	*mezzo-soprano*
STELLA, AN OPERA SINGER	*speaking part*
THE MUSE OF POETRY	*speaking part*

Chorus of students

★   ★   ★

Acts I, II and III

SPALANZANI, A PHYSICIST AND INVENTOR	*tenor*
HOFFMANN	*tenor*
COCHENILLE, SPALANZANI'S SERVANT	*tenor*
NICKLAUS	*mezzo-soprano*
DR COPPELIUS, A SPECTACLES-MAKER	*baritone*
OLYMPIA, SPALANZANI'S 'DAUGHTER', LOVED BY HOFFMANN	*soprano*
ANTONIA, A CONSUMPTIVE GIRL, LOVED BY HOFFMANN	*soprano*
CRESPEL, HER FATHER, A COUNCILLOR	*baritone*
FRANZ, CRESPEL'S SERVANT	*tenor*
DR MIRACLE, AN EVIL PHYSICIAN	*baritone*
A VOICE (ANTONIA'S MOTHER)	*mezzo-soprano*
GIULIETTA, A VENETIAN COURTESAN, LOVED BY HOFFMANN	*soprano*
SCHLEMIL ⎫ TWO OTHER ADMIRERS	⎰ *bass*
PITTICHINACCIO ⎭ OF GIULIETTA	⎱ *tenor*
DAPERTUTTO, AN EVIL MAGICIAN	*baritone*

Chorus of guests at Spalanzani's house and of Venetian
ladies and gentlemen, etc.
*In the Prologue and Epilogue the scene is laid in
Nuremberg, and in the three Acts respectively in Paris,
Munich and Venice, in the early nineteenth century*

E. T. A. Hoffmann (1776–1882) was a German novelist and amateur
composer; his writings occupy an important place in the German
literary romantic movement and he wrote a famous 'romantic'
interpretation of Mozart's *Don Giovanni*. So it is appropriate that a
strain from *Don Giovanni* is quoted in Offenbach's opera, of which
Hoffmann is the hero. Hoffmann himself appears as story–teller in
the prologue and epilogue: between come the three acts (each

founded on one of the real Hoffmann's stories) which tell of his different loves.

Because Offenbach left the work unfinished at his death, Ernest Guiraud (1837–92) undertook its orchestration; he also supplied it with recitatives. (He did similarly for *Carmen*: see page 320.) But in recent years there has been a tendency for opera houses to eliminate the recitative and to give the work with spoken dialogue, as Offenbach intended. Moreover, though the published vocal score gives the three acts (with three different heroines in the order Olympia – Guilietta – Antonia, it was Offenbach's intention to have the 'Guilietta' act last, as a reference in the prologue and another in the epilogue make clear. Various modern productions have adopted this authentic order, and we do so in the following synopsis.

Ideally, all three heroines – being dramatically treated as different incarnations of Hoffmann's beloved – should be sung by the same soprano. This has occasionally, but not often, been done. But it is normal, on the same dramatic grounds, for the four 'villain' roles (Lindorf, Coppelius, Dr Miracle and Dapertutto) to be sung by the same baritone, as an incarnation of the evil genius who foils Hoffmann at every turn. Certain other roles may also be doubled.

The voice of Stella must be the only example of a role in opera which is that of an opera-singer and which calls for no singing! The role of Nicklaus is given to a mezzo-soprano, representing a youth; it has been observed that Nicklaus is apparently never addressed by anyone in the opera except Hoffmann – as if he were, so to speak, a projection of Hoffmann, his 'better self', pressing the claims of conscience and duty on a being who is ruled by passion.

★　　★　　★

PROLOGUE: In Luther's beer-cellar at Nuremberg (sited next to an opera house, where the celebrated singer Stella is appearing in *Don Giovanni*), voices are heard singing in praise of beer and wine. Lindorf – a married man, but pursuing Stella – enters, and bribes Stella's servant Andreas into handing over a letter addressed by Stella to Hoffmann. The letter encloses the key of her room and Lindorf eagerly looks forward to keeping the assignation in Hoffmann's place.

Luther comes in with waiters to prepare the room for a crowd of students, who soon arrive, singing lustily, led by Hermann and Nathaniel. Nathaniel proposes a toast to Stella, then Hermann and he ask Luther where Hoffmann is: just then Hoffmann arrives with his friend Nicklaus, who ironically quotes from the music of Leporello's opening song in *Don Giovanni* and applies the words to the way Hoffmann's escapades tire him out night and day – 'Notte e giorno faticar'.

Hoffmann is at first in reflective mood. In response to eager requests he sings a comic song about a dwarf, Kleinzach – but his romantic musings lead him astray in the middle and he sings of his pursuit of love. Soon after, Hoffmann sees Lindorf, who mocks him; Hoffmann recognizes in Lindorf the force of evil which has always dogged him, and the two exchange insults. The conversation turns to the students' girls: Hoffmann talks of his three loves (all now embodied in Stella). Disregarding Luther's warning that the curtain is about to rise on the next act of the opera, the students prepare to listen as Hoffmann relates the stories of his three encounters . . . 'The first was called Olympia . . .'

ACT I: In Paris, the physicist and inventor Spalanzani boasts a 'daughter', Olympia. Hoffmann, who has become Spalanzani's pupil and fancies himself in love with Olympia, comes in. Spalanzani, after giving orders to his servant Cochenille, leaves Hoffmann alone. Hoffmann peeps behind a curtain and sees Olympia, apparently sleeping. Enraptured, he sings: 'Ah! vivre deux' ('Ah! to live with you'). Nicklaus enters and tells Hoffmann that Spalanzani's sole interest is science and that he makes lifelike dolls: 'Une poupée aux yeux d'émail' ('A doll with enamel eyes').

But Hoffmann fails, or refuses, to take the obvious hint. Coppelius, an inventor and Spalanzani's rival, arrives. He sings of his scientific wares and sells Hoffmann a pair of magic 'eyes' through which Olympia seems still more wonderful. Spalanzani returns, and, out of earshot of Hoffmann, Coppelius claims his share of the income which Spalanzani will earn from Olympia, for Coppelius made her eyes. Spalanzani pays Coppelius with a cheque drawn on a banker whom he knows is bankrupt.

The guests now begin to arrive for Olympia's splendid coming-out dance. Nicklaus and Hoffmann look forward to seeing the beautiful girl. Soon Spalanzani leads her out, to the admiration of all assembled, especially Hoffmann. Spalanzani offers to have her sing to her own harp accompaniment. She sings a coloratura aria – 'Les oiseaux dans la charmille' ('The birds in the arbour') – but there is a strange running-down in the middle which Spalanzani has to remedy by winding up a mechanism. Hoffmann, utterly enchanted, and still not realizing what Olympia is, wishes to take her to supper, but Spalanzani cunningly asks him to stay behind with her. The guests go down. Hoffmann, alone with Olympia, sings lovingly to her: as he touches her shoulder she makes a mechanical response. Finally, he takes her hand: she rises, moves around in various directions and goes off, to Hoffmann's dismay. Nicklaus comes in and tries to tell him the truth about her, but he will not listen.

Coppelius enters: he has found that Spalanzani's cheque is worthless and is eager for revenge. He disappears, to conceal himself in Olympia's room and wait for her. The guests reassemble and the dance begins. Hoffmann takes Olympia as his partner; they dance for a while, whirling more and more rapidly, until Spalanzani taps her and stops them (after Nicklaus has tried and failed). Hoffmann has fallen and is dazed: his spectacles (the 'eyes' Coppelius gave him) are broken. As he begins to recover, there is a sound of breaking machinery. Coppelius, in an inner room, has destroyed Olympia. Hoffmann, aghast, begins to realize that she was only a puppet. As Coppelius and Spalanzani shower one another with abuse, the guests deride the deluded Hoffmann.

ACT II: The second story takes place in Munich. Antonia, whom Hoffman loves, is seated at the harpsichord in her room, singing unhappily: 'Elle a fui, la tourterelle' ('She has fled, the turtle-dove'). Her father, Crespel, enters and reminds her of her promise never to sing – she inherits her mother's voice and also her mother's fatal tendency to tuberculosis, which her singing aggravates. She goes off, renewing her promise. Crespel, worried that Hoffmann is disturbing her peace of mind, orders his deaf servant Franz to admit no one. After a comic song for Franz, Hoffmann arrives with Nicklaus, and Franz, having misheard his instructions, admits them.

Hoffmann sings a snatch of the love-duet he and Antonia used to sing. Antonia comes and the lovers embrace passionately; Nicklaus leaves them to express their love. She mentions that she is forbidden to sing, but he presses her; she goes to the harpsichord and they sing a duet (incorporating the strain which Hoffmann had previously sung). At the end she becomes faint, then, hearing her father coming, she goes off to her room. Hoffmann hides.

Franz comes in and announces Dr Miracle. Crespel orders him to be sent off – he does not want his daughter killed by Miracle's treatment, just as his wife was. But he enters and insists on treating her, to the fear of both Crespel and the concealed Hoffmann. By magical means he diagnoses her illness in her absence and, despite Crespel's angry protests, prescribes for her. As if she hears Miracle's command, 'Chantez!' ('Sing!'), her voice is heard. Miracle remains unruffled during Crespel's furious attempts to eject him, returning through the wall when pushed out by the door. Eventually he leaves, followed by Crespel.

Antonia returns to find Hoffmann alone. Before he goes, he warns her to forget her dreams of becoming a singer. She agrees never to sing again ('Je ne chanterai plus'). Then Miracle returns, as if by magic: he takes up her words, reproaching her for wasting so great a telent and telling her of the dazzling future in store for her as a singer. She is disturbed and looks to her mother's portrait for comfort. It comes to life and speaks to her, bidding her sing, and Miracle plays wildly on a violin to rouse her excitement. At the end, Miracle disappears into the earth, the portrait resumes its old form and Antonia falls, dying.

Crespel comes in, exchanging only a few words with his daughter before she dies. As Hoffmann enters, Crespel turns on him and accuses him of being responsible. Hoffmann merely tells Nicklaus to fetch a doctor, in response to which Miracle appears. He pronounces her dead.

ACT III: Hoffmann's third tale is enacted in Venice. The setting is a palace overlooking the Grand Canal; a Barcarolle is sung by Nicklaus and the courtesan Giulietta with the assembled company. Hoffmann sings a cheerful drinking-song: 'Amis, l'amour tendre' ('Friends, tender love'). He loves Giulietta but her accepted companion is at present Schlemil. Now Giulietta introduces Hoffmann to Schlemil and also to another admirer of hers, Pittichinaccio, and suggests a game of cards.

They go off, leaving Nicklaus and Hoffmann alone: Nicklaus warns his friend not to be foolish, but Hoffmann is in love with Giulietta and will not easily be restrained. As they depart Dapertutto enters – a sorcerer who uses Giulietta to enslave his victims. He has already enslaved Schlemil and is determined to capture Hoffmann. He exhibits the diamond with which he will again bribe Giulietta to do his will: 'Scintille, diamant' ('Glitter, diamond').

Giulietta enters and Dapertutto asks her to captivate Hoffmann so that he can capture his soul by stealing his reflection in her mirror. Hoffmann, coming in as Dapertutto departs, sings passionately of his love for her. She warns him of Schlemil's jealousy but says she loves him; then she begs him to look in her mirror, so that when he goes she can retain his likeness for ever. He is mystified but consents.

Schlemil enters with Pittichinaccio, Nicklaus, Dapertutto and others. Dapertutto hands Hoffmann a mirror: he is horrified to find that his reflection has vanished. Nicklaus tries vainly to lead the distracted Hoffmann away. Hoffmann proclaims that he both hates and adores Guilietta, and the others comment on the situation. Now (in spoken dialogue, as the Barcarolle is heard again in the background) Hoffmann demands of Schlemil the key to Giulietta's room: they fight, Hoffmann using Dapertutto's sword, and Schlemil is killed. Hoffmann grabs the key and rushes off to Guilietta's room – but returns as Giulietta approaches, below, in a gondola. She is alone. But instead of accepting Hoffmann as a lover, she abandons him as a victim to Dapertutto and takes Pittichinaccio into her arms. Nicklaus drags the disillusioned Hoffmann away.

EPILOGUE: Back in Luther's inn, Hoffmann tells his friends that his tales are finished. In the distance, cheers are heard, which Luther says are for Stella. Lindorf slips out. In answer to a remark of Nathaniel's, Nicklaus explains that Stella is the embodiment of Olympia, Antonia and Giulietta, and all drink to her. At first this infuriates Hoffmann, but then he decides that drowning his sorrows in punch is the only solution. The students go off, leaving Hoffmann slumped over the table, dead drunk. In a vision, the Muse of Poetry appears and asks him to devote his life to her, to which he joyfully consents.

Stella enters and sees Hoffmann. Nicklaus explains that he is drunk; Lindorf comes in and draws her towards him. The students' voices, raised in a drinking-song, are heard again.

⋆   ⋆   ⋆

The puppet Olympia is characterized by an aria that is fully expressive yet capable of being delivered (by a skilled soprano) in a slightly mechanical, left-hand-then-right-hand sort of way. It is also extremely difficult to sing accurately in tune (ex. 1).

Ex. 1

In complete contrast, Antonia introduces herself with a rather slow, intense song about a turtle-dove (ex. 2), with the most delicately-hinted accompaniment.

Ex. 2

Giulietta has, rather remarkably, no comparable solo – but the Barcarolle, which Nicklaus begins and in which Giulietta presently joins, is the strongest indication of her (and Venice's) seductive charms. Notable in this act is the 'diamond aria' for Dapertutto (showing the power of the evil genius who confronts Hoffmann). Hoffmann's own romantic, expansive nature is shown in the opening of his duet with Giulietta (ex. 3), where he is intoxicated with love. Although Hoffmann and Giulietta sing ecstatically together later in the duet, Giulietta's feeling for Hoffmann is merely a courtesan's fancy; so Offenbach never gives her the phrase of genuine passion we have quoted from Hoffmann's part.

Ex. 3

The celebrated Barcarolle, perhaps unexpectedly assigned to two women's voices (at the opening of Act III), was transferred from Offenbach's unsuccessful opera *Rheinnixen* ('Sprites of the Rhine') produced at Vienna in 1864.

CAMILLE SAINT-SAËNS

1835–1921

One of the most prolific and versatile composers of his day, and blessed with a finely polished technique, Saint-Saëns wrote large quantities of orchestral, chamber, keyboard, sacred and secular choral music, and songs, as well as thirteen operas. Only one of his operas, however, has remained in the repertory. For all his command of form and his true and faithful setting of words, he seems to have lacked sufficient dramatic flair for the subjects he chose. But *Samson et Dalila*, with its familiar story and many stretches of vigorous and appealing music, has never been long away from the stages of the principal opera-houses. Once it got there, that is: for it was declined by the Paris Opéra, for which it was written, and had its première instead at Weimar; objections to its biblical plot kept it from London until 1909.

SAMSON ET DALILA
Libretto by Ferdinand Lemaire

First performed: Weimar, 1877
Three Acts

Cast in order of singing:

SAMSON	*tenor*
ABIMELECH, SATRAP OF GAZA	*bass*
HIGH PRIEST OF DAGON	*baritone*
TWO PHILISTINES	*tenor, baritone*
MESSENGER	*tenor*
AGED JEW	*bass*
DELILAH	*mezzo-soprano*

Chorus of Jews and Philistines
The scene is laid in Gaza in biblical times

Samson et Dalila was planned, in the first place, as an oratorio, but at
an early stage the librettist persuaded Saint-Saëns to let it be an opera,
although stage performances of biblical works were discouraged and
even prohibited in some countries (including Britain, where Edward
VII personally intervened to ensure the lifting of the Lord Chamber-
lain's ban). Many remnants of oratorio style – doubtless suggested
by the topic and the kind of music usually associated with it, rather
than because of Saint-Saëns's original plans for the work – have a
place in the opera, most of all in the choral music, where Handelian
fugues are to be found. The work was first heard at the court theatre
at Weimar, where Liszt promoted its production; it reached France
thirteen years later, in a performance at Rouen, and Paris later the
same year, 1890.

★   ★   ★

ACT I: In Gaza, in a square by the temple of Dagon, a crowd of Jews
are mourning their defeats and their oppression at the hands of the
Philistines. From among them, Samson tells that he has heard God's
voice and that the time for their delivery is approaching ('Arrêtez, ô
mes frères' . . . 'L'as-tu donc oublié?' – 'Cease, O my brethren!' . . .
'Have you then forgotten?'). The Jews are at first disbelieving, but
then are aroused, and the tone in their voices attracts the attention of
Abimelech who enters with Philistine soldiers. Abimelech taunts
them and their God, and Samson, provoked, calls to God for
vengeance and to the Jews to rise against their oppressors.
Abimelech attacks him, but Samson seizes the Philistine's sword and
kills him. The High Priest comes out of the temple and commands
the soldiers to quell the revolt, but they cannot; and now a Messenger brings news of its spread across the countryside. The High Priest
calls forth hatred on the Jews: 'Maudite à jamais soit la race' ('Cursed
for ever be the race').

The Jews sing in praise of God for their deliverance, led by an
Aged Jew. Delilah, with a retinue of Philistine maidens, arrives to do
pretended homage and celebrate the Jews' victory ('Je viens célébrer
la victoire'); Samson calls on God to protect him from his weakness
for her, and the Aged Jew exhorts him to turn from her. After a
dance for the priestesses, Delilah addresses him warmly: 'Printemps
qui commence' (Spring is beginning'); Samson is spellbound.

ACT II: By her house in the fertile Valley of Sorek, Delilah contemplates her power over Samson, whom once she loved, and her planned ensnaring of him for the Philistines ('Amour, viens aider ma faiblesse' – 'O love! come and help my weakness'). The High Priest comes to strengthen her resolve. But that is scarcely necessary, she says, as she already loathes Samson; they join in calling for his death, and the High Priest demands that she discover the secret of his strength. The High Priest leaves, and Delilah goes back into her house, anxious that she may have lost her power over Samson and that he may not come.

But Samson duly comes, drawn by her irresistible power over him. His thoughts are chiefly of freeing his people, but she speaks to him of love and of her passion for him: 'Mon cœur s'ouvre à ta voix' ('My heart opens to your voice'). As a thunderstorm gathers, she presses him for his secret, but he spurns her and calls on God's aid. Finally, taunting him, she rushes into her house; Samson hesitates, then follows. Philistine soldiers arrive, and wait in readiness; eventually Delilah appears at a window, and calls them – the deed is done and Samson is at their mercy.

ACT III: Samson, shackled, blinded and shorn of his hair, is turning the mill wheel in the prison at Gaza and appeals to God's compassion: 'Vois ma misère, hélas' ('Behold my misery, alas!'). The Jews reproach him for betraying them, and worse, for doing so for a Philistine woman. Philistines come and take Samson away.

In the Temple of Dagon, festivities are afoot, and a bacchanal is danced. The High Priest mocks Samson's plight; so too does Delilah. Samson calls on God to give him power to avenge the insults to his name. The High Priest and Delilah sing in praise of Dagon, and finally demand that Samson join their celebration. He is led to the pillars at the centre of the hall. He again calls on God: and this time his call is answered as he tears down the pillars and the rejoicing Philistines – as well as Samson himself – are crushed as Dagon's temple falls in ruins.

★   ★   ★

Hans von Bülow, the German conductor, follower of Wagner, and first husband of Cosima Liszt (later Cosima Wagner), said of Saint-Saëns that he was 'the only contemporary musician to have profited usefully from the theories of Wagner without being led astray by them'. Yet Saint-Saëns was no Wagnerian; his style was too eclectic to be labelled, and his operas range from lightweight 'opéra-

comique' to *Samson*, his nearest approach to the Meyerbeer tradition
of the *grand opéra*, typically taking as its topic the destiny of a people.
Its most famous number, by far, is Delilah's song 'Mon cœur s'ouvre
à ta voix', in which he touches on a depth of sensual feeling that is
rare in his urbane, polished music. And here, interestingly, one can
find an example of Wagnerian technique: the transformation of a
theme to convey a relationship between one dramatic context and
another. The second part of Delilah's song is an impassioned plea to
Samson, as her voice descends (ex. 1); later in the opera, after her

Ex. 1

betrayal of him, she taunts him with memories of their former love,
and does so to a corruption of this phrase and in particular its
attendant harmony, so that the music itself actually conveys the
betrayal of love (ex. 2).

Ex. 2

To meet the conventions of French grand opera, Saint-Saëns took care to introduce dance music of a colourful and spectacular kind, inviting parallel colour and spectacle on the stage. All the dance music goes to the Philistines, who are portrayed as a pleasure-seeking people as compared with their enemies, the Jews. This recalls, not surprisingly, Handel's treatment of similar situations in his oratorios; the mourning chorus and in particular its concluding fugue represent solemn prayer, and the use of the old-fashioned style here conveys something of the gravity of their situation as well as their earnestness (ex. 3).

Ex. 3

sé - es   Et   les gen - tils   pro-fa-nant   ton au -

vu   nos cit - és   ren-ver-sées   Et les gen-tils   pro-fa-nant ton au -

Et sous leur   joug   nos tri-bus   dis - per - sé - es

- tel.   Nous   a - vons   vu nos ci -[tés]

- tel   Et sous leur joug   nos   tri - bus   dis - per -[sées]

GEORGES BIZET

1838–75

Oriental subjects, with opportunities for exotic-sounding music, were much favoured in nineteenth-century Paris. In 1883 Paris saw the première of an opera about the daughter of a Brahmin priest in love with a British officer in India – *Lakmé* by Léo Delibes (1836–91). It is still performed today, though it has hardly the 'classic' status of Delibes's two celebrated ballets, *Coppélia* (on the story by E. T. A. Hoffmann which also furnished the 'Olympia' episode in Offenbach's *Les contes d'Hoffmann*) and *Sylvia*.

Oriental subjects were also used by Georges Bizet in two operas: *Les pêcheurs de perles* ('The Pearl Fishers', 1863) and *Djamileh* (1872; one act, unsuccessful). And Bizet found another 'orient' (that is, a setting giving dramatic opportunity for an exceptional, exotic touch in the music) at the very door of France: in Spain. *Carmen* was produced in 1875; displeased most of the critics; was reckoned a failure. Tchaikovsky, visiting Paris at the time, prophesied that within ten years it would be the most popular opera in the world. He overestimated, but not by much. Incidentally, Tchaikovsky's own use of a boys' chorus imitating soldiers at the opening of *The Queen of Spades* is the frankest of tributes to Bizet's masterpiece.

Among Bizet's other works is the opera *La jolie fille de Perth* ('The Fair Maid of Perth', 1867), based on Scott's novel.

CARMEN

Librretto by Henri Meilhac and Ludovic Halévy,
after Prosper Mérimée

First performed: Paris, 175
Four Acts

Cast in order of singing:

MORALES, A CORPORAL	*baritone*
MICAELA, A PEASANT GIRL FROM NAVARRE	*soprano*
DON JOSÉ, A CORPORAL FROM NAVARRE	*tenor*
ZUNIGA, A LIEUTENANT	*bass*
CARMEN, A GIPSY	*mezzo-soprano*
FRASQUITA, A GIPSY	*soprano*
MERCEDES, A GIPSY	*soprano*
ESCAMILLO, A TOREADOR	*baritone*
EL DANCAIRO, A SMUGGLER	*baritone*
EL REMENDADO, A SMUGGLER	*tenor*
TWO GIPSIES	*mezzo-soprano, baritone*

Chorus of soldiers, street-boys, townspeople,
cigarette girls, gipsies, smugglers
The scene is laid in Seville in the 1820s

Say 'seductive Spanish gipsy' and we think of Carmen; say 'Toreador' and we think of Escamillo's swaggering tune. Bizet's opera has come to have an almost proverbial status. Its ever-fresh score has combined with its dramatic story to preserve its popularity the world over.

Indeed, its tunes are now so well loved, its plot so well understood, and its heroine so widely recognized as respresenting a whole type of female behaviour, that we scarcely think of what a shocker the opera originally seemed. Girls smoking on the stage (in 1875); such a disgusting death for the heroine – and on the stage of the Opéra-Comique, dedicated by tradition to much less sordid fare!

Not that 'opéra-comique' in France means precisely 'comic-opera'. As we have noted in considering Gounod's *Faust* (see page 296), its distinguishing feature was the use of spoken dialogue – in place of recitative, which was used in works presented at the larger theatre, the Paris Opéra. Later (after Bizet's death) *Carmen* was performed and published in an all-sung version, with recitatives added by Bizet's friend Ernest Guiraud (1837–92). The modern tendency is to restore the spoken dialogue, which makes the action much clearer, and to restore certain parts of Bizet's original score which were omitted from the published version (more dubiously, as the accepted version may well have had his assent).

★　★　★

ACT I: The curtain rises on a square in Seville, with a tobacco factory on one side and a guard-house on the other. Soldiers, led by Morales, sing as they lounge and watch the bustle of people in the street. Micaela, a simple country girl, comes to ask Morales if he knows a corporal called Don José, who is her sweetheart; he tries to flirt a little with her and tells her that José will soon come, when the guard changes. She goes, and the soldiers briefly resume their song.

Trumpets off-stage signal the approach of the new guard, a crowd of urchins following and imitating them admiringly. The children sing as the guard is changed, José commanding the relief. Morales tells José that a girl has inquired after him.

Zuniga, an officer only recently posted to Seville, asks José about the girls in the cigarette factory. They are 'fast' by reputation, but they do not interest José, who loves only Micaela. A bell sounds and the girls come out of the factory smoking, watched by a crowd of men, with whom they exchange pleasantries. The last girl to appear from the factory is Carmen, a seductive gipsy beauty. Only José ignores her. She sings a habanera: 'L'amour est un oiseau rebelle' ('Love is like a rebellious bird'). All the young men sue for her favours, but her eye has fallen on José, and she tosses a flower to him before going back into the factory.

José, left alone, is disturbed by the incident. Then Micaela arrives: she has come to give José a letter – and a kiss – from his mother. In their duet, 'Parle-moi de ma mère' ('Tell me about my mother'), the two sing nostalgically of the village which was his home. When she goes he reads the letter, which urges him to marry Micaela.

Suddenly there is a commotion in the factory and girls come running out, chattering about a quarrel involving Carmen. Zuniga sends José with two soldiers to investigate. He soon comes out with Carmen, who sings an impudent 'Tra-la-la!' in reply to Zuniga's questions. It seems that she attacked another girl with a knife, so Zuniga sends her off to prison, in José's charge.

Carmen and José are left alone in the square. She speaks seductively to him; he forbids her to speak to him, so she sings – to herself, she pretends – a seguidilla, 'Près des remparts de Séville' ('Near the ramparts of Seville'). Soon José is entirely captivated. In response to her promise that she will give him her love at Lillas Pastia's inn, he loosens the cord round her wrists. Zuniga returns with the warrant for her arrest. As the crowd watches, José begins to march Carmen away. But suddenly she turns, gives him a push (as she had arranged with him) and rushes away, to the crowd's amusement. [In stage performances, José is usually put under arrest immediately by Zuniga for permitting Carmen's escape.]

ACT II: It is two months later. In Lillas Pastia's tavern, where Carmen had told José she would wait for him, gipsies are dancing. Carmen sings the Gipsy Song, 'Les tringles des sistres tintaient' ('Guitar strings were ringing'), in which Frasquita and Mercedes join. Zuniga is present and tries to lead Carmen off, but she refuses to go; he mentions that José, who had been imprisoned for permitting Carmen's escape, has just been released. Soon Escamillo, a famous toreador, arrives. He is cheered by all present and sings the Toreador's Song, 'Votre toast' ('Your toast') with their support, and before he leaves he makes a bid for Carmen. Zuniga and the rest of the crowd soon follow, hurried off by the innkeeper, leaving Carmen, Frasquita and Mercedes.

Two smugglers, Dancairo and Remendado, enter and ask the three women for immediate help in a venture. Carmen refuses, knowing that José will come – but she agrees to try to persuade him to desert and join them. The others leave Carmen as José is heard approaching: 'Dragon d'Alcala' ('Dragoon of Alcala'). He comes and declares his love. She is dancing for him when, hearing bugles calling him to duty, he prepares to leave. She is angry and sarcastic – this is love that can be quelled by a bugle-call! He tries to assure her of his love, telling her that he has kept, throughout the imprisonment, the flower she threw to him: 'La fleur que tu m'avais jetée' ('The flower you threw to me') – the Flower Song. She tempts him with visions of a free and happy life together among the smugglers and gipsies in the mountains.

He resists and is about to leave when there is a knock at the door and Zuniga enters. He asks Carmen if she prefers a common soldier to an officer, and orders José back to camp. José refuses and draws his sword against his officer. The smugglers, who have been in hiding, disarm Zuniga and send him off in the custody of some gipsies. By defying his officer José has turned his back on the army. To leave with Carmen is now the only way for him, and he joins in a chorus in praise of the free life.

ACT III: In the smugglers' mountain lair, preparations are being made for an exploit, led by Dancairo. By now Carmen is tiring of José, who is unhappy at the kind of life he is leading; she suggests that he should leave them, but he is bitterly jealous and threatens her angrily. As the men rest, Frasquita, Mercedes and Carmen read their fortunes in the cards. Carmen sees only death for herself – 'and later for him'.

Dancairo leads the smugglers off, singing of their plans; the women go with them, to beguile the customs officers. The stage is empty when a figure appears in the darkness: it is Micaela, who has paid a guide to take her to the smugglers' lair and prays that God will help her to lead José back to his mother: 'Je dis que rien m'épouvante' ('I say that nothing frightens me'). She sees him approaching; then, as a shot rings out, she hides. José had seen a man coming and only just missed him. The man identifies himself as Escamillo, who has been in the region rounding up bulls for his next fight. In a duet Escamillo says he has come to see Carmen, who is tiring of her latest lover, a soldier ('her affairs last only six months'). José's jealousy is aroused; he challenges Escamillo, who then realizes that José is the man, and they fight.

José is about to kill his rival when Carmen arrives and seizes his arm. Dancairo tells Escamillo to go, which he does, but not before he has taunted José, who has to be held back by the smugglers. They are leaving again when Remendado finds Micaela in hiding. She pleads with José to come away with her. Carmen and the smugglers too tell him to go, but he swears that only death can part him from Carmen. But when Micaela says that his mother is dying he consents to leave, and even then he threateningly tells Carmen that they will meet again. Escamillo's voice is heard from a distance and Carmen moves towards him, but José menacingly bars her way.

ACT IV: Tradesmen, gipsies, children and townspeople are seen filling the square in Seville, outside the amphitheatre where a bullfight is to be held. Zuniga is there, making small purchases from the gipsies. Soon the colourful procession of those taking part in the bull-fight starts, hailed by the bystanders (including children); Escamillo brings up the rear in triumph, to shouts of his name. After a brief love-duet with Carmen, who is with him, he goes off to prepare for the fight. Frasquita and Mercedes have seen José in the crowd and warn Carmen to take care, but she is unafraid.

José intercepts Carmen as she moves towards the arena. He begs her to return to him, to go away with him, forgetting the past; but she says that her love is dead. From the arena, cheers for Escamillo are heard. Carmen tries to enter but he bars her way, determined that she shall not go to her new lover. More cheers are heard. José becomes more violent. She demands that he kill her or let her pass. Then she throws his ring at him and tries to slip past him, but he catches her and plunges his knife into her back. As she falls dead the crowd, singing the Toreador's Song, comes out of the amphitheatre and sees her. Kneeling by her lifeless body, José gives himself up.

★   ★   ★

The cigarette-girls come out of the factory with a studiedly languid air as they puff at their cigarettes, and the music which they sing is languid too. Then, suddenly loud and with an abrupt change of tempo (ex. 1), Carmen enters. Even operagoers familiar with *Carmen* would not necessarily recognize this tune, played here on the violins, but it is metamorphosed later in the scene into a theme that is unforgettable (ex. 2).

Ex. 1

Ex. 2

This has already been heard in the prelude, and is first heard in the opera when Carmen throws the flower at Don José, thus establishing her power over him; it recurs at various points, up to the very end of the opera when José gives himself up for her murder. But this recurrence is not part of a general web of leading-motives used symphonically; it is a unique 'fate' motive.

The Toreador's Song is also requoted. It is the best-known piece in the opera, and has to be delivered with swagger by Escamillo: Bizet marked it to be sung 'with fatuity' – which shows just how he viewed Escamillo's character.

The habanera sung by Carmen is an adaptation of a Spanish-American song by Sebastian Yradier (1809–65); and the entr'acte before Act IV and the snatch of melody with which Carmen defies Zuniga in Act I are also borrowings from Spanish sources (ex. 3).

Ex. 3

But the atmosphere which is so striking in this opera is not mainly a matter of borrowing but of a daringly original mind working on his material. When Carmen dances for José in Lillas Pastia's tavern she has her own tune (sung to 'la'); with this she (or a performer in the orchestra) plays the castanets in a typically Spanish rhythm; and at the same time two bugles (Bizet specified that instrument, not trumpets) sound the retreat, summoning José back to barracks. The three strains intertwine in a whole which represents exactly what is in José's mind.

As remarkable as anything in the work is the characterization of Micaela. As the opposite of Carmen she might have been simpering and pale. But her music is strong (ex. 4). Note the force of the unorthodox harmony at ★.

Ex. 4

nuit et   jour_____   à l'ab - sent_____

*

Dramatically, Micaela is strong partly because she represents not only herself but also José's mother from whom she comes. This is one of the incidental virtues of a libretto which, in itself, is one of the best ever written.

JULES MASSENET

1842–1912

Much of Massenet's music may seem today too obvious in its sensuous charm, and we need not look for a revival of most of his operas: he wrote no fewer than twenty-seven, excluding those unfinished and unperformed. The mixing of the religious and the erotic (which had already provided two major operatic successes in Wagner's *Tannhäuser* and Gounod's *Faust*, and was to reach its musical climax in Richard Strauss's *Salome*) was congenial to Massenet. His *Hérodiade* ('Herodias'; 1881) and *Thaïs* had considerable success and are still considered by the French as part of their national repertory. Internationally, at any rate until recently, preference has been given to *Manon*, another work in which religious and erotic impulses are intertwined. But the later *Werther*, a work of quite different type (more intense, less expansive), is at least as powerful a demonstration of his art. Berlioz and Gounod had turned to Goethe for the supernatural passions of the Faust story; Massenet found in another work by Goethe the essential true-to-life picture of middle-class family life streaked by tragic, unfulfilled love. In 1894 (two years after *Werther*) the composer wrote *Le portrait de Manon*, a one-act sequel to the earlier work.

MANON
*Libretto by Henri Meilhac and Philippe Gille, after
the novel by the Abbé Prévost*

First performed: Paris 1884
Five Acts

Cast in order of singing:

GUILLOT DE MORFONTAINE, MINISTER OF FINANCE,
    AN OLD ROUÉ   *tenor*
DE BRÉTIGNY, A NOBLEMAN   *baritone*
POUSSETTE ⎫   *soprano*
JAVOTTE   ⎬   DESCRIBED AS ACTRESSES   *soprano*
ROSETTE   ⎭   *mezzo-soprano*
INNKEEPER   *baritone*
LESCAUT, OF THE ROYAL GUARD, MANON'S COUSIN   *baritone*
TWO GUARDSMEN   *tenors*
MANON LESCAUT   *soprano*
THE CHEVALIER DES GRIEUX   *tenor*
THE COUNT DES GRIEUX, HIS FATHER   *bass*

Chorus of citizens, travellers, postilions, porters,
street-vendors, worshippers, gamblers, soldiers
*The scene is laid in France (Amiens, Paris
and near Le Havre) in 1721*

The Abbé Prévost (1697–1763) was a soldier (in his youth), a novelist, and a translator into French of Richardson's English novels, as well as a member of the Benedictine order. His most famous work is the novel *Manon Lescaut* (1731), a classic treatment of the bad girl as literary heroine (dying in the end, of course). It has the peculiar distinction of having inspired four operas over ninety-six years, from *Manon Lescaut* by Auber (1856) to Hans Werner Henze's *Boulevard Solitude* (a modern-dress adaptation, 1952) – with the two best known examples in between, Massenet's *Manon* (1884) and Puccini's *Manon Lescaut* (1893).

Dramatically, a notable difference between these two is that Puccini follows the novel in showing Manon as dying in the wilds of America, after her sentence of transportation; in Massenet's opera she dies before the planned embarkation at Le Havre. Massenet gives his heroine much sentimental charm, and the same kind of appeal goes into the musical portrayal of the hero, in the romantic dilemma of having to choose between passion and priesthood.

★　★　★

ACT I: In the courtyard of an inn at Amiens, two well-to-do clients, Guillot and De Brétigny, have arrived with their merry companions,

Poussette, Javotte and Rosette – described as actresses, really Guillot's mistresses. They clamour impatiently for a meal. Soon the innkeeper announces that it is ready and they go a pavilion to eat.

People gather to watch the arrival of the stage-coach, and the innkeeper comments on it. Lescaut, a young guardsman, enters with two travelling-companions whom he sends off into the inn while he awaits the coach. (He is to meet his young cousin Manon, who is travelling in the coach on her way to entering a convent.) The coach arrives and there is a general bustle of passengers, porters and others. Lescaut finds Manon among the crowd and they introduce themselves to one another; he comments on her beauty. Rather confused after the journey, Manon tells Lescaut of her feelings: 'Je suis encore tout étourdie' ('I am still absolutely stunned'). Once more there is a flurry of activity as preparations are made for the coach's departure. Lescaut goes off to fetch Manon's baggage; Guillot offers to elope with her; she laughs at him and his companions call him back. But he tells Manon that his coach will call in a few minutes and is at her service.

Lescaut comes back and Guillot rejoins his friends. Intending to go and play cards with the guardsmen, Lescaut solemnly warns Manon not to listen to any frivolous propositions. Left alone, she sings with sad resignation of her dreams as she sees the prettily dressed 'actresses' at the inn: 'Restons ici' ('Let us remain here').

The Chevalier Des Grieux enters, musing on his coming reunion with his father. Suddenly he sees Manon, and is at once enchanted by her. Within a few moments both are deeply in love. She tells him that she is destined for a convent, but he begs her to come to Paris with him and they sing together rapturously. The coach ordered by Guillot arrives and they decide to go to Paris together in it.

From inside the inn, the girls' laughter is heard, and Lescaut's voice. Lescaut and Guillot come out. In fury, Lescaut charges Guillot with the abduction of Manon. The innkeeper tells Lescaut that Manon went off with a young man in Guillot's coach. The bystanders mock Guillot as he vows revenge on the eloping pair.

ACT II: Des Grieux and Manon are living in a small Paris apartment. He is writing to his father, asking his consent to his marriage with Manon, and he and Manon read the letter over together. (From it we learn that she is only just sixteen.) Two men in soldier's uniform are brought in by the maid. One is Lescaut; the other, pretending to be Lescaut's fellow-guardsman, is De Brétigny, who hopes to become Manon's lover. (Manon recognizes him; Des

Grieux does not.) Des Grieux and Lescaut at first quarrel angrily;
Manon is afraid, and De Brétigny tries to restrain his friend. But Des
Grieux assures Lescaut of his honourable intentions. While he shows
him the letter he was writing, De Brétigny draws Manon aside and
tells her that Des Grieux's father plans to take him away from Paris
by force that very evening. De Brétigny dissuades her from warning
her lover; would she not prefer a life of luxury with De Brétigny to
poverty with Des Grieux?

The visitors depart and Des Grieux goes to send off his letter.
Alone, Manon refects on her weakness in failing to reject De
Brétigny's offer and on the coming end of her idyll with Des Grieux:
'Adieu, notre petite table' ('Farewell, our little table'). Des Grieux
returns and finds her in a sad mood. As they have their supper he tells
her of a dream he has had, a dream of happiness with her: 'Instant
charmant' ('Delightful moment'). He is interrupted by a knock on
the door. Manon is distressed and asks him not to answer it. But he
goes. Sounds of a scuffle are heard and he does not return.

ACT III: At the Cours-le-Reine, a place of promenading for fashionable Paris, street vendors are crying their wares amid a general
bustle. Poussette, Javotte and Rosette come out of a pavilion where
they have been dancing. Lescaut arrives, makes some purchases and
leaves. Guillot arrives and then De Brétigny, who speaks of Manon,
with whom he is now living. Presently Manon herself enters. She is
much admired by all the men present and sings a coquettish song to
them – expressing her mood in the gavotte 'Profitons bien de la
jeunesse' ('Let us make the most of youth').

Eventually Manon moves off to make some purchases. Meanwhile De Brétigny meets an old acquaintance, the Count Des Grieux
(father of Manon's previous lover), who tells him that his son has
gone to a seminary to train for the priesthood, after an unhappy love
affair. Manon overhears part of their conversation and, with some
embarrassment, questions the Count, pretending that his son's lover
was a friend of hers. The Count tells her that his son has now begun
to overcome his unhappiness.

Guillot arrives, with some friends (including Lescaut) and the
ballet dancers from the Opéra – brought by him to amuse and
impress Manon, whom he in turn hopes to win from De Brétigny.
Greeted by the crowds, the dancers perform a ballet. But Manon is
uninterested, thinking only of Des Grieux; she asks Lescaut to call
her carriage and, to Guillot's stupefaction, goes off to the St Sulpice
seminary.

The scene changes to the St Sulpice seminary. Worshippers are gathered there, praising the oratory of 'the Abbé Des Grieux'. He enters and his father talks to him, trying to dissuade him from entering the priesthood. But he will not be dissuaded. Left alone, he sings of his new desire – to forget Manon and find heavenly peace: 'Ah! fuyez, douce image' ('Oh flee, sweet vision'). He goes. Manon arrives at the seminary and, while the sound of prayer is heard from the chapel, she gives money to a porter who fetches Des Grieux. In their long duet which follows, he at first rejects her and tries to send her away. But she begs him to have pity and eventually he gives way: he can no longer overcome his love for her, and they go off together.

ACT IV: At a gambling-hall in Paris, Lescaut, Poussette, Javotte and Rosette are among the crowds. Guillot enters, soon followed by Manon, who has brought Des Grieux, against his better judgment. Manon and Lescaut try to persuade the unwilling Des Grieux to retrieve his fortunes at the tables. Singing of her love for him, she eventually succeeds, and when Guillot challenges him to a game he agrees. They play, watched excitedly by Manon and the three girls, for extravagant stakes.

Des Grieux consistently wins, and at length Guillot rises from the table and suggests he has been cheated. Des Grieux challenges him, but order is restored and Guillot goes off, threatening the lovers. The agitated crowd points suspiciously at Des Grieux. Soon there is a knock at the door: Guillot has returned with the police, to arrest Des Grieux for cheating and Manon as his accomplice. Des Grieux's indignation changes to remorse when his father enters. In an ensemble, Guillot rejoices in the prospect of revenge while the others plead for mercy. The Count promises his son that he will soon be freed, but he has no pity for Manon; the two are separated and taken off.

ACT V: Des Grieux is waiting on the road to Le Havre, where Manon and other women are to be taken for deportation as prostitutes. Lescaut comes. They had hoped to hold up the convoy of deportees and rescue Manon, but the plan has gone awry. The soldiers approach with their charges. The sergeant says that one of the girls (Manon) is half-dead and Lescaut bribes him to let him take her away, promising to bring her back later.

Lescaut leaves her and Des Grieux alone together. Des Grieux promises to contrive her rescue, but she is full of remorse. Her only consolation is a remembrance of their past happiness. Desperately

ill, she has no strength left to escape; she dies, and with a cry Des
Grieux falls over her body.

★　★　★

In *Manon*, Massenet makes telling use of a number of recurring
motives associated with his various characters, even though the
work is made up of separate musical numbers. A feature of the score
is the way in which, repeatedly, the orchestra takes on the role of
commentator and itself utters the motives. This was enough to gain
for the work the hostile label 'Wagnerian' from those who did not
really appreciate Wagner. But, with the hindsight of today we might
just as reasonably relate this trait to Puccini's method, particularly in
the way the orchestra proclaims, for example, De Brétigny's characteristic theme at the end of Act II – for although De Brétigny is now
off-stage, this is 'his' act: during it, he has won Manon. His theme is
shown in ex. 1.

Ex. 1

Manon is a girl in pursuit not of money or power but of pleasure.
She harbours no good-will or ill-will or any moral feeling. Her
music has a simple, light appeal; with complete naturalness of idiom
she tells Des Grieux of her past, ending: 'And that is the story of
Manon Lescaut!' (ex. 2). With this very phrase, at the end of the
opera, she dies.

Ex. 2

Des Grieux's music, happy or despairing, never loses its noble character, and at first seems to be able to match Manon's own capricious lightness (ex. 3). But Des Grieux, alas, is poor; poverty

Ex. 3

Nous vi - vrons à Pa - ris, Tous les deux, tous les deux

will diminish pleasure; and pleasure-loving Manon accepts the rich De Brétigny. She queens it at the Cours-la-Reine; this scene, with a ballroom off-stage, introduces the musically picturesque style of the eighteenth century – a minuet first of all, and later Manon's famous gavotte (ex. 4). The music of this scene is used to open the prelude (Massenet prefers this term to overture). The prelude also quotes other themes in the work – notably two which we do not hear again until the last act.

Ex. 4

Pro - fi - tons bien de la jeu - nes - se

WERTHER

*Libretto by Edouard Blau, Paul Milliet and
Georges Hartmann, after Goethe*

First performed: Vienna, 1893
Four Acts

Cast in order of singing:

THE BAILIFF		baritone or bass
JOHANN	FRIENDS OF THE BAILIFF	baritone or bass
SCHMIDT		tenor
SOPHIE, SECOND DAUGHTER OF THE BAILIFF		soprano
WERTHER, A VISITOR		tenor
CHARLOTTE, THE BAILIFF'S ELDEST CHILD		mezzo-soprano

BRÜHLMANN	⎫		⎧	*tenor*
KÄTCHEN	⎬	YOUNG LOVERS		*mezzo-soprano*
ALBERT, ENGAGED TO CHARLOTTE	⎭			*baritone*

Six younger children of the Bailiff; townsfolk; a manservant
The scene is laid in Wetzlar, near Frankfurt-on-Main, 'from July to
December in 178 . . .'

Goethe's *The Sorrows of Young Werther* (1774) was a novel which immediately made an impression on cultivated taste. Its hero shoots himself in unfulfilled love for a married woman – a deed said to have inspired several examples of actual suicide in its time. The novel waited more than a century for its successful operatic adaptation; it is not surprising that it received its first performance on a German-speaking stage, only in the following year being given in Paris and in French. The German names, when sung, are set by the composer with French stresses (Werther himself on the second syllable instead of, properly, the first) which sounds odd to non-French ears; so does 'Bacchus', similarly accented on the second syllable. The society depicted is of a bourgeois family with a cultivated taste for music and literature; a reference to Ossian's verse will be noted. Poetry ascribed to this ancient Gaelic bard was published in the 1760s and achieved a European fame: it was later judged to be virtually a forgery at the hand of its editor and supposed translator into English, James Macpherson.

In the cast-list, 'Bailiff' as a translation of Massenet's 'Bailli' is used in one of its historic English senses, a steward managing an estate for its owner.

★   ★   ★

ACT I: Although it is July, the Bailiff's six younger children are already being rehearsed in a Christmas carol by their father. They are in the garden. Their singing is careless until they are admonished to remember that Charlotte, their beloved elder sister, is listening to them from indoors. The Bailiff's friends Schmidt and Johann arrive a greet a younger sister, Sophie, who comes out from the house. The men speak of Werther, a young man in the Prince's service, and of Albert, Charlotte's fiancé. The two cronies leave with their favoured refrain, 'Vivat Bacchus!', by which they anticipate the pleasure of drinking at the inn.

All the others have gone inside when Werther, guided to the place by a peasant, arrives on his first visit. He is immediately enraptured by the peaceful beauty of the garden and the house beyond: 'Je ne sais si je veille ou si je rêve encore' ('I do not know whether I am awake or am still dreaming'). Glimpsed through a half-open door, the sight of the children (still carolling) entrances him further. They crowd round their adored sister Charlotte when she enters, and promptly she cuts a loaf and serves their evening meal before being introduced to Werther by her father. The Bailiff chaffs two young, utterly self-absorbed lovers, Brühlmann and Käthchen, who are also visiting him. Charlotte bids the children greet Werther warmly, as a 'cousin'. Werther again ecstatically contemplates this 'spectacle idéal d'amour et d'innocence'. He and Charlotte pass into the house and the Bailiff leaves ('Vivat Bacchus!') for the inn.

As darkness falls, Albert, who has been away, unexpectedly returns and is joyfully received by Sophie. But he declines to go in; he wishes to rejoin them all early next morning. Werther and Charlotte reappear from the house: his words to her take on a rising passion. Her reference to the dead mother whom she replaces in caring for the children only increases his fervour and his feelings of 'rêve, ecstase, bonheur' ('dream, ecstasy, happiness'). Charlotte, who has been swept away by his ardour, suddenly comes to herself: 'Nous sommes fous!' ('We are mad!') At that moment the Bailiff, having returned and learnt the news from Sophie, is heard calling out that Albert is back. Left alone, Werther voices his despair: 'Un autre . . . son époux!' ('Another . . . her betrothed!': *époux* also means, and later in this opera *will* mean, 'husband').

ACT II: At the inn on a Sunday morning, while the organ is heard from the church nearby, Schmidt and Johann drink and praise the Lord 'en exaltant ses dons' – by making the most of his gifts, i.e. the wine. Charlotte and Albert, now three months married, sit down in happy understanding, then go towards the church. Werther arrives, distraught: 'Un autre est son époux!' ('Another is her husband!'). He pours out his self-pity as he thinks of the embraces that might have been his. Schmidt and Johann now try to console Brühlmann, whose seemingly devoted sweetheart has left him. Albert comes out of the church and, with frank affection, recognizes and forgives Werther's tormented longing. In equal friendship Werther promises that his dream is now past and forgotten.

The intense mood is broken as the merry, simple-hearted Sophie enters with a bouquet. The Pastor's golden wedding is to be celebrated by a ball and she engages Werther, with mock seriousness, for 'the first minuet': her refrain is 'Tout le monde est joyeux!' ('Everyone is joyful!'). What irony for him!

Alone, Werther admits to himself that he lied to Albert. His passion for Charlotte is not dead: if he is to escape its consequences, he must go away. When she arrives she indeed asks him to go . . . but to return, as a friend, at Christmastime. Alone again, Werther wonders if he might be kindly received at another home (that is, if he should leave the world and come into the presence of God). The wild thought is interrupted by the re-entrance of Sophie. Abruptly, Werther leaves. Sophie weeps. As the procession for the golden wedding approaches, Albert sombrely guesses Werther's true feelings.

ACT III: On Christmas Eve, Charlotte is at home, thinking of the absent Werther: she takes out some of his letters and begins reading aloud: 'Je vous écris de ma petite chambre' ('I write to you from my little room'). While she anxiously ponders his hints of suicide, Sophie enters unexpectedly. Although the two houses are evidently at only a day's distance, Charlotte has not lately visited them and is sadly missed. Sophie wishes that her sister would laugh as she used to: 'Ah, le rire est béni' ('Ah, laughter is blessed').

When Sophie has left, Charlotte prays for guidance. As she finishes, softly, Werther appears at the door. He looks again round the familiar room, with the harpsichord ('Voici le clavecin') which used to accompany their singing together. He recalls a poem by Ossian in his own translation: 'Pourquoi me réveiller, ô souffle du printemps' ('Oh, why awaken me, thou breath of spring?'). She joins her voice to his; he repeats his love for her but at the point of yielding she breaks away and rushes from the room. Werther himself leaves the house.

Albert enters. The empty room with the street door open makes him suspicious, even when Charlotte returns. A servant enters with a note from Werther: will Albert lend him his pistols for a distant journey ('un lointain voyage')? Coldly, Albert obliges Charlotte to hand the pistols to the waiting servant. As Albert leaves the room, Charlotte thinks only of whether she can reach Werther's lodgings before the fatal deed is done.

ACT IV: In Werther's lodgings, on Christmas Night, the sight that greets Charlotte, as she rushes in, is his body outstretched and mortally wounded. To her anguished cries he responds faintly, asking for pardon. Once again he says 'I love you'; now, at last, she confesses the same. Outside the window the lights in the Bailiff's house can be seen. From the house come the clear voices of children in their carol. Werther takes its words as a symbol of redemption, and hopes that his grave will be blessed by a woman's tears. He dies and Charlotte falls in a faint. Through the window float the sounds of 'Noël! Noël!' and of laughter and happy cries.

* * *

Orchestral episodes (among them a prelude to each of the first three acts and a 'Christmas Night Symphony' before the fourth) have a strong part in establishing the atmosphere and in reinforcing themes which have been, or will be, associated with significant words. The other strong 'recall' is that of the carol – cheerfully rehearsed in the opening scene, and sung in the opera's last bars by children unaware of the tragic scene which their music reaches.

A jovial orchestral phrase, just after Schmidt and Johann have first entered, foreshadows their (and the Bailiff's) drinking-song, later given words (ex. 1). Later in the first act as Charlotte and Werther,

Ex. 1

Vi - vat Bac -chus! sem - per vi - [vat]

having first met, re-enter the garden, there is a tune which rises and falls with the simplest of contours, the simplest of harmonies, on the final notes of which Charlotte joins with the words 'Il faut nous séparer' ('Now we must part') – a daring musical depiction of a pure, naive companionship which cannot be sustained.

Charlotte's reading to herself of Werther's letters (Act III) may be regarded as the emotional core of the work comparable to Tatyana's *writing* her letter in Tchaikovsky's *Eugene Onegin* (page 364). The words which she recognizes as threatening suicide bring a heightened musical emotion. The orchestral strings shudder as she reads the words: 'Do not accuse me, but weep for me!' (ex. 2). The stage direction is 'Reading it over in terror, fearing to understand'. This motive reappears ominously in the orchestral movement which links this scene to Werther's death-scene, and also in the latter scene itself as Charlotte enters. The two light-hearted songs for the younger Sophie (fifteen years old against Charlotte's twenty, and soprano against mezzo-soprano) admirably set off Charlotte's own passionate outpourings.

Ex. 2

CLAUDE DEBUSSY

1862–1918

For part of his career, Debussy was a practising music critic as well as a composer, and what he wrote about other composers helps to define his own attitudes. Gluck he attacked as standing for 'Wagnerian formulas in embryo, which is unbearable'; Massenet and Gounod he defended, Bizet he exalted; Puccini and his Italian contemporaries he described as employing 'a film formula, whereby the characters fling themselves on one another and tear their melodies from each other's lips'; and one of Grieg's works was 'a pink bon-bon filled with snow'. Most significant was his love-and-hate affair with 'the arch-poisoner, Wagner'. He enormously admired Wagner's musical genius and his harmonic boldness, but totally rejected his symphonic method of composing operas in a texture woven out of leading-motives. In Debussy's view, the attempt to parallel the dramatic development with musical development is undramatic: 'Either the music gets out of breath in running after a character, or else the character sits down on a note to allow the music to catch up with him'.*

PELLÉAS ET MÉLISANDE
*Libretto: Maurice Maeterlinck's play, slightly adapted by
the composer*

First performed: Paris, 1902
Five Acts

*These translations are by Oscar Thompson, from his book *Debussy, Man and Artist* (1937).

Cast in order of singing:

GOLAUD, GRANDSON OF ARKEL	*baritone*
MÉLISANDE	*soprano*
GENEVIÈVE, ARKEL'S DAUGHTER-IN-LAW,	
MOTHER OF GOLAUD AND PELLÉAS	*mezzo-soprano*
ARKEL, KING OF ALLEMONDE	*bass*
PELLÉAS, GRANDSON OF ARKEL, HALF-BROTHER	
OF GOLAUD	*tenor*
YNIOLD, GOLAUD'S SON BY HIS FIRST MARRIAGE	*soprano*
	(or boy treble)
A SHEPHERD	*baritone*
A DOCTOR	*bass*

The scene is laid in the imaginary kingdom of
Allemonde in medieval times

Debussy and the Belgian dramatist Maurice Maeterlinck (1862–1949) were born in the same year. Maeterlinck's play *Pelléas et Mélisande* (1892) immediately commended itself to Debussy for an opera: he set the actual text of the play (very slightly cut and altered), not a conventional opera libretto worked up from it. This must be one of the few operas with singing parts for four generations: Yniold is son to Golaud, who is son to Geneviève, who is daughter-in-law to Arkel. One other play by Maeterlinck gave rise to an opera of some success: *Ariane et Barbe-Bleue* (1899), set in 1907 by Paul Dukas (1865–1935).

Debussy completed no other operas. He found nowhere else the inspiration which Maeterlinck had given him – the inspiration for a shadowy, legendary, understated tragic drama, in which the real and the symbolic intertwine, and in which the personages submit to fate. Ironically, Maeterlinck (after first having consented to the opera's being composed) publicly wished failure to the première: he had presumed that his wife would be chosen for the part of Mélisande, and she was not! The Scottish singer, Mary Garden, was.

The almost hypnotic, impressionistic appeal of Debussy's well-loved orchestral pieces – *L'après-midi d'un faune*, the *Nocturnes* – is felt too in this opera. There are no heroics, only the muted music suited to a remote kind of vision.

★   ★   ★

ACT I: In a forest, Mélisande is alone by a well. Golaud, who had been hunting in the forest and is now lost, chances upon her. He finds her trembling with fear and weeping, afraid even to be touched ('Ne me touchez pas!', she says). It emerges that she has been hurt, though she will not tell him by whom. Visible at the bottom of the well is a golden crown that fell from her head while she was weeping. She wishes to stay in the forest alone, but he insists that she comes with him.

In a room in the royal castle, several months later, Geneviève is reading to her father-in-law King Arkel a letter from her son Golaud to her other son Pelléas, in which he tells his half-brother how he discovered Mélisande and eventually made her his wife. He has asked Pelléas to find out whether Arkel, who had intended him to make a different marriage, would forgive him and receive them. Arkel agrees to do so. Pelléas enters, asking his grandfather for permission to visit a dying friend but, as his own father is ill and his brother just returning, Arkel tells him to wait, and to light the lamp signifying that Golaud's ship has permission to land.

Later, Golaud and Mélisande are understood to have landed. In front of the castle, Geneviève is in discussion with Mélisande. Pelléas enters and talks with them. In the distance the sound of boatmen in the harbour can be heard, and through the mist the ship which brought the newcomers can be seen setting sail again. Geneviève goes, leaving Pelléas to take Mélisande to the castle. In their brief moment alone together the seeds of love between them are sown.

ACT II: Pelléas and Mélisande are together by a well at a shaded spot in a park. Mélisande longs to touch the water but cannot reach. As she plays with the ring Golaud gave her, she drops it in the well; soon it is beyond their grasp and irretrievably lost. What shall they tell Golaud? 'La vérité!' ('The truth!'), says Pelléas.

Back in a room in the castle, Golaud is in bed. He was hurt in a riding accident – at noon, just the moment the ring was lost. By his bedside, Mélisande tries to make him comfortable. Suddenly he sees that she is weeping: in response to his kindly questions, she says she is unhappy in the gloomy surroundings of the castle and asks to be taken away. Golaud takes her hand, and sees that the ring is missing. He is much distressed and sends her out, in the dark, with Pelléas, to a cave by the shore where she untruthfully says it slipped off.

Pelléas takes her down to the cave (so that she will at least be able to describe it to Golaud). It is sinister and dark, and Mélisande is frightened, especially when the light of the moon discloses three aged paupers asleep. Pelléas leads her off, determining to come back another time.

ACT III: Mélisande is by herself at a window of one of the towers of the castle, singing as she combs her long hair. Seeing her from the path below, Pelléas is entranced by her beauty. At his request she leans far out and he takes her hand; then her hair tumbles down and envelops him, filling him with excitement. Doves fly around them. He refuses to let go of the long, soft tresses: 'Je les noue, je les noue' ('I am knotting them'), he sings. He finds they are caught in the branches of a tree; then Golaud comes, and tells them to stop playing childlishly so late at night.

Golaud, alone with Pelléas, shows him the dank vaults of the castle and then leads him up to the terrace. There he tells Pelléas that he witnessed what happened the previous night and is disturbed by the relationship between Pelléas and Mélisande; he asks Pelléas to spend less time in her company, and mentions that she may soon become a mother.

In front of the castle, Golaud, plagued by jealous suspicions, asks his child Yniold what happens when Pelléas and Mélisande are together. The child's replies are innocent: they talk, he says, about a door, or a light, or how he (Yniold) wil grow up into a big boy; once they kissed, when it was raining. There is nothing to anger Golaud, nothing to reassure him. A light goes on in Mélisande's room. Golaud holds Yniold up so that he can see in: Pelléas is there, he says, they are looking at one another, they are not close; but he begs to be put down, as this is hurting him. At length Golaud does so, and leads him off.

ACT IV: In a room in the castle, Pelléas and Mélisande meet. He tells her that he has been with his ailing father, who is now rather stronger. His father has told him to go on a journey. They arrange to meet that evening by the well, and Pelléas goes out.

Arkel enters. He has noticed Mélisande's unhappiness in the gloomy surroundings and is anxious about her. Then Golaud comes in, with blood on his forehead. Speaking angrily to Mélisande, he asks for his sword. He comments on her large, beautiful eyes; Arkel sees in them only 'a great innocence'. But Golaud derides her 'innocence'. Becoming more and more angry and agitated, he eventually seizes her by her hair, pulls her to her knees and drags her across the room in a passionate, jealous rage. Arkel stops him: he suddenly feigns calmness, while Mélisande weeps pitifully: 'Je ne suis pas heureuse!' ('I am not happy!')

By the well in the park, Yniold is playing. The bleating of sheep is heard as a shepherd and his flock pass nearby: the sheep are suddenly silent as the shepherd directs them away from their accustomed fold (they are to be slaughtered). Yniold goes. Pelléas arrives, soliloquizing: he understands now that he and Mélisande are deeply in love and that he must go away as soon as possible, to live only on his fading memories of her. Mélisande arrives. First he and then she admits their love: 'Je t'aime' . . . 'Je t'aime aussi'. It is dark and they can scarcely see one another. In the distance they hear the castle doors being barred and know that they are now certain to be discovered: 'Tout est perdu, tout est sauvé!' ('All is lost, all is won!'). They embrace. A moment later they hear and see Golaud, watching nearby; they keep calm, reconciled to the inevitable; as he comes they embrace, passionately, then again, still more passionately, for the last time. Golaud leaps at them, killing Pelléas, while Mélisande flees in terror.

ACT V: In a room in the castle, Mélisande is ill in bed, watched over by a doctor, Arkel and Golaud. She was wounded by Golaud, but the wound, the doctor says, is very slight, and not the cause of her illness. She has also given birth to a child. Golaud is repentant; he now believes that their embraces were not those of guilty lovers. She becomes conscious, but answers Arkel only vaguely. Golaud asks to be left alone with her. He begs for forgiveness, which she, not really comprehending, readily grants; then he asks whether her love with Pelléas was guilty, which she denies, but he presses her again and she returns to half-consciousness. Arkel comes in with the physician and talks to her, showing her the baby, which she is too weak to hold.

The servants silently assemble along the walls. Golaud again becomes impassioned and demands to be left alone with his dying wife. Arkel tries to calm him. The servants all fall to their knees as Mélisand's life ebbs away, and Arkel quietly observes her final tranquillity.

★   ★   ★

There are musical themes related to particular characters in *Pelléas et Mélisande*, of which we may instance the oboe theme before the curtain rises (ex. 1), which is to be associated with Mélisande (and last returns, also on the oboe, as she dies at the very end of the opera).

Ex. 1

But the method is not Wagnerian. Here we may quote from that authoritative Wagner scholar, Ernest Newman, in his *Opera Nights* (1943):

> It is characteristic of Debussy's entirely non-Wagnerian way of handling his motives that he should use the motive of Mélisande to accompany both her own words descriptive of Golaud, 'Oh, you hair is so grey' and Golaud's remark about herself, 'I am looking at your eyes. Do you never close your eyes?' Wagner would have shuddered at the thought of employing Mélisande's motive when it was a case of describing Golaud!

The declaration of love between Pelléas and Mélisande (Act IV) is in a sense both the climax of the opera and the ultimate expression of Debussy's method. At the opposite pole from conventionally rapturous, expansive operatic declarations of love we have Pelléas's low-toned confession: 'You do not know that it's because . . .' – and then he breaks off, inconsequentially as lovers do, to utter the crucial words. Mélisande follows him at the same level of pitch, an extraordinary effect (ex. 2).

Ex. 2

Notice the orchestral part with its repetition and variation of harmony. The placing of words in short, conversation-like phrases (the
antithesis of soaring Italian melody) also plays a notable part in the
dramatic expression, as in Mélisande's 'He doesn't love me any more
– I am not happy' in the previous scene (ex. 3).

Ex. 3

The harmonic language of the opera – especially sequences of
block chords outside the usual harmonic relationships – owes something to Musorgsky's *Boris Godunov*, a score of which came into
Debussy's hands in Paris about 1893.

BEDRICH SMETANA

1824–84

Debussy's opera shows an element of positive revolt against conventional notions of what opera should be. We turn back now to an earlier phenomenon of musical revolt: the desire of Czech and Russian composers to establish their own national music, often *against* the conventions of Italian opera and German symphony. Such revolutionary ideals in music often went along in sympathy with revolutionary politics too – as in the case of Smetana, now regarded as the founder of a Czech national style in concert-hall and opera-house.

Sympathizing with Czech national feeling against the dominion of the Austrian Empire, Smetana found the atmosphere of Prague oppressive after the crushing of the abortive revolution of 1848. He worked in Sweden from 1856 to 1861, but returned when an easing of Austrian rule made it possible for the Czechs to found in Prague a theatre for plays and opera in their own language. Smetana's work became the cornerstone of Czech opera and still remains so. Although his other seven operas are cherished by his countrymen and several (notably *Dalibor* and *The Kiss*) have justified themselves at festivals and in recordings, only *The Bartered Bride* entered the international repertory and remains there.

The operas of Antonin Dvořák (1841–1904) are also chiefly the preserve of Czechoslovak theatres, though *Rusalka* (1901) is occasionally heard elsewhere: the title-role is that of a water-nymph.

THE BARTERED BRIDE
(Prodaná Nevěsta)
Libretto by Karel Sabina

First performed: Prague, 1866
Three Acts

Cast in order of singing:

JENÍK, A PEASANT, SON OF MICHA BY HIS FIRST WIFE	*tenor*
MAŘENKA, DAUGHTER OF KRUŠINA AND LUDMILA	*soprano*
KECAL, A MARRIAGE BROKER	*bass*
KRUŠINA, A PEASANT	*baritone*
LUDMILA, HIS WIFE	*soprano*
VAŠEK, SON OF MICHA BY HIS SECOND WIFE	*tenor*
THE MANAGER OF A TROUPE OF STROLLING PLAYERS	*tenor*
ESMERALDA, A DANCER ⎫	*soprano*
THE INDIAN ⎬ MEMBERS OF THE	*tenor*
HÁTA, MICHA'S ⎭ TROUPE	*mezzo-soprano*
SECOND WIFE	
MICHA, A LANDLORD	*bass*

Chorus of villagers, actors and children
The scene is laid in a Bohemian village, on the Patron
Saint's day, in the first half of the nineteenth century

Lively rustic jollification, with catchy airs and invigorating dances
– this, rather than any dramatic subtlety or opportunity for vocal
fireworks, is provided by *The Bartered Bride*. We give this opera the
title fixed by custom, but the Czech would be more literally
rendered *The Sold Fiancée*.

★　★　★

ACT I: The exuberant overture sets the mood for the opening
scene: a village with an inn and – for it is a festive day – a fair.
Among the cheerful villagers only Mařenka is sad. Her sweetheart,
Jeník, asks why: because her parents are planning her marriage with
a man she cannot love, she tells him – Vašek, the dull-witted son of
Micha. Jeník, she feels, does not show sufficient concern; she asks
him whether his mysterious past includes a love-affair. He reassures her, explaining that he was turned out after his father's second
marriage. They sing about the strength of their love and their
confidence in the future.

They go off and Mařenka's parents, Krušina and Ludmila, enter
with Kecal, a marriage broker, who is haranguing them about
keeping to the bargain they have made. The husband, he says, is
Micha's son, not the good-for-nothing one who disappeared, but
Vašek: in the solo and trio which follow he assures them to their

satisfaction that although the boy is a bit slow and odd he has every other virtue in abundance.

Mařenka enters. They tell her what they are planning, but Ludmila makes it clear that they will not insist on the marriage without Mařenka's consent. Mařenka objects that she has a lover to whom she has sworn fidelity. Confident of overcoming this trifling obstacle, Kecal determines to go off to the inn to have a word with her lover, Jeník, but is not entirely pleased when Krušina decides that Mařenka should at least meet Vašek.

The scene changes to the village inn, where young people dance and sing in a lively polka.

ACT II: At the inn, the young men are singing in praise of beer, while Jeník praises love; Kecal, watching them, praises only money. They dance a Furiant. Then Vašek enters – a ridiculous, stuttering figure. Mařenka arrives. She tells Vašek (who does not know her) that everyone pities him for having to marry such a disagreeable girl as Mařenka, especially as someone else is pining for him – implying it is herself. She runs off, with him in pursuit.

Kecal approaches Jeník, promising to find him a rich wife and, in a duet, emphasizes the importance of money in marriage. Then he offers Jeník a hundred crowns to give up Mařenka. When the offer has trebled, Jeník agrees – on condition that Mařenka marries no one other than Micha's eldest son. While Kecal goes to draw up the contract with this added clause, Jeník expresses his surprise that the broker could imagine that he would give her up so readily. Kecal returns with the contract, and with Krušina and many villagers as witnesses, Jeník signs. All are astonished and disgusted that he should have bartered his bride-to-be so readily.

ACT III: Vašek, alone on the village green, anxiously bewails his prospective fate as husband of the terrible Mařenka. A group of strolling players is about to perform and their manager calls out all the attractions. The 'Dance of the Show-people' (or 'of the Comedians') follows. Vašek is interested by the troupe, especially by Esmeralda, the Spanish dancer. The Indian in the troupe comes to the manager with news that the man who plays the dancing bear is drunk. Esmeralda, with hints of love, entices Vašek to take his place and she and the manager start showing him what he has to do.

Vašek's parents, Micha and Háta, arrive with Kecal, who has the marriage contract. To their consternation, Vašek refuses to sign because of what he has heard about Mařenka. Mařenka, distraught at Jeník's apparent perfidy, enters with her parents, who, with Kecal and Vašek's parents in support, try to obtain her signature to the contract. Vašek, who had wandered off, is called back, and he recognizes Mařenka as the girl who spoke to him in the morning; he is now willing to sign, but Mařenka wants time to think it over. The four parents and Kecal agree to leave her alone for a few minutes. She sings, with bitter nostalgia, of her dreams of happiness with Jeník.

Jeník enters. Mařenka will not hear a word from him, cutting off contemptuously all his efforts to explain. In a lively duet he complains of her obstinacy, while she upbraids him. Kecal arrives. Jeník mentions the clause in the contract about her marrying Micha's son, gently assuring her that Micha's son will always love her.

The villagers and the four parents return and ask Mařenka what she has decided: to annoy Jeník, she says, she will marry Vašek. All congratulate her, including Jeník himself. Háta and Micha are disconcerted to see him – especially when Jeník greets Micha as his father (the significance of the added clause now becomes clear). Kecal too is taken aback. Háta sneers at Jeník but Mařenka, free to choose and at last realizing what has happened, of course chooses Jeník, to Kecal's annoyance and Háta's fury. The villagers join in the laughter at Kecal's expense.

Suddenly there are cries of confusion, as a 'bear' appears. It is Vašek, to Háta's rage and embarrassment. She leads him off, while Ludmila, Krušina, Micha and the villagers congratulate the united lovers.

★   ★   ★

Though the plot of *The Bartered Bride* hangs so perilously on one improbability (why does Jeník not tell Mařenka of his plan?), the opera lives by the racy cut of its melodies. They are closely related to those of the dance, even when not actually danced to on the stage. Smetana's gift was to find a great variety of exact musical characterizations, all within this melodic type.

Kecal the marriage-broker is the confident business-man, seemingly sharper than these village folk but really not so sharp as he thinks (ex. 1). Note the *sforzando* slaps-on-the-back in the orchestra!

Ex. 1

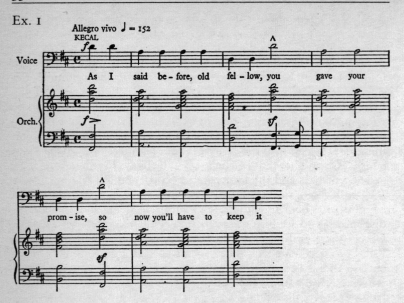

Vašek stutters nervously, opening his song (ex. 2) – and again, note the orchestral accompaniment with its continuation of the stuttering (bar 5).

Ex. 2

Though hero and heroine are allowed their music of real sentiment, even they are perhaps most memorably caught in the bickering duet of the last act (ex. 3). The tune is one which is naturally performed with a pulling-back of the rhythm at first and then a gradual resumption of tempo.

Ex. 3

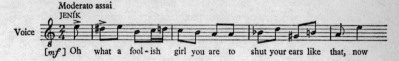

But to deduce that the score uses only a simple kind of music would be wrong. The cleverness of Smetana's art may be seen in the echoing of voices (not strictly in canon) in the lovers' Act I duet, and in the similar give-and-take in Kecal's and Jeník's matchmaking duet in Act II, which in the theatre is perhaps the most taking number in the whole score.

ALEXANDER BORODIN

1833–87

The first Russian operas to become internationally famous were those of Mikhail Ivanovich Glinka (1804–57): *A Life for the Tsar* (1836, now performed in Russia under Glinka's first intended title, 'Ivan Susanin') and *Ruslan and Lyudmila* (1842). The nationalist-historical element in the first and the Russian-legendary element in the second were prophetic of much that was to follow in Russian opera. So was the literary inspiration of Pushkin (in *Ruslan and Lyudmila*) and Glinka's use of musical elements drawn from Russian folksong.

Borodin, like Musorgsky and Rimsky-Korsakov (see pages 357 and 375), was a member of the nationalist group of composers called 'The Five' or 'The Mighty Handful'. A professor of chemistry, he had a severely limited time available for music; but the fact that his only opera, *Prince Igor*, was left unfinished at his death appears partly due to other reasons. For nearly five years he left it almost untouched. It was completed after his death by his close associates, Rimsky-Korsakov and Alexander Glazunov (1865–1936): the over-ture was written out and orchestrated by Glazunov, to whom Borodin had often played it on the piano.

PRINCE IGOR
(Knyaz Igor)
Librettor by the composer

First performed: St Petersburg, 1890
Prologue and four Acts

Cast in order of singing:

IGOR, PRINCE OF SEVERSK		*baritone*
PRINCE GALITZKY, HIS BROTHER–IN–LAW		*bass*
SKULA ⎫ PLAYERS OF THE GUDOK★ AND		⎰ *bass*
YEROSHKA ⎭ DESERTERS FROM IGOR'S ARMY		⎱ *tenor*
YAROSLAVNA, IGOR'S SECOND WIFE		*soprano*
A NURSE IN YAROSLAVNA'S HOUSEHOLD		*soprano*
A POLOVTSIAN MAIDEN		*soprano*
KONCHAKOVNA, DAUGHTER OF KHAN KONCHAK		*mezzo-soprano*
VLADIMIR, IGOR'S SON BY HIS FIRST MARRIAGE		*tenor*
OVLUR, A BAPTIZED POLOVTSIAN SOLDIER		*tenor*
KHAN KONCHAK, A PRINCE OF THE POLOVTSI		*bass*

[The role of Khan Gzak is silent.]

Chorus of Russian and Polovtsi (soldiers, people,
prisoners, etc.)
*The scene is laid in Putivl (a town of the Seversk region)
and in the camp of the Polovtsi, in 1185*

Prince Igor sketches, in bold musical contours, a tale of war and peace, honour and dishonour. It makes dramatic and musical use of the picturesqueness of the orient, sometimes for barbaric effect. Its story is set in the twelfth century when Russia – at that time a loose federation of principalities – was under pressure from the Tatars. The Tatar (otherwise Mongol) power, known as the 'Khanate of the Golden Horde', became even stronger in the next century and actually established sovereignty over Russia. The Polovtsi were one of these Tatar peoples.

In the opera, Prince Igor, ruling at Putivl, leads the Russians; he falls prisoner to Konchak, one of the Khans (princes) who rule the Polovtsi. The Russians are Christians (they were converted about 990); the Polovtsi are pagan, but among them is one, Ovlur, who has accepted Christianity and treacherously offers to help Igor escape.

It is an opera of spectacle, especially in the famous Polovtsian Dances with chorus, which end the second act. Dramatically it displays noble enemies in opposition. The three leading male characters – Igor, Konchak, Galitzky – are baritone, bass and bass, which

★An old Russian bowed instrument with three strings.

lends a distinctive vocal colour to the score; and frequently the same singer doubles the two bass roles.

★　　★　　★

PROLOGUE: Outside the cathedral in Putivl, Prince Igor is acclaimed as he prepares to march to war against the Polovtsian Khans. An eclipse of the sun takes place, which Galitzky (Igor's brother-in-law) and others regard as a bad omen. Igor nevertheless sets out amid further acclaim. Two merry ne'er-do-wells, Skula and Yeroshka, desert from Igor's army, preferring to serve under Galitzky and avoid a foreign campaign. Igor bids farewell to his sorrowing wife Yaroslavna; his son Vladimir, who is to serve with his father, joins in. Igor appoints Galitzky to rule in his absence, then sets off on horseback with his army.

ACT I: In Galitzky's home his retainers are rejoicing, Yeroshka and Skula among them. Now that Igor is away, Galitzky too rejoices. If only he were really the ruling prince, what a merry reign would be his! A group of girls enters to complain that one of their number has been abducted by Galitzky's men. He refuses to give her up, and leaves. Skula and Yeroshka mock the petitioners, then embark on a drinking song with chorus in Galitzky's honour. They and their fellows wish Galitzky were their real ruler.

Meanwhile, in her home, Igor's wife Yaroslavna pines for her husband. Ushered in by a nurse, the girls who have vainly implored Galitzky's justice now ask Yaroslavna's help. They leave, and Galitzky enters: Yaroslavna argues with him fiercely until he promises to free the abducted girl. He leaves.

A group of noblemen enters with sad tidings for Yaroslavna: her husband and his men are prisoners of the Polovtsi. Moreover, the alarm bells sound even now and distant fires are seen; the enemy is marching on Putivl.

ACT II: In the camp of the Polovtsi, at evening, young girls are singing (with solo) and dancing. Konchakovna, the daughter of the Khan Konchak, is looking forward to seeing the man she loves. She tells the girls to give food and drink to a group of Russian prisoners-of-war who now enter. A patrol of Polovtsian soldiers, providing guards for the night, sings and departs – except Ovlur, a Christian convert among the Polovtsi. He remains on guard, unobserved, when Vladimir (a prisoner like his father) enters and calls for his beloved. It is Konchakovna. She enters: they declare their love for one another and leave.

Igor himself appears, singing of his longing to be free. Ovlur, discloses himself and offers to help Igor escape; but Igor, deeming such behaviour dishonourable, declines.

Konchak enters, treating his captive as an esteemed noble guest, offering him treasure and slave-girls, and asking him to stay and become his ally – or to go home, on condition of not renewing the war. Igor declines the condition. Konchak admires his honourable behaviour, and entertains his guest with male and female dancers and singers (the Polovtsian Dances).

ACT III: A march introduces a scene in the Polovtsian camp. The Polovtsi (basses) hail the arrival of the men of an allied army (tenors) under Khan Gzak. Konchak proclaims the success of the campaign. The victors leave for a feast, after which they will decide on the next military steps. The Russian prisoners, downcast, believe that only if Igor were free could a Russian force turn back their enemies.

The Polovtsian soldiers guarding the prisoners begin to sing and dance; they become drunk and fall down, asleep. Ovlur enters, and this time Igor, realizing his countrymen's dependence on him, accepts his help: he and his son will try to escape.

Konchakovna enters, seeking to persuade Vladimir to stay while his father urges their departure. Vladimir decides to leave with his father – but, as they try to make their escape, the lovesick Konchakovna raises the alarm. The Polovtsi, with Konchak following, rush in. Igor has escaped but Vladimir is recaptured. Konchak gives his orders: let Vladimir be free, and marry his daughter, but let the guards who permitted the escape be hanged. The crowd hails Konchak and the coming campaign.

ACT IV: Seated atop the city walls of Putivl, Yaroslavna laments the plight of her people and herself. A group of countryfolk appears, having fled before the oncoming Khans. But Yaroslavna sees a Russian prince approaching, ready to lead the defence of the city. She recognizes him: it is Igor. They embrace.

Yeroshka and Skula, tipsy and playing their gudoks, enter with a song about the happiness they have been enjoying while Igor has been a captive – only to behold him then, in conversation with his wife as he enters the citadel. They decide that it is not worth running away and instead start sounding the bells to announce Igor's return. The crowd assembles joyfully. All acclaim Igor as he and his wife emerge in state from the citadel, ready to lead the people once more.

★　★　★

The celebrated overture contains some of the most stirring tunes of
the opera. The rapid alternation of trumpets comes from the reunion
of the triumphant Polovtsi and their allies in Act III; and two bold
tunes which come later are both taken from Igor's soliloquy in Act II
(ex. 1).

Ex. 1

The 'oriental' element in the music, familiar in the concert-hall in
the Polovtsian Dances, is also reflected in the music of Konchakovna. Her invocation to the absent Vladimir in Act IV (ex. 2)
uses one characteristic melodic interval (in this case from D sharp to
C natural) which also served Verdi as an orientalism in *Aida*.

Ex. 2

MODEST MUSORGSKY

(1839–81)

Musorgsky was a Russian army officer and later an unimportant
civil servant. He did not study music systematically and the composer's technique which he forged was very much his own. But his
willingness to tolerate a certain 'roughness' of sound, without the
gloss that might have been brought by academic training, fitted his
desire to reproduce Russian speech-inflexions in his music and to use
the folk-music idioms of the Russian people.

Musorgsky's masterpiece is the opera *Boris Godunov*. Out of
mistaken devotion, his friend Rimsky-Korsakov applied himself
after Musorgsky's death to 'correcting' what he conceived to be
crudities in the score of the opera; but Rimsky-Korsakov's version,
though persisting by the sheer idolence of some singers and opera
companies, is now recognized as falsifying Musorgsky's conception. A version by Shostakovich (1940) imposes a new orchestration
on the original melodies and harmonies; but in 1975 an edition by
David Lloyd-Jones restored all aspects of Musorgsky's original.

Living a disorderly life, succumbing to drink, and dying early,
Musorgsky left his other operas unfinished; they therefore had to
come under someone else's hand if they were to be produced. *The
Khovansky Affair* (in Russian, *Khovanshchina*) was completed and
characteristically retouched by Rimsky-Korsakov, and produced in
1886; a later completion, truer to Musorgsky, has been made by
Shostakovich. *Sorochintsy Fair*, left much less complete, has been
finished in at least four different versions by different hands; *The
Marriage*, also left very incomplete, was not performed until 1931 in
Moscow in a version finished by Mikhail Ippolitov-Ivanov
(1859–1935).

BORIS GODUNOV
Libretto by the composer, after Pushkin

First performed: St Petersburg, 1874
Prologue and Four Acts

Cast in order of singing:

A POLICE OFFICER	*baritone*
MITYUKHA, ONE OF THE CROWD IN MOSCOW	*bass*
SHCHELKALOV, SECRETARY OF THE STATE COUNCIL	*baritone*
PRINCE SHUISKY, A LEADER OF THE NOBLES	*tenor*
BORIS GODUNOV, TSAR	*baritone*
PIMEN, A MONK AND CHRONICLER	*bass*
GRIGORI, AFTERWARDS KNOWN AS DMITRI, THE PRETENDER	*tenor*
HOSTESS OF AN INN	*mezzo-soprano*
MISSAIL ⎱ VAGABOND MONKS	⎰ *tenor*
VARLAAM ⎰	⎱ *bass*
AN OFFICER	*bass*
XENIA, BORIS'S DAUGHTER	*soprano*
FYODOR, BORIS'S SON (A YOUNG CHILD)	*mezzo-soprano*
NURSE TO BORIS'S CHILDREN	*contralto*
A BOYAR (NOBLEMAN) IN WAITING	*tenor*
MARINA MNISZEK, A POLISH PRINCESS	*soprano*
RANGONI, HER CONFESSOR, A JESUIT	*bass*
A SIMPLETON	*tenor*
LAVITZKY ⎱ JESUITS	⎰ *bass*
CHERNIKOVSKY ⎰	⎱ *bass*
KRUSHCHOV, A NOBLEMAN	*bass*

Chorus of Russian people, boyars, Poles, etc.
The scene is laid in Russia and Poland in 1598–1605

Boris Godunov himself – a tsar tormented not only by political intrigue but by his own conscience – is one of opera's most subtle and most commanding roles. Yet neither Boris nor anyone else is allowed to dominate Musorgsky's opera. We are shown a slice of history, and in history rulers come and go like other mortals. Historical fact is at the basis of Pushkin's chronicle-play (in twenty-four scenes) on which the opera is founded. Boris Godunov reigned as tsar from 1598 to 1605. In 1604 a pretender arose who claimed to be Dmitri, the supposedly murdered son of a previous tsar. He gained support among the Poles, intriguing with the Polish princess Marina Mniszek, and eventually usurped the throne for a brief period.

The opera is concerned with Boris's coronation, his guilty conscience, his relationship with his children, and his death; and with Dmitri (who is here depicted as a runaway monk, Grigori) and his relationship with Marina and his bid for the throne. Another major participant is the People – buffeted by political change, compelled to cheer when the police order it, breaking out in wild acts of rough justice, and producing the symbolic, pathetic figure of the Simpleton (or 'the Idiot', as he is sometimes called).

Originally Musorgsky gave his opera no love interest and Marina did not appear. This original version (1868–9) had only seven scenes; the seventh showed the death of Boris, and the previous one was set outside St Basil's Cathedral in Moscow, introducing the Simpleton.

In this form the opera was rejected by the organization of the Imperial Theatres in St Petersburg. Musorgsky thereupon expanded and revised his scheme. He rewrote the scene for Boris and his children; he put in a 'Polish act', bringing in Marina; he scrapped the scene outside St Basil's; and *after* the death of Boris he placed a new scene, set in a wood-clearing near Kromy, introducing the Simpleton here instead.

This revised version (1871–2) is regarded as the definitive one: the synopsis which follows corresponds to it. It was slightly cut by the composer in a vocal score published in 1874. There is a case for performing either this definitive version or the earlier, more terse version (without the love interest).

★   ★   ★

PROLOGUE: Outside the Novodevichy monastery in Moscow, the crowd in obedience to a policeman utters lamentations. Inside is Boris Godunov, who – as Shchelkalov, secretary of the State Council, now declares sadly – has declined the throne, despite the wishes of the nobles and clergy. A band of pilgrims arrives and enters the monastery. The police officer orders the crowd to appear at the Kremlin at dawn next day.

Next day the people are assembled in the courtyard of the Kremlin. Shuisky hails Boris, who has at last consented to become tsar and who now emerges, crowned. He speaks, revealing his troubled mind. The people hail him.

ACT I: In a monastery at Chudov, by night, an old monk, Pimen, is writing a chronicle of Russia. Dawn nears; the chanting of monks is heard. Grigori Otrepyev, a young monk sleeping in the cell, awakens. He asks and receives Pimen's blessing, then speaks of a dream that haunts him; he sees a crowd in Moscow pointing with scorn at him. Pimen speaks how he himself saw, twelve years before, the body of the young Prince Dmitri, son of the late Tsar, who had been killed by order of the usurping Boris Godunov. Grigori (with cries of 'Boris, Boris!') is strongly impressed – and Pimen has mentioned that, were Dmitri still alive, he would be just of Grigori's age.

In a roadside inn, the hostess is singing to herself. Travellers arrive: two vagabond monks, Missail and Varlaam, followed by Grigori, who is now in peasant's clothes. The monks drink. Varlaam sings a racy song, 'Kak'vo gorode bilo vo Kazani' ('Thus it was at the town of Kazan'), about the military exploits of Tsar Ivan. Grigori is restive: planning to pose as Dmitri and to claim the Russian throne, he wants first of all to cross the nearby frontier into Lithuania (part of the kingdom of Poland at this time).

Frontier guards knock, enter, and announce that they have a warrant for the arrest of one Grigori (short form, Grishka) Otrepyev. The illiterate guard hands the warrant to Grigori who reads out the description of the wanted man, but falsely, to make it correspond to Varlaam. Eventually Varlaam himself manages to read it out correctly, but in the nick of time Grigori escapes.

ACT II: In a room in the Kremlin, Boris's daughter, Xenia, is weeping for her dead fiancé. Her young brother Fyodor is engrossed by a mechanical clock. The old nurse tries to comfort Xenia with a song about a gnat. After another song (by the nurse and Fyodor) Boris suddenly enters. Xenia and the nurse leave; Fyodor with a globe proudly shows his father the Russian empire on it. As Fyodor withdraws, Boris sings of the unhappiness he foresees and how the thought of the murdered Dmitri haunts him: 'Dostig ya vishe vlasti' ('I am supremely powerful').

A noise is heard outside. A boyar (nobleman) in waiting enters with news of a civil disturbance caused by Shuisky. Fyodor re-enters and tells his father how the noise outside was caused by a pet parrot misbehaving.

Shuisky enters, and Boris accuses him of plotting. Shuisky says a

Pretender has arisen in Lithuania under the name of Dmitri – a name that shakes Boris, who seeks confirmation from Shuisky that the true Dmitri was in fact killed. Left alone, agitated, Boris imagines that the moving figures on the mechanical clock – which now begins to strike – are a vision of the murdered child.

ACT III: At Sandomir Castle in Poland, Princess Marina is being adorned by her attendants. But she does not care for the idle flattery of their song. She wants to hear of Poland's glory and hopes that Dmitri (with whom she has fallen in love) will make her empress in Moscow. Her confessor, the Jesuit Rangoni, tells her to lead Dmitri on and win his allegiance to the Roman Catholic Church. Marina curses Rangoni's artfulness, but gives way.

In the castle garden by moonlight the lovesick Grigori – or Dmitri, as he now calls himself – is awaiting Marina. Rangoni appears, addressing him as Tsarevich, and asking to be accepted as his spiritual guide. A polonaise is heard. Marina, who is entertaining guests, passes by with an old nobleman; the guests sing of Poland's coming triumph over the Russians.

Marina re-enters. Obedient to Rangoni, she pretends to spurn Dmitri's promises of love and demands assurance of a throne. They quarrel, then are reconciled; Rangoni, aside, is gleeful.

ACT IV: The State Council of Boyars is meeting in the Moscow Kremlin. The secretary of the council, Shchelkalov, announces Boris's wish for support against the Pretender. They give it. Shuisky (whom the others suspect of rebellion) enters and reports that he secretly observed Boris trembling, declaring he saw the ghost of the murdered Dmitri, and calling 'Chur, ditya' ('Out, child!').

Boris himself, ill, lurches in and speaks those very words. He sits down. Shuisky, having asked permission, withdraws to bring in a monk who has sought audience. It is Pimen, who declares that he had become blind but, on revisiting the grave of the murdered Tsarevich Dmitri, was miraculously cured.

Boris falls. Knowing that death is near, he sends for his son and dismisses the boyars. Bells toll. He tells Fyodor to mistrust the boyars and to champion the people and the Russian Church. Distant voices are heard; the boyars re-enter, and Boris dies.

In a forest clearing near Kromy, the rebellious crowd are baiting Krushchov, a captured boyar who is a supporter of Boris. A simpleton enters and sings religious words. Urchins mock him and tap the old pan he wears for a hat. Missail and Varlaam (the vagabond monks) enter and lead the crowd in praise of Dmitri; two

Jesuits, Lavitzy and Chernikovsky, also praise Dmitri – in Latin – but the crowd turn against them and take them into the forest to hang them.

Heralded by a trumpet-call, Dimitri enters on horseback. The crowd hail him. Krushchov shakes off his bonds and hails him too. Dmitri urges all: 'To Moscow!'. The voices of the Jesuits, in prayer, are heard off-stage. All follow Dmitri off, leaving only the simpleton singing of unhappy Russia.

★ ★ ★

Boris Godunov is remarkable for its reproduction of ordinary speech-rhythms – the music thus being asymmetrical, with frequent changes of time-signature. Musorgsky also uses actual folk-tunes, notably ex. 1, which becomes the crowd's salute to Boris on his coronation.

Ex. 1

When in Act II the monk Pimen is writing his chronicle, a graphic musical figure 'describes' the slow moving of the pen over parchment – first continuously, then intermittently as the work draws to an end and Pimen comments on the approaching dawn. Later, as Pimen tells Grigori the story of the murdered Dmitri, we hear ex. 2.

Ex. 2

The accompaniment figure in that last bar characterizes Dmitri throughout – that is, the real murdered Dmitri and also Grigori, as the Pretender. Other themes recur in the opera, though less prominently. But one theme associated with Boris recurs (in the bass of the accompaniment) at the beginning of the death scene (ex. 3). The unemphatic vocal line given to Boris is typical: the role calls not for great vocal range or agility but for the ability to bring out the dramatic intensity behind notes which look, on paper, as ordinary as this.

Ex. 3

PYOTR ILYICH TCHAIKOVSKY

1840–93

Tchaikovsky completed eight operas, three of them based on the writings of his country's greatest poet, Alexander Pushkin (1799–1837). Of these three, two have entered and remained in the international repertory, and in Russia today are regarded as stable favourites. *Eugene Onegin* (1879) is the more lyrical; Tchaikovsky was utterly absorbed in the purely human passion of his heroine, Tatyana. *The Queen of Spades* (1890) is on a broader canvas. Less well known is a one-act opera which has a fairy-tale atmosphere and is known from its French heroine's name as *Yolande* or, in Russian, *Iolanta* (1892).

As a composer, Tchaikovsky is far better known for his ballets than for his operas, but his operatic style is at its best compelling. While Musorgsky, in his setting of Russian words, aimed at a representation of the realism of speech, Tchaikovsky preferred a romantic idiom with formal numbers. Both *Eugene Onegin* and *The Queen of Spades* include ballroom scenes with brilliant dance music, giving scope for ballet.

EUGENE ONEGIN
Libretto by the composer and K. S. Shilovsky,
after Pushkin's narrative poem

First performed: Moscow, 1879
Three Acts

Cast in order of singing:

TATYANA	} DAUGHTERS OF MME LARINA	{ *soprano*
OLGA		{ *contralto*

FILIPEVNA, THEIR OLD NURSE	*mezzo-soprano*
MME LARINA, A LANDOWNER	*mezzo-soprano*
VLADIMIR LENSKY, ENGAGED TO OLGA	*tenor*
EUGENE ONEGIN, HIS FRIEND	*baritone*
TIKHON PETROVICH BUYANOV, A CAPTAIN	*bass*
TRIQUET, A FRENCH TUTOR	*tenor*
ZARETSKY, A FRIEND OF LENSKY	*bass*
PRINCE GREMIN	*bass*

[The role of Guillot, a coachman, is silent.]

The scene is laid on a Russian country estate
near St Petersburg in the 1820s

For many, the most remarkable character of the opera is not that of the title-role; it is the heroine, Tatyana, with her romantic longings. Tchaikovsky himself almost fell in love with his creation. The action is placed at a time when the English romantic novel swept the literary taste of Europe. 'Oh, Grandison! . . . Oh, Richardson!' sighs Tatyana's mother, Mme Larina. *Sir Charles Grandison* is the title of a novel (1753) by the English writer Samuel Richardson.

Tatyana (sometimes referred to by the pet forms Tanya and Tanyusha), is also a novel-reader, and her literary, romantic conception of love is contrasted with the matter-of-fact approach of her sister Olga.

'Prince' in imperial Russia indicates the highest rank of aristocracy but *not* royalty. 'Larina' is the feminine form of the surname Larin.

* * *

ACT I: Mme Larina, assisted by Filipevna (her children's old nurse), is making jam on a portable stove in her garden. From inside the house a song is heard: Larina's two daughters, Tatyana and Olga, are singing a duet. The voices of Larina (reminiscing about her youth and marriage) and Filipevna are added and continue when the girls' song has ended.

The singing of peasants is heard. They approach and offer Larina a decorated sheaf as a symbol of the collected harvest. They sing and dance for her, then leave. Tatyana and Olga come out. Olga sings of her merry disposition. Larina bids Filipevna provide the peasants with refreshment. Tatyana looks sad – because of the tragic novel she is reading, she explains.

Filipevna announces the arrival of Lensky, Olga's betrothed; Onegin, a new neighbour whom they have not formally met, is with him and is presented. Larina and Filipevna leave the four young people together. Tatyana is romantically impressed by Onegin; Onegin, blasé, is mildly taken with Tatyana.

Lensky approaches Olga with loving words, and they walk away. Onegin asks Tatyana whether country life does not bore her; she replies that she daydreams. They stroll off. Lensky returns with Olga and declares his love for her ('Ya lyublyu vas'). Larina and Filipevna come out of the house again and beckon the others in. Filipevna comments to herself on Tatyana's bashful appearance: has she taken a fancy to this 'new gentleman'?

The scene changes to Tatyana's bedroom. She is in her nightdress, but does not feel sleepy and lets Filipevna tell her of her own strange marriage. Then she bids her go. Left alone, she writes a letter to Onegin, having difficulty in finding the right words. In it she confesses her love for him.

Dawn comes. Filipevna re-enters. Tatyana gives her the letter to send – and Filipevna pretends at first not to know for whom it is intended.

Next day, in a far corner of the Larins' garden, peasant girls sing as they gather berries, then move off. Tatyana enters, agitated, for Onegin is approaching: he speaks courteously but coldly to her of the letter she sent him, making it clear that he does not return her passion. She is mortified and silent. The peasant girls' chorus is heard again.

ACT II: At a ball at the Larins' to celebrate Tatyana's name-day, a waltz is danced amid conversation. Captain Buyanov, acting as host, is surrounded by girls; Onegin dances with Tatyana and overhears ill-natured gossip about himself. Bored, he determines on an idle revenge on Lensky for bringing him here. He takes Olga away from Lensky for a dance – 'Proshu vas!' ('Allow me!') – and flirts with her. The other guests' gay comments are resumed over the waltz. When it is ended, Lensky confronts Olga and Onegin angrily but they go off for another dance.

Triquet, the old French tutor, is brought forward and sings an old-fashioned song of compliments to Tatyana.

A cotillion begins. Onegin and Lensky, not dancing, quarrel:

Lensky challenges Onegin to a duel. Larina protests at such an upset in her house. 'V vashem dome' ('In your house') says Lensky, bitterly recalling his former pleasure there; all the guests join in. Tempers rise; Lensky calls Onegin a seducer and Onegin hurls himself on Lensky. The pair leave separately, Lensky bidding Olga a final farewell.

Early the next morning, by a river bank, Lensky is waiting with his second, Zaretsky, for Onegin to appear for the duel. Zaretsky withdraws, and Lensky, alone, laments the bygone golden days – 'Kuda, kuda . . .?' ('How distant, how distant') – and laments for Olga, whom he still loves.

Onegin appears, lacking a 'gentleman' as second but bringing his coachman, Guillot, instead. The seconds retire to arrange the formalities. Lensky and Onegin sing (apart and aside from each other) of their new and perhaps ridiculous enmity. On three claps of Zaretsky's hands, both men fire. Lensky falls. 'Ubit?' ('Dead?') asks Onegin. Zaretsky confirms it. Onegin is struck with horror.

ACT III: It is some years later. Onegin, after much travelling abroad, is at a ball in St Petersburg. A polonaise is danced. Onegin, aside, declares himself bored by the occasion; he is still pursued by the memory of Lensky's death.

The guests dance an écossaise, then comment as Prince Gremin enters. On his arm (to Onegin's astonishment) is Tatyana, who converses with others but notices Onegin. Gremin tells Onegin that Tatyana is his wife, and speaks of the great comfort she has brought him: 'Lyubvi vsye vozrasti pokorni' ('To love, all ages submit'). He presents Onegin to her; they acknowledge each other only as former neighbours in the country, but as Tatyana and her husband leave, Onegin feels powerfully drawn towards her.

Later, at her house, Tatyana is alone, holding a letter from Onegin. To herself she admits that her passion for him has reawakened. Onegin enters and kneels to her. She bids him rise, asking why he pursues her now. Although she attempts to be cold, Onegin seizes her hand and declares himself passionately; momentarily overcome, she allows herself to utter the words 'Ya vas lyublyu' ('I love you').

But she will not leave her husband: bidding Onegin go, she leaves the room. Onegin, overcome with despair, quickly departs.

* * *

As Tatyana in the first scene tells how sympathetically she reacts to

Ex. 1

the lovers' tragedy in the novel she is reading, we hear in voice and orchestra a theme (ex. 1) which has been foreshadowed in the overture. In the following scene, when she is in her room, the theme is heard again from the orchestra; then, when left alone, Tatyana bursts out with a second theme (ex. 2) – her purposeful as opposed to her dreamy side – as she prepares to write to Onegin.

Ex. 2

Later in this Letter Scene Tatyana asks, as she writes, 'Are you [Onegin] my guardian angel or a wily tempter?' – to a third theme (ex. 3), heard a moment earlier in the orchestra.

Ex. 3

Here are three Tchaikovsky's most memorable themes, all musically interrelated and all devoted to portraying his beloved Tatyana. The music for Lensky, the last-act aria for Gremin, the popular dance-music and the peasant choruses are almost equally memorable. The duet for Lensky and Onegin before their duel is a canon, an apt musical illustration of two men separated, not speaking to one another, yet thinking along the same lines.

THE QUEEN OF SPADES
(Pikovaya Dama)
Libretto by Modest and Pyotr Tchaikovsky, after Pushkin

First produced: St Petersburg, 1890
Three Acts

Cast in order of singing:

CHEKALINSKY		*baritone*
SURIN	GENTLEMEN OF ST PETERSBURG	*bass*
TOMSKY		*baritone*
HERMAN, A YOUNG OFFICER		*tenor*
PRINCE YELETSKY, ENGAGED TO LISA		*baritone*
LISA, GRAND-DAUGHTER OF THE COUNTESS		*soprano*
THE COUNTESS, AN OLD WOMAN		*mezzo-soprano*
PAULINA, A FRIEND OF LISA'S		*contralto*
GOVERNESS IN THE COUNTESS'S HOUSEHOLD		*mezzo-soprano*
MAJOR-DOMO IN THE HOUSE OF A RICH OFFICIAL		*tenor*
MASHA, LISA'S MAID		*soprano*

| CHAPLITZKY | GENTLEMEN AT THE | | tenor |
| NARUMOV | GAMBLING HOUSE | | bass |

In the Pastoral (Act II, *Scene 3*)

PRILEPA, A SHEPHERDESS	*soprano*
MILOZVOR, A SHEPHERD	*contralto* (PAULINA)
ZLATOGOR, A RICH SUITOR	*baritone* (TOMSKY)

Promenaders, children, nurses, governesses, servants,
dancers, professional choristers
*The action takes place in St Petersburg
at the end of the eighteenth century*

The source, once again, is Pushkin – but whereas the original of
Eugene Onegin was a verse narrative, the original of *The Queen of
Spades* was in prose, a kind of short novel or long-short story. A tone
of detachment of irony pervades the story but is missing from the
opera libretto, which was prepared for the composer by his brother.
The resultant opera is less concise, less realistic, than the earlier
Eugene Onegin. It nevertheless gives sharp, powerful focus to three
portrayals – Lisa, crazed with love; Herman, obsessed with gambling; and the old Countess, frail in body but brusque and authoritative in manner, dying of shock and reappearing in Herman's mind as
a (falsely) prophetic ghost.

★   ★   ★

ACT I: In the Summer Garden, St Petersburg, children are playing
and adults are strolling in the sun. Chekalinsky and Surin, two
gentlemen, refer to the curious, moody character of their acquaintance, Herman: at the card-table he watches endlessly, but never
plays. Herman himself, a young officer, enters. To his friend, Count
Tomsky, he discloses that he is in love – and tormented because the
girl, whom he has only seen and never spoken to, belongs to a class
above him.

Prince Yeletsky enters and receives congratulations on his newly
announced engagement. His fiancée, Lisa, approaches in the company of her grandmother, an old countess. Herman's torment is
increased, for this is the girl he has loved from afar. She is evidently
affected on seeing him – an unknown, tormented man.

Tomsky explains to his friends how an episode in the Countess's
youth, when she used to live in Paris, gave her the nickname of the

Queen of Spades: 'Odnazhdi v Versailles, au jeu de la reine'. (There are some French phrases in the Russian text of this opera.) A certain Count Saint-Germain was in love with her, but she ignored his advances until, one night at Versailles, she lost all her money at cards and the Count promised – in return for her favours – to tell her the magic secret of three winning cards. The secret worked, and in due course the Countess passed it on to two others. But she had a ghostly warning that she will die when a third man comes to learn the secret. The story fascinates Herman's already disturbed mind. He determines to win Lisa away from the Prince.

The scene changes to Lisa's room. Paulina and other girls are with her. Lisa and Paulina pass the time in song; then, while the pensive Lisa sits apart, the other girls start a merry dance and song which brings in the Governess, who reprimands them for their rowdy behaviour. They leave. It is a fine night, and Lisa tells her maid, Masha, to leave the balcony door open. She sings a sad soliloquy: 'Otkuda eti slyozi?' ('Whence come these tears?').

Suddenly Herman is at the window. He pours out his love to Lisa, drawing out a pistol and threatening to shoot himself if she gives the alarm to the house. She is beginning to yield when there is an imperious knock at the door. She hides Herman and the old Countess enters. The sight of her reminds Herman of the mysterious secret of the cards. When the Countess goes he again pours out his desperate entreaty to Lisa. At last she confesses that she loves him too.

ACT II: At a masked ball in a wealthy private house, there is singing, dancing and (announced by the Majordomo) a firework display. Chekalinsky and Surin, aware that the story of the Countess's past has fascinated Herman, determine to tease him by making apparently ghostly suggestions about the 'third man' who comes to learn her secret. Prince Yeletsky sees that Lisa is unhappy, and reiterates his devotion to her.

A pastoral entertainment, *The Faithful Shepherdess*, is performed for the guests at the ball. Paulina (in the male role of a modest young shepherd) and Tomsky (as a rich, unsuccessful suitor) take part.

In response to a note left by Lisa, Herman waits for her. She gives him the key of her garden door: he can get through the Countess's room to her own. She asks him to come the following evening. No, he says, he will come this very night. Having just glimpsed the Countess again, he is more and more obsessed by the possibility of learning the secret of the three cards. Excitement invades the party with the announcement that the Empress is about to enter the ballroom.

The scene changes to the Countess's room, Herman hides himself as the Countess enters. Her attendants fuss round her. Her mind runs back to the elegance of her young days in Paris. She drowsily sings an old French song from an opera she heard in her youth. Revealing himself, Herman asks her for the secret of the three cards. She is terrified but silent. He draws a pistol. She falls back. Still having said nothing, she is dead.

Lisa enters, sees the dead body and accuses Herman. He hurries out, leaving her.

ACT III: In his room in the barracks, some days later, Herman reads a note he has just received from Lisa. Realizing she may have blamed him unjustly for intending the Countess's death, she asks him to meet her on the quayside before midnight. Herman meanwhile is tortured in his mind, particularly by what happened at the Countess's funeral, when the dead woman's eye seemed to wink at him. The mysterious sound of a distant church choir now adds to his terror. The ghost of the Countess appears and announces that for the sake of Lisa, she will tell him the three winning cards: three, seven, ace ('Troika, ṣemyorka, tuz').

On the quayside, midnight strikes and Lisa is in despair: Herman has not come. He arrives, but after only a brief expression of his love he presses Lisa to hurry with him to the gaming-house, now that he possesses the secret of the three cards. Lisa realizes that the man to whom she has enslaved herself is indeed a murderer: 'Tak eto pravda' ('So it is true!'). She makes a last bid to save him but Herman pushes her away. She throws herself into the river.

At a gaming-house, the assembled gamblers (including Tomsky, Surin, Chekalinsky. Chaplitzky and Narumov) are surprised to see Yeletsky, who has never been there before. The company breaks for supper and songs (one by Tomsky), then returns to the faro table. Suddenly Herman enters, with wild looks. He stakes the huge, unheard-of sum of forty thousand roubles on the three and it wins. He stakes again on the seven and it wins. He sings with wild emotion about the turns of fortune: 'Chto nasha zhizn? Igra!' ('What is our life? a game!').

Chekalinsky, who has been the banker, refuses a further bet. But Yeletsky, who, of course, came precisely in order to challenge Herman because of Lisa's death, accepts the bet. Again Herman claims a win, for has he not staked on the last card mentioned to him by the Countess, namely the Ace? No, says Yeletsky: the card in Herman's hand is the Queen of Spades. The Ghost of the Countess (the Queen of Spades herself) appears again to Herman, whose madness is now complete. He stabs himself.

★ ★ ★

The period of the opera – the era of Catherine the Great, at the end of the eighteen century – is musically evoked at several points. One of them is the Countess's singing to herself (Act II, Scene 2) an air from Grétry's opera of 1784, *Richard Cœur de Lion*; another is the pastoral masque (Act II, Scene 1), on a tale which is, with Russian names, the equivalent of the myth of Daphnis and Chloe. Earlier, the duet for Lisa and her friend Paulina is a party-piece, accompanied by Lisa at the harpsichord, ending with a prolonged trill in old-fashioned style. The words describe the gentle quivering of nature as the night breezes blow (ex. 1). Such decorous prettiness is a foil to the strong passions linked to the Queen of Spades (the Countess) herself. When

Ex. 1

Herman is told by his mocking friends, Chekalinsky and Surin, about the 'third man' who can obtain the faithful secret from the Countess, a repeated three-note figure is heard from the lower orchestral instruments (ex. 2).

Ex. 2

The three notes may incidentally provide a numerical symbol for the three cards, but it is their musical sense of hidden menace which turns out more important. The theme reappears at various times when the drama demands it – the last time, naturally, being at the moment when Herman realizes that the final card in his hand is not the ace but the Queen of Spades.

NIKOLAI RIMSKY-KORSAKOV

1844–1908

Although at first a naval officer, Rimsky-Korsakov developed a very full musical career – as conductor, teacher (his pupils included Stravinsky), promoter and editor of others' works, and a prolific composer. His fifteen operas are nearly all based on historical or legendary Russian material. As Tchaikovsky excelled in the operatic portrayal of emotions from within, so Rimsky-Korsakov excelled in the depiction of scenes from without – transforming, as it were, visions and colours into music, and making considerable play with eastern and other exotic elements.

His most important operas are *May Night* (1880), *The Snow Maiden* (1882), *Sadko* (1898), from which comes the so-called Hindu Song, really 'The Song of the Indian Merchant', *The Tale of Tsar Saltan* (1902), from which comes 'The Flight of the Bumble-Bee', *The Legend of the Invisible City of Kitezh* (1907) and *The Golden Cockerel* (1909).

THE GOLDEN COCKEREL .
(Zolotoy Petushok)
Libretto by V. Belsky after a story by Pushkin

First performed: Moscow, 1909
Three Acts

Cast in order of singing:

THE ASTROLOGER	*tenor-altino*
KING DODON	*bass*
PRINCE GVIDON, HIS ELDER SON	*tenor*

GENERAL POLKAN, IN SERVICE TO THE KING   *bass*
PRINCE AFRON, THE KING'S YOUNGER SON   *baritone*
THE GOLDEN COCKEREL   *soprano*
AMELFA, HOUSEKEEPER TO THE KING   *contralto*
THE QUEEN OF SHEMAKHAN   *soprano*

Chorus of soldiers, courtiers, people, etc.
The place and time of the action are left unstated

A fable, a fairy-tale, a thing of fantastic and sometimes garish music: superficially, *The Golden Cockerel* might seem to be no more than that. But the fantastic plumage conceals the barbs of satire. Indeed, the Tsarist censor at first forbade the production of *The Golden Cockerel*: its mocking exposure of stupid despotism perhaps struck too near home. It was not produced until the year after the composer's death.

The requirements for the cast include a 'tenor-altino', 'a type of voice which Rimsky-Korsakov said 'is rarely found' and which is not listed under that name in the chief British or Italian musical dictionaries. The Soviet *Encylopedic Musical Dictionary* (1959), however, appears to define it simply as a very high tenor. Rimsky-Korsakov's part rises to an E above the usual tenor 'top C', but his score also includes an alternative without quite such high notes in case the part needs to be given to 'a lyric tenor with a good, strong falsetto' as the next best thing.

*   *   *

ACT I: In a brief prologue in front of the curtain, the Astrologer tells the audience it is about to see a moral tale.

The curtain rises to show the ageing King Dodon with his Council of State. He asks for advice on how to deal with the foreign attack which threatens from all sides. His elder son, Gvidon, produces a brilliant idea: let the enemy invade the surrounding country while the king and his army remain secure in the central citadel and devise some way of repelling them. The king and his courtiers applaud, and the king is angry with General Polkan when he declares the plan inadequate.

The king's younger son, Afron, has an even better idea: disband the army, then suddenly mobilize it again for a surprise attack! Once again king and courtiers applaud – and once again General Polkan doubts the plan and is abused and even physically attacked. Well, what is to be done? Consult an augury, perhaps – but then the courtiers begin to quarrel on rival methods of foretelling the future. At the height of the quarrel a mysterious Astrologer enters. To solve the difficulty, he offers a golden cockerel who will crow to indicate an alarm and point to the direction from which it comes.

The bird now crows ('Kiriki, kirikuku' in Russian) and adds that the king may for the present sleep soundly. King and courtiers hail the prodigy, and the king offers to do the Astrologer any service he wishes. The Astrologer says he may take advantage of this later, but not yet, and withdraws. The king dismisses his Council, gets into a big bed, accepts delicacies from his housekeeper Amelfa, plays with a parrot, then (lulled by the golden cockerel's repeated cry that all is safe) goes to sleep, dreaming of an unknown beautiful woman.

Suddenly the cock crows to raise the alarm, which is taken up all round. Polkan rushes in; then Dodon's sons, armed, go off none too willingly to fight. A military march is heard from outside; but the atmosphere becomes calm again and the cock crows that the danger is averted.

Dodon tries to sleep again and, having remembered that he had a most pleasant dream but having forgotten what it was, asks Amelfa to make conjectures. At the third time she guesses rightly, and Dodon falls asleep again. Once more the cockerel sounds the alarm; Polkan dares to arouse the sleeping king; with difficulty he puts on his rusty armour and goes to mount a horse (making sure it is a docile one). Then, to the acclamation of his subjects, he rides away to fight.

ACT II: It is night. The battle has gone badly. The corpses of the king's two sons are seen; riderless horses stand motionless. Some surviving soldiers lament their state. King Dodon joins them, bewailing his sons and his army. General Polkan enters and tries to raise the soldiers' spirits; but they cannot attack the enemy because they do not even know where he is.

Suddenly the morning mists begin to disperse and a mysterious, luxurious tent is seen. In a ridiculous manner the soldiers fire a cannon at it. But it is unharmed, and the soldiers flee when it opens to reveal a beautiful woman. Accompanied by four slaves each bearing a musical instrument, she sings a hymn to the sun.

To Dodon's inquiries she reveals that she is the Queen of Shemakhan. She makes the men comfortable (the corpses are timidly taken away) but they are still uneasy in their minds. Polkan tries valiantly to make sociable conversation but the queen, carried away by the memory of a dream of love which she had the previous night, finds him gross and gets Dodon to send him away. She comes close to the embarrassed Dodon and sets out to conquer him with sensuous melody and words.

She makes Dodon sing in turn, which he does to a brief, ridiculous tune. Then she tearfully confesses her wish to find a man to dominate her. Dodon volunteers for the role and tells her to stop weeping ('Perestan plakat'). She now insists that he shows his manliness by dancing. Extremely reluctant (in fact, consenting only when she threatens to take Polkan in his place), he dances while she instructs him, herself dancing with a tambourine in her hand. The dance music becomes more furious, and she laughs at Dodon, who falls down exhausted.

As soon as he recovers he offers her his heart and his kingdom, magnanimously offering also to have Polkan (whom the queen dislikes) beheaded. Dodon's chariot is brought in and the pair ride away – Dodon ecstatic, the queen's female slaves reflecting their mistress's attitude as they sing of this latest, ridiculous conquest of hers. Dodon's soldiers may be poor fighters, but now they sing 'Hurrah!' very well.

ACT III: Back in Dodon's city, with the golden cockerel still keeping watch, there is a general sense of foreboding, but Amelfa assures the people that Dodon is returning in triumph with a girl he has rescued. Trumpets sound his approach. First there enters the queen's procession, with giants, dwarfs and other grotesque participants. Then a chariot brings Dodon and the queen herself, to whom the crowd wishes long life ('Dolgo zhit tebya!').

Suddenly the Astrolger appears. The queen, seemingly disturbed, asks who he is. Dodon greets him warmly. The Astrologer reminds him of his promise of a gift and now asks, as this gift, the queen. Dodon remonstrates but the Astrologer persists, saying he wants to get married and refusing alternative gifts. Growing furious, Dodon hits him on the head with his sceptre and the Astrologer falls dead.

Dodon is troubled. The queen seems to make light of the affair, but when the reassured Dodon turns to embrace her she repulses him, telling him to vanish ('Propadi ti') and his stupid nation as well! Dodon starts to remonstrate gently, but the golden cockerel crows suddenly and attacks the king on his head with its beak. He too falls dead, amid a peal of thunder. Darkness descends. The laughter of the queen is heard. When the darkness lifts, both queen and cockerel have disappeared; the people intone a long lament and throw themselves despairingly on the ground.

The story is over. The curtain falls. But in front of it comes the Astrologer: only he and the queen were real people, he says, and the rest were creatures of the imagination.

★   ★   ★

As in others of his operas, Rimsky-Korsakov here borrows from Wagner the use of vividly descriptive leading-motives, but rejects Wagner's symphonic, ever-developing texture in favour of a more regular and symmetrical musical line.

The very opening of the orchestral introduction gives us two of the most important motives, instantly recognizable when they return in the opera itself. First we have the cockerel, on a muted trumpet, followed by the Queen of Shemakhan in a sensuous melody on the cellos (ex. 1). This theme – which occurs in the opera

Ex. 1

not only when the queen appears but, before that, when Dodon is in bed dreaming of love – leads to a prefiguring of the queen's 'Hymn to the Sun' in Act II. Next in the overture, with a complete change of mood, a mysteriously tinkling sound with an off-beat tune for the glockenspiel and harps (ex. 2) introduces the Astrologer – and then the Astrologer himself comes to deliver the prologue.

Ex. 2

GIACOMO PUCCINI

1858–1924

We now resume the story of Italian opera. Verdi, in his middle years, reigned without substantial challenge. Almost the only opera by another Italian composer of that period to survive (just!) in the repertory of non-Italian countries is *La Gioconda* (1876) by Amilcare Ponchielli (1834–86), the teacher of both Puccini and Mascagni.

'Puccini looks to me more like the heir of Verdi than any of his rivals.' That was the verdict of a young London music critic called Bernard Shaw in 1894 – a verdict made, remarkably, on the evidence only of Puccini's first successful opera, *Manon Lescaut* (1893). Shaw pointed to Puccini's combination of a symphonic style (that is, a style of continuously developing music, like Wagner's) with a vein of traditional Italian melody.

Puccini thereafter turned out a chain of operatic successes unequalled since his day. He pursued and extended this symphonic method; he extended also his range of poignant and biting harmonies, learning from Debussy as well as Wagner. Dramatically he cared little for subtlety of character but much for the power of erotic or brutal impulses seen or suggested on the stage – impulses which are powerfully suggested in the high points of his music. Puccini's characteristic genre is thus what in English is called *melodrama* (it is amusing to recall that this word descends from the Italian *melodramma*, which simply means opera!). The comedy of *Gianni Schicchi* stands as an exception.

LA BOHÈME
(Bohemian Life)
*Libretto by Giuseppe Giacosa and Luigi Illica,
after the novel by Henry Mürger*

First performed: Turin, 1896
Four Acts

Cast in order of singing:

MARCELLO, A PAINTER	*baritone*
RODOLFO, A POET	*tenor*
COLLINE, A PHILOSOPHER	*bass*
SCHAUNARD, A MUSICIAN	*baritone*
BENOÎT, THEIR LANDLORD	*bass*
MIMÌ	*soprano*
PARPIGNOL, A TOY SELLER	*tenor*
MUSETTA	*soprano*
ALCINDORO, A COUNSELLOR OF STATE	*bass*
A CUSTOMS OFFICIAL	*bass*
SERGEANT	*bass*

Chorus of people, students, work-girls, shopkeepers,
street vendors, soldiers, waiters, children, etc.
The scene is laid in Paris about 1830

La Bohème, the tunes and the pathos of which have made it one of the
most successful operas ever written, was Puccini's fourth opera.
Preceding it were the unsuccessful *Le villi* ('The Wilis') and *Edgar*,
produced in 1884 and 1889 respectively, and the successful *Manon
Lescaut* (1893).

Mimì, the heroine of *La Bohème*, dies of consumption (i.e. in
modern language, pulmonary tuberculosis) like the heroine of *La
traviata*. But whereas *La traviata* is concerned with social taboos of
love and marriage, *La Bohème* does not speak of marriage at all. The
girls have Bohemian lovers and live with them in near-poverty or
leave them for others who can provide more luxurious living – a
point less clear in the opera than in its literary inspiration, Henry
Mürger's prose work *Scènes de la Bohème* (1854). (A play on the
subject was called *Scènes de la vie de Bohème*.) The period of Mürger's
writings is retained in the opera, the libretto of which mentions
Guizot, the French Prime Minister during the reign of Louis Philippe
(1830–8). 'La Bohème' is defined in a French dictionary as:
'Bohemia; wild and disorderly people (*or* life), the loafing fraternity;
vagrants, tramps'.

Following Italian custom, Puccini's librettists italianized the
original names 'Rodolphe' and 'Marcel' into Rodolfo and Marcello.
The name 'Musetta' (meaning a bagpipe and indicating the girl's
stridency and roughness, in contrast to the mildness and sweetness

of Mimì) is an invention of the librettists, the character not having an
exact counterpart in the French original.

★   ★   ★

ACT I: Marcello and Rodolfo, in the Parisian garret which they
share with Colline and Schaunard, are doing their best to keep warm
on a freezing Christmas Eve. With no fuel for their stove, they think
of burning a chair, then Marcello's latest painting, but finally settle
for the manuscript of the play Rodolfo has been writing. Act I is
blazing when Colline enters. As the closing scene is reduced to ashes,
Schaunard arrives, with attendants carrying food, wine and fuel, to
the others' astonished delight, and flings some money on the floor.
While he tells how he earned it – from an Englishman who wanted
music lessons – they set the table; but Schaunard insists that they dine
out.

As they are having a drink before leaving, the landlord, Benoît,
comes in, asking for his rent: they offer him wine, then tease him
about a woman they have seen him with, and finally hustle him out
in mock disgust at such behaviour in a married man. Then, when the
others go off to the Café Momus, Rodolfo says that he will follow in
five minutes – he has an article to finish.

He is making little progress. Suddenly there is a knock on the
door. Mimì, a frail young girl who lives in a room above, is on the
threshold, half fainting; her candle has blown out and she wants it
relighted. Rodolfo helps her to a chair and gives her wine. She soon
feels better and starts to go; but she loses her key and her candle again
goes out. His conveniently goes out too and they are soon both in the
dark, groping for the key which Rodolfo finds and hides. Their
hands meet; Rodolfo takes her in his. 'Che gelida manina' ('What a
freezing little hand!'), he exclaims, and while warming it into life he
introduces himself. Will she now tell him about herself, he asks? 'Sì.
Mi chiamano Mimì' ('Yes , I'm called Mimì'), she begins; she tells
him that she works in solitude, embroidering artificial flowers, but it
is nature's flowers that delight her.

His friends call from the street below; he asks them to keep a place
at the Café. In the duet 'O soave fanciulla' ('O lovely girl'), Rodolfo
and Mimì find themselves falling in love. He agrees to take her with
him to the Café (with a hint, too, of what he expects when they
return), and their voices are heard as they go together down the
staircase.

ACT II: In the square outside the Café Momus, in the Latin Quarter, there is a large crowd, with street vendors crying their wares, students, a mother calling her children; their noises mingle with those from the Café, where customers, some of them at tables outside, are calling to the waiters. Rodolfo and Mimì have arrived to join their friends. Schaunard is buying a horn, Marcello flirting with passing girls, Colline buying books and having some clothes repaired. They sit down for their meal at a table outside the Café, and Rodolfo introduces Mimì to his friends. Meanwhile, there is a further commotion in the street, as the toy-seller Parpignol comes along, followed by children (calling Parpignol's name delightedly) and their mothers. The friends order their meal and talk gaily.

The vivacious Musetta, obviously known to the passers-by, enters. Formerly Marcello was her lover, but now she comes with an elderly admirer, Alcindoro, whom she treats like a tame dog. She spots the 'Bohemians', insists on taking the table next to them, and, to Alcindoro's embarrassment, she tries harder and harder to attract Marcello's attention, singing her Waltz Song: 'Quando me'n vo' ('As I go along'), Marcello becomes more and more inflamed.

Eventually Musetta sends Alcindoro off on an errand, pretending one of her shoes is hurting, and she and Marcello embrace passion-ately. The waiter brings the bill, which the friends cannot pay. Now soldiers, with a band, approach: windows are flung open, and children pursued by their mothers come out into the street. In the general excitement the friends rush off, Marcello and Colline carry-ing the half-shod Musetta, leaving Alcindoro to pay both bills on his return. They sing Musetta's praises as the crowd sings those of the drum-major.

ACT III: Two months have elapsed. It is early morning at the Barrière'd'Enfer, one of the gates of Paris, with street sweepers, a customs official (who opens the gate) and milkmaids and carters passing. Singing is heard from a nearby inn, with Musetta's voice prominent. Day is just dawning when Mimì arrives and asks a sergeant to point out the inn where a painter is working. He does so, and she asks there for Marcello. Soon he comes out, and tells her that he and Musetta have been living there for a month, he as a jobbing painter and she teaching singing. She asks if Rodolfo is there: on learning that he is, she refuses to enter and bursts into tears. They still love one another, she tells Marcello, but Rodolfo is fiercely jealous. He advises them to part, and she agrees that they must. Her persistent cough alarms him.

Rodolfo, who has been asleep, now comes out. As he talks to

Marcello, Mimì conceals herself. At first he says that he wants to leave Mimì as she is such a coquette, but eventually he gives the true reason – her failing health, which is further aggravated by their life together in his chilly room. Mimì can control her tears no longer, and Rodolfo hears her. They embrace, then bid each other a sad farewell in the duet 'Donde lieta uscì' ('The place which she left in happy mood') – while in the background Musetta and Marcello have a lively quarrel.

ACT IV: Marcello and Rodolfo have both left their girls and are back sharing the garret. They are pretending to work. Each lately happens to have seen the other's girl; on hearing the news each pretends no longer to care. But memories of former happiness overwhelm them. Schaunard and Colline arrive, carrying food (four loaves and a herring!) of which they make a mock-sumptuous meal. They then hold a mock dance, Rodolfo taking Marcello for his partner. Then Colline and Schaunard fight a duel, with tongs and shovel.

Suddenly Musetta enters, highly agitated. She has found Mimì, in utter exhaustion. They bring her in and prepare a bed for her; soon she feels rather better, but there is no food or drink in the house and it is clear that she is dying. Musetta takes off her earrings, to be sold to provide food and medical attention, and she promises a muff, to warm Mimì's icy hands. She and Marcello leave. Colline sings a farewell to his old coat ('Vecchia zimarra'), intending to sell it to buy necessities for Mimì. He leaves with Schaunard.

The lovers, left alone, sing of their happy memories of their first meeting: 'Torna al nido la rondine' ('The swallow returns to its nest'). Mimì has a convulsive fit of coughing just as Schaunard, then Musetta and Marcello, return. Mimì delightedly takes the muff, sinking back a moment later into unconsciousness. Musetta mutters a prayer.

As Colline returns with money for the doctor, who is already on his way, Schaunard murmurs to Marcello that Mimì is dead. Rodolfo thinks she is resting peacefully: then he sees their expressions and the truth dawns. He flings himself on the bed, sobbing over her lifeless body.

★   ★   ★

'Che gelida manina' (which, as sung in English, became 'Your tiny hand is frozen'), which is one of the world's most famous operatic songs, starts with one note nine times repeated – than which, in itself, nothing could be less 'inspired'. Plainly it is not entirely in melody in its purest sense that Puccini's power lies. In fact the success of *La Bohème* partly depends on a very strong, very distinctive harmonic style and on a structural development which interweaves various strands symphonically, sometimes with Wagner-like concentration. This harmonic and this structural trait combine in their effect: a theme that recurs is recognized by its well-defined harmonic background (and sometimes by characteristic orchestration) as well as by its 'tune'. Such recognition is, for most people, subconscious, but it is worth examining it in eighteen bars from the final pages of the vocal score. The failing Mimì is recalling her first meeting with Rodolfo.

Ex. 1

MIMI

hand   then   you   clasp – èd.
man   tu   mi   pren – de – vi

RODOLFO   (raising her up in alarm)   **26** *a tempo*

Oh! God!   Mi – mi!____
Oh! Dio!   *Mi – mi!*____

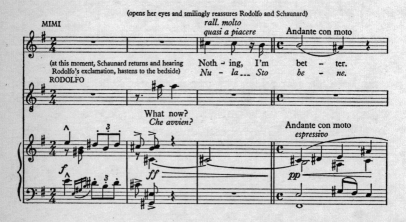

MIMI

(opens her eyes and smilingly reassures Rodolfo and Schaunard)

Noth – ing,   I'm   bet – ter.
Nu – la... Sto   be – ne.

(at this moment, Schaunard returns and hearing Rodolfo's exclamation, hastens to the bedside)
RODOLFO

What now?
Che avvien?

Note:
bar

1 single note which originally preceded Rodolfo's 'Your tiny hand is frozen'
2 Mimì begins to quote the same
7 Mimì ceases to quote and returns to her present conversation, but the orchestra goes on quoting
12 sudden change to the theme associated with Mimì's coughing and illness in Acts I and III
16 the return of Schaunard is signified by his own cheery theme, and
17 as Mimì tries to reassure Rodolfo and Schaunard that she has regained her old self, her old theme – 'Mi chiamano Mimì' – returns in the orchestra. Significantly this theme has (and originally had) a one-note orchestral introduction, one of the signs of its kinship to 'Che gelida manina'.

TOSCA
*Libretto by Giuseppe Giacosa and Luigi Illica, after
the play by Victorien Sardou*

First performed: Rome, 1900
Three Acts

Cast in order of singing:

CESARE ANGELOTTI, LEADER OF THE PROSCRIBED REPUBLICAN PARTY	*bass*
A SACRISTAN	*baritone*
MARIO CAVARADOSSI, A PAINTER	*tenor*
FLORIA TOSCA, A FAMOUS SINGER	*soprano*
BARON SCARPIA, CHIEF OF POLICE	*baritone*
SPOLETTA, POLICE AGENT	*tenor*
SCIARRONE, A POLICE OFFICER	*baritone*
A GAOLER	*bass*
A SHEPHERD BOY	*boy's voice (or contralto)*

Chorus of choirboys, soldiers, police agents, ladies,
nobles, citizens, artisans, etc.
The scene is laid in Rome, in June 1800

Political struggle and sexual struggle: it is a proven good mixture for
the stage, and the French playwright Victorien Sardou (1831–1908)
used it with great success in *La Tosca* (1887). Moreover he was
writing of a time and place (Rome, 1800) when religious and political
attitudes were strongly intertwined – which allowed him to add
religious conflict to his ingredients. Puccini's opera, based on the
play, makes the political and religious struggle less clear: not until
the moment when Cavaradossi, about to face the firing-squad,
refuses the services of a priest do we gather the force of his conviction
as a free-thinker, and we miss the point of Cavaradossi's doing a
painting in a church (in the play an intended ruse to conceal his true
political convictions).

But the sexual battle – Scarpia torturing Cavaradossi in earshot of
Tosca so that she, who loves Cavaradossi, should be willing to give
herself to Scarpia to earn mercy for her lover – is presented in
Puccini's opera with great dramatic violence and the maximum force
of his musical language. These three characters, each with their
dramatic solos, are memorably brought to theatrical life.

*   *   *

ACT I: In the church of Sant' Andrea della Valle, a painter's gear and
a large, covered picture are to be seen. Angelotti, an escaped political
prisoner, runs in, dishevelled and exhausted. He glances round and,
seeing an image of the Madonna, he looks under it and eventually
finds a key (left there for him by his sister, the Marchesa Attavanti);
with it he opens the door to the Attavanti family chapel and goes
within, closing the door behind him.

A sacristan enters with some paintbrushes for Cavaradossi, the
painter who has been at work. But Cavaradossi is not there to take
them. The Angelus is rung, and the sacristan kneels in prayer.
Cavaradossi enters, uncovers his unfinished picture of the Magdalen
and contemplates it; the sacristan is somewhat horrified by its
resemblance to a lady whom he has seen at worship in the church (in
fact Angelotti's sister). Cavaradossi says that it is modelled on her.
He starts painting, stopping to contrast with the portrait a miniature
of Tosca: 'Recondita armonia' ('Hidden harmony').

The sacristan soon departs and Angelotti, believing the church
empty, comes out of the chapel. He sees Cavaradossi and immediately recognizes him as a supporter of his own Republican party.
Tosca's voice is heard outside, and Cavaradossi hurries Angelotti
back into the chapel with the basket of food prepared for himself. He

lets Tosca in. She momentarily suspects that he was not alone – perhaps with another woman – but is quickly reassured. She adorns the Madonna's image with flowers, then turns to him, suggesting an assignation for the evening. The two sing tenderly of their love. As she is about to leave she sees his portrait of the Magdalen, recognizes its model, and is furiously jealous. He once more assures her that there is no cause for jealousy, and they again sing of their love.

After bidding Tosca an affectionate farewell, Cavaradossi lets Angelotti out of the chapel. He determines to hide Angelotti in his villa to help him escape from Scarpia, the evil chief of the Roman police. As Angelotti prepares to leave the church a cannon sounds – the sign that a prisoner's escape has been discovered – and the two hurry off.

The sacristan and a crowd of boys enter the church, excited at the news of Napoleon's defeat, which is to be celebrated by a cantata at the palace with Tosca as soloist.

Suddenly they are interrupted (and terrified) by the arrival of the sinister Scarpia and his men. Scarpia tells his assistant, Spoletta, to search the building, while he himself questions the sacristan. They discover the Attavanti chapel unlocked; in it is a fan, bearing the Attavanti arms, and the empty food basket. Then Scarpia recognizes the Marchesa Attavanti in Cavaradossi's picture.

Tosca returns, disturbed to learn from the sacristan that Cavaradossi has left. Scarpia speaks to her, showing her the Marchesa's fan; he insinuatingly suggests to her that Cavaradossi has gone to meet the Marchesa. Her jealousy is easily aroused, and she goes off angrily to his villa, followed, on Scarpia's instructions, by Spoletta.

The church is filling with people, and against the sound of the organ and chanted prayer, with jubilant bells and cannon shot in the background. Scarpia sings of his two objectives – the death of Angelotti and the possession of Tosca.

ACT II: 'Tosca è buon falco' ('Tosca is a good decoy'), muses Scarpia, alone in his room in the Farnese Palace, at supper. He summons Sciarrone, his henchman, and hands him a note for Tosca. He sings of his plan to make Tosca his mistress (actually, as he says, preferring force to more gentle methods) and to hang both Angelotti and Cavaradossi.

Spoletta returns and tells how he and his assistants followed Tosca to Cavaradossi's villa. They have brought back Cavaradossi, but (to Scarpia's annoyance) they could not find Angelotti despite an extensive search. At this moment the cantata is heard from the royal apartments below. Cavaradossi is brought in, protesting. Scarpia starts questioning him about Angelotti (they pause for an instant as Tosca's voice is heard floating above the others) but he gives no information and, to Spoletta's and Scarpia's irritation, only laughs when they mention the searchers' vain efforts. Scarpia closes the windows so that the music cannot be heard, and resumes the questioning more forcefully, but still to no result. Tosca enters and embraces Cavaradossi, who whispers to her to keep silent. Scarpia sends him into the torture chamber, with a judge to take his deposition.

Left alone with Tosca, Scarpia tries unsuccessfully to obtain information from her about who was at the villa. He asks Sciarrone if Cavaradossi has yet given way, but he has not. Then he horrifies Tosca by revealing that Cavaradossi is at that moment being tortured. She hears his groans and calls to him: Scarpia charges her to keep silent, pressing her to give way by threatening more excruciating tortures. The door is opened and now she can hear all her lover's groans. As Spoletta kneels in prayer, Cavaradossi cries out in intolerable pain and Tosca can stand no more: she tells Scarpia that Angelotti is hidden in the well in the garden of the villa. Terribly mauled, Cavaradossi is brought in. Tosca tries to comfort him, but when he realizes from a remark of Scarpia's that she has betrayed Angelotti he angrily repulses her. Then Sciarrone arrives to tell Scarpia that Napoleon has defeated the royal troops, to Cavaradossi's great delight: 'Vittoria' he sings. Scarpia, infuriated, sends him away under guard.

Tosca begs Scarpia to spare him. He says he might and offers her wine. Pushing it contemptuously aside, she asks him realistically for his price: 'Quanto?' ('How much?'). His price is her body. She proudly refuses. Distant drums are heard as men march to the scaffold: she can choose whether or not Cavaradossi will be among them, he tells her. In her song 'Vissi d'arte' ('I lived for my art') she indicates her helplessness and prays to heaven. Scarpia remains adamant.

Spoletta comes in to say that Angelotti took poison as he was captured. He asks for instructions for dealing with Cavaradossi; Scarpia looks at Tosca, who has no choice but to consent. In Tosca's hearing he orders only a mock execution for Cavaradossi, but secretly he conveys to Spoletta his real meaning – that Cavaradossi is, in fact, to be shot. Keeping up the deception, he writes and hands to Tosca a safe-conduct so that she and Cavaradossi can afterwards leave the country. Then he turns to her, 'Tosca, finalmente mia' ('Tosca, mine at last'). But she has picked up a knife, and plunges it into his heart.

Dying, he calls for help, unavailingly. 'E avanti a lui tremava tutta Roma!' ('And before him trembled all Rome!'), remarks Tosca. She places a crucifix and candles by the body, and leaves with the safe-conduct.

ACT III: From a platform on the roof of Fort St Angelo, where Cavaradossi is due for execution, a shepherd boy's voice is heard in the distance as the new day dawns. Matin bells sound. A group of soldiers arrives with Cavaradossi and a gaoler tells him he has one hour to live. The gaoler allows him to write his last letter to Tosca; as he does so he remembers the past: 'E lucevan le stelle' ('And the stars shone').

Tosca arrives with the safe-conduct and shows it to Cavaradossi, who is sobbing with emotion. She tells him what took place and warns him that, to keep up the appearances of the mock-execution, he must fall down at the shot and not stand up too soon, 'just like Tosca on the stage' ('come la Tosca in teatro'). The firing-squad arrives and takes up its position.

She watches tensely. The shots ring out. He falls realistically and does not move. As the soldiers depart, she discovers in horror that the execution was a real one. There is tumult below. Spoletta and Sciarrone arrive, having found out that Tosca has killed Scarpia. Tosca pushes Spoletta away as he comes to arrest her. She leaps up on the parapet and flings herself to her death.

★　★　★

The opera is called *Tosca*, but it starts by proclaiming 'Scarpia!' – in three menacing chords (ex. 1). The curtain at once rises on the entry of the escaped Angelotti. The same motive of three chords

Ex. 1

signals the arrival of Scarpia at his first entrance interrupting the
jubilation of the choristers); it occurs in his big soliloquy in Act II;
altered into a less positive succession of chords (ending with the
minor instead of the major) it accompanies his dying words after
Tosca has stabbed him; and it returns in its original form, but
subdued in power, when (in Act III) Tosca tells Cavaradossi what
has happened. There are other recurrences too. Such recurrences
and metamorphoses of motives is an essential part of Puccini's
operatic construction: some sixty such motives have been detected
in *Tosca*.

Cavaradossi has the first big lyric outpouring of the opera – the
celebrated 'Recondita armonia' ('Hidden harmony') – which Puccini, in the interests of dramatic continuity, 'accompanies' by the
mutterings of the sacristan against unbelievers like Cavaradossi
himself. (Concert performances of the solo, and recorded versions,
of course miss this.) His aria near the end of the opera constitutes
Cavaradossi's second great moment of self-revelation. His voice
steals in on one repeated note as though he is quietly thinking alone.
But the orchestra has already begun to play as a background the tune
which will come from Cavaradossi's voice a few moments later (ex.
2).

Ex. 2

By the nature of opera we should expect Tosca to have a climactic,
sustained outburst at the point where her psychological tensions are
highest – when Scarpia is bartering with her for Cavaradossi's

freedom – and instead she sings 'Vissi d'arte' (ex. 3). It is not an utterance of protest or resolution but of helplessness: having lived only for art and love, why should she be placed in such terrible torment? Indeed, it has been well said that Tosca is not really a tigress, even if some prima donnas like to play her so, but a 'little woman' like Mimì and Butterfly, forced to one deed of violence – like Butterfly, again.

Ex. 3

MADAMA BUTTERFLY
Libretto by Giuseppe Giacosa and Luigi Illica, after the play by David Belasco, itself based on a story by John L. Long

First performed: Milan, 1904
Two Acts

Cast in order of singing:

LIEUT. B. F. PINKERTON, US NAVY	*tenor*
GORO, A MARRIAGE BROKER	*tenor*
SUZUKI, BUTTERFLY'S SERVANT	*mezzo-soprano*
SHARPLESS, AMERICAN CONSUL	*baritone*
MADAMA BUTTERFLY (CHO-CHO-SAN)	*soprano*

THE IMPERIAL COMMISSIONER	*bass*
THE OFFICIAL REGISTRAR	*baritone*
THE BONZE (PRIEST), BUTTERFLY'S UNCLE	*bass*
PRINCE YAMADORI	*tenor*
MRS KATE PINKERTON	*mezzo-soprano*

Chorus of Butterfly's friends and relations, servants, sailors
The scene is laid in Nagasaki at the beginning of the twentieth century

In the summer of 1900 Puccini was in London and saw a performance of a new, successful American one-act play – *Madame Butterfly*, by David Belasco, adapted from a short story by John Luther Long – and he immediately conceived the idea of basing an opera on it. The hero-villain of the play, a US Navy lieutenant who deserts his trusting Japanese wife, was surnamed Pinkerton. In the original story his initials were B. F. (for Benjamin Franklin), but for English audiences he had become F. B., and in the libretto of the opera his full name is mentioned as Sir (!) Francis Blummy Pinkerton. This, however, was in the first version of the opera (in two acts with one interval) which was for various reasons a complete failure when given in February 1904, and had only a single performance. The successful revised version (Brescia, May 1904), in which the second act is itself divided into two parts, drops the incredible Sir Francis Blummy and restores the B. F.

Butterfly herself (on whom, almost entirely, the opera rests) is a most appealing figure, particularly because she is absolutely alone in her plight – her husband has deserted her, her relatives have renounced her, the sympathetic Consul gives her advice she cannot take, and her servant Suzuki cannot grasp her noble single-mindedness. The poignancy of her situation is added to – with a sentimentality which would occasion giggles in the theatre today if the music were not there to support it – by the appearance of her infant son, Trouble, to whom she gives a Stars and Stripes as a plaything before she bandages his eyes and stabs herself. This Trouble *is* a trouble, by the way: the child is supposed to be between two and three, a very difficult age to represent on the stage either by a dummy or otherwise. Butterfly has proudly given her son not a Japanese but an American name (*Dolore* in the Italian text). Butterfly's own Japanese name is represented in English as Cho-cho-san, in Italian as Cio-cio-san.

*   *   *

ACT I: The obsequious marriage-broker, Goro, is showing Pinkerton round the house he is buying as his matrimonial home in Japan. He is introduced to the three Japanese servants hired for him by Goro, including Suzuki, who compliments him. They depart and Goro watches for the arrival of Butterfly, Pinkerton's bride, her family and the others who will be at the wedding.

First to come is Sharpless, the American Consul. While Goro fetches refreshments, Sharpless admires the house and garden and the fine view of the harbour and ocean. Pinkerton expresses his easy-going attitude to life and to his forthcoming marriage, ending with 'America for ever!' (English words in the Italian original) while the orchestra blares out a phrase from 'The Star-Spangled Banner'. He sends Goro to fetch Butterfly and praises her charms, but makes Sharpless uneasy about his irresponsibility, especially when he drinks to a future 'real, American wife' ('una vera sposa americana').

Butterfly and her friends are heard approaching. When Goro brings them in, she sings of coming to Pinkerton at the call of love, and on her instruction they all kneel ceremoniously before 'B. F. Pinkerton', as she names him. In conversation with Sharpless, she mentions that she comes of good family, is fifteen years old and has a mother but her father is dead. Now Goro announces the arrival of Butterfly's relations, including her mother, a cousin, an uncle (Yakuside) and an aunt. There is a great deal of chatter from the assembled friends, most of it inconsequential and slightly malicious, while servants provide food and drink. Sharpless warns Pinkerton not to trifle with Butterfly.

Soon Butterfly bids them all bow low before the two Americans. Rather embarrassed, Butterfly asks if he minds her bringing a few personal possessions, which she has in her baggy sleeves. (Among the most cherished is a knife sent to her father by the Mikado, Goro explains, with a message – which was obeyed.) She tells Pinkerton, out of her relatives' hearing, that the previous day she went to the Mission and embraced Christianity, to make her fit to be his wife.

The Imperial Commissioner, who has been in the background, comes forward, reads the marriage contract and hands it to Goro, who has it signed by Pinkerton, Butterfly and her relations. Congratulations are offered to the bride, first by her girl-friends and then by the Commissioner and the Official Registrar, who now depart. So does Sharpless, warning Pinkerton to be careful. The guests are beginning to drink a Japanese toast to the couple ('O Kami! O Kami!') when the old Bonze (a priest), Butterfly's uncle, arrives. He demands to know what Butterfly was doing at the Mission, accusing her of renouncing her religion and her relatives. The relatives are scandalized: they immediately refuse to have anything more to do with her, and Pinkerton orders them off. Their accusing voices die away in the distance.

From within, Suzuki is heard muttering her prayers. A moment later she emerges with her mistress's white nightgown; Butterfly retires to a corner and prepares herself. Alone, as evening falls, the couple sing a long, tender love-duet.

ACT II (Part I): It is three years later. Suzuki is praying, with a prayer-bell, asking the gods to stop Butterfly's weeping. Pinkerton has not returned since being recalled to America soon after the wedding, and they have hardly any money left. Butterfly, still believing he will come back, tries to persuade the more sceptical Suzuki; she looks forward to his return, imagining the scene: 'Un bel dì ('One fine day').

Goro arrives, with Sharpless. Butterfly (who insists on being called Madama Pinkerton) is excited to see them and makes them welcome, but her nervous, bubbling chatter prevents Sharpless from telling her news he has received in a letter from Pinkerton. She asks him at what time of year the robins nest in America – explaining that Pinkerton had promised to return at the robins' nesting time. She mentions that Goro has tried to persuade her to marry the rich Prince Yamadori – who enters at that moment to pay court to her. Goro explains to Sharpless that Butterfly could divorce Pinkerton for desertion under Japanese law, but she interposes by saying that she is an American citizen.

Alone with Butterfly, Sharpless starts to read the letter: her initial excitement changes to dismay when he hints that Pinkerton will not return. Sharpless is deeply touched when Butterfly produces her small son, Trouble, and says that she would rather kill herself than return to her old occupation of dancing to earn them enough to subsist on. Promising to tell Pinkerton of the child's existence, Sharpless leaves. A moment later Suzuki drags in Goro, who has been spreading tales that no one knows who is the child's father. Butterfly threatens him with a dagger, then pushes him away in disgust.

A cannon shot is heard, the sign that a ship is entering the harbour. Butterfly and Suzuki see that it is a man-o'-war, it is American, and its name is *Abraham Lincoln* – it is Pinkerton's ship! At last he is returning to her! She and Suzuki set about decorating the house with flowers, then Suzuki helps her to prepare herself, making up her face and slipping on her wedding garment. They make three holes in the screen for the two women and the child to watch for Pinkerton's coming. As night falls, distant humming voices are heard, and in the moonlight it can be seen that the child and Suzuki have fallen asleep; only Butterfly is awake, still patiently watching.

ACT II (Part II): As the new day dawns, the voices of the sailors can be heard from the harbour. Butterfly is still watching. Suzuki wakes and sees that it is daylight; she insists that Butterfly goes upstairs, with the child, promising to call her when Pinkerton comes. A moment later there is a knock and Pinkerton enters with Sharpless. Hearing that Butterfly stayed up all night, and seeing the scattered flowers, Pinkerton is greatly troubled and cannot face her. Suzuki sees a woman outside in the garden and Sharpless tells her that it is Pinkerton's American wife, Kate. Sharpless asks Suzuki to tell Butterfly that Mrs Pinkerton is willing to adopt the child. Suzuki, in anguish, remonstrates but then leaves, and Sharpless chides Pinkerton for his heartless behaviour. He is now remorseful: 'Addio, fiorito asil!' ('Farewell, flowery refuge!').

Pinkerton goes out as Kate enters with Suzuki, promising to treat the child as if it were her own. Butterfly calls Suzuki from upstairs, then comes down, eagerly looking for Pinkerton. Seeing Sharpless and Kate, and Suzuki in tears, she guesses the situation, and Suzuki confirms her fears. She realizes that Kate is Pinkerton's wife and in response to their request she says she will hand over the child if Pinkerton will come in half an hour's time. Sharpless and Kate leave.

Suzuki tries to comfort the desolate Butterfly, but is sent away. Butterfly takes her father's knife from its case and reads its inscription: 'Con onor muore chi non può serbar vita con onore' ('He dies with honour who cannot stay alive with honour'). In an effort to restrain her mistress, whose intention she has guessed, Suzuki pushes the child in. Butterfly smothers him with kisses, singing to him 'Tu! Tu! Piccolo iddio'. ('You! You! my little god!'). She gives him an American flag and a doll to play with, binds his eyes gently, goes behind a secreen and stabs herself. As Pinkerton arrives with Sharpless, she stumbles out, points to the child, and dies.

* * *

Puccini incorporated a number of Japanese melodies into his score.
(For a full examination, see *Puccini: A Critical Biography*, by Mosco
Carner.) We may quote one (ex. 1). It occurs just at the moment
when Butterfly, approaching from offstage with her girl friends, is
seen for the first time (ex. 2).

Ex. 1

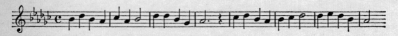

Ex. 2

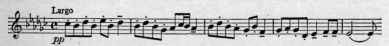

'One fine day', Butterfly's own most famous aria, is additionally
effective on the stage because it suggests 'acting within acting'.
Puccini expressly says that Butterfly must 'act the scene [of Pinkerton's hoped-for return to her] as if it were actually taking place';
and the accompaniment is marked 'as if from a distance'. Note that in
the accompaniment the melody is doubled at a lower octave and so
becomes the bass part as well, a typical Puccini device (ex. 3).

Ex. 3

LA FANCIULLA DEL WEST
(The Girl of the Golden West)
Libretto by Guelfo Civinini and Carlo Zangarini
after the play by David Belasco

First performed: New York, 1910
Three Acts

Cast in order of singing:

JOE	⎫	*tenor*
HANDSOME	⎬ MINERS	*baritone*
HARRY	⎭	*tenor*
NICK, BARTENDER AT THE POLKA TAVERN		*tenor*
HAPPY	⎫	*baritone*
SID	⎬ MINERS	*baritone*
TRIN	⎪	*tenor*
SONORA	⎭	*baritone*
JIM LARKENS		*bass*
JACK RANCE, SHERIFF		*baritone*
JAKE WALLACE, A TRAVELLING BALLAD-SINGER		*baritone*
ASHBY, AGENT FOR WELLS FARGO		*bass*
MINNIE, PROPRIETRESS OF THE POLKA TAVERN		*soprano*
POST-BOY		*tenor*
DICK JOHNSON, ALIAS RAMERREZ, A BANDIT		*tenor*
JOE CASTRO, A HALF-CASTE		*bass*
WOWKLE, MINNIE'S RED INDIAN SERVANT		*mezzo-soprano*
BILLY JACKRABBIT, A RED INDIAN		*bass*

Chorus of men in the mining camp
The scene is laid in a mining camp in California
during the gold rush of 1849–50

David Belasco's play about the Californian gold rush, *The Girl of the Golden West*, made a strong impression on Puccini when he saw it in New York in 1907 – as Belasco's *Madame Butterfly* had made on him in London. Although the word 'golden' does not occur in the Italian title it is customarily retained in English references to the opera.

Minnie in *La fanciulla del west* is a 'strong' heroine – who takes out a pistol and defies a crowd of angry men. The drama takes place in an exotic setting emphasized in the Italian text by the use of English expression such as 'Hello' to convey atmosphere. The Wild West is still an unusual enough setting for opera to have an appeal on its own, apart from Puccini's typical strength of melody. Incidentally, the refrain 'Dooda–dooda–day' is heard, but not to Stephen Foster's well-known tune; and the tune said by commentators to be a folksong 'The Old Dog Tray' (quoted in ex. 1 below) is not Foster's 'Old Dog Tray'. Puccini stipulates a horse on the stage – thus gratifying an Italian operatic audience as well as adding to the authenticity of his Wild West.

★   ★   ★

ACT I: It is evening, in the Polka; off-stage is a dance-hall. Voices are heard from outside as Nick, the bartender, lights the lamps. Joe, Handsome and Harry (miners) enter singing, followed later by Trin, Sonora and others. A game of cards begins. Only Larkens is solitary and miserable; he is (as Nick comments) homesick for 'his old Cornwall' ('la sua vecchia Cornovaglia'). Sonora and Trin both ask Nick about Minnie, the owner of the tavern, and Nick tells each separately that Minnie favours the questioner.

Jake Wallace, the travelling ballad–singer, approaches with a song, 'Che faranno i vecchi miei' ('What'll happen to my old folk?'), accompanying himself on the banjo. The men, caught by the nostalgia of the song, join in. Larkens bursts out sobbing; the men whip round for money to send him back home. He leaves with it gratefully. The card-game is resumed, and Sid is caught cheating. The men would hang him but Rance, as Sheriff, intervenes: 'Andiam, ragazzi' ('Come on, lads'). At his suggestion they pin his card on him to identify him as a cheat. They kick him out.

Ashby, agent for the Wells Fargo company, enters and converses with Rance about Ramerrez, the bandit for whose capture his company has offered a reward. All the men drink to Minnie, whom Rance says is shortly to be the new Mrs Rance – a boast which evokes a jealous outburst from Sonora, now drunk, who fires a pistol shot. Suddenly Minnie herself enters and quietens everyone. Joe, Sonora and Harry offer her presents, and Sonora pays his outstanding account with a bag of gold.

The men form an attentive group round Minnie as she starts 'school' with them, reading from the Psalms about the pure in heart. She also admonishes Billy Jackrabbit, the Red Indian who hangs round the camp, to marry Wowkle (of whose child he is the father).

The post-boy arrives and distributes mail. Ashby announces to

Rance that he will shortly catch Ramerrez. Joe is saddened by news
of his grandmother's death. Outside a stranger has arrived and has
asked for water with his whisky – to the amazement of the hard
drinkers present. Rance, left alone with Minnie, courts her (although
he has a wife already). He tells her that once he valued only gold –
'Dalla mia casa son partito' ('I left my home'); but now he offers a
thousand dollars for a kiss. Minnie repulses him: she seeks real love
and recalls the love her mother knew – 'Laggiù nel Soledad' ('Back
there in Soledad').

Dick Johnson enters – the stranger who ordered water with his
whisky. He and Minnie recognize each other from a past meeting
and speak warmly together. Rance is angry, but Minnie persuades
the others to accept Johnson, and Johnson leads her off to dance.

Joe Castro, a half-caste member of Ramerrez's gang, has been
captured and is brought in. He pretends to be ready to betray
Ramerrez's whereabouts – but in fact surreptitiously tells Johnson
(who *is* Ramerrez) that his gang is near. The rest of the men,
dragging Castro with them, leave. Minnie and Johnson, left
together, feel the awakening of love between them; but a shrill
whistle (the signal from his gang) makes Johnson depart. Before he
goes he tells Minnie that she has an angelic face ('Avete un viso
d'angelo') – a phrase that she repeats with a sigh, alone, as the curtain
falls.

ACT II: An hour later, in Minnie's cabin, her maid Wowkle is
singing as she rocks her baby. Billy comes in and promises to marry
Wowkle. Minnie enters, orders supper for two and decks herself for
Johnson, who arrives. She wonders why he came to the Polka – had
he mistaken the path for the one leading to Nina Micheltorena,
loose-living girl living not far away? But soon Minnie loses herself in
describing her enjoyment of the Wild West landscape: 'Oh, se
sapeste' ('Oh, if you knew').

Johnson passionately approaches Minnie, who, having dismissed
Wowkle, yields to his kisses. He denies that Nina Micheltorena has
been his mistress. Snow outside traps them within, and Minnie gives
him permission to sleep in her room. A noise is heard outside – the
other men, in pursuit of Ramerrez. Minnie hides Johnson and lets the
men in: they disclose that Johnson is Ramerrez and that Nina, his
former lover, has betrayed him. The men leave.

Minnie accuses Johnson of lying to her. He protests his love, and
leaves. A shot rings out. Unable to control herself, Minnie opens the
door and helps the wounded Johnson in. She confesses she still loves

him and helps him up to the loft to hide. Rance comes in, pursues Minnie – 'Ti voglio' ('I want you') – but does not find Johnson until blood drips down from the loft, disclosing the hiding-place.

Minnie proposes a game of poker with Rance – if she wins, she and Johnson are free; if she loses, Rance can have both her and his prisoner. They play. Minnie cheats (unnoticed by Rance) and wins. Rance leaves, Minnie laughs and weeps.

ACT III: Later, the hunt is on again for Johnson, alias Ramerrez. In a forest camp, Rance converses with Nick. An alarm is raised. Ashby is excited at the thought of catching his prey; Rance gesticulates with jealousy towards Minnie's cabin: 'Minnie, ora piangi tu' ('Minnie, now weep!'). Eventually Johnson is captured (off-stage). The men exult: 'Dooda-dooda-day!'

Johnson is brought in. The men, led by Rance, prepare to hang him. He asks for a moment's grace, pleading 'Ch'ella mi credi libero' ('Let her think me free').

Johnson's neck is in the noose when Minnie rushes in. With a pistol she defies the crowd. Then she appeals to the men individually by all that she has done to help them in the past – and finally she throws away her pistol. Sonora is the first to capitulate to her appeal. The others follow. As the men mourn her departure she leaves on Johnson's arm.

★   ★   ★

The travelling ballad-singer enters in Act I with ex. 1 (heard in the distance first of all), to which words of homesickness are attached. There is dramatic point in the verse, because the emotion of home-sickness is seen to be very strong in these 'forty-niners', and Minnie's role among them is really to supply 'home' amid their homelessness. When she pleads for her lover in the final scene it is her sisterly, homely services to the men that she bids them recall. And when they allow Johnson and her to go, and all sing a farewell to her, it is quite appropriately this tune that they repeat.

Ex. 1

Minnie's first entrance, in which she performs the violent action of snatching Sonora's pistol before she sings a note, is accompanied in the orchestra by her characteristic theme (ex. 2).

Ex. 2

In the hero's famous song in Act III there is a curious exotic touch, seemingly almost oriental in its melody and its harmonization: note how the melody is continued by the orchestra when the singer makes a brief break. We quote a part (ex. 3) shortly after the aria begins, to the words 'She will await my return and her days will pass by . . .'. Such a style seemed suitable to Puccini in treating the oriental scenes of *Madama Butterfly* and (later) *Turandot*; here it serves to delineate what must have been, for Puccini, another 'orient' – equally remote and strange – located paradoxically in the Golden West.

Ex. 3

IL TRITTICO

(The Triptych)

'Il trittico' (a three-panelled painting: in English 'triptych'): this was how Puccini viewed the three one-act operas on which he began work in 1913. The three were to represent different aspects of life and together were to make up an evening's entertainment. They indeed shared a single evening at their first performance, but nowadays are rarely all performed together. This is partly because such an evening is very long (as Puccini himself came to recognize), and partly because the middle opera seems to many to fall below the other two in quality.

The first opera is an adaptation from a French play by Didier Gold, *La houppelande* ('The Cloak'), the title literally translated by Puccini as *Il tabarro*. It is a tense and terse drama, strongly in the 'realist' tradition.

Puccini adopted the Italian convention of italianizing the French names, Louis becoming Luigi, and so on. The three nicknames used are also italianized: Il Tinca (originally 'Le Goujon') means 'The Gudgeon', Il Talpa (originally 'La Taupe') means 'The Mole', La Frugola (originally 'La Furette') means 'The Rummager'.

Suor Angelica ('Sister Angelica') has a cast only of women. It is a romantic opera, having as its climax a miracle shown on the stage. No 'realism' here! The opera is notable for a strongly drawn female villain, the Aunt, who (unless we count Suzuki in *Madama Butterfly*) is Puccini's only major characterization for a mezzo-soprano.

Gianni (short for Giovanni) Schicchi was an actual Florentine who is among the souls in purgatory mentioned in Dante's *Divine Comedy*: Puccini's *Gianni Schicchi* retains the name, the period and the background. This is a comic opera: and just as the normally 'tragic' Verdi excelled himself in the comedy of *Falstaff*, so Puccini shows a superb sureness (both in the main character and in the total handling of the action) in the comic roguery of *Gianni Schicchi*.

IL TABARRO
(The Cloak)
Part I of *Il trittico*
Libretto by Giuseppe Adami, after a play by Didier Gold

First performed: New York, 1918
One Act

Cast in order of singing:

GIORGETTA, AGED 25	*soprano*
MICHELE, HER HUSBAND, A BARGEMASTER, AGED 50	*baritone*
LUIGI, A BARGEMAN, GIORGETTA'S LOVER, AGED 20	*tenor*
IL TINCA, A BARGEMAN, AGED 50	*bass*
IL TALPA, A BARGEMAN, AGED 50	*bass*
A SONG-SELLER	*tenor*
LA FRUGOLA, TALPA'S WIFE, A RAG-PICKER, AGED 50	*mezzo-soprano*
TWO LOVERS	*tenor and soprano*

Chorus of bargemen and midinettes
The action takes place in a barge on the river Seine, in Paris

The curtain rises before the music starts. The scene is set in a barge on the river Seine, with famous Parisian landmarks visible in the background and Parisian noises audible (including a motor-horn, written into the score). Giorgetta, doing various little jobs on the barge, talks with her husband Michele as he watches the sunset. Some bargemen can be heard from below, where they are emptying the hold; Giorgetta suggests a glass of wine to refresh them. Michele asks her for a kiss, but she is cold towards him, and he goes below.

Luigi, one of her husband's crew, comes aboard and Giorgetta goes to fetch wine and glasses, giving some of each of the bargemen, including Il Tinca and Il Talpa, who have been grumbling good-humouredly about the back-breaking work. An organ-grinder happens to come along and Giorgetta dances – at first with Il Tinca, rather stiffly, and then with Luigi, in a languid, yielding fashion. Michele returns: Luigi pays the organ-grinder and the men go back to work, while Michele and Giorgetta discuss plans for their departure and she chides him for his morose moods. While they talk, a song-seller on the shore is trying to find buyers for his ballads, and he sings one of his songs, to the accompaniment of a companion who plays a little harp. 'E la storia di Mimì' ('It's the tale of Mimì'), he says, as the strings of the orchestra play a quotation from *La Bohème*. A group of midinettes, having brought the song, echo his singing.

La Frugola, Il Talpa's wife, arrives with a sack full of odds and ends. She talks to Giorgetta of her life and her cat. Michele asks Luigi to be present for a job the next day. Il Talpa and Il Tinca come up: La Frugola reprimands Il Tinca for his drinking, but he complains that drink is all he has to live for. Luigi angrily echoes his despair at the hard lot of the working man: 'Per noi la vita'. Il Tinca goes off.

La Frugola sings wistfully of her dream of happiness: 'Ho sognato una casetta' ('I dreamed of a cottage'). Giorgetta takes up the theme of longing: 'E ben altro il mio sogno! ('My dream is different!') – a nostalgic one for her early days in Belleville, a Paris suburb. Luigi lived there too; they recall it happily together. La Frugola and Il Talpa go off, singing of their dream cottage. Distant, impersonal voices are heard.

Giorgetta and Luigi are left alone. They are lovers, and he moves towards her, but she warns him to go as Michele will soon be back. They have exchanged only a few words of love when Michele comes: Luigi asks if he can be taken as far as Rouen, to seek work, but Michele says he would be better off in Paris and he agrees to stay. Michele goes into the cabin, and the lovers sing a passionate duet: 'Hai ragione' ('You are right'). Before he leaves, they arrange for him to return, later, when she shows a light to indicate that all is clear.

Michele comes up. They talk awhile, Michele desiring Giorgetta and reminding her of how in their happier days she used to nestle under his cloak, but she is cold and unresponsive – to his barely suppressed fury. She goes down to bed as Michele arranges the barge's lights. A pair of lovers passes by. A cornet sounds a military call from a barracks. Michele soliloquizes on his torment. He guesses that his wife is unfaithful and determines to wait, discover who her lover is, and kill him. He lights his pipe. Luigi, seeing a light, comes on to the barge. Michele watches him and lies in wait: suddenly he pounces and seizes him by the throat. As Michele strangles Luigi he forces him to confess repeatedly that he is Giorgetta's lover.

Giorgetta comes up from below as Luigi dies. Michele quickly wraps the body in his cloak. She is in a nervous mood; she apologizes for her earlier heartlessness and wants to come close to him. 'Dove? Nel mio tabarro?' ('Where? Under my cloak?'), he asks. As she

comes closer, he rises, and undoes the cloak so that Luigi's body rolls
out: then he seizes her and pushes her against her lover's face.

★   ★   ★

Here realism in the plot – in the sense of sordidness – is combined
with musical realism (the sound of a motor-horn, the imitation of a
cat). The whole opera preserves a hard intensity of mood; to the
characterization of the participants Puccini adds what seems a
characterization to the scene itself, in impressionist musical terms
influenced by Debussy. The opening (ex. 1) is hypnotic, and its
'wavy' motion surely represents the onward yet unchanging course
of the Seine in Paris.

Ex. 1

The first two bars are given to strings only with one flute, one
clarinet, and a bass clarinet – one of the many remarkable touches of
instrumentation in this work, which calls for four trombones instead
of the usual three. It is this opening theme which the unseen
impersonal voices sing later (before Luigi and Giorgetta's love-
duet). The construction of the whole work is thematic, in Puccini's
habitual way, and Michele's two references to his cloak (*tabarro*) – in
his plea for Giorgetta's love and his final gesture of disgust towards
her – have the same theme in different guises.

SUOR ANGELICA
(Sister Angelica)
Part II of *Il trittico*
Libretto by Giovacchino Forzano

First performed: New York, 1918
One Act

Cast in order of singing:

SISTER ANGELICA, A NUN	*soprano*
THE MONITOR (LA SUORA ZELATRICE)	*mezzo-soprano*
A LAY SISTER (LA CONVERSA)	*soprano*
THE MISTRESS OF THE NOVICES	
(LA MAESTRA DELLA NOVIZIE)	*mezzo-soprano*
A LAY SISTER (LA CONVERSA)	*mezzo-soprano*
SISTER OSMINA	*soprano*
SISTER GENOVIEFFA	*soprano*
THREE OTHER NUNS	*two sopranos, mezzo-soprano*
SISTER DOLCINA	*soprano*
THE NURSING SISTER (LA SUORA INFERMIERA)	*mezzo-soprano*
The ALMS SISTERS (LE CERCATRICI)	*two sopranos*
THE ABBESS (LA BADESSA)	*mezzo-soprano*
THE PRINCESS, ANGELICA'S AUNT	
(LA ZIA PRINCIPESSA)	*mezzo-soprano*

Chorus of nuns and angels
*The scene is laid in a convent, at the end of the
seventeenth century*

The scene shows the cloister of a convent, with a garden, and the door of a chapel, through which the voices of nuns at prayer can be heard. Two lay sisters, then the young Sister Angelica, go into the chapel. Her voice is clearly audible from within. When the service ends the sisters come out of the chapel, two by two, bowing to the Abbess.

After the Monitor has reprimanded three nuns for minor offences (the Mistress of the Novices explaining this to her charges), Sister Genovieffa draws the sisters' attention to the rays of the setting sun, which will soon make the font glow as if the water is golden. This happens just three evenings in the year. The sisters resolve to sprinkle some 'golden water' on the tomb of one of their number who has lately died. In the course of a conversation about worldly desires, Genovieffa admits that, as a former shepherdess, she longs to see and hold a lamb. Genovieffa asks Angelica if she desires anything. No, she replies ('Io no, sorella, no'): but all are aware that this is not the truth and that she is constantly sad at having heard no word from her family in her seven years in the convent.

The nursing sister comes in, agitated: one of the sisters has been stung by wasps. She asks Angelica, who understands curative potions, for help, and Angelica gives her a herbal mixture. Then two alms sisters arrive with provisions, which the others unload with pleasure from a donkey. One of the alms sisters mentions that a very grand carriage is drawn up before the entrance. Angelica, flustered, asks her ('Ah! ditemi, sorella') to describe the carriage, but she cannot. The sisters watch her with kindly pity: as the visitors' bell rings they assemble, excited, each one wondering if the visitor is for herself. Genovieffa tells Angelica, who is praying for help, that all hope it is for her. The Abbess enters and summons Angelica. The others go off towards the cemetery, with 'golden water': their prayers can be heard while the Abbess tells Angelica that her aunt, the Princess, has come.

The Abbess goes and the stern figure of the Princess enters. Angelica is much moved, and goes to embrace her aunt. But the Princess coldly stares straight ahead, only offering Angelica her hand to kiss and beginning to recite Angelica's history: 'Your father, Prince Gualtiero . . .' She tells Angelica she has come to obtain her signature to a document, in which she renounces all claims to the money left by her parents in favour of her younger sister, who is to be married. Angelica looks to her aunt for some sign of pity or kindness, but the Princess is inexorably harsh, only reminding her of the disgrace she brought upon the family and the eternal penance due from her. Angelica says she is repentant, but nothing can make her forget her son – the son she has seen only once. She asks her aunt for news of him. The old woman is at first silent, then – when Angelica's demand is repeated with increasing emotion – she explains: two years ago he was taken ill, and died. Angelica falls to the ground, sobbing.

It is now becoming dark. Without words a sister brings an oil-lamp, the Abbess a pen and ink, and Angelica signs the document; the Princess takes it and moves towards Angelica, who shrinks away; then she leaves, glancing back at her niece.

Angelica is once more alone. As the sisters light the lanterns on the tombstones in the cemetery, she bursts into tears, and sings of her child: 'Senza mamma, o bimbo, tu sei morto' ('Without your Mummy, darling baby, you died'). Genovieffa and the other sisters come in and comfort her. Angelica, now in a state of mystical ecstasy, tell them that heavenly grace has descended on her, and that she knows what she must do. They all give thanks to God and the Virgin and move off to their cells.

Angelica comes from her cell. Alone, she mixes a poisonous potion from some flowers, using water from the font. Then she sings of the peace her draught will bring; she bid the sisters farewell, and in a state of exaltation she drinks. Now her serenity fades, and she returns to reality: in anguish she cries 'Ah, son dannata!' ('Oh, I am damned!') and she prays for forgiveness for her terrible sin.

Distant voices, of angels, are heard. Suddenly the chapel is miraculously suffused with light. The church doors open: the Blessed Virgin appears; in front of her is a child, clad in white, whom she pushes towards Angelica. Angelica rises her arms to the child, who steps towards her, as the voices sing 'Salve, Maria!' She falls to the ground and dies, and the miraculous vision fades.

★　　★　　★

The moments before the second-act curtain of *Tosca*, in which the heroine performs with tremendous effect her dumbshow action with candles and crucifix to orchestral accompaniment, are paralleled in *Suor Angelica*. Here a much longer dumbshow action involving four people (Angelica, another nun, Angelica's aunt, and the Abbess) takes places and lasts for several minutes (more than forty bars of music): the action is minutely described in the score. The resulting tension is immediately released in Angelica's aria, the climax of Puccini's portrayal of his heroine, where she pours out her feelings on learning that the illegitimate child she bore is dead (ex. 2). Note the modal touch in melody and harmony (the flat seventh, that is the G natural in the tonality of A – characteristic of Puccini's idiom in this opera, where he plainly hints at old church music. The modal touch is also used – but for its oriental associations, with quite different effect – in *Madama Butterfly* and *Turandot*.

Ex. 2

GIANNI SCHICCHI
Part III of *Il trittico*
Libretto by Giovacchino Forzano

First performed: New York, 1918
One Act

Cast in order of singing:

ZITA, BUOSO DONATI'S COUSIN, AGED 60	*mezzo-soprano*
SIMONE, BUOSO'S COUSIN, AGED 70	*bass*
RINUCCIO, ZITA'S NEPHEW, AGED 24	*tenor*
MARCO, SIMONE'S SON, AGED 45	*baritone*
CIESCA, MARCO'S WIFE, AGED 38	*soprano*
GHERARDO, BUOSO'S NEPHEW, AGED 40	*tenor*
NELLA, GHERARDO'S WIFE, AGED 34	*soprano*

BETTO OF SIGNA, BUOSO'S IMPOVERISHED BROTHER-IN-LAW,
    OF UNCERTAIN AGE   *bass*
LAURETTA, GIANNI SCHICCHI'S DAUGHTER, AGED 21   *soprano*
GHERARDINO, GHERARDO AND NELLA'S SON, AGED 7   *contralto*
                                            (or boy's voice)
GIANNI SCHICCHI, AGED 50   *baritone*
SPINELLOCCIO, A BOLOGNESE PHYSICIAN   *bass*
SER AMANTIO DI NICOLAO, A NOTARY   *bass*
PINELLINO, A COBBLER   *baritone*
GUCCIO, A DYER   *tenor*

The scene is laid in Florence, in 1299

The relatives of Buoso Donati are assembled in prayer and tears
around the bed where he has just died. 'Povero Buoso' ('Poor
Buoso') – this and similar laments go up from Buoso's cousin Zita,
with her nephew Rinuccio; another cousin, Simone, with his son
Marco and his wife Ciesca; Buoso's nephew Gherardo, with his wife
Nella and their seven-year-old son, Gherardino; and Betto, Buoso's
brother-in-law. The small boy, bored, is being a nuisance, and all
silence him from time to time.

Betto whispers that rumours are afoot in Signa, where he lives, that
Buoso has left all his money to a monastery instead of to the family.
Simone, as the senior relative, declares that they are lost if the will is
already in the lawyers' hands, but if it were hidden in the room . . .
whereupon a frenzied search begins, ending when Rinuccio finds the
will in a cupboard. Before they open it, he asks whether, if they are
all now rich, he could marry Lauretta, Gianni Schicchi's daughter.
Zita, as his aunt, reluctantly consents. While they are opening the
will (with difficulty, for Betto has pocketed the scissors), Rinuccio
sends the small boy to fetch Gianni Schicchi and Lauretta. As they
light more candles in his honour, they all mutter 'Poor Buoso' again,
and each hopes for the prize possessions – the house, the mills at
Signa and the mule.

They all gather round and read the document, their mouths
moving but saying nothing aloud, with mounting horror and
dismay. 'Dunque era vero!' ('So it was true!'), exclaims Simone,
promptly extinguishing the candles. They all join in an outburst of
hate directed at the fortunate monks. How the monks will laugh at
the Donatis, they exclaim, their mock laughter changing almost to
tears. They begin to think of ways of getting round the will, but to

no avail. The only person to help, says Rinuccio, is Gianni Schicchi – and he's coming, says Gherardino, rushing in. First Zita, then the others object to the outsider, especially as he is not a Florentine, but Rinuccio talks them round: in his song 'Firenze è come un albero fiorito' ('Florence is like a flowering tree') he points out that Florence has traditionally derived her strength from newcomers.

Schicchi enters with Lauretta. As Rinuccio and Lauretta snatch a lovers' greeting, Schicchi sees the sad faces and at first thinks Buoso must be recovering; then he realizes that he is dead, and thinks what good actors they are; and finally the truth is explained to him. Zita says she will not let her nephew marry Lauretta, who has no dowry. A lively quartet ensues, Zita and Schicchi quarrelling vigorously while the lovers beg not to be parted. All join in the argument. Schicchi, offended, tries to take Lauretta away. Rinuccio, however, asks his help in circumventing the will; but he refuses, only giving way when Lauretta adds her plea in order that she and Rinuccio may marry: 'O mio babbino caro' ('Oh my beloved daddy').

Schicchi takes the will and studies it. At first he says that nothing can be done (the lovers lament); then an idea dawns. He sends Lauretta out to feed the birds, and discloses his scheme. After making sure that no one else knows Buoso has died, he tells them to take out the body and remake the bed. Then there is a knock at the door. It is the doctor, Spinelloccio (who speaks with a nasal voice and in a Bolognese accent – Bologna is the site of a famous faculty of medicine). Hurriedly they darken the room, and Schicchi hides behind the bedcurtains. They admit Spinelloccio and tell him Buoso is resting. With an imitation of Buoso's voice convincing enough to startle the relatives, Schicchi asks the doctor to come back in the evening, as he feels very sleepy. Spinelloccio goes.

Schicchi comes out and explains his plan. He himself will pose as the dying Buoso while a notary takes down his last will and testament. Zia sends Rinuccio off for the notary and the delighted relatives embrace one another. But they are less affectionate when it comes to dividing the spoils. Five parts of the estate are claimed by the four men and Zita: but violent quarrels break out over the three prize items, starting when Simone claims them on grounds of seniority.

The tolling of a funeral bell interrupts the uproar: they are terrified that Buoso's death might have been discovered. (Here Lauretta comes in for a moment – the birds are sated – but Schicchi dispatches her again.) Soon Gherardo brings welcome news that someone else has died, and they breathe again, with a very happy 'Requiescat in pace'! Schicchi dresses himself in Buoso's night attire, with a kerchief and nightcap; first Zita, then Simone, Betto, Nella and Ciesca in turn offer him bribes to leave them the three controversial items. 'Sta bene!' ('So be it!') he answers each one, and each one is satisfied. The three women stand back and admire him in his disguise, singing him a mock lullaby. As he gets into bed, he warns them all of the legal punishment for falsifying a will – the loss of a hand and exile: 'Addio, Firenze' ('Farewell, Florence'), he sings, and makes them join in, glancing through the window at the familiar landmarks of the town.

There is a knock, and the notary, Amantio, enters with two of Buoso's friends, Pinellino and Guccio, to act as witnesses. Pinellino expresses his sorrow at seeing Buoso in such a state. Amantio reads the opening rigmarole in Latin, to which Schicchi is careful to add a sentence revoking all previous wills, to the relatives' admiration. First he decides on an economical funeral; then five lire to the monks – rather a little, Amantio suggests, which Schicchi counters by saying that when people leave large sums of money to the Church they are suspected of having come by it dishonestly. Then he goes on to the five items as arranged, with profuse thanks from each beneficiary. Now for the mule – he leaves it 'to my devoted friend Gianni Schicchi' ('al mio devoto amico Gianni Schicchi'). (The lawyer writes, repeating the words in Latin.) The relatives jump up in surprise: Simone protests but is quickly silenced by Schicchi, while the others mutter. Then the house goes – to Gianni Schicchi. There are loud protests this time, quelled by Schicchi singing his 'Farewell, Florence' and flapping an empty sleeve of his nightshirt – an eloquent warning. Finally, the mills at Signa: again to Gianni Schicchi, but between every few words comes a phrase of 'Farewell, Florence'. The notary and witnesses depart sadly, bidding the relatives bear up.

A riot breaks out the moment they have gone – 'Ladro, Ladro!' ('Thief, thief!') – as all the relatives set about Schicchi, who defends himself with a stick. Then they do their best to ransack the house, while Schicchi orders them off 'his' property. As their angry voices fade away into the distance, Rinuccio opens the balcony window from outside, where he and Lauretta are embracing and singing of their love. Schicchi, who has been chasing the rapacious relatives, comes back and sees them, smiles, and turns to the audience. (Now he speaks, not sings.) Who could think of a better use for the money? For this escapade he has been sent to perdition, and so be it: but, with

Dante's permission, if the audience have enjoyed themselves, may he be allowed to plead 'extenuating circumstances'?

★   ★   ★

The sweetmeat in the score belongs not to the title-role but to Lauretta: it is 'Oh my beloved daddy' (ex. 3). Note that she naturally uses the colloquial form 'babbino', not 'padre' – 'daddy', not 'father', though many singers of the English version try to 'refine' it.

Ex. 3

But the title-role is the commanding one, with two extraordinary theatrical strokes in it: first, when Schicchi (impersonating Buoso) recites the final and vital clauses of 'his' will in a half-spoken, impersonated voice but intersperses it by recalling his warning to the relatives ('Farewell, Florence') in a normal singing voice; second, when he turns at the very end to the audience and (speaking, not singing) pleads that, if his action was criminal, at least there were extenuating circumstances. (The published English version says 'Not Guilty'. This is both false to the original and nonsense in itself.)

TURANDOT
Libretto by Giuseppe Adami and Renato Simoni,
after the play by Carlo Gozzi

First performed: Milan, 1926
Three Acts

Cast in order of singing:

A MANDARIN	*bass*
LIÙ, A SLAVE GIRL	*soprano*
THE UNKNOWN PRINCE (CALAF)	*tenor*

TIMUR, CALAF'S FATHER, A DETHRONED KING   *bass*
THE PRINCE OF PERSIA   *tenor*
PING, THE GRAND CHANCELLOR   *baritone*
PONG, THE GENERAL PURVEYOR   *tenor*
PANG, THE CHIEF COOK   *tenor*
THREE OF TURANDOT'S HANDMAIDENS   *sopranos*
THE EMPEROR ALTOUM   *tenor*
PRINCESS TURANDOT   *soprano*
[The role of the executioner is silent.]

Chorus of soldiers, attendants, children,
priests, mandarins and people
The scene is laid in Peking, in legendary times

In *Turandot* Puccini returned to an oriental scene (as in *Madama Butterfly*) and to a strongly stressed connection between sex and cruelty (as in *Tosca*). In fact, on any normal consideration, the story is perhaps the most repulsive that any opera audience is regularly called on to enjoy. Richard Strauss's Salome is at least killed for her perversion, but the love-triumph of Turandot and Calaf is a triumph based on the acceptance of the torture and death of Liù, the only character of the story who shows any positive action for good.

Moreover, there are several incidental touches in Puccini's opera (not in Gozzi's original play of 1762, *Turandotte*) which specially emphasize horror and cruelty – among them the personal appearance of the executioner and the procession taking the previous rejected suitor to the scaffold. But it is not difficult in the theatre to let moral scruple be overpowered by the force of Puccini's resplendent score.

Puccini died in November 1924: he had not completed the love-duet and the ensuing final scene, though he had left sketches for them. On Toscanini's advice the completion was entrusted after his death to Franco Alfano (1876–1954), a composer whose style had been influenced by Puccini and who had once himself meditated an opera on the same subject. This completion has itself, until recent times, been given in a truncated and weaker form, but Alfano's stronger ending is now to be preferred.

★　★　★

ACT I: By the walls of Peking, a mandarin reads out a decree to the assembled crowd. In accordance with the law, he proclaims, the Princess Turandot will only marry if a prince of royal blood comes forward who can solve her three riddles: failure to solve them means death; and death awaits the Prince of Persia, who has just failed. The crowd is crying for his blood. Guards push back the people who rush towards the palace, calling the name of the executioner, Pu-Tin-Pao.

In the crush an old man has fallen. Liù, the slave-girl who is his devoted companion, calls for help and a man, the Unknown Prince, runs up. He recognizes the old man, Timur, as his father, and Timur greets his son. (Both are fugitives from a usurper of the throne in their own country, and have to remain unknown.) While the bloodthirsty shouts of the crowd continue in the background, Timur tells his son how he has been cared for by Liù; and she explains her devotion – it was because the Prince himself once smiled at her.

Preparations for the execution proceed, with the sharpening of the blade. The crowd continue their savage chanting. Their mood changes as darkness descends and they wait for the moon to appear, but again they call for Pu-Tin-Pao. Voices of children are heard. Then the procession appears: the people, seeing the pale young Prince of Persia, now beg for pity for him (with the Unknown Prince adding his voice). Turandot appears on the balcony; all the people fall on their faces except the executioner and the two princes. She makes a decisive gesture – the death sentence. She utters no sound.

The Unknown Prince is dazzled by his brief glimpse of her beauty. As the procession passes, with priests, the Prince determines to remain, despite the pleas of Timur and Liù. From a distance, the Prince of Persia's voice is heard in one final call, 'Turandot'; then there is a scream from the crowd as he is executed. The Prince resolves to try to win her himself and goes to strike the ceremonial gong as a signal.

Ping, Pang and Pong, three of Turandot's ministers, clad in grotesque masks, intercept him and try to dissuade him. Ping says that Turandot is just a woman, like any other – it isn't worth the risk, and he is sure to fail, like all her previous suitors. Their chatter is disturbed by Turandot's handmaidens, who demand quiet as she is resting. But the ministers soon resume their stream of words. Shadows of Turandot's dead suitors flit by. The Prince eventually shakes off the three 'masks', but his father again tries to draw him away, and finally Liù tries – 'Signore, ascolta' ('My lord, listen') – saying that she and Timur must die if the Prince persists. He is much moved – 'Non piangere, Liù ('Do not weep, Liù') – but remains resolute, though all five repeatedly beg him to give way, supported by hidden voices warning him of certain death. At the climax he calls Turandot's name three times, and sounds three strokes on the gong, committing himself finally as a suitor – for her hand or for death.

ACT II: In a pavilion, Ping, Pang and Pong are ready to make arrangements for a wedding or a funeral, as may be required. At some length, they muse on the happy days before Turandot's bloody reign, Ping recalling his house on the Lake of Homan, Pang his forests at Tsiang, Pong his garden at Kiu. They think once again of Turandot's innumerable beheaded suitors; if only they could have the pleasure of preparing a nuptial couch instead of an execution! Sounds from the palace and the assembling crowd recall them to their duties.

The scene changes to the square before the palace, where the crowds gather for the asking of the fateful riddles. At the head of an imposing staircase the aged Emperor Altoum appears, on a huge throne, and the people prostrate themselves. In a weary, trembling voice, he too tries to dissuade the Prince, but again without avail. A mandarin, as before, proclaims the decree, and the voices of children are heard calling to Turandot. She enters, clad in gold. In her song 'In questa reggia' ('In this palace') she explains the reason for her savage edict – it is in revenge of an event a thousand thousand years ago, when a princess was carried off and cruelly ravished by a barbarian. She menacingly advises him to withdraw, but he determinedly refuses.

She poses the first riddle: he quickly answers 'Hope' ('La speranza'). The wise men open their scrolls and check; it is right. He takes longer over the second, but again answers correctly: 'Blood ('Il sangue'). The crowd's suspense mounts. To the third riddle – 'What is the ice that fires you?' ('Gelo che ti da foco?') – he hesitates yet more, but then answers: 'Turandot'. To universal delight he has triumphed: the Emperor and people declare that the oath is binding and Turandot must give way.

She protests wildly, asking whether he wants her by force. He does not, he replies; and he gives her an opportunity of escape – if she can discover his name by morning he is prepared to die. The Emperor prays that the Prince will be his son by morning. As the court rises, the people prostrate themselves and sing in his praise.

ACT III: From the garden of the palace, heralds can be heard in the distance proclaiming Turandot's decree that 'Nessun dorma' ('Let no one sleep'); the Prince's name must be discovered, on pain of death. The Prince takes up the words in an aria in which the off-stage voices join. Ping, Pang and Pong approach, trying to persuade him (pushing forward a bevy of beautiful girls and coffers of gold and jewels) to accept an alternative to Turandot and abandon his suit which is bringing such terror to Peking. The people add their voices, but despite threats of torture he stands firm.

Suddenly, soldiers drag in Timur and Liù, who had earlier been seen with the Prince: 'Eccolo il nome' ('Here is the name'), they exclaim. The Prince declares they know nothing, but the people ignore them. Turandot is summoned. Ping offers to wring the name out of them; then Liù steps forward, declaring that she alone, not the old man, knows it. The people clamour to have her tortured. Ping repeatedly demands the name, but despite cruel tortures she will not answer. Tied up, the Prince cannot intervene.

Turandot asks Liù how she can endure: through her love, she answers. The tortures are renewed and the executioner appears. Then Liù says she will speak. In her song 'Tu che di gel sei cinta' (You who are circled in ice'), she predicts Turandot's eventual capitulation to the Prince – and her own (Liù's) death. As she finishes she seizes a dagger, stabs herself, and falls, dying, at the Prince's feet, the name still undisclosed. Timur, helpless without her, holds her hand: 'Liù, bontà! Liù, dolcezza!'. ('Liù, so good! Liù, so gentle!'). The crowd, now repentant, ask her spirit to pardon them.

[At this point Puccini's music ends.]

All depart, except the Prince and Turandot. He chides her for her hardness, and tears the veil from her. She at first repulses him, protesting that she is sacred and he must not profane her; but he seizes her and kisses her passionately. As women's voices are heard in the distance, she begins to melt. Children's voices sing a hymn to the morning. Deeply ashamed that he has triumphed over her, Turandot sheds her first tears. She asks him to leave her now, victorious, his name still unknown. But he tells her his name – Calaf, son of Timur; she may kill him if she wishes.

The brief final scene takes place before the palace, where crowds are paying homage to the Emperor. Turandot brings in Calaf, telling her father that she knows the name of the stranger: 'Il suo nome è Amor' ('His name is Love'). The people sing jubilantly.

★　★　★

Turandot is objectively the richest (that is, the biggest and most complex in sound) of Puccini's scores. Its harmony is more advanced than that of any of his previous works. As well as a very large orchestra in the pit (including tuned gongs and other unusual percussion) there is an off-stage band of brass, two alto saxophones, percussion and organ. The two saxophones double the melody (ex. 1) sung by the children in the first act ('There, on the mountains to the east, the stork sings'). This is one of several authentic Chinese

Ex. 1

tunes incorporated in the score: in its melody and in Puccini's striking harmonization (plus the effect of children's voices) it denotes serenity. It is thus directly contrasted with the violent, 'tortured' chromatic themes like the one which thunders out in the first two bars of the opera (ex. 2) and portrays Turandot's cruelty.

Ex. 2

An extraordinary battle of keys takes place in the Riddle Scene (Act II). We translate literally:

Turandot: The riddles are three, death is one!'

Prince: No, no! the riddles are three, one is life.

The theme proclaimed by Turandot is 'trumped' by the Prince who sings it in a higher key; then when Turandot tries to 'trump' him with a higher key still, he keeps up with her, as it were matching force with force (ex. 3).

Ex. 3

Liù is one of Puccini's most touching characters – her torture, her aria 'Tu che di gel sei cinta', her heroic suicide and then her funeral procession constitute the big moment of compassion in the opera.

But the dominating tune in the work remains the Prince's: it is
'Nessun dorma', with words that continue: 'But my mystery is
enclosed within me; my name no one shall know' (ex. 4).

Ex. 4

The sonorous richness is increased by a variation of the harmony
later. Alfano, in completing the work, was acting entirely in accord
with Puccini's own principles in insisting on it – *with* the enriched
harmony – in the final pages.

RUGGERO LEONCAVALLO

1858–1919

The exploration of low life (as in *La Bohème)* and of the extremes of emotional agony (as in *Tosca*) are marks of 'realistic' opera. The Italian word *verismo*, sometimes encountered in English contexts, simply denotes realism in its theatrical and literary sense. The soprano–tenor–baritone plot of *Tosca* was curiously foreshadowed four years earlier in *Andrea Chénier* (1896) by Umberto Giordano (1864–1948). Giordano and Francesco Cilea (1866–1950), composer of the celebrated *Adriana Lecouvreur* (1902), and perhaps Alfredo Catalani (1854–93), now chiefly remembered for *La Wally* (1892), are among the leading contemporaries of Puccini attached to the *verismo* tradition.

Theatrical realism attracted another of Puccini's contemporaries, Ermanno Wolf-Ferrari (1876–1948), in *I gioielli della Madonna* ('The Jewels of the Madonna', 1911); but Wolf-Ferrari also composed two longer-lasting comedies in a mock-formal vein which looks back to the eighteenth century – *I quatro rusteghi* (1906; known in Britain in Dent's translation as 'School for Fathers') and *Il segreto di Susanna* ('Susanna's Secret', 1909).

Among Italian composers, one who made a more radical approach to musical composition was Ferruccio Busoni (1866–1924) who wrote four operas, with librettos (in German) by himself: *Die Brautwahl* ('The Bride-Choosing'; 1912), *Arlecchino* (1917), *Turandot* (1917) and *Doctor Faust* (unfinished, completed by Philipp Jarnach and performed in 1925). The last is the most highly regarded, but intellectual regard rather than theatrical success has been Busoni's lot.

Celebrated in the realist tradition of Italian opera are '*Cav* and *Pag*' – to use the colloquial English names for the two works which form an almost invariable double bill. *Cavalleria rusticana* by Pietro Mascagni and *Pagliacci* by Ruggero Leoncavallo are treated here in reverse order, since Leoncavallo was slightly the older composer.

Leoncavallo wrote an unsuccessful *La Bohème* at the same time as Puccini's, but *Pagliacci* is his only well-known piece.

PAGLIACCI
(Clowns)
Libretto by the Composer

First performed: Milan, 1892
Two Acts

Cast in order of singing:

TONIO (IN THE PLAY, TADDEO, A CLOWN)	*baritone*
CANIO (IN THE PLAY, PAGLIACCIO)	*tenor*
A VILLAGER	*baritone*
BEPPE (IN THE PLAY, ARLECCHINO)	*tenor*
A VILLAGER	*tenor*
NEDDA, CANIO'S WIFE (IN THE PLAY, COLOMBINA)	*soprano*
SILVIO, A VILLAGER	*baritone*

Chorus of villagers and peasants
The scene is laid near Montalto, in Calabria
1865–70

A play within a play: the device is an ancient one (Shakespeare has made it familiar to us). The comic scene enacted for a village audience by a group of strolling players becomes a tragic drama of real life.

Additionally, the composer (who was his own librettist) introduces a prologue spoken by one of the actors in costume but supposedly giving a message direct from the author. This is, of course, also an ancient theatrical device, and its effect of providing a frame (and thus an effect of theatrical 'remoteness') for the subsequent action is similar to the mid-twentieth-century use of a prologue or epilogue (as in Britten's *The Rape of Lucretia* and Stravinsky's *The Rake's Progress*). In its own period it was particularly bold, and it is still very telling.

The title of the work is just *Pagliacci* (Clowns). The usual introductory *I* (The) is unauthentic. In the standard English version the familiar English harlequinade-names of Punchinello, Harlequin and Columbine replace Pagliaccio, Arlecchino and Colombina.

* * *

ACT I: The orchestral introduction is interrupted by the singer who is about to play the role of Tonio. He pushes his head between the curtains and then steps forward, telling the audience that he is the Prologue. He announces that the drama they are to witness, though represented by actors, is nevertheless about real human beings with ordinary feelings. The curtain rises.

On the afternoon of the Feast of the Assumption, a troupe of travelling actors has arrived, and villagers, in festive mood, come to greet them. Canio, leader of the troupe, steps down from the wagon and thanks the villagers for their welcome, announcing that a performance will take place at eleven o'clock that evening in the improvised theatre. Canio's wife, Nedda, begins to alight from the wagon and Tonio – a hunchback, vainly in love with her – moves to help her; but Canio angrily pushes him aside and lifts her down himself. The people laugh at Tonio, who mutters that he will avenge his humiliation.

A villager invites Canio and his colleagues to come to the tavern. Beppe says he will come too, but Tonio declines. Another villager jocularly remarks that Tonio is staying so as to make love to Nedda. Canio solemnly warns that although such a situation might be funny on the stage, in real life it would not: 'Un tal gioco' ('Such a joke'). Nedda hears and is anxious, but Canio assures the villagers that he does not really suspect her. Bagpipes are heard, then bells: as evening descends, the villagers go off, imitating the clang of the bells and singing of love.

Alone, Nedda sings nervously of her husband's suspicious, then, carried away by the sound of the birds, she breaks into happy song: 'Stridono lassù' ('Trilling up there'). As she finishes, Tonio appears. She mocks heartlessly at the hunchbacked clown and his declaration of love; eventually he can bear no more and tries to force a kiss from her, but she has picked up a donkey-whip and strikes him across the face. In pain and humiliation, he goes off, swearing revenge.

A moment later Silvio, a villager who is Nedda's real lover, appears. He pleads with Nedda to fly with him, but she begs him not to tempt her. Eventually she gives way. During their long duet Tonio enters, unseen but not unseeing. He fetches Canio, too late to see the departing Silvio but just in time to hear her words: 'A stanotte e per sempre tua sarò' ('Tonight and for ever I shall be yours'). Tonio tells Nedda that it was he who brought Canio back. Canio demands to know her lover's name, which she refuses to give. In his fury he almost stabs her, but Beppe intervenes, calms him and leads Nedda off, while Tonio promises to watch for the man. Beppe returns for a moment, telling Canio to dress for the performance and Tonio to beat his drum to attract the crowds. Left alone, Canio faces the fact that despite his private tragedy he has still to be the clown and amuse his public: 'Vesti la giubba' ('Put on the costume').

ACT II: Later that evening the crowd begins to assemble for the performance, Tonio calling on them to 'Walk up! Walk up!' ('Avanti, avanti'). Beppe helps to sort out the seating, and in the general confusion Nedda and Silvio manage to exchange a few words. The people are beginning to get impatient when the bell rings and the curtain rises on the play.

To a mock eighteenth-century minuet, Colombina (Nedda) is seen on her own. Her husband, Pagliaccio, is away, she says, and and the clown Taddeo is at market, so all is safe. Soon the serenade of Arlecchino (Beppe) is heard. But before he can enter, Taddeo (Tonio) comes in and makes a grotesque declaration of love, in the course of which Arlecchino enters by the window. Arlecchino throws out Taddeo, who promises to keep watch for them. They sing a little love-duet (in gavotte rhythm) over their supper, but are interrupted by a warning from Taddeo – Pagliaccio (Canio) is approaching. Arlecchino leaves, and as Pagliaccio enters he hears Colombina say 'A stanotte e per sempre tua sarò' (the very words Canio had heard Nedda use earlier in reality).

At this point Canio, unnerved, hesitantly tries to go on with the play, and in his role of Pagliaccio accuses Colombina of having a lover; she says that her visitor was only Taddeo, whom she brings in, and Taddeo assures Pagliaccio with a meaningful sneer that his wife is true to him. Now Canio can stand no more; he forgets the play and fiercely demands to know her lover's name. She tries to laugh it off, calling him Pagliaccio. 'Nò! Pagliaccio non son!' ('No! I am no clown!'), he bursts out in fury.

The audience (but not Silvio) suppose this is really splendid, true-to-life acting, and call 'bravo'. Nedda for a moment replies in her own nature, but when once more he demands her lover's name she tries to resume the play. Thinking she is mocking him, he threatens to kill her. The audience begin to get agitated as they realize that the actors are no longer acting. During their angry, impassioned

dialogue Silvio tries to rush forward; then Beppe, restrained by
Tonio, tries to make a move. Canio stabs Nedda; she call to Silvio
for help, and as he rushes to her aid Canio stabs him too. Turning to
the audience, he says: 'La commedia è finita!' ('The entertainment is
over').

★   ★   ★

The notion of a play within a play, which is the fundamental
dramatic point of the opera, also provides the two strongest and
best-known musical excerpts – the baritone's prologue and the
tenor's 'Vesti la giubba' (long known to British audiences as 'On
with the motley'). The one, in fact, melodically anticipates the other.
The prologue's final line, 'Incominciamo!' ('Let us begin!'), takes the
baritone to a splendidly effective high G – not in the score (where the
note is D) but in all performances.

The inner play features the traditional characters of the harlequinade, and the point is musically made by the old-fashioned,
artificial style of music. Ex. 1, for instance, is Arlecchino's serenade
to Colombina, with pizzicato strings imitating a serenader's guitar.

Ex. 1

PIETRO MASCAGNI

1863–1945

One work made Mascagni famous, the one-act *Cavalleria rusticana*: and, very remarkably, it was his first opera. He wrote fourteen more, none as successful – though *L'amico Fritz* (1891), *Iris* (1898, set in Japan) and one or two others are occasionally still given.

CAVALLERIA RUSTICANA
(Rustic Chivalry)
Libretto by Giovanni Targioni-Tozzetti and Guido Menasci,
after a short story by Giovanni Verga

First performed: Rome, 1890
One Act

Cast in order of singing:

TURIDDU, A PEASANT	*tenor*
SANTUZZA, A PEASANT GIRL	*soprano*
MAMMA LUCIA, TURIDDU'S MOTHER,	
KEEPER OF AN INN	*contralto*
ALFIO, A CARRIER	*baritone*
LOLA, ALFIO'S WIFE	*mezzo-soprano*

Chorus of villagers
The scene is laid in a Sicilian village

Two bold theatrical touches distinguish the score of *Cavalleria rusticana*. Within the overture, which is based on tunes to be heard in the opera itself, a serenade is sung behind the curtain – supposedly the secret serenade sung by Turiddu to his illicit love, Lola. It is as though we are not just hearing an overture but are sensing, through the closed curtains, the life going on in the Sicilian village which is soon to be visually revealed. (In fact, Lola makes her first entrance with a song that seems like a recollection of this.)

Then, later in the opera, an intermezzo is played *with the curtain up*: our eyes concentrate on the empty stage, stimulated by the orchestra to recall what we have seen.

The meaning of the title is really 'The Rustic Code of Honour': the opera shows this code operating in a working village community, as earlier operas had shown the operation of codes of honour in aristocratic society. The climax is violent, with a duel off-stage; the soprano, tenor, and baritone express in powerful solos the fierce pride from which the violence results; and a strong choral part emphasizes the collective strength of village life.

★   ★   ★

Early on the morning of Easter Day, the church bells are ringing and people are entering church. Their songs in praise of spring are heard. Santuzza, heartbroken at being deserted by her lover, Turiddu, comes to his mother's inn to ask if he is there. He is away buying wine, says his mother, Lucia, but Santuzza says he was seen in the village the previous night.

Alfio the carrier enters with his horses, singing gaily, and the square fills with people, who echo his song before they move off or enter the church. He asks Lucia for wine: she replies that she has none – Turiddu has gone to get some. He is surprised, since he saw him near his own cottage that morning. Lucia is about to exclaim but Santuzza quickly silences her. Alfio leaves. The sound of the organ and prayers are heard from the church, echoed by the people in the square, led by Santuzza and Lucia in the Resurrection Hymn.

Left alone as all the others enter the church, Lucia asks Santuzza why she silenced her earlier. Santuzza explains – 'Voi lo sapete' ('You know it') – that Turiddu had been engaged to Lola before he went away to war; then Lola had married Alfio, and Santuzza became Turiddu's lover; but now the jealous Lola, although married, has drawn Turridu's affection away from Santuzza.

Lucia goes into the church and Turiddu enters. Santuzza reproaches him for his conduct with Lola: at first he denies it, then tells her that no amount of pleading will move him. Lola approaches, singing 'Fior di giaggiolo' ('Flower of iris') – converses with them briefly, mocking at Santuzza, and passes into the church, inviting Turiddu to follow. He is on the point of following but Santuzza begs him to hear

her (Turiddu, ascolta!). She passionately begs him to return to her
('No, no, Turiddu'), but he says that all is over between them. As he
goes off into the church he throws her to the ground in fury.

Alfio enters and the jilted Santuzza tells him of his wife's infidelity
with Turiddu. He swears to avenge his honour in blood, and both
depart.

The stage is empty (nearly all the villagers are in the church) as the
Intermezzo is played. Then, the service over, the people come out of
church and happily head for their homes. Turiddu asks Lola to join
the group outside his mother's inn, and he sins a gay Brindisi
(drinking song), 'Viva il vino' ('Long live wine'). Then Alfio arrives.
He insultingly declines the glass that Turiddu fills for him. The
women, sensing sinister happenings, lead Lola off. Alfio and Turiddu exchange a few words, then Turiddu bites Alfio's ear, the
traditional Sicilian manner of accepting a challenge to a duel. Turiddu tells Alfio not to blame Lola for what has happened, and
expresses his fear for Santuzza should he be killed.

As the others go off, Lucia enters. Turiddu asks her for her
blessing and charges her to look after Santuzza if he fails to return.
Terrified, she guesses what is happening and calls after him desperately as he goes. Santuzza enters and the two women embrace.
An agitated crowd gathers. In the distance a woman's voice is heard
saying that Turiddu has been killed. Santuzza, Lucia and the
assembled crowd scream, and the two women fall to the ground.

★   ★   ★

Cavalleria rusticana is a story of love stolen and avenged, but there is
no love-song in it after the serenade behind the curtain (before the
opera starts) and no love-duet at all. The big duet (ex. 1) expresses
Santuzza's love for Turiddu, it is true, but on Turiddu's part it
expresses his indifference towards her. Its striking melody (to the
words 'Stay, stay, Turiddu') partly depends for its impact on a
strong descending bass.

It is noteworthy that the opera's other memorable vocal line, part
of the Easter Hymn, 'Let us sing a hymn – the Lord is not dead . . .':
ex. 2), has very much the same heavy support in a trudging bass, and
also has the characteristically insistent triplet movement for a background.

Ex. 1

Ex. 2

ENGELBERT HUMPERDINCK

1854–1921

Wagner influenced operatic composers everywhere – composers as dissimilar as Puccini, Dvořák and Sullivan. On German and Austrian composers his influence was, naturally, direct. Of these, Humperdinck was Wagner's professed disciple, and worked with him at Bayreuth on the production of *Parsifal*. *Hänsel und Gretel*, the first of Humperdinck's own six operas, was the only one to enjoy lasting success.

HÄNSEL UND GRETEL
(Hansel and Gretel)
Libretto by Adelheid Wette, after the Brothers Grimm

First performed: Weimar, 1893
Three Acts

Cast in order of singing:

GRETEL	*soprano*
HÄNSEL	*mezzo-soprano*
GERTRUD, THEIR MOTHER	*mezzo-soprano*
PETER, THEIR FATHER, A BROOM-MAKER	*baritone*
THE SANDMAN (SLEEP-FAIRY)	*soprano*
THE DEW FAIRY	*soprano*
THE WITCH	*mezzo-soprano*

Chorus of children

Adelheid Wette, the composer's sister, modified a familiar fairy-tale of the Brothers Grimm to make the libretto of *Hänsel und Gretel*. (The boy's name is Hänsel, but the form and pronunciation 'Hansel' has become standard in English performances.) Never before had an opera for children won such an international success. The two child roles need to be impersonated by women, however: it was left for Benjamin Britten to write successful operas with children singing leading roles – in *The Little Sweep* (the core of *Let's Make an Opera!*), *The Turn of the Screw* (see page 548) and *Noye's Fludde*.

There is thus a marked preponderance of women's voices in the original score. But some German productions have successfully used a tenor as a comically grotesque witch, and the part of the Sandman might well be given to a baritone instead of a soprano. In any form the opera retains a great charm, simple on the surface but with a good deal of musical subtlety beneath.

★　　★　　★

ACT I: Hänsel and Gretel are seen in a small, improverished-looking broom-maker's hut. Gretel is knitting, Hänsel is making brooms; both are hungry and their parents are away. They try hard to keep cheerful, Gretel taking the lead. Eventually they dance, more and more energetically, until they tumble on to the floor. At that moment their mother comes in. She is annoyed to find them playing when they should have been hard at work. In her anger she knocks down and breaks a jug, full of milk which was to have served as the supper. So she despatches them to the Ilsenstein woods with a basket, telling them to bring it back full of strawberries instead.

Alone, she sits down, exhausted, wondering how to provide food for her starving family. Soon the father comes in, in merry mood, having had a successful day's business and a few drinks on the way home. At first she is irritated, but irritation changes to delight when he unpacks, a large basket of food. He asks about the children: she tells him that they were misbehaving, and about the milk jug (over which they can now laugh) and that she sent them to the Ilsenstein woods. He is horror-struck, for in the woods, he tells her, there is a fearsome witch who rides on brooms (he illustrates with one of his besoms) and cooks and eats little children. They both rush off to bring Hänsel and Gretel back.

ACT II: In the forest, the two children are singing quietly as Gretel makes a garland and a nosegay of roses and Hänsel fills the basket with strawberries. They hear a cuckoo, and in imitation of the pirate 'bird they steal a few strawberries from the basket. Quickly they finish the whole lot, then realize that they must refill the basket and that it is getting too dark to see clearly. They begin to get a little afraid at the strange shapes in the twilight, and they call for help – to be answered only by echoes and by the cuckoo, now mysterious. Their fear grows as it becomes misty.

Then suddenly the mist partly rises, to disclose the Sandman, who calms them with his song and settles them down to sleep. They say their prayers, 'Abends will ich schlafen gehn' ('At evening I want to go to sleep'). As sleep finally overcomes them, a bright light breaks through the darkness and the mist and fourteen angels, in shining white, come down a ladder and group themselves round the children in a 'Dream Pantomime'.

ACT III: The Dew Fairy comes to arouse the sleeping children. Gretel wakes first, than calls Hänsel. They talk of the dream of angels, which they both had. As the distant mist lifts, they excitedly see that they are near a gingerbread house. Naturally, they go towards it, not without a little trepidation at first on Gretel's part, and as they reach it they begin to eat bits of it. A voice from inside asks who is eating the house: 'Knusper, knusper, Knäuschen!' ('Crunch, crunch, mousekin'). But they ignore it. Suddenly the witch comes out, throwing a rope round Hänsel's neck, and draws them towards her. She promises them quantities of delicious food. Hänsel tries to escape, but she invokes a spell to bind them to the spot.

The witch takes Hänsel to a kennel and shuts him in, leaving Gretel while she fetches food for him; he needs fattening, but Gretel does not! Then the witch sends Gretel indoors to set the table (having first broken the spell that kept her motionless). Hänsel, pretending to sleep, overhears the witch planning to push Gretel into the oven so as to cook her and eat her. In her excitement the witch goes for a quick ride on a broomstick, singing 'So hop, hop, hop, gallop, lop, lop!' She goes back to Hänsel, inspects him, finds him still rather lean and calls Gretel to bring him more food. While the witch feeds him, Gretel pronounces over him the spell of disenchantment – 'Hokus, pokus, Holderbusch' – which she had earlier heard the witch use.

Then the witch tells Gretel to peep into the oven to see if the gingerbread is ready. Hänsel, now able to move, slips out of the kennel and warns Gretel to be careful. She pretends not to understand how to look into the oven, and asks the witch to demonstrate; as does so, they push her in and bang the door closed. In relief, the two sing a merry waltz: 'Juchhei! Nun ist die Hexe tot' ('Hooray! Now the witch is dead').

The children go back into the house to eat their fill. The oven starts crackling and explodes, and suddenly they find they are surrounded by a troop of motionless children, who a moment earlier had been cakes. When Gretel touches them, they are able to open their eyes, and when Hänsel pronounces the formula for breaking the spell they jump up and thank Hänsel and Gretel for saving them and restoring them to life. Then Hänsel's and Gretel's parents appear, and the family are happily reunited. Two children bring out the witch – now baked into a cake – and all join in thanks to God.

★　★　★

Hänsel und Gretel is usually said to be Wagnerian, and so it is in the way that motives recur throughout. But, unlike Wagner, Humperdinck preserves a structure of clearly separated numbers and uses tunes which are complete in themselves (often appropriately like those of nursery rhymes) rather than fragments of Wagner's 'endless melody'.

In the opening scene, when Hänsel interrupts his playing with Gretel to mention how hungry he is, Gretel replies by recalling the words of comfort their father always speaks: 'When our need is at its greatest, then God will stretch out his hand' (ex. 1).

Ex. 1

'Wenn die Not auf's Höch-ste steigt, Gott der Herr die Hand ___ auch reicht!'

Then Hänsel and Gretel start their dance (ex. 2) with tapping of feet and clicking of fingers.

Ex. 2

Brü-der-chen, komm tanz' mit mir, bei-de Händchen reich' ich dir,

Ein-mal hin, ein-mal her, rund her-um, es ist nicht schwer!

The first half of ex. I becomes the first line of the children's prayer
before they go to sleep in the wood in the second act. And when,
almost at the end of the opera, the relieved father greets the children,
what he sings (ex. 3) uses the rhythm of the dance-tune above; and
after that he recalls his habitual words of comfort which are repeated
by the assembled company.

Ex. 3

Kin - der, schaut das Wun-der an,,   wie   die He - xe he - xen kann,

wie sie hart,   knu-sper hart   sel - ber nun zum ku - chen ward!

The episode when, in the wood, the children become frightened
by the dark and are answered only by echoes and by the cuckoo
(formerly a friendly sound, now a mysterious one) is evidence of a
truly poetic imagination at work in the theatre. The witch herself –
whose ride on a broomstick is orchestrally depicted in a prelude to
Act II – is not too horrifically portrayed.

RICHARD STRAUSS

(1864–1949)

Following Wagner, Richard Strauss embraced a method of composing with recurrent thematic motives and with an opulent orchestral texture which can often stand independently on its own. But Strauss made his operas faster and more concentrated in action. *Salome* and *Elektra* (1909) each play in one continuous scene. *Der Rosenkavalier*, a realistic comedy, takes up three long acts but crams them full of detail: and in place of Wagner's characteristically slow-paced delivery we have fast dialogue-in-music. Moreover, Strauss – not for nothing a contemporary of Zola, Ibsen and Wilde – made deliberate use of plots intended to deliver a shock in the theatre. They duly shocked – and succeeded.

Before these operas (his most famous), Strauss wrote *Guntram* (1894) and *Feuersnot* ('Dearth of Fire', 1901). Afterwards followed *Ariadne auf Naxos* (see page 455); then the philosophical *Die Frau ohne Schatten* ('The Woman without a Shadow', 1919); *Intermezzo* (1924), to his own text – it is a portrait of Strauss's marriage; *Die ägyptische Helena* (The Egyptian Helen', 1928); *Arabella* (1933), the last of his operas to words by Hugo von Hofmannsthal who exercised so profound an influence on him; *Die schweigsame Frau* ('The Silent Woman', 1935, to a libretto by Stefan Zweig after Ben Jonson); *Friedenstag* ('Peace Day', 1938); *Daphne* (1938); *Die Liebe der Danae* ('The Love of Danae', completed 1940, rehearsed 1944, but not staged until 1952); and *Capriccio* (1942), a delightfully self-indulgent 'conversation piece' about the rivalry of a poet and a musician.

SALOME
Libretto by Hedwig Lachmann from Oscar Wilde's play

First performed: Dresden, 1905
One Act

Cast in order of singing:

NARRABOTH, CAPTAIN OF THE ROYAL GUARD	*tenor*
PAGE TO HERODIAS	*contralto*
TWO SOLDIERS	*two basses*
JOHN THE BAPTIST (Jokanaan)	*baritone*
A CAPPADOCIAN	*bass*
SALOME, DAUGHTER OF HERODIAS (by Herodias's former marriage to the brother of Herod, now killed by Herod's command)	*soprano*
A SLAVE	*soprano or tenor*
HEROD, THE TETRARCH	*tenor*
HERODIAS, HIS WIFE	*mezzo-soprano*
FIVE JEWS	*four tenors, bass*
TWO NAZARENES	*tenor, bass*

[The role of the executioner is silent.]

The scene is laid in Palestine in biblical times

Richard Strauss put all his power of musical descriptiveness into *Salome*; we are invited to feel the neurotic sexuality of the heroine as both alluring and repulsive. The opera is based on Oscar Wilde's play *Salome* (1894), written in French. Wilde made Salome infatuated with John the Baptist, and King Herod infatuated with Salome (his step-daughter) – two additions to the New Testament narrative. The play, literally translated into German and slightly cut, forms the libretto for Richard Strauss's one-act opera. Salome herself is supposed to be only in her teens, an impression which sopranos with the necessary stamina for the part do not find it easy to convey. Many, but not all, singers of the role use a stand-in for the Dance of the Seven Veils.

In the German pronunciation of 'Salome', the accent falls on the first syllable.

★   ★   ★

On a terrace outside the banqueting hall of Herod's palace, Narraboth, captain of the guard, is with a page and two soldiers (who are guarding the cistern in which John the Baptist is imprisoned). Narraboth, looking into the hall, expresses his admiration of Salome; the page warns him of the danger of looking at her thus. John's voice is heard from the cistern in impassioned prophecy of one 'who will follow me' ('Nach mir wird Einer kommen'). The soldiers and a Cappadocian converse.

Soon Salome comes out of the banqueting hall: she is irritated by the Romans, Egyptians and Jews at Herod's feast and by Herod's lascivious glances at her. Hearing the prophet's voice, she is curious to see him; she knows that he has persistently reviled her mother. A slave comes to recall her to the feast, but she dismisses him. Her curiosity is further stimulated when she learns that John is a young man. Obeying Herod's order, the soldiers refuse to let her speak with him, but Narraboth, in response to her promises to look favourably on him, eventually orders them to let the prophet out.

As he comes forth, repulsive in appearance after his imprisonment, he fiercely denounces the evil acts of Herod and especially Herodias. Salome is both fascinated and repelled. He shows no interest in her and merely tries to send her away, but this only inflames her fascination, which soon turns into lust. She expresses luridly her compulsive desire to touch his body, then his hair, then to kiss his mouth: he refuses, to her frustration and fury. Narraboth vainly tries to restrain her, and, when Salome continues to express her desire to kiss John, Narraboth stabs himself and falls to the ground between them.

Telling Salome that she is accursed, John the Baptist descends into the cistern again. Herod and Herodias, with attendants, enter. Herod is seeking Salome, to Herodias's annoyance; he comes upon Narraboth's body and orders it to be taken away. Then he invites Salome to share with him wine, then fruit and eventually his throne. But she is cold towards him. John the Baptist's voice is heard again, to Herodias's discomfiture; but Herod is afraid of the prophet and refuses to have him silenced or to hand him over to the Jews. Among a group of Jews present a dispute breaks out, in which two Nazarenes (talking of the coming of the Messiah), and eventually Herod, join. John's denunciation of 'the daughter of Babylon' ('Tochter Babylons)' is taken by Herodias as an attack on her.

Now Herod asks Salome to dance for him. She is at first unwilling, and Herodias orders her not to dance. But the desperate Herod promises her anything she desires; she makes him swear it, and then, despite her mother's protests, she dances the Dance of the Seven Veils. At the end of it, the inflamed Herod asks her what she desires. She ask for the head of John the Baptist ('den Kopf des Jokanaan') on a silver charger.

Herod, aghast, at first refuses. He thinks this is the doing of
Herodias (who is delighted) but Salome assures him it is not. He does
all he can to dissuade her from her request, promising her fabulous
jewels or anything else she wants, but she steadfastly insists on
holding him to his oath and having John's head. Eventually Herod
gives way, full of foreboding. Herodias takes the ring of death from
his finger, giving it to a soldier; he passes it to the executioner, who
descends into the cistern.

Salome waits tensely to hear John's cry, but there is none. She
imagines that the executioner is afraid and has not killed John, and
tells the page to go to summon soldiers. But then the huge black arm
of the executioner appears from the cistern; in his hand is a silver
shield, with John's head upon it. Hungrily she kisses its lips, gloating
in the triumph of her lust. Herod, repelled and full of fear, decides to
go indoors. The lights are extinguished. Before going in, Herod
turns and sees Salome, in the light of the moon, still gloating, her
passion sated. He orders the soldiers to kill her ('Man töte dieses
Weib!'), and they crush her beneath their shields.

★   ★   ★

An impressive contrast is created musically between the lascivious,
spiritually corrupt atmosphere which embraces Herod, Herodias
and Salome, and the uprightness of John the Baptist with his
certainty of prophecy. The characteristic themes of the former group
are nervous, angular and shifting in key; but when John first speaks
(ex. 1), prophesying that One will follow him who is stronger than
he ('I am not worthy to loosen the laces of his shoes'), the orchestra
too conveys the feeling of utter firmness, the voice joining in.

Ex. 1

The rising figure marked 'espressivo' stands as a 'prophecy motive' throughout the work.

When John is brought out of his cistern Salome remarks of him: 'He's horrible' (ex. 2: note the expressiveness of the *pianissimo*!). The little musical motive here tossed between voice and orchestra,

Ex. 2

expressing Salome's fascination with John (turning from horror to sexual desire), is one of the motives later used in the Dance of the Seven Veils and then again when Salome demands her reward ('I want you to bring me now, on a silver charger . . .': ex. 3).

Ex. 3

But what does she want on the silver charger? The suspense is
intensified when Herod interrupts with delight, saying how
charming is the choice of such a container to hold the promised gift.
Only when he has finished does Salome shatter him by naming her
choice – and there again, just preceding the words 'John's head' (den
Kopf des Jokanaan) the little motive seen in the last two examples
recurs.

ELEKTRA
Libretto by Hugo von Hofmannsthal, after Sophocles

First performed: Dresden, 1909
One Act

Cast in order of singing:

FIVE MAIDSERVANTS	*contralto, mezzo-sopranos and sopranos*
OVERSEER	*soprano*
ELECTRA	*soprano*
CHRYSOTHEMIS, HER YOUNGER SISTER	*soprano*
CLYTEMNESTRA, WIDOW OF AGAMEMNON	*mezzo-soprano*
CLYTEMNESTRA'S CONFIDANTE	*soprano*
CLYTEMNESTRA'S TRAIN-BEARER	*soprano*
A YOUNG SERVANT	*tenor*
AN OLD SERVANT	*bass*
ORESTES	*baritone*
ORESTES' TUTOR	*bass*
AEGISTHEUS	*tenor*

Chorus of servants
The scene is laid in Mycenae in ancient times

If *Salome*, with its lurid sexuality, shocked the audiences of its day, then *Elektra* went a stage further – but in a different direction, for here Strauss's huge orchestral and virtuoso vocal apparatus are applied to the obsessive hatred of Electra for her mother (murderess, long before the action of the opera, of her father Agamemnon on his return from the Trojan war) and Electra's craving for her mother's death at the hands of her brother Orestes: and we do not need Freud to point out the sexual component in her feelings. Like Salome, Electra dies, sated with her triumph, as the opera ends. When it was first heard, the opera alarmed its audiences not only in this respect but also for its sheer volume and psychological intensity. Many stories have been told, true or no, of Strauss, at rehearsals for the première, exhorting the orchestra to play louder and louder as the singers could still be heard. For the Electra herself, above all, the opera is a colossal assignment: she is on the stage virtually from start to finish, required to encompass a vast range of feeling, to rise above a dense, immensely detailed orchestral score, and even to execute a grotesque dance of triumph.

★   ★   ★

In an inner courtyard of Agamemnon's palace at Mycenae, now ruled by his widow Clytemnestra and her paramour Aegistheus, five serving-maids are drawing water from a well. Four of them discuss the degradation of Electra, her obsessions and her hateful behaviour towards them; when the fifth speaks up on her behalf she is sent within by the overseer, and her cries as she receives a beating are soon heard. The women depart, and Electra emerges from the house. She calls on the spirit of her father to avenge his murder, the history of which she recalls; she goes on to prophesy that the moment for vengeance is approaching, that blood will flow and that she and her brother and sister will dance in celebration.

Chrysothemis enters and tells Electra that Clytemnestra and Aegistheus plan to confine Electra in a prison tower. She talks of her longings and her fears, like a fire burning in her breast ('Ich hab's wie Feuer in der Brust') and particularly of her desire for marriage and children. Sounds are heard within; Clytemnestra must be coming out. Chrysothemis hurries off to avoid her.

A procession is seen, through the palace windows, of servants, priests and prisoners; finally Clytemnestra arrives, sallow, bloated, heavily bedecked with jewels. She looks with loathing at her daughter, complaining about her to her attendants. Then she

descends into the courtyard to ask Electra what remedy there is for
horrific dreams that torture her; would a sacrifice bring her peace of
mind? Yes, says Electra, but a very particular kind of sacrifice.
Clytemnestra presses her eagerly for the details; who or what must
be killed? when? where? by whom? It must be a human sacrifice, says
Electra, of a married woman, slain by her own kin: her meaning is
plain, but not to her mother. Electra talks of her brother, whose
name is taboo; she knows that her mother has tried to have him
killed, and lives in terror of his vengeance for his father.

Eventually Electra leaps out from the darkness towards her
mother, and in a wild outburst tells her that she, Clytemnestra, must
be the victim, how she will be pursued by her own son and done to
death by him; Electra expresses her wild elation at the prospect.
Clytemnestra is overtaken by spasms of fear; but then lights appear
in the palace, the Confidante appears, followed by serving-maids,
and delivers a whispered message to the queen who, now gloating
with triumph, returns into the palace. Chrysothemis now comes out
of the palace and tells Electra the news: Orestes is reported dead.
Electra refuses to believe it. A servant appears, demanding a horse:
he has to hasten to tell Aegistheus the glad tidings. Now, Electra tells
Chrysothemis, they will have to carry out the deed of revenge; for
the purpose, Electra has kept the axe with which Agamemnon was
killed. She draws herself to Chrysothemis, praises her sister's youthful strength and tries to cajole her; but Chrysothemis, repelled, frees
herself and rushes off. Electra throws a curse after her.

Electra, left alone, starts digging feverishly in the courtyard. A
man appears. She asks him his business. He says he has to see the
queen; he and another man bear the news of Orestes' death. She
reacts with a bitter, emotional lament. He is alarmed at this and
inquires who she is; she tells him. Now he assures her that Orestes is
in fact still living – and servants now come from the palace and greet
him. 'The dogs in the yard recognize me,' he says, 'but not my own
sister.' She greets him now with profound tenderness. But she
refuses his embrace, ashamed at the coarse, ravaged state she has
chosen for herself in expiation of her father's murder. The two of
them resolve that the deed of vengeance must be done, and Electra
talks of giving him the axe. Orestes' tutor now joins them and calls
him to perform the act for which they have come.

A servant and the Confidante appear, and they invite the two men
into the palace. They enter, leaving Electra in the courtyard in state
of wild excitement. She realizes that the axe remains hidden. But

then a shriek is heard from within, and another. Chrysothemis and servants come running out, crying out with alarm and calling for Aegistheus; they return into the palace. He comes and calls for lights, talks briefly to Electra, who confirms the news of Orestes' death; he notes the change in her as she bears a torch to light his way into the palace. A moment later his cry is heard. Chrysothemis and the women rush out again. Electra breaks into a wild, demented, maenadic dance of triumph: at the end, she falls dead, in a colossal climax of elation. Chrysothemis, who has watched her, rushes to the door and batters on it, crying 'Orestes!'

★   ★   ★

Agamemnon, former king of Mycenae, is dead before the opera starts; but Strauss leaves us in no doubt that he dominates the opera, for the motif associated with him runs through the score. It is first of all identified as his when Electra, in her first words when she is left alone on the stage, calls on her dead father (ex. 1*a*); but the falling interval of a fourth, returning to the original note, has been heard several times before, indeed in the very opening bar (ex. 1*b*), and it continues to be, up to the very last bar (ex. 1*c*) – it is worth noting

Ex. 1

that the mode is minor at the start but major at the finish after Agamemnon's spirit has been avenged. It is also insistently heard during Electra's final dance of triumph.

This motif is not the only one associated with the former king. The single memorable idea in the work, in fact, is the theme that seems to stand for the love between father and daughter, Agamemnon and Electra, and which first appears, with a heart-aching poignancy, during Electra's first monologue as she calls on him not to leave her alone and to greet his child (ex. 2); it returns at another climatic moment, the height of her duet scene with Orestes, where it represents the bond between father and children. It is significant that it appears only fragmentarily in the scenes for Chrysothemis.

Ex. 2

Except in the Recognition Scene, there is little lyrical music for Electra; the chief lyrical role is really that of Chrysothemis, who is in the true tradition of Strauss's lyrical, impassioned sopranos, although there is a tortured quality to much of what she sings. Not as tortured, however, as Clytemnestra, whose corruption and decadence are manifest in everything she has to sing – the tense rhythms and the angular lines – and in the frenetic textures and harmonies of her accompanying music. But 'accompanying' is hardly the word. For *Elektra* is almost a Strauss tone-poem for orchestra, so vivid and rich is the score, so sharply does it portray the drama. It represents, in fact, an ultimate point in Strauss's musical expression, in its preoccupation with morbidity and horror, with its intense elaboration, and one from which he turned back. His next opera, *Der Rosenkavalier*, shows the application of similar techniques to an altogether more urbane, 'civilized' range of topics. It was left to others – like Schoenberg and Berg – to carry further the operatic idiom of *Elektra* into the dark worlds of the human psyche that at this very time were being explored in Freud's Vienna.

DER ROSENKAVALIER
(The Knight of the Rose)
Libretto by Hugo von Hofmannsthal

First performed: Dresden, 1911
Three Acts

Cast in order of singing:

OCTAVIAN, COUNT ROFRANO, A YOUNG GENTLEMAN OF NOBLE FAMILY	*mezzo-soprano*
THE FELDMARSCHALLIN, PRINCESS VON WERDENBERG	*soprano*
BARON OCHS AUF LERCHENAU, THE FELDMARSCHALLIN'S KINSMAN	*bass*
MAJOR-DOMO TO THE FELDMARSCHALLIN	*bass*
FOUR FOOTMEN TO THE FELDMARSCHALLIN	*two tenors, two basses*
THREE POOR ORPHANS	*soprano, mezzo-soprano, contralto*
MILLINER	*soprano*
ANIMAL-SELLER	*tenor*
VALZACCHI, AN ITALIAN INTRIGUER	*tenor*
ITALIAN TENOR	*tenor*
ATTORNEY TO THE FELDMARSCHALLIN	*bass*

ANNINA, VALZACCHI'S COMPANION	*contralto*
HERR VON FANINAL, A NOUVEAU-RICHE, RECENTLY ENNOBLED	*baritone*
MARIANNE LEITMETZERIN, DUENNA TO SOPHIE	*soprano*
MAJOR-DOMO TO FANINAL	*tenor*
SOPHIE, FANINAL'S DAUGHTER	*soprano*
LANDLORD OF AN INN	*tenor*
FOUR WAITERS	*tenor, three basses*
FOUR CHILDREN	*sopranos*
COMMISSIONER OF POLICE	*bass*

The scene is laid in Vienna in the early years of the reign of Empress Maria Theresa (mid-eighteenth century)

'A comedy for music' – such is the original description of the libretto which Hugo von Hofmannsthal wrote for Richard Strauss. There is comedy here indeed but also (especially in the young lovers' music and the final trio) a melting pathos which represents Strauss's late-flowering romantic art at its best.

In *Der Rosenkavalier* we encounter a youth who retains a boy's voice (and so is impersonated by a female singer) and who is called on by the plot to dress up as a girl. The double operatic transvestism was classically brought off by Mozart with the subsidiary role of Cherubino in *Le nozze di Figaro* – but Strauss goes further, applying it to one of the main characters, so that the sole love-interest of the work involves no male singer at all. Strauss later wrote another famous breeches-part in the role of the Composer in the second version of *Ariadne auf Naxos* (see page 455).

The breeches-part in *Der Rosenkavalier* is that of Octavian, who is chosen in the plot to be a 'Rosenkavalier' – that is, the bearer of a ceremonial silver rose from a nobleman to his betrothed. Octavian is at this stage in love with a woman older than himself, the Feldmarschallin.

Older, but not *so* much older. We may gather that Octavian (who is seventeen) was not her first lover nor will be her last. 'Feldmarschallin' (abbreviated to Marschallin) means 'wife of the Field-Marshal', following the custom in German whereby a woman uses a female form of her husband's title. The feminine ending '-in' was also formerly applied to surnames: the duenna is thus referred to as 'Leitmetzerin', though her true surname is Leitmetzer.

★   ★   ★

ACT I: The morning sun streams into the Feldmarschallin's bed-room. Octavian is still kneeling beside her bed, embracing her and pouring out endearments. (She calls him by the French nickname, Quinquin; he calls her Marie-Thérèse or Bichette.) Tinkling bells are heard, and Octavian hides as breakfast is brought for the Feldmar-schallin by Mahomet, her black pageboy. In tender mood, they share it. They hear a man approaching and Octavian hides again. For a moment they think it is her husband, returned from the hunt, but in fact it is her kinsman Baron Ochs, who enters with a footman. Octavian emerges from hiding, disguised in a chambermaid's clothes, and the lecherous Ochs is much taken with 'her'. He has come to tell the Feldmarschallin that he is planning to marry the daughter of the wealthy Herr von Faninal and to ask her advice on the choice of a man to act as his 'Rosenkavalier', bearing the ceremonial silver rose to his betrothed.

The Major-Domo enters and tells the Feldmarschallin that various people are waiting to see her. Meanwhile, Ochs flirts outrageously with 'Mariandel', really Octavian in disguise. The Feldmarschallin mildly takes him to task, but he tries hard to justify the eternal pursuit, boasting coarsely of his prowess and experience. The Feldmarschallin offers the services of her kinsman, Octavian, as the Rosenkavalier, showing Ochs a medallion of him; he comments on the resemblance to 'Mariandel'.

The morning's callers are now admitted. First, three poor, high-born girl orphans, ushered in by their mother, present their petition; then a milliner offers her hats and an animal-seller his apes and parrots; then an Italian intriguer, Valzacchi, offers a scandal sheet. The orphans bow themselves out, thanking the Feldmarschallin for her generosity. Her hairdresser enters and starts work on her hair, while a flautist comes in and plays, followed by an Italian tenor who sings an aria ('Di rigori armato'). All this time the Baron has been conferring with the attorney about his marriage contract: their voices are now heard, with the Baron in irritable mood, and continue while the flautist plays again and the tenor sings another verse. The bustling scene comes to an end as the Feldmarschallin waves them all off. Valzacchi and his companion Annina, however, take the opportunity to ingratiate themselves with Ochs, who asks them to find out all about 'Mariandel' for him. Ochs leaves the silver rose, brought by his servants, in the Feldmarschallin's care.

Left alone, the Feldmarschallin thinks of how the days are passing and how she must eventually be referred to as 'the old Princess' ('die alte Fürstin'). Octavian returns, in his own clothes, and finds her in pensive mood. She tries to explain to the passionate youth that their love can only be ephemeral. In answer to his protests, she says he must leave her now, and perhaps see her later. Reluctantly but obediently he goes. Suddenly realizing that she has dismissed him without a farewell or a last kiss, she starts up violently: she summons four footmen to call him back, but they report that he went too fast to be caught. The black pageboy is summoned, to take the silver rose to Octavian.

ACT II: Faninal is just leaving his house, about to bring Ochs to meet his daughter for the first time. Sophie's duenna, Marianne Leitmetzer, tells him that his fine new carriage is awaiting him and the Major-Domo hurries him off – etiquette demands that the bride's father must not be present when the Rosenkavalier arrives as the bridegroom's messenger. Sophie prays for protection from the sin of pride, interrupted by Marianne's commentary from the window.

Calls of 'Rofrano' are heard and Marianne tells Sophie that the Rosenkavalier has arrived. His resplendent entry follows: he is clad all in white and silver, followed by his servants, in white and green, some with plumes and swords. As he advances with the silver rose, he and Sophie are each taken aback by the other's grace. He presents the rose to her and the two talk for a few breathless moments.

The servants withdraw and the two, with Marianne nearby, sit down to converse. They are strongly attracted – youth to youth. Then Faninal brings in Ochs. His coarsely condescending behaviour distresses Sophie (whom Marianne tries to comfort) and infuriates Octavian. Soon Ochs asks Sophie to sit on his knee and he behaves with gross familiarity. The fawning Faninal is delighted to have both a Lerchenau and a Rofrano in his house but his daughter is sickened by the Baron's manner: she tears herself angrily away as he becomes more and more importunate. But Ochs is untroubled, reminding her cheerfully of an old song in waltz time, 'Mit mir' ('With me'). Meanwhile, the attorney and his clerk have arrived, and Faninal shows Ochs into an ante-room with them to draw up the contract.

Sophie and Octavian turn to one another, she begging him for help. Then there is a commotion among the servants (Ochs's ill-mannered men are chasing Faninal's maids); the Major-Domo comes for help and Marianne goes off. Alone, Sophie and Octavian are free to express their mutual feelings and sing a tender duet, culminating in a declaration of their love.

Suddenly they are seized from behind by Valzacchi and Annina, who call Ochs. He enters, confronts the young couple and asks Sophie for an explanation ('Eh bien, Mam'zelle?'). She will not answer; but, after sarcastic remarks from Ochs, Octavian tells him that Sophie will not marry him. Ochs, brushing aside the protests, starts to lead her off; Octavian, enraged, challenges him. Still Ochs takes no notice, so Octavian insults him vigorously. Ochs whistles for his servants, but Octavian draws and for a moment they fight. Octavian's sword scratches Ochs's arm, whereupon his servants rush on Octavian and Ochs yells 'Mörder!' ('Murder!').

Now confusion reigns. Servants bustle round, tending Ochs's scratch; Annina and Marianne express their varying concern. Faninal comes in and takes command, ordering someone to fetch a surgeon, apologizing profusely to Ochs and raging at Octavian and Sophie. He orders Octavian out and, in response to Sophie's downright refusal to marry Ochs, says he will force her to take him or she will go to a convent. Marianne takes her to her room. With more apologies to Ochs, Faninal rushes off.

Ochs, left alone with his servants and the doctor – and some wine – gradually recovers his humour, even beginning to waltz. His humour is further improved when Annina (now in Octavian's pay) comes with a letter from 'Mariandel', suggesting an assignation. He agrees with delight and sends Annina away – but without her expected tip.

ACT III: In a private room at an inn, the scene is prepared in dumb show during the orchestral introduction for Ochs's encounter with 'Mariandel' – in which Octavian plans to trap and expose Ochs. Octavian (ready in female clothes for his role), Valzacchi and Annina hide various assistants behind trapdoors opening into the room. When eventually all is ready, Octavian leaves the room. Dance music is heard in the distance and Ochs arrives, leading 'Mariandel'. Valzacchi greets Ochs with silent feigned respect, pointing out a bed in a recess. The landlord and waiters ask obsequiously if everything is all right, and answer a few of Ochs's queries before he sends them and Valzacchi off.

Now the téte-à-tête begins, 'Mariandel' speaking in raw, peasant fashion. Ochs offers 'Mariandel' wine, which she declines ('Nein, nein, nein, nein! i trink kein Wein'); she runs off as if afraid – into the recess, where she sees the bed and feigns great wonder at who sleeps there. They sit down and Ochs is about to kiss her when he notices, with discomfiture, the striking resemblance to Octavian. A moment later a head appears through a trapdoor, to Ochs's alarm.

A servant brings in the supper (the distant music becomes clearer when the door opens). 'Mariandel', to Ochs's perturbation, is rather melancholy in mood, but giving him an occasional languid glance. Soon the faces start appearing in mysterious places at an alarming rate, unseen, apparently, by 'Mariandel', but terrifying to Ochs, who rings the bell. Annina, in disguise, suddenly rushes in, pretending to claim Ochs as her husband, and followed by the landlord and three waiters. He protests vigorously, but the landlord and waiters are scandalized, especially when four children come in, calling 'Papa, Papa, Papa!'.

The Police Commissioner enters, and is suspicious of Ochs. Who, he wishes to know, is the girl? Ochs says that she is his fiancée, Sophie von Faninal. At this moment Faninal himself arrives. He identifies Ochs but is furious at the suggestion that the girl is his daughter.

Hunting around the room for his wig, which he had discarded earlier, Ochs runs into the children, who resume their cries. Sophie, whom Faninal has sent for, enters. Faninal, humiliated, faints and is carried out to the next room, with Sophie and the landlord following, and the police remove everyone except Ochs, 'Mariandel', Annina and the children.

Ochs now asks to be allowed to escort 'Mariandel' home, but she refuses to go with him. She whispers a few words to the Commissioner, then disappears into the recess. Female clothes are thrown out, one by one, to Ochs's fury. The landlord announces the Feldmarschallin, who has been summoned to Ochs's aid by one of his servants.

Octavian emerges in his proper clothes. Sophie, who has re-entered, angrily passes on to Ochs her father's instruction that he must never come near the Faninal house again. The Feldmarschallin advises Ochs to depart and assures the police officers that they can go, as what has happened was merely a prank. She asks Octavian to explain the position to Ochs, who now sees why the resemblance between Octavian and 'Mariandel' was so strong – and begins to understand rather more about the relationship between Octavian and the Feldmarschallin. Since he now realizes that the evening's events were a masquerade, Ochs hopes to resume his plans of marriage; but the Feldmarschallin says decisively that he must forget them.

The concealed trap-door-manipulators now emerge, Annina removes her disguise and Valzacchi leads out his accomplices – all to

Ochs's astonishment. They remind him ironically of what has passed. The musicians, the coachmen, the 'boots', the waiters and the landlord start pestering him and he is only too glad to get out.

Only the Feldmarschallin, Sophie and Octavian remain. The two women each understand the claim of the other on Octavian. But the Feldmarschallin is strong enough to wipe away her tears and approach Sophie kindly. Sophie, abashed, curtseys. Octavian is deeply moved by the Feldmarschallin's goodness but the Feldmarschallin cuts short his thanks with the words 'Ich weiss nix, gar nix' ('I know nothing . . . nothing').

Now, standing apart from the lovers, the Feldmarschallin expresses the poignancy of her situation: 'Hab mir's gelobt' ('I vowed to myself'): it is the beginning of a long trio for her and the lovers. The Feldmarschallin leaves; the lovers fall into each other's arms with the words 'Ist ein traum' ('It is a dream'). The Feldmarschallin re-enters, now with Faninal, who leads her away again. The lovers end their song, embrace, and go. The room is left empty.

But Sophie has dropped her handkerchief. Who comes to fetch it? It is Mahomet, the Feldmarschallin's pageboy. With tripping footsteps he runs out again and the opera is over.

★ ★ ★

Before the curtain rises the orchestra 'tells' us of the night of love of the Feldmarschallin and Octavian. The very opening gives us two themes, representing the boy's youthful ardour (*a*) and the full, sensual passion of the mature woman (*b*) (ex. 1).

Ex. 1

The unconcealed eroticism of the whole plot goes with an equally unconcealed eroticism in the music. This is linked to another major element of sensuous appeal: the use of Viennese waltz-tunes. Here the spirit of Johann Strauss was taken by his namesake to enliven (with triumphant anachronism) a scene set in Vienna a hundred years before Johann Strauss's day. There are several of these waltzes in *Der*

Rosenkavalier, which have been made into various suites for concert-hall use. The most famous (ex. 2) is what might be called Ochs's theme-song: he first sings it when trying to fondle Sophie in Faninal's house.

Ex. 2

Before this, Octavian has presented the silver rose to the accompaniment of a strange chord-sequence in an orchestration that itself sounds 'silvery' (ex. 3: flutes, harps, solo violins, celesta). We quote it (*a* below) not at its first appearance but as Strauss brings it back – with an utter simplicity of telling effect – when the young lovers are finally each other's, and are singing their duet just before the end of the opera. Sophie's words may be translated: 'It is a dream, it cannot be true that we two are together.'

Ex. 3

ARIADNE AUF NAXOS
(Ariadne on Naxos)
Libretto by Hugo von Hofmannsthal

Original version first performed: Stuttgart, 1912
Revised version first performed: Vienna, 1916
Revised version: Prologue and One Act

Cast in order of singing:

THE MAJOR-DOMO		*speaking part*
THE MUSIC MASTER		*baritone*
A LACKEY		*bass*
AN OFFICER		*tenor*
THE COMPOSER		*soprano*
THE TENOR (later Bacchus)		*tenor*
A WIG MAKER		*bass*
ZERBINETTA, AN ACTRESS		*soprano*
THE DANCING MASTER		*tenor*
THE PRIMA DONNA (later Ariadne)		*soprano*
NAIAD		*soprano*
DRYAD	THREE NYMPHS	*contralto*
ECHO		*soprano*
HARLEQUIN		*baritone*
BRIGHELLA	CHARACTERS IN THE	*tenor*
TRUFFALDINO	HARLEQUINADE	*bass*
SCARAMUCCIO		*tenor*

The scene is laid in Vienna in the early eighteenth century

In *Ariadne auf Naxos* we see a curious marriage between Strauss's fondness (like Wagner's) for mythological or other ancient stories and his leaning to realistic comedy. *Ariadne auf Naxos* was at first designed as a one-act opera, to be performed as the divertissement in a condensed version of Molière's comedy *Le bourgeois gentilhomme* (for which Strauss also provided incidental music). In this form it was not particularly successful; moreover, the difficulty of providing separate companies of actors and singers made it prohibitive for most theatres. So Strauss and his librettist wrote a musical prologue to replace the play. The original 'opera' was retained, in slightly revised form; but now, instead of being offered as M.

Jourdain's entertainment for his dinner guests, it is offered by a Viennese *nouveau riche* to his.

It is in the revised form – to which the following synopsis adheres – that the work is generally given today. The prologue introduces the supposed artists who are to perform the entertainment for the wealthy patron's guests; it also introduces the particularly sympathetic character of the Composer himself (a soprano role, representing a youth). To fit in with its eighteenth-century conception and inspiration, *Ariadne* is scored for a far smaller orchestra than Strauss's previous operas. In it the charm of a mock old-fashioned harlequinade is set beside a virtuoso handling of three types of soprano: coloratura (Zerbinetta), lyric (Composer) and dramatic (Ariadne).

★   ★   ★

PROLOGUE: Back-stage in the private theatre of a Viennese mansion, the Music Master agitatedly approaches the Major-Domo, complaining that the serious opera (*Ariadne auf Naxos*) by his pupil the Composer, to be given that evening, will be spoilt if followed, as is proposed, by a comic opera or harlequinade. The Major-Domo tells him that the plans will not be changed, and that the opera will need to be shortened; he goes off, and the Music Master follows.

A lackey brings in an officer, who goes into the room where Zerbinetta, the actress of the harlequinade, is dressing. The Composer enters, anxious about rehearsing his opera. He is irritated when the lackey goes off and leaves him; but then a melody occurs to him and he tries to write it down. One of the dressing-room doors suddenly flies open and the Tenor angrily ejects a wig-maker; then Zerbinetta comes out of her room with the officer, and is joined by the Dancing Master; and then the Prima Donna comes out of hers, with the Music Master. The Music Master tells the Composer, who has noticed – and been attracted by – Zerbinetta, of the plans for the evening. The Composer is outraged at the demands made on him, but recovers as another 'inspiration' comes to him. Zerbinetta, her troupe around her, talks with the Dancing Master, and finishes her make-up; meanwhile, the Prima Donna makes slighting remarks about the comedians.

The Major-Domo returns and creates further consternation by announcing that, on his master's orders, the two entertainments are to be given simultaneously. The Composer is horrified, but the Dancing Master and the Music Master agree that a compromise must be managed. Both the Prima Donna and the Tenor demand that any necessary cuts shall be in the other's part – on which both are reassured (separately) by the Music Master.

The story of Ariadne is explained to Zerbinetta, who, not believing in a woman who truly longs for death when deserted by a lover, treats it somewhat cynically when telling it to her troupe. The Composer, idealistically, tries to explain it to Zerbinetta, and as they talk he is strongly drawn to her. She goes off; then the Prima Donna returns and, to the Music Master, renews her protests at having to appear alongside a comic troupe. The Composer, seeing the harlequinade players, is once more aghast at the pollution of his art, and rushes off in despair.

OPERA: On a stage within the stage, the scene is set for the opera of *Ariadne* – a seashore, with a cave, and wings made from rocks and trees. The three nymphs (Naiad, Dryad and Echo) comment on Ariadne's sadness, while she reclines on the shore asleep. She awakes, recalling her love for Theseus: 'Ein Schönes war' ('There was once a beautiful thing'). From the wings, Harlequin, Zerbinetta and the other comedians comment; Ariadne continues as if she has not heard them. Soon the comedians, uncomprehending, give up; Ariadne, rising, sings to herself of the happy prospect of death: 'Es gibt ein Reich' ('There is a land').

The comedians return, to try to enliven Ariadne with singing and dancing: 'Die Dame gibt mit trübem Sinn' ('The lady feels sad'). Zerbinetta enters, sends them away and approaches Ariadne: 'Grossmächtige Prinzessin' ('All-powerful princess'). She tries to talk to her as woman to woman; Ariadne pointedly ignores her and retires into the cave, but Zerbinetta continues at some length her attempt to console her, relating the story of her own love-life.

Harlequin enters and attempts to make love to Zerbinetta. She resists him coquettishly. The other three enter, also in pursuit of her, while she dances around them; soon she and Harlequin, who has remained in the background, go off together, to the annoyance of the others.

As they go, the three nymphs return, commenting on what they have just seen – a young god approaching the island. It is Bacchus. He enters, singing of his escape from the enchantress Circe (which the nymphs had recalled). Ariadne comes from the cave happily; she believes her visitor to be Hermes, the messenger of death, and welcomes him.

The nymphs go off, leaving Bacchus and Ariadne toether. He is

entranced by her beauty; as they sing together, their feelings warm
into love. He eventually kisses her and she believes she is dying. She
revives, and with a sense of wonderment they move off together into
the cave. As their loving voices are heard, the nymphs comment,
and Zerbinetta enters to remark characteristically on the inevitability
of the outcome.

★   ★   ★

Ariadne is an opera full of contrasts. Most of Strauss's operas are
much concerned with the essential nature of Woman: here two
different feminine types (or different aspects of femininity) are
powerfully contrasted by musical means. Ex. 1 shows how the
'faithful–unto–death' Ariadne recalls her happiness with Theseus.

Ex. 1

Compare this with ex. 2, the music allocated to the fickle,
light-hearted Zerbinetta – in perhaps the most brilliant and intensely
difficult coloratura aria in the entire repertory – as she sings of her
past love affairs. Then she breaks into a cheerful rondo: 'Like a god
came each one of them, and his step made me dumb' (ex. 2).

Ex. 2

Note the more 'serious' transformation of Zerbinetta's rondo theme (ex. 3) as, in the opera's closing pages, she applies the same idea to Ariadne ('When a new god comes to us, we are captive, dumb').

Ex. 3

The other marked contrast is between what one might call the 'satellites' of the two women. Ariadne's are the three nymphs, whose trios are like those of Wagner's Rhinemaidens, but lighter, more translucent, in texture (Echo, by the way, is often an echo in fact as well as name). Zerbinetta's – the four men of the harlequinade – are on quite another level: indulging in all kinds of frivolous antics and singing in lively, dancing rhythms.

LEOŠ JANÁČEK

1854–1928

Like Smetana, Leoš Janáček is considered by his countrymen an intensely national composer. At first his works made little international headway, but after the Second World War his operas became prominent in the theatres of German-speaking countries and in Britain. *Jenůfa* (1904) had embarked rather earlier on an international career – it was given in Vienna in 1918 and in New York six years later. It was first given at Covent Garden in 1956; five years earlier, Sadler's Wells had given *Katya Kabanova*, and British audiences have now also seen stage productions of *The Cunning Little Vixen* (1924), in which all the characters are animals, *Mr Brouček's Excursions* (1920), and the last two of Janáček's operas, *The Makropoulos Case* and *From the House of the Dead* (first performed posthumously, in 1930).

One of the reasons why Janáček's operas took so long to achieve their due place in the repertory is that they are so closely linked in their idiom and their diction to the Czech language; he aimed to use a naturalistic idiom based on the rhythms and the pitch patterns of his native tongue, just as Musorgsky had with Russian. English (or for that matter German or French) words do not naturally sit on Janáček's music. The composer was a 'Slavophile' generally and was much influenced by Russian literature; *From the House of the Dead* is based on Dostoevsky, *Katya Kabanova* on Ostrovsky's *The Storm* (a play to which Tchaikovsky had written incidental music).

KATYA KABANOVA
Libretto by V. Cervinka after the play by Ostrovsky

First performed: Brno, 1921
Three Acts

Cast in order of singing:

VANYA KUDRASH, TEACHER AND CHEMIST — *tenor*
GLASHA, A SERVANT TO THE KABANOV FAMILY — *mezzo-soprano*
SAVEL PROKOFIEVICH DIKOY, A MERCHANT — *bass*
BORIS GRIGORIEVICH, HIS NEPHEW — *tenor*
FEKLUSHA, A SERVANT TO THE KABANOV FAMILY — *mezzo-soprano*
MARFA IGNATYEVNA KABANOVA (known as Kabanikha),
    WIDOW OF A WEALTHY MERCHANT — *contralto*
TIKHON IVANOVICH KABANOV, HER SON — *tenor*
KATERINA (Katya) KABANOVA, HIS WIFE — *soprano*
VARVARA, ADOPTED DAUGHTER OF THE KABANOV
    FAMILY — *mezzo-soprano*
KULIGIN, A FRIEND OF KUDRASH — *baritone*

Chorus of people
*The scene is laid in the Russian town of Kalinov
on the Volga in the 1860s*

The storm which rages through the small Russian town of Kalinov echoes the storm in the mind of Katya – married to a weak husband under the thumb of his cruel mother, and guiltily in love with a man too weak to rescue her. The tortured mind of Katya is contrasted with the carefree youthfulness of Varvara, the adopted daughter in the household of Katya's mother-in-law; and their music contributes to a strange but compelling atmosphere in which the cruelties and torments of small-town life find subtle operatic expression.

The Czech title of the opera is correctly written *Kát'a Kabanová*. But as this (and the other names in the Czech score) are merely Czech spellings of the Russian names of the original Russian play, we give here the usual English forms for the original Russian spelling.

★　★　★

ACT I: By the Kabanov family house on the banks of the Volga, Kudrash sits watching the river, talking to the Kabanovs' servant Glasha. They move aside as Dikoy and Boris enter; as usual, Dikoy is rating his nephew. Dikoy leaves and Boris talks with Kudrash, explaining that he has to live with his uncle in order that he may eventually inherit a legacy. People are returning from church, among them Feklusha, another servant of the Kabanovs, who talks

to Glasha. Boris confides his unhappiness to Kudrash, and his eyes
are fixed on Katya Kabanova, returning with her husband Tikhon
from church. Boris is, he confesses, in love with her.

Tikhon is under the thumb of his mother, known as Kabanikha,
who tells him he should go away at once on business. She reprimands him for treating her with little affection since his marriage,
but he protests his love and respect of her, and Katya does likewise.
Kabanikha turns fiercely on Katya, who goes into the house; she
follows after warning her son to act more sternly towards his wife.
Varvara expresses to Tikhon her pity for Katya.

The scene changes to a room in the Kabanov house, where Katya
is talking to Varvara about how sad she has become lately and recalls
her carefree younger days. Growing agitated, she mentions her
guilty love for another man. Varvara asks if she will meet the man
while Tikhon is away, an idea she at once rejects. Tikhon enters,
followed by Glasha and Feklusha. Katya begs him not to leave her,
and when he says he must go she begs him to take her with him.
Despite her repeated pleas, Tikhon is only irritated, and refuses.
Desperately, she asks him to make her swear not to speak to any
stranger.

Kabanikha interrupts, entering to say that all is ready for his
departure. She demands that Tikhon should tell his wife how to
behave in his absence; reluctantly and with embarrassment, he does
so, following his mother's instructions, to Katya's deep humiliation.
Before he leaves, they sit down for a moment together, following
Russian custom. As he kisses Katya goodbye, she embraces him
passionately – to Kabanikha's disgust.

ACT II: It is evening, and as Kabanikha, Katya and Varvara work at
their embroidery Kabanikha rebukes Katya for not showing more
obvious grief at her husband's departure. Kabanikha leaves, and
Varvara announces her intention of going out – she has obtained the
key of the locked garden gate, and offers to summon Boris to meet
Katya. Katya, much agitated, rejects the idea; but left alone (with
Kabanikha's voice briefly heard from outside) she decides that she
will see him, only for a moment, and she goes. A moment later
Kabanikha enters with Dikoy, who is maudlin drunk; Kabanikha
comforts him.

Later that evening in the wooded garden behind the Kabanov
house, Kudrash is alone, singing a serenade and playing his guitar as
he waits for Varvara. Boris enters; a girl, he says, had come up to
him and told him to come for an assignation. Kudrash warns him of

the dangers of loving a married woman. Soon Varvara approaches, singing a song by which her sweetheart will know her; joyously, Kudrash answers her in song. Varvara tells Boris that Katya will come, and goes off with Kudrash. Boris waits anxiously. Soon Katya arrives. She is still tortured by her conscience, but eventually gives way to her emotions; they embrace and go off together, just as Varvara and Kudrash return. Their loving voices are heard in the distance, while Varvara and Kudrash talk, then sing another happy song. It serves to call Katya back, for the time has come for the women to go in. Boris and Katya part wordlessly, too moved even to bid one another goodnight.

ACT III: It is a stormy afternoon and people are hurrying to shelter in a large decrepit building near the river bank. Kudrash and his friend Kuligin watch. Dikoy enters, everyone making way for him; Kudrash tries to persuade him of the value of lightning conductors, which he dismisses angrily, irritated by Kudrash's scientific and irreligious attitude to the elements. A moment later Boris comes in, then Varvara, who anxiously tells Boris that Katya, with her husband now returned, is almost deranged by her sense of guilt. The storm goes on and Katya, Tikhon and Kabanikha come in. Boris conceals himself. Katya's overwrought state is observed by the crowd and by Dikoy, who comment on it and on her beauty. She notices Boris, and can bear it no longer; she bursts out with a desperate confession of her guilty love, and rushes off.

At a deserted spot by the Volga, night is falling as Tikhon and Glasha, carrying a lantern, come searching for Katya. Tikhon, though he still loves her, talks of the punishment she deserves. As they move off, Varvara and Kudrash enter. Varvara is full of foreboding; she agrees to go away with him, and they depart. In the distance, Tikhon's and Glasha's voices are heard calling Katya. Just then she enters, from the opposite direction; she only wishes now to see Boris once again. Kuligin passes and mysterious, wordless voices are heard from afar. Katya speaks wildly, wishing half for death, half to see Boris again. Then Boris enters. They embrace passionately, and talk of the future: Boris has been sent away by his uncle, and Katya will have to bear the taunts of her mother-in-law and the town. Boris goes. The distant voices are heard again. Katya, utterly distraught, throws herself into the river. People quickly gather – Kuligin, a passer-by, then Dikoy, Glasha, Tikhon and Kabanikha. 'You killed my wife!' says Tikhon bitterly to his mother, who prevents him from diving in after Katya. The body is pulled out of the river and Dikoy places it on the bank, where Tikhon falls upon it. Kabanikha formally thanks the people present for their kind assistance.

★ ★ ★

Janáček's realistic setting of Czech words – realistic in the sense that it flows in irregular patterns, like the prose of ordinary speech – is complemented by his similarly 'irregular', asymmetrical, and subtle treatment of recurring motives. In the first scene as Boris begins to divulge to Kudrash his love for Katya a little theme steals in first high on the oboe, then repeated by violins; then, when Katya herself enters with her husband and family (orchestra without voices), the flute takes it over (ex. 1). This symbolizes not only Boris's love for

Ex. 1

Katya but also hers for him, and recurs with that dual significance. Note the similar phrase '*x*' (and compare the previous example) at the point when, in the garden, she finally lets her passion express itself to Boris; her words ('Tvoje vule nade mnou vládne') show her anguish (ex. 2).

Ex. 2

The strongest contrast with this idiom is provided by the songs (that is, musical material sung *as* interpolated songs) given to the 'happy' pair of lovers in the garden scene. They are in the spirit of Czech folksong and one (the first 'answering'-duet) has a dance-like beat but an unexpected phrase-rhythm (ex. 3).

Ex. 3

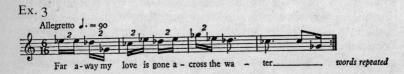

THE MAKROPOULOS CASE
Več Makropulos
Libretto by the composer after Karel Čapek

First performed: Brno, 1926
Three Acts

Cast in order of singing:

VÍTEK, A SOLICITOR'S CLERK	*tenor*
ALBERT GREGOR	*tenor*
KRISTINA (Krista), VÍTEK'S DAUGHTER	*soprano*
KOLENATÝ, A LAWYER	*baritone*
EMILIA MARTY	*soprano*
JAROSLAV PRUS	*bass*
JANEK, HIS SON	*tenor*
CLEANING WOMAN	*mezzo-soprano*
CARPENTER	*baritone*
COUNT HAUK SENDORF	*tenor*
MAID	*soprano*

[The role of the Doctor is silent.]

The scene is laid in Prague in 1922

The flood of inspiration that drew from Janáček, in the last years of his life, a stream of intensely characteristic masterpieces led him into increasingly eccentric operatic topics. There is *The Cunning Little Vixen*, with its world of animals and nature, and *From the House of the Dead*, in the hermetic setting of a prison camp. Between them comes *The Makropoulos Case*, the story after a play by Karel Čapek (Janáček saw it three weeks after it opened, in 1922) of a woman who took an elixir in 1591 and is still living in the twentieth century. Its central character, Elina Makropoulos, was the sixteen-year-old daughter of a Greek (Cretan) physician at the Prague court of the Habsburg emperor Rudolf II; her father was commanded to produce an elixir, and tried it out on his daughter, who was seriously ill (her father was imprisoned, and the emperor did not take the elixir); but she escaped and took with her the formula. She has become a great singer, and concealed her longevity by changing her name while retaining the initials E. M. – thus she has been Eugenia Montez, a Spaniard, Elian

MacGregor, a Scotswoman, and many more; now she is Emilia Marty, a Czech.

The Czech title, *Več Makropulos*, literally means 'The Makropoulos Document', but its implications are wider, and 'affair', 'matter' or 'case' served better to convey them – as long as 'case' is not taken to signify the lawsuit that takes place during the action. So here we use the form of title that has been used for recent productions of the work in Britain, though we favour the normal English transliteration ('–poulos' rather than '–pulos') from the Greek name.

★   ★   ★

ACT I: In the offices of the lawyer Dr Kolenatý, a clerk, Vítek, is arranging the files of the famous case *Gregor v. Prus*, which began in 1827 and now seems likely to be resolved after ninety-five years. Albert Gregor, for whom Kolenatý is acting, enters; he asks Vítek to phone Dr Kolenatý and see what news there is from the court, but Kolenatý has left. Kristina (Krista) rushes in and tells her father with enthusiasm about the singer Emilia Marty whom she heard in a rehearsal at the opera-house (where she is a young singer). Then Emilia herself enters, with Kolenatý: she has come to discuss the Gregor case, and Kolenatý introduces Gregor to her. She inquires about the case, and Kolenatý explains. Baron Joseph Ferdinand Prus ('Peppi') died intestate in 1827 and his large estate was taken over by his cousin, but a claim was made by Ferdinand Karel Gregor, who had certain evidence that he had some entitlement; the cousin, however, objected that the deceased had expressed a deathbed wish that the estate should pass to 'Mach Gregor', and another relative found someone called 'Gregor Mach'. Emilia, who has shown a surprising knowledge of events so long past, tells Kolenatý that Ferdinand was Joseph's son, by an opera singer called Elian MacGregor. What is more, there is evidence, in a yellow envelope in a particular drawer in a cabinet at the Prus home, that Joseph wished to leave the rich Loukov estate to his son. Kolenatý and especially Gregor are excited and amazed, but the sceptical lawyer thinks she is duping him; Gregor, however, insists that Kolenatý should go to the Prus house, and he reluctantly agrees.

Gregor and Emilia are left alone. He is enchanted by her – profoundly grateful for her miraculous appearance just when he was about to lose his case, and infatuated by her presence and her beauty. He says he will do anything for her, and she asks him to give her the Greek document (the formula for the elixir) that she knows will be found in his ancestor's papers. Now Kolenatý returns, with Jaroslav Prus: the will has been found, with other papers. But still the situation is not quite clear, for the will mentions only a son Ferdinand, with no other name, and Prus requires written proof that this is Ferdinand Gregor. Emilia offers to provide such proof.

ACT II: The next morning, backstage at the opera-house, a cleaner and a stage carpenter are discussing the tumultuous reception Emilia received the previous evening. Prus arrives to see her, and decides to wait. The cleaner and carpenter go, but now Krista arrives, with Janek, Prus's son – the two are in love, though Krista protests that she must give him up to concentrate on her art. Emilia arrives; Prus introduces his son, who is tongue-tied. Then Gregor comes, with Vítek, and presents her with a bouquet and a jewel-box – she returns the box, throws down the flowers, and gives Gregor a handful of money (which he passes on to Vítek). Emilia calls forth admiration from all, speaks slightingly of great singers of the past and is generally ill-mannered to those assembled. Then the elderly half-demented Count Hauk Sendorf enters, with a bouquet: he falls to his knees before Emilia, and tells her how like she is to the Spanish beauty, Eugenia, whom he loved fifty years ago. Emilia recognizes him, of course, for she was Eugenia, and offers him a kiss and endearments before sending him off. At Vítek's request she signs a photograph for Krista, then sends off everyone except Prus.

Prus comments to Emilia on her knowledge of the letters and the will in a locked cabinet in his house; he mentions – to her excitement – that something else was there too. He refers to Elian MacGregor and her passionate letters, and aks if Emilia knows her real name – the letters were signed 'E. M.', which, he says, could stand for 'Emilia Marty' or 'Elina Makropoulos', and this last name is the one given in the Loukov parish register as the mother of Ferdinand, an illegitimate child born in 1816. Unless, he says, someone called Makropoulos comes to light, the estate will remain in the Prus family. Emilia asks his price; but Prus merely bows and leaves. Now Gregor returns, and pleads his passionate desire for her. She rejects his advances, but asks him to obtain the document she has written and sent to Kolenatý: Prus's discovery means that it needs to bear the name Makropoulos. As he again begs for her love, she, wretched and weary, subsides into sleep. The cleaning woman sees him, and he leaves. Janek enters, and Emilia, waking, takes the opportunity to ask the young man, who also is infatuated with her, to perform a service: will he bring her the sealed envelope that his father has?

Janek nervously agrees; but then his father, who has been listening in concealment, emerges and despatches him. Prus agrees to bring the envelope to her room that night.

ACT III: It is daybreak. Emilia comes out of her hotel bedroom into the room adjoining; she is wearing her nightgown. Prus, in dinner jacket but collarless, follows. She demands the envelope, which he hands over; but he is filled with disgust after his night with this cold, loveless woman. A maid comes to do Emilia's hair, and delivers a note for Prus: he reads it, and learns that Janek has killed himself. Emilia comments cynically and continues dressing. As Prus leaves he collides with Hauk, who has come to take Emilia back to Spain and has taken his wife's jewels for the purpose. She makes to go with him; but then a crowd of people enter, among them Hauk's doctor, who leads him away. In front of Gregor and Prus, Kolenatý questions her about the document she has sent him, but she swears it was written by Elian MacGregor and declines to be further drawn. She goes off to breakfast, and the men immediately start examining her possessions: all bear 'E. M.' names – Eugenia Montez, Else Müller, Elian MacGregor, Ekaterina Myshkin. Emilia returns, in evening dress, with a bottle of whisky. Kolenatý questions her again: she tells him her true name, her father's name, her date and place of birth, and the truth about the parentage of Ferdinand Gregor. Increasingly drunk, she goes on to tell them how she left the Makropoulos document – the formula for the elixir – with Joseph Prus, and has only now returned for it in order to secure another 300 years of life; she relates the story of her father, Rudolf II and the elixir. Kolenatý still refuses to believe her, but as she collapses, muttering Greek prayers, he and all present acknowledge that she must indeed be Elina Makropoulos, 337 years old. They ask her forgiveness; and she at last recognizes that her life is empty, lonely and without pleasure or warmth, and should be allowed to end. She hands the Makropoulos secret over to Krista, urging her to use it: Krista burns it as Emilia dies.

★　　★　　★

Like most of Janáček's scores, that of *The Makropoulos Case* is built out of numerous motifs, most of them brief and suggestive, and nearly always cast in the speech rhythms and melodic shapes of the Czech language. They are not exactly leitmotifs, in a Wagnerian sense, nor simply thematic labels; they have a certain character and identity, like for example the fussy, slightly pompous little figure

Ex. 1

(ex. 1) associated with the lawyer Kolenatý, or the four-note phrase (ex. 2) that seems to parallel the word 'Makropoulos' and comes at critical junctures when the name is used – it should be noted, by the way, that in Czech the stresses fall on the first and third syllables.

Ex. 2

Ma - kro - pou - los

The special character of the score, however, derives not only from this motive structure, with its high nervous tension, its restlessness, its abruptness of diction, its awkward-sounding (at least to a non-Czech) rhythms, but also to its scoring: Janáček's tendency to use instruments at extreme parts of their compass – busy high woodwind and high violins in particular – and thus give something of a strained effect, along with his avoidance of ordinarily warm and rich sound, constantly heightens the dramatic tension that comes over to the listener. It is in this context that the opera's final scene is so intensely moving, as the music tells us unmistakably of the cold, hard, dried-up Emilia coming to terms with the ending of her grotesquely prolonged life: a marvellous dissolution of emotion in music, showing how far the composer of opera can go beyond the spoken dramatist, in terms of the evocation of human feeling.

IGOR STRAVINSKY

1882–1971

Born a Russian, afterwards taking French and then American nationality, Igor Stravinsky had a musical career of extraordinary variety and extraordinary success. In the 1950s he began writing serial and then strict twelve-note music – to which he had been attracted by the work not of Schoenberg but of Schoenberg's disciple, Anton Webern (1883–1945). Stravinsky's operas date from before this 'conversion'; the most important of them belong to what is called his 'neo-classical' period.

But others were written still earlier. *Solovey* ('The Nightingale'); words in Russian by the composer and S. N. Mitusov after Hans Andersen, (but first produced in France as *Le rossignol* in 1914) is cast in a glittering Russian style worthy of a Rimsky-Korsakov pupil; there is also the half-hour comedy *Mavra* (Russian text by Boris Kochno after Pushkin, first given in French in 1922). The burlesque *Bayka* ('Reynard'; words in Russian arranged by the composer, composed in 1915–16 and first given in France as *Renard* in 1922) and *Histoire du soldat* ('The Soldier's Tale'; words by C. F. Ramuz, 1918) both involve dance and instrumental music, the former singing and the latter speech, but are not true operas. Nor in a sense is the 'opera-oratorio' *Oedipus Rex*, chosen for detailed comment here none the less because it represents so striking and so important a break with operatic traditions, though *The Rake's Progress* (1951) is equally significant for the ways in which it picks those traditions up.

OEDIPUS REX
(King Oedipus)
Libretto by Jean Cocteau (after Sophocles),
translated into Latin by J. Daniélou

First performed: Paris, 1927
Two Acts

Cast in order of singing:

OEDIPUS, KING OF THEBES	*tenor*
CREON, JOCASTA'S BROTHER	*bass-baritone*
TIRESIAS, A SEER	*bass*
JOCASTA, OEDIPUS'S WIFE	*mezzo-soprano*
A MESSENGER	*bass-baritone*
A SHEPHERD	*tenor*

[A narrator also takes part, as indicated in the synopsis.]

Chorus of men of Thebes
The scene is laid in Thebes in classical times

Significantly Stravinsky set a version of Sophocles' *Oedipus Rex* not in the author's own Greek nor the composer's own Russian nor in the language of modern France (where the work was to be staged) but in Latin – a language which Stravinsky described as 'a medium not dead, but turned to stone, and so monumentalized as to have become immune from all risks of vulgarization'. The libretto was therefore written in French (by Cocteau) and translated into Latin. A narrator is required to interrupt the action by telling the story in the audience's own language.

The work is described as an 'opera-oratorio', and the novelty of the form was doubtless a deliberate challenge to tradition and especially to the idea that opera should be realistic. The characters of *Oedipus Rex* are costumed, but (according to the original scheme) restricted in their movements: Oedipus, Creon and Jocasta use masks and move only their arms and heads.

It is fitting to this conception that the music, too, should seem severe and monumental. But such is the skill of the music – not only in itself but in the way its variety of mood and pace reflect the drama – that the piece comes over in the theatre with impressive power.

* * *

ACT I: [Narration] King Oedipus is begged by the people of Thebes to save them from the plague, which is destroying the city. He promises to do so, saying that he has sent Creon, his wife's brother, to ask the oracle of Apollo what is to be done. Creon appears and is greeted by the people.

[Narration] Creon tells Oedipus and the people the god's answer: the Thebans must discover the murderer of the previous king, Laius;

he must be driven out of the city, for it is he who is causing the city's misery. Oedipus boasts to the people that he will find the guilty man.

[Narration] The chorus pray that Oedipus will succeed. They greet the seer Tiresias, whom Oedipus decides to consult; but Tiresias declines to speak, asking not to be compelled to do so. Oedipus, made suspicious by his silence, accuses him of being the murderer himself. In indignation, Tiresias resolves to speak, and he tells Oedipus what the god has said: 'Regis est rex peremptor' ('The king's murderer is a king'). Oedipus, believing Tiresias to be in league with Creon in a plot against himself, turns angrily on him. Then the queen, Jocasta, appears, to be greeted by the people in a jubilant chorus.

ACT II: [Narration] The chorus repeat their greeting to Jocasta. She rebukes the princes for quarrelling in the plague-ridden city. She tells Oedipus not to trust oracles ('Ne probentur oracula'): she knows that they can lie – for they predicted that her son would kill her husband, the previous king, whereas he was in fact murdered by a thief at a meeting of three roads (the chorus echo the word 'trivium').

Oedipus becomes uneasy: he remembers killing an old man once at a meeting of three roads. (He believes, however, that he is the son of the Corinthian king, Polybus; he had left Corinth as it was predicted that he would kill his father and marry his mother.) In a long duet, Jocasta tries to lead him away, but he is bent on discovering the truth and sends for the shepherd who witnessed his crime.

[Narration] The chorus announce the arrival of a messenger, who bears news of the death of Polybus. He relates that Polybus was not Oedipus's true father; he, the messenger, had brought Oedipus, exposed on a mountainside in his infancy, to Polybus. The truth seems clear, but the people still hope that some miraculous explanation will come to light. The shepherd then comes forward and tells how the infant son of Laius and Jocasta had been abandoned in this way on a mountainside.

Jocasta has departed, Oedipus, not comprehending the truth, at first believes she does not wish to hear of his humble ancestry. But at last he realizes the terrible facts: he is the son of Jocasta, and has murdered his true father, Laius, and married his mother. He leaves.

[Narration] The messenger returns with news of the death of Jocasta: 'Divum Jocastae caput mortuum' ('Dead is the sacred head of Jocasta'). The people tell of how Jocasta hanged herself and of how Oedipus cut her down, then put out his eyes with her brooch. He reappears, to their horror; but when they see their king's blind mutilated face their horror turns to pity as they bid him farewell.

★   ★   ★

Though the music is both hard in texture and apparently rigid in shape (which is what we mean by the 'monumental' aspect of Stravinsky's work in this vein), it is nevertheless varied not only between characters but even within their utterances. Oedipus, at the beginning, is vain and self-confident: his promise to deliver his people ('Ego vos liberabo') is uttered with flaunting coloratura. But when he discovers the terrible truth about himself, he is reduced to (ex. 1). These words ('Light has come!') bear their own terrible irony: in a few minutes we shall hear that Oedipus has put out his eyes.

Ex. 1

Jocasta's earlier utterance in distrust of oracles (ex. 2) shows Stravinsky's characteristic rough-riding over the natural rhythms of language to create musical and dramatic tension.

Ex. 2

THE RAKE'S PROGRESS
Libretto by W. H. Auden and Chester Kallman

First performed: Venice, 1951
Three Acts

Cast in order of singing:

TRULOVE, A COUNTRY GENTLEMAN	*bass*
ANNE, HIS DAUGHTER	*soprano*
TOM RAKEWELL	*tenor*
NICK SHADOW	*baritone*
MOTHER GOOSE, A BROTHEL-KEEPER	*mezzo-soprano*
BABA THE TURK	*mezzo-soprano*
SELLEM, AUCTIONEER	*tenor*
KEEPER OF THE MADHOUSE	*bass*

Chorus of whores, roaring boys, servants, citizens, madmen
The scene is laid in eighteenth-century England

For his last opera, and indeed his only mature, full-length one, Stravinsky carried his neo-classical ideas to an extreme point. He lived in America and was now published by a British firm; he resolved to write his opera in English and to base it on the series of engravings by William Hogarth, made in the early 1730s, called *The Rake's Progress* (which he had seen in 1947 in a Hogarth exhibition in Chicago). His Hollywood neighbour Aldous Huxley proposed W. H. Auden as the librettist; Stravinsky invited Auden to Los Angeles, where the two men worked out a scenario, and then Auden went away and, with Chester Kallman, wrote the text, adding to Hogarth's characters the additional one of Nick Shadow – which transforms the fable from a tale about a foolish man's self-motivated downward progress into something more Faust-like.

* * *

ACT I: In the garden of Trulove's country house, Tom Rakewell, a young and impecunious country gentleman, is courting Anne. Her father watches, more or less approvingly, then sends Anne off into the house while he tells Tom that he has made inquiries about a job for him in the city. Tom, however, has higher hopes for himself, and declines; Trulove is disconcerted at the prospect of a wastrel son-in-law. Left alone, Tom states his cheerful determination to entrust himself to fortune while he is still young and strong. 'I wish I had money,' he mutters; and Nick Shadow appears and tells him that he has good news to impart. Tom calls Anne and her father, and in their presence Nick announces that Tom has been left a fortune by a rich uncle who lived abroad. In a quartet, all give thanks, and Nick (whom Tom engages as his servant) leads Tom off to London to settle his business affairs, Tom and Anne bidding one another a fond farewell and Tom promising to call Anne and Trulove to London as soon as he can.

'The Progress of a Rake begins', exclaims Nick as the first scene ends; and the second is set in Mother Goose's brothel in London. The roaring boys and the whores are celebrating their lifestyle, toasting Venus and Mars. Tom and Nick are present, Nick urging Tom to all sorts of indulgence. Nick presents his young recruit to the company, and Tom sings an aria: 'Love, too frequently betrayed'. The whores are charmed by him, but Mother Goose asserts her proprietorial rights and takes him away for herself.

In Trulove's garden, Anne reflects on Tom's silence and resolves to take herself, perilously and alone, to London in order to rescue him.

ACT II: Tom is at breakfast in the morning-room of his house in a London square. He is discontented with his way of life: 'Vary the song, O London'. Nick enters with a handbill about the bearded lady, Baba the Turk. Does Tom desire her, is he obliged to her? As he is not, says Nick, he should marry her. With impeccable sophistry, he proves to Tom's satisfaction that he should, and Tom, vastly intrigued at the idea, agrees with mounting enthusiasm.

It is twilight in the street outside Tom's house. Anne is there, anxious and hesitant. She sees, and wonders at, a procession of servants carrying packages into the house, and then a sedan chair, from which Tom alights. He sees her and, ashamed, tries to send her away; she cannot understand. Then, from the chair, a head – richly coiffed and heavily veiled below the eyes – appears: it is Baba, waiting impatiently to be helped down and into the house. Tom is full of remorse, Anne deeply distressed, Baba irritated by the delay. Anne hurries off, and people gather to see the famous Baba the Turk go into Tom's house – pausing, before she does so, to remove her veil and disclose a flowing black beard.

In Tom's morning room, now cluttered with bric-à-brac, Baba is chattering away interminably over breakfast. Infuriated at Tom's sulky silence, she bursts out in a rage and starts destroying objects in the room. Eventually he rises and places his wig firmly over her head; she falls silent, and the despairing Tom turns to sleep. Now Nick enters, with a fantastic machine; as he sings, he places pieces of stone in one end, a loaf of bread in the other, turns a wheel and the loaf drops out, giving the transparent illusion that the stone has turned into bread. Tom awakes: he tells Nick of his strange dream about a machine that converts stones into bread. Nick discloses his machine; it is the one Tom had dreamt of. He inserts a stone, and out there duly falls a loaf of bread. The excited Tom talks of banishing hunger and poverty. Nick points out some of the practical difficulties of exploiting it: they need backers of wealth and reputation – and they go off to visit the ones who, Nick says, have already expressed interest.

ACT III: Tom's morning-room is covered with dust; Baba is still there, under the wig, and a crowd is present examining the various objects to be sold – Rakewell is ruined, and an auction is about to begin. Anne enters, seeking him, but no one can help her. Sellem enters, mounts a dais, and embarks on the auction. A few objects are sold, and then Sellem approaches a mysterious one for which the bidding is especially lively. It goes at 100, is uncovered, and bursts into furious song – for it is Baba, who tries to send everyone away. Out in the street the voices of Tom and Nick are heard. There is an encounter between Anne and Baba, who advises the girl to seek Tom as he still loves her. Anne is much touched ('He loves me still'); Baba decides to go back to the stage. The auction is called off as the voices are again heard, and Anne, encouraged by all present, determines to find Tom.

Tom and Nick are in a graveyard. A year and a day have passed, Nick announces; and in his true capacity as the Devil he claims his wages – not Tom's money but his soul. Tom, too late, repents all he has done. The clock strikes: Tom has until midnight to kill himself. At nine strokes Nick halts the chimes; he will allow Tom's fate to hang on a game of cards. Tom guesses the first card right: his thoughts of Anne prompt him to say the Queen of Hearts. Second, as he is pondering, the spade by the graveside crashes – 'The deuce!' he exclaims, and settles correctly on the Two of Spades, to Nick's fury. Third and last, he can think of nothing better than the Queen of Hearts again. Nick, enraged, sinks into the grave, but as he does so he curses Tom to perpetual insanity.. The dawn rises; Tom is sitting on a green mound where the grave had been, singing: 'With roses crowned'. He thinks he is Adonis.

Tom is in Bedlam, with other madmen and madwomen. He is singing of the prospect of a visit from Venus, his lover. The mad people deride his expectations: 'Leave all love and hope behind'. The Keeper enters, with Anne, whom Tom greets as Venus; they sing together: 'In a foolish dream'. Soon Tom is weary, and Anne sings him to sleep. The Keeper admits Trulove, who draws Anne away. Tom awakes, protesting at Venus's absence; he falls dead, mourned by his companions.

In an epilogue, Anne, Baba, Tom, Nick and Trulove point the moral – 'For idle hands and hearts and minds the devil finds a work to do'.

★　★　★

For his opera inspired by the eighteenth century, Stravinsky chose a musical language with an eighteenth-century basis, though drawn from a generation later than Hogarth. The score of *The Rake's Progress*, it should first be said, is totally and umistakably Stravinskian, and belongs entirely to its own day. But it uses techniques of Mozart's time: recitative (some accompanied by the orchestra, some with merely a harpsichord), and there are set-piece arias, several of them following the slow–fast pattern in the manner of early nineteenth-century Italian composers like Bellini or Donizetti. There are several specific echoes of Mozart, some from his piano music, and some from *Così fan tutte*, of which one from the Act I mock-farewell quintet (see page 87) comes several times in slightly different guises (see, for example, ex. 1). Then there are hints of *Don Giovanni*, in the Graveyard Scene for man and master and in the Epilogue, so closely akin to Da Ponte and Mozart's in its moral about the fate of the sinner. And the introductory fanfare even harks back to Monteverdi's *Orfeo*.

Ex. 1

Some critics have cried down *The Rake's Progress* as a semi-pastiche or as a heartless, cold work dominated by its rigid forms. Neither view is true or perceptive. At this stage of his life Stravinsky was reaching increasingly towards strict, clear-cut musical forms, and the conventional framework was far from a restricting influence on him – rather, it was liberating one, for each aria (and in this he is just like an eighteenth-century master, a Handel or a Mozart) has its well-defined, circumscribed expressive content, enabling Stravinsky to handle strong emotion in a precisely controlled manner. And, for all the Mozartisms, Bellinisms and so on, he remains wholly himself, as is shown by, for example, the writing in Nick's aria in the first scene of Act II, with its taut, motoric rhythms, its sharply etched decorative writing, its wilful and pointed distortion of natural verbal rhythms to set up a tension between music and words (ex. 2). The music that stands for the onset of Tom's madness,

Ex. 2

in Act III, is equally telling, with the curiously distorted logic of its lines (ex. 3). The music of *The Rake's Progress* often teases and always fascinates; and, for all its cool and controlled surface, it can also be uncommonly moving.

Ex. 3

ALBAN BERG

1885–1935

The distance between the first performances of Richard Strauss's *Ariadne auf Naxos* and Alban Berg's *Wozzeck* is a mere twelve years – but these twelve years include those of World War I, and for most music-lovers the gap between the two works is the gap separating 'old' from 'modern' music. Of all the pioneers and innovators of modernism in music, the most influential has proved to be the Viennese, Arnold Schoenberg (1874–1951), of whom Berg was a disciple.

Schoenberg himself composed four operatic works. The one which, philosophically as well as musically, might have stood as the cornerstone of his career was *Moses und Aron* ('Moses and Aaron'), to his own libretto. But he completed only two of its three acts. It was nevertheless brought to the stage, incomplete, in 1957 and subsequently, attracting considerable interest. He also composed three shorter works, each of less than a full evening's length: *Erwartung* ('Expectation'), completed in 1909 though not produced until 1924, *Die glückliche Hand ('The Lucky Hand')*, composed 1910–13; and *Von heute auf morgen* ('From today till tomorrow'), composed 1930. Of these *Erwartung*, the best-known, is a 'monodrama', i.e. for one character only. The character is female, as in another celebrated single-voiced, one-act opera, *La voix humaine* ('The Human Voice'), composed by Francis Poulenc (1899–1963) to a libretto by Cocteau and produced in 1958.

But Schoenberg never established himself with the public as an opera composer. His influence and method were to triumph only at one remove, in Berg's double legacy to the stage. In *Wozzeck* and *Lulu* Berg depicted the extremities, not to say perversities, of human feeling. The musical grammar of these two works is not the same. *Wozzeck* has (for nearly all of its length) turned its back on the old major/minor key-system, being literally 'keyless' or 'atonal'; in the later *Lulu*, Schoenberg's newly-invented 'twelve-note technique' has been used to impose a new ordering in place of the lost major/minor. But it is fair to say that the listener feels the idiom of both works as jagged, angular, distorted – an impression comparable to that produced in painting by cubism and other non-realistic, twentieth-century approaches.

WOZZECK
Libretto by the composer, after Georg Büchner

First performed: Berlin, 1925
Three Acts

Cast in order of singing:

THE CAPTAIN	*tenor*
WOZZECK, A SOLDIER, ORDERLY TO THE CAPTAIN	*baritone*
ANDRES, ANOTHER SOLDIER, HIS FRIEND	*tenor*
MARIE, A WOMAN LIVING WITH WOZZECK	*soprano*
MARGRET, MARIE'S NEIGHBOUR	*contralto*
THE DOCTOR	*bass*
THE DRUM-MAJOR	*tenor*
TWO APPRENTICES	*baritone (or tenor) and bass*
AN IDIOT	*tenor*
MARIE'S AND WOZZECK'S CHILD	*treble*

Chorus of soldiers, apprentices, servants and children
The scene is laid in a German town in the early nineteenth century

In its depiction of the agony of the unbalanced, persecuted individual at the hands of unfeeling society, *Wozzeck* seems so modern that it is hard to realize that it is based on a play written before Victoria came to the throne. This play was *Woyzeck* (that was the original spelling), left unfinished by its German author, Georg Büchner, who died in 1837 at the age of 23.

Wozzeck is a simple soldier, distinguished neither by intelligence nor any other special gift: an anti-hero, in fact. Yet he wins our sympathy – ill-treated as he is by his superiors, deceived by the woman with whom he lives. Even this woman, however, has her glimpses of redemption. Theirs is a pathos which they themselves cannot express articulately, but it is a pathos which becomes intensely moving in the theatre. Berg's music (orchestral as well as vocal) seems to convey the fears and fantasies of Wozzeck's mind as well as the frustrations of his material existence.

★　★　★

ACT I, *Scene 1:* The Captain is being shaved by the agitated, nervous Wozzeck, his batman. He teases Wozzeck, reproaching him for having a child out of wedlock. Wozzeck attempts to justify himself: 'Wir arme Leut' ('We poor folk') cannot afford the morality of the rich.

Scene 2: Wozzeck and his friend Andres are cutting wood in a field. Andres is singing gaily while Wozzeck, confused in his mind, believes the place to be haunted and sees strange visions.

Scene 3: Marie is minding her small child and talking through the window of her room with a neighbour, Margret. As a military band passes by, Marie waves to the Drum-Major. Margret comments on Marie's friendliness with men and the two quarrel. Marie sings her child a lullaby: 'Mädel, was fangst Du jetzt an?' ('Girl, what are you starting now?'). The child falls asleep. Soon there is a knock at the window. Wozzeck, still agitated, looks in, talks for a moment with Marie, and rushes off again. Soon after, the distressed Marie breaks out in anguish and goes out.

Scene 4: In his study, the Doctor talks to Wozzeck, who has consented for a small extra wage to be subjected to the Doctor's medical experiments. The Doctor hectors him, then listens to Wozzeck's descriptions of his strange world – he hopes to become famous through the medical discoveries arising from his studies of Wozzeck.

Scene 5: Outside her house, Marie talks with the handsome, bearded Drum-Major and admires his physique. He is strongly attracted by her and tries to embrace her: at first she resists, then, with a shrug, she leads him indoors.

ACT II, *Scene 1:* In her room, Marie is impatiently trying to get her child to sleep, intermittently admiring herself (wearing a pair of gold ear-rings) in a broken mirror. Wozzeck enters and is suspicious on seeing the ear-rings. He looks at the sleeping child, gives Marie some money which he has received from the Captain and the Doctor, and goes off, leaving her in remorse over her infidelity.

Scene 2: In the street, the Captain catches up with the Doctor, who is in a hurry. The Doctor makes the Captain uneasy by talking about disease and death. They stop Wozzeck as he passes and, with allusions to soldiers wearing beards, tease him cruelly about the Drum-Major. He goes off distracted, soon followed by the Captain and the Doctor.

Scene 3: In front of her house again, Marie greets Wozzeck. He questions her and reproaches her angrily for her behaviour with the Drum-Major. Before she goes off, she says 'Lieber ein Messer in der Leib, als eine Hand auf mich' ('Better a knife in my body than lay a hand on me').

Scene 4: Soldiers, girls and apprentices are drinking and dancing in a tavern to the music of a band. Two drunken apprentices sing of brandy. Wozzeck enters and is enraged to see Marie and the Drum-Major among the dancers; he is about to rush at them when the dance ends and the soldiers and apprentices, led by Andres, sing a hunting song: 'Ein Jäger aus der Pfalz' ('A hunter from the Pfalz'). Andres and Wozzeck talk for a moment, then one of the drunken apprentices climbs on to a table and delivers a rambling sermon. An idiot approaches Wozzeck and talks to him of blood, the thought of blood preys on Wozzeck's mind as the dancing is resumed.

Scene 5: Soldiers are asleep in the barrack room. Wozzeck, still tortured by thoughts of the dance-hall, talks to the half-sleeping Andres. The Drum-Major, drunk, enters noisily, boasting of his possession of a woman and hinting at her identity. He torments Wozzeck and offers him brandy: in reply Wozzeck merely whistles. Angrily, the Drum-Major seizes him and they fight, the Drum-Major completing his humiliation by pushing him to the floor and beating his face.

The Drum-Major goes and the disturbed soldiers settle themselves again, Wozzeck sitting on his bed and staring before him.

ACT III, *Scene 1:* Marie, alone with her child in her room, reads her Bible by candlelight. She is in penitent mood and prays for mercy.

Scene 2: At dusk, Wozzeck and Marie are walking by a pool. She is nervous and wishes to go home, but he insists on their sitting down. He recalls their first meeting and kisses her; then he draws his knife and cuts her throat.

Scene 3: Apprentices and girls are dancing a polka in a tavern. Wozzeck watches them. He sings raucously and calls Margret over, starting to make love to her. Then he asks her to sing, which she does, accompanied by an out-of-tune piano: 'In's Schwabenland' ('To Swabia'). She notices a dark red stain on his right hand. He says that he had cut his arm; but the crowd gathers round him and he rushes off.

Scene 4: Back by the pool, Wozzeck is searching for the knife with which he killed Marie. He comes upon her corpse. Finding the knife, he throws it in the pool; and as the blood-red moon shows through the clouds, wades in after it as if to wash off his own blood. He drowns. Arriving at that moment, the Captain and the Doctor pause, thinking that they heard something. Then the Captain, disturbed by the uncanny atmosphere, drags the Doctor off.

Scene 5: In front of Marie's house, a crowd of children, among them Marie's, is playing. News comes of the discovery of Marie's body and they hurry off to see it, one of them telling Marie's child that his mother is dead. He goes on riding his hobby horse for a while, then, finding himself alone, runs off after the others.

★　★　★

'We poor folk': the basic dramatic motive of the opera is musically characterized by Wozzeck in the opening scene (ex. 1).

Ex. 1

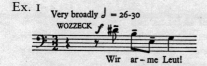

As distinct from ordinary notation, parts of the opera employ a device called 'Speech-song' (*Sprechgesang*) which Schoenberg devised. In it the singer does not sustain the pitch of the note indicated but just touches it: the effect is something of a compromise between speech and song. This is only one of the ways in which Berg develops a peculiarly intense expression for the words, away from older conventions of what is beautiful and regular in music.

On occasion Berg comes close to a 'popular' musical style (lullaby, military march, hunting song) but deliberately distorts the kind of melody we should expect. Thus Marie, singing to her child in Act I has ex. 2. Here is the typical rocking of the traditional lullaby, and indeed a typical lullaby melody – except for the violent distortion induced by the out-of-key notes in the phrases marked '*x*'.

Ex. 2

A similar kind of 'distorted reality' is achieved by the tavern orchestra in Act II and the out-of-tune piano in Act III. But it is not only in the unusual instruments required here that Berg's use of the orchestra is original and impressive. Notable are the huge orchestral *crescendo* on the single note B, after Marie's murder – an overwhelming effect in the theatre – and the interlude between the two final scenes of the opera. It is this interlude (not atonal, but in the key of D minor) which seems to sum up Wozzeck's tragedy and to speak directly from composer to audience. The chorus is also sometimes used orchestrally – that is, for its power of sheer tone-colour and atmosphere, notably in the 'snoring' heard when Wozzeck returns to his barrack-room in Act II.

The scenes are composed by Berg in what are usually considered instrumental forms – fugue, variations, etc. – though it is the dramatic, not the formal, development which we sense in the theatre.

LULU
Libretto by the composer, after two plays by Frank Wedekind

First performed (incomplete): Zurich, 1937
First performed (complete): Paris, 1979
Prologue and Three Acts

Cast in order of singing or speaking:

AN ANIMAL-TAMER	*bass*
ALWA, A COMPOSER	*tenor*
DR SCHÖN, ALWA'S FATHER, A NEWSPAPER EDITOR-IN-CHIEF	*baritone*
LULU	*soprano*
THE PAINTER	*tenor*
THE PROFESSOR OF MEDICINE	*speaking part*
SCHIGOLCH, AN OLD MAN	*bass*
THE PRINCE, AN AFRICAN EXPLORER	*tenor*
A DRESSER IN A THEATRE	*contralto*
A THEATRE MANAGER	*bass*
COUNTESS GESCHWITZ	*mezzo-soprano*
RODRIGO, AN ACROBAT	*bass*
A HIGH-SCHOOL BOY	*contralto*

A MANSERVANT	*tenor*
BANKER	*bass*
JOURNALIST	*baritone*
MARQUIS	*tenor*
GROOM	*contralto*
LADY ARTIST	*mezzo-soprano*
MOTHER OF GIRL	*contralto*
FIFTEEN-YEAR-OLD GIRL	*soprano*
A MANSERVANT	*tenor*
A POLICE LIEUTENANT	*speaking part*
A NEGRO	*tenor*
JACK	*baritone*

[The role of 'the professor' (in Act III) is silent.]

The scene is laid in a German-speaking city, in Paris, and in London towards the end of the nineteenth century

Lulu is Woman. Female sexuality had never before been so frankly treated on the opera stage, without apology or moralizing. The composer found in Wedekind's *Earth Spirit* and *Pandora's Box* a character whom he could show as the irresistible but somehow innocent enslaver of many men, rising in fortune and then sinking to prostitution and brutal death. No less remarkable is the sympathetic depiction of Countess Geschwitz, who worships Lulu with unrequited lesbian passion.

The opera was originally published and performed in only two acts, not encompassing the heroine's downfall, and it was widely believed that the final act had been abandoned in an impracticably unfinished state. But after the death of the composer's widow (in 1977, forty-two years after her husband!) it was shown that the remaining work, involving editing and some orchestration, was indeed practicable on the basis of the materials that Berg had left. It was accomplished by Friedrich Cerha.

The use of 'twelve-note' technique is supplemented in *Lulu* by a formalized dramatic plan, full of parallels in the action and in the construction of the music. The characters whom Lulu receives in her final desperate state as a prostitute are played by performers who took earlier parts as her husbands or wealthy admirers; the performer she shot dead (as 'Dr Schön') now knifes her (as 'Jack' – i.e. Jack the Ripper). In the second act, an orchestral interlude covering Lulu's arrest for murder, her imprisonment and escape takes the form of a piece which comes to a halfway point and then is played backwards: the composer suggested, as a visual counterpart, a film with a similar reverse order of symbols.

The third act is considerably longer than the others and its party scene gives some impression of happening on a different dramatic level. The two-act version (which actually served to establish the opera) was strong in consistency and development even if failing in the composer's intended cyclical effect.

★　★　★

PROLOGUE: An Animal-Tamer, as from a circus, introduces the story in terms of crude animal characteristics, with Lulu as a snake.

ACT I: Lulu is married to Dr Goll, a professor of medicine, but is the mistress of Dr Schön, a newspaper editor-in-chief. Dr Schön and his son Alwa, a composer, are present while Lulu is having her portrait painted. When the two of them leave, the Painter pursues Lulu amorously. Her husband unexpectedly arrives and dies from shock at what he sees.

The portrait of Lulu at the height of her youthful beauty reappears in every successive scene. In the next scene she is married to the Painter and is visited by Schigolch, a decrepit old manwho evidently shares her past, and by Dr Schön. Although he intends to make a socially respectable marriage, Dr Schön cannot throw off the fascination that Lulu exerts on him. The Painter has not realized that his wife has been living under the 'protection' of Dr Schön; he now learns it and kills himself. Lulu is unmoved.

The scene changes to a dressing-room in a theatre. Lulu, as a solo dancer, is called on stage. Suddenly, realizing that Dr Schön and his fiancée are in the audience, she returns and refused to perform; only when she has totally humiliated Dr Schön, compelling him to write a letter of renunciation to his fiancée, does she consent to continue the show.

ACT II: Dr Schön is now married to Lulu but racked by jealousy of her admirers, even the lesbian Countess Geschwitz. Leaving the house for a little while, he returns to find Lulu surrounded by adoring males – his own son Alwa, an Acrobat, a Schoolboy. Dr Schön produces a revolver and demands that she shoot herself. She kills him.

An orchestral interlude bridges the gap in time. We next see the same room, some months later. Lulu's associates are at the point of effecting her escape from prison – to which she was condemned for murdering Dr Schön. Countess Geschwitz, self-sacrificingly, goes to smuggle herself into prison in Lulu's place. The Acrobat plans to take Lulu away with him as a circus performer, but on her arrival he realizes with disgust that she has grown too thin and weak. Instead it is Alwa who confesses his love for the woman who killed his father. They agree to go away together.

ACT III: In their new and luxurious Paris home, Lulu and Alwa are entertaining guests, Gambling, eating and drinking, the company is confident of prosperity, thanks to the ever-rising value of their railway shares. But, because she is still wanted by the German police as an escaped murderess, Lulu is blackmailed by the Acrobat and by a pimp, the Marquis, who wants to sell her to a brothel in Cairo. Suddenly, news comes that the railway shares have crashed. The company breaks up in recriminations. By quickly changing clothes with a young groom, Lulu manages to escape with Alwa just before the police arrive to arrest her.

Finally, Lulu is seen living in dire poverty in a London attic with Alwa and Schigolch, and reduced to casual prostitution. Countess Geschwitz arrives, bringing the portrait which she salvaged from Paris. A Black client of Lulu's kills Alwa. While Jack, another client, is with Lulu, the Countess resolves to start a new life as a champion of women's rights. Suddenly there is a scream: Jack has killed Lulu. On his way out he also stabs the Countess, who utters her devotion to Lulu and dies.

★　★　★

Lulu is probably notated with more exactitude than any other opera: it is as if the composer was obsessed by the need to control to the full every moment and every detail of the performance. When Dr Schön is compelled to write the letter renouncing his financée, the notes which fit his *silent* writing are to be found (but are not sung) in the score; when Lulu fires the five shots which kill him, the exact semiquaver on which each shot falls is marked.

But if Berg is here a super-individualist, he also follows the traditional operatic device of 'labelling' his characters by musical means, both by the manner of their utterance (Schigolch's yawn, for instance) and by motives which may occur either vocally or orchestrally. Thus the Animal-Tamer's first indication of Lulu as a snake, a temptation (ex. I), has a particular shape that recurs when Lulu at her first appearance asks Dr Schön ('very sarcastically', says the score) to

Ex. 1

ANIMAL - TAMER
cantabile

Sie ward ge-schaf-fen   Un - heil___ an - zu-stif - ten,

convey her good wishes to his fiancée (ex. 2), and indeed is
repeatedly though not constantly associated with her.

Ex. 2

Und ich... las - se mich... *(dolce)* un - be - kann - ter - wei - se Ih - rer

Braut   em - pfeh - len!

Countess Geschwitz (her name is accented on the first syllable) is intensely portrayed: hers is the only pure, selfless devotion to Lulu. It is she who closes the opera with a profession of love which the dead Lulu cannot hear and which is followed a few seconds later by her own death. The extremes of vocal range in a single phrase are as characteristic of Schoenberg as of Berg himself (ex. 3).

Ex. 3

GESCHWITZ

Mein En - gel   Laß dich noch ein - - mal sehn!
sempre espr.

SERGEY PROKOFIEV

1891–1953

Although his operas have never quite managed to gain a secure footing in the standard repertory, Prokofiev was both productive and wide-ranging as an opera composer. His first mature opera, *The Gambler*, was written in 1915–17 (though not performed until 1929); this was followed by his entertaining fable *The Love for Three Oranges* (written 1919, performed 1921), after Gozzi, a typical product of the post-World War I period when the composer, influenced by the theatrical experimentation of the time, was enjoying a cosmopolitan existence in the West. No less experimental or original was his next, *The Fiery Angel* (written in the 1920s but not performed complete until 1954); it is an impassioned tale of medieval demonic possession. But after his return to the USSR in the 1930s Prokofiev's operatic career inevitably took a different course – though scarcely a smoother one. There was first *Semyon Kotko* (1939), an attempt at a realistic patriotic opera, then *The Duenna* (or *Betrothal in a Monastery*), after Sheridan, composed 1941, performed 1946; but neither of his last two operas was staged in complete form in his lifetime. These are *The Story of a Real Man* (1948) and *War and Peace*, written between 1941 and 1952.

WAR AND PEACE
(Voyna i mir)
Libretto by the composer and Mira Mendelson, after Tolstoy

First performed: Leningrad, 1946
Thirteen scenes and epigraph

Cast:

(For the sake of clarity, the very large cast is divided into two
groups, principal and subsidiary singers. For each group, the
scene in which a singer first appears is shown.)

Principal singers

1

PRINCE ANDREY BOLKONSKY	*baritone*
NATALYA ROSTOVA (Natasha)	*soprano*
SONYA, HER COUSIN	*mezzo-soprano*

2

COUNT ILYA ROSTOV, NATASHA'S FATHER	*bass*
MARIA DMITRIEVNA AKHROSIMOVA, HER AUNT	*contralto*
HÉLÈNE BEZUKHOVA, WIFE OF PIERRE	*mezzo-soprano*
PRINCE ANATOL KURAGIN, HER BROTHER	*tenor*
DOLOKHOV, AN OFFICER	*baritone*
COUNT PYOTR BEZUKHOV (Pierre)	*tenor*

7

COLONEL VASSKA DENISOV	*baritone*

8

FIELD MARSHAL PRINCE MIKHAIL KUTUZOV	*bass*

9

NAPOLEON BONAPARTE	*baritone*

11

PLATON KARATAYEV, AN OLD SOLDIER	*tenor*

Subsidiary singers

2

PRINCE YEKATERINSK	*tenor*
HIS MAJOR-DOMO	*tenor*
MADAME PERONSKAYA	*soprano*

3

MAJOR-DOMO TO PRINCE NIKOLAI BOLKONSKY	*baritone*
MAID	*soprano*
VALET	*baritone*
PRINCESS MARYA BOLKONSKAYA	*mezzo-soprano*
PRINCE NIKOLAI BOLKONSKY	*baritone*

5

BALAGA, A TROIKA DRIVER	*bass*
MATRYOSHA, A GYPSY	*mezzo-soprano*

6

DUNYASHA, NATASHA'S MAID	*soprano*

GAVRILA, AKHROSIMOVA'S BUTLER — *bass*

7

MÉTIVIER, A FRENCH DOCTOR — *baritone*
A FRENCH *ABBÉ* — *tenor*

8

TIKHON SHERBATSKY, A PARTISAN — *baritone*
FYODOR, A PARTISAN — *tenor*
TWO PRUSSIAN GENERALS — *speaking roles*
PRINCE ANDREY'S ORDERLY — *tenor*
TWO RUSSIAN GENERALS — *speaking roles*
KAIZAROV, KUTUZOV'S AIDE-DE-CAMP — *tenor*

9

ADJUTANT TO GENERAL COMPANS — *tenor*
ADJUTANT TO MARSHAL MURAT — *treble*
MARSHAL BERTHIER — *baritone*
GENERAL BELLIARD — *baritone*
ADJUTANT TO PRINCE EUGÈNE — *tenor*
NAPOLEON'S AIDE-DE-CAMP — *bass*
ORDERLY — *tenor*
DE BEAUSSET — *tenor*

10

GENERAL BENNIGSEN — *bass*
PRINCE BARCLAY DE TOLLY — *tenor*
GENERAL YERMOLOV — *baritone*
GENERAL KONOVNITSIN — *tenor*
GENERAL RAYEVSKY — *baritone*

11

CAPTAIN RAMBALLE — *bass*
LIEUTENANT BONNET — *tenor*
MAVRA KUSMINICHNA, THE ROSTOVS' HOUSEKEEPER — *contralto*
IVANOV, A MUSCOVITE — *tenor*
CAPTAIN JACQUOT — *bass*
GÉRARD — *tenor*
MARSHAL DAVOUST — *bass*
A FRENCH OFFICER — *baritone*
THREE MADMEN — *tenor, baritone, speaking part*
TWO FRENCH ACTRESSES — *sopranos*

Chorus of the Russian people, dancers, soldiers, partisans
The scene is laid in Russia, 1809–12

War and Peace lies squarely in the great tradition of Russian epic opera, related as it is to the epic novel. The opera, like *Boris Godunov*, is a series of scenes rather than a continuous narrative, some personal, some public, though within the public ones the fates of the central characters are pursued and the impact on their lives of the great events taking place around them are observed. Prokofiev became enthused with the idea of an opera on Tolstoy's novel early in 1941, and its composition acquired a powerful extra significance when later that year the Germans invaded the Soviet Union and created situations analogous to those portrayed in the work. He devised the libretto himself, with his mistress the poet Mira Mendelson, and composed the music while evacuated from Moscow to the Caucasus and then Central Asia. Although the first version was completed in 1942, orchestrated in 1943 and officially approved for production later that year, there were repeated postponements, and Prokofiev supplied additional scenes in response both to official requests and advice from musician friends. There were concert performances in 1944 and 1945, and its first stage performance – of only the first eight scenes – in Leningrad in 1946. Prokofiev continued to revise it; but the postwar repression of experiment in Soviet music in 1948 precluded any further performances and it was not until 1955, after Prokofiev's death, that a fuller version, in eleven scenes, was given, again in Leningrad. A thirteen-scene version, though with internal cuts, was given in Moscow two years later. To a Westerner, the prolonged doubts surrounding the opera in the Soviet Union must seem puzzling, for it is a stirring epic about the heroism of the Russian people in defiance of a foreign invader; and much is made of the inspiration drawn by the people from the wise and resourceful figure of Kutuzov – clearly modelled on the official view of Stalin.

The synopsis below gives the opera in its complete form. The choral Epigraph has been differently placed in some performances, and that and Scenes 2 and 10 are later additions to the original plan. In some stage versions Scenes 7 and 11 have been omitted.

PART I: PEACE

Epigraph: The Russian people sing of the violation of their sacred land by invaders from many European countries and their determination to defeat and destroy their enemies.

Scene 1: It is a peaceful night in the spring of 1809 on the country estate of the Rostov family at Otradnoye. Prince Andrey Bolkonsky, mourning his late wife, is visiting the Rostovs on business; he reflects sombrely and despairingly on nature, spring and happiness. Then he hears the voice of Natasha, daughter of the household, in spirited conversation with her cousin Sonya; she talks of the beauty of nature. Andrey is much moved.

Scene 2: At the end of 1810, a New Year's Eve ball is in progress at the house in St Petersburg of a courtier of the former empress, Catherine the Great. Count Rostov and his family arrive. Natasha and Sonya eagerly survey the crowd, who are dancing a polonaise. Pierre and Hélène Bezukhov enter; he is an intellectual and a freemason (and thus an object of derision): she a famous, even notorious beauty. Natasha's aunt Akhrosimova warns against too close an acquaintance with Hélène, who is with her dissolute brother Anatol and his friend Dolokhov. The Tsar arrives with his mistress and is greeted by the choir. The dancing continues: a waltz is called, and Pierre introduces Andrey to Natasha. They talk and dance together, to their mutual pleasure, and Count Rostov afterwards invites Andrey to call on them. Meanwhile Anatol has noticed Natasha and expressed to his sister his interest in a flirtation with her.

Scene 3: It is February 1812. Andrey and Natasha are now betrothed but Andrey's father has required that he spend a year away in the army. Count Rostov has brought Natasha to the Bolkonsky mansion to meet the old Prince. But he is a peppery character and does not want to receive her – she is neither wealthy nor sufficiently well born. They are announced, but an old valet conveys his refusal. Instead they are greeted, with some embarrassment, by Andrey's sister Marya; the Count goes off, leaving Natasha with her. Then the old Prince enters, in dressing-gown and nightcap, greets Natasha with obviously feigned apologies and then talks slightingly of her to Marya. He goes, and the Count returns, to Natasha's relief; she resents her treatment by the Bolkonskys, and rejects with some poise the belated attempt at warmth from the old-maidish Marya as they leave.

Scene 4: Three months have passed. Natasha is a guest at a ball in the Bezukhov home. Hélène tells Natasha, to the background of dance music, that Anatol is sighing for her; she is embarrassed but flattered. Count Rostov, uneasy in the atmosphere of the household, comes to take Natasha and Sonya home, but Hélène contrives to delay them. Natasha finds herself momentarily alone with Anatol, who professes passionate love for her; she tries, as the fiancée of another man, to turn him away. But he succeeds in kissing her and handing her a letter, which, now observed by Sonya, she reads; clearly she is infatuated by Anatol although Sonya warns her that he is a deceiver. The Count returns and takes them away from the house – no place, with its free-and-easy ways, for his daughter.

Scene 5: It is 12 June 1812. Anatol is in the apartment of his friend Dolokhov, preparing for his elopement with Natasha. Dolokhov has supplied Anatol with money, a passport, a false priest (for the 'marriage') and a witness, but warns him of the risks he is taking (for Anatol is already married). Anatol dismisses his arguments, and when the coachman Balaga comes, determined to drive hard and make good speed on the journey, he departs – first bidding farewell to his gypsy mistress Matryosha and taking the sable coat he had given her.

Scene 6: Natasha is waiting anxiously at her aunt's house. Her maid Dunyasha hurries in to tell her that she has been betrayed by Sonya; the household is alerted to the planned elopement. Anatol and Dolokhov arrive – and are greeted by the valet, Gavrila. They grasp the situation and rush off just as Natasha, ready for the journey, comes in. She is sharply rebuked by her aunt, Akhrosimova, for her foolish behaviour; frustrated and despairing, she is only angry, and runs off, sobbing. Then Pierre Bezukhov arrives; Akhrosimova tells him what has happened.

She leaves him with Natasha, to whom he explains that Anatol is already married; Natasha asks him to beg Andrey (she had broken off her engagement) to forgive her. As he leaves Pierre says that, were he free, he would himself ask for her hand. Deeply ashamed, she goes off, then calls the unhappy Sonya to help her.

Scene 7: Later than evening Hélène, Anatol and two French guests (Dr Métivier and an *abbé*) are playing cards in Pierre's study. Pierre enters and speaks sternly to his wife, who leads off her guests; but he detains Anatol, questions and threatens him. He demands that Anatol hand over any letter from Natasha, leave Moscow at once, and never mention the affair to anyone. Anatol agrees and departs. Pierre's reflections on the aimlessness of his life are interrupted when Denisov arrives, with news from the frontier: Napoleon's troops are drawn up, and war is imminent.

PART II: WAR

Scene 8: It is 25 August 1812. By the Rayevsky Redoubt, near Borodino, Russian militia men are digging trenches, singing confidently of their determination to save Moscow. Andrey, now a senior officer, is present. Colonel Denisov arrives and asks where he can find Field-Marshal Kutuzov: he has a plan to put to the commander-in-chief for harrying the enemy's communication and supply lines. Andrey directs him, noting that Denisov had once been engaged to Natasha, in whom he had reposed such fair hopes. The men sing of their devotion and their eagerness to defend Russia. Pierre now appears: he wants to witness the forthcoming battle. Two German generals stroll by, theorizing about widening the battle area; Andrey expresses his contempt (after all, the Prussian army has been routed) and his confidence in the Russians' ability to defend their own soil. He bids Pierre farewell as the soldiers reaffirm their determination. Now Kutuzov enters, to lusty cheers, and watches as several regiments file past. He invites Andrey to join his staff, but Andrey, hoping to end his grief by dying for his country in battle, declines. A shot is heard: the battle of Borodino has begun.

Scene 9: In the Shevardino Redoubt, Napoleon and his staff are watching the progress of the battle. Messengers come from various of Napoleon's generals, mostly telling of the enemy's courage and asking for reserve forces; the battle is not going Napoleon's way and he is worried and indecisive – so much so that he sharply refuses when pressed by De Beausset to take luncheon.

Scene 10: Two days later, the Russian generals are gathered in a peasant's hut at Fili for a council of war: should they fight before Moscow, in an uncertain position, and risk their entire army? or should they withdraw, preserving their strength and stretching the enemy lines? The generals present various views, and Kutuzov decides: they will retreat and abandon Moscow; their only hope lies in this sacrifice. In the distance the confident singing of the soldiers is heard as Kutuzov, left alone, reflects on his decision and its implications.

Scene 11: It is autumn. The French now occupy Moscow, but they find the city practically deserted and are desperately trying to control the fires started by the people of the city. A group of Muscovites – joined by Pierre – express their anger at the looting by the French soldiery; among them is the Rostovs' housekeeper, Kusminichna, who mentions that Natasha and her family have left Moscow and are caring for the wounded, and that (unknown to Natasha) Andrey is among them. French soldiers enter; Pierre tries to stop them from maltreating the Muscovites and is arrested as a suspected incendiary. Davoust orders that some prisoners be shot, but most are reprieved, and Pierre has time to exchange some words with a resigned old soldier, Karatayev, before they are marched off. Three lunatics, escaped from an asylum, appear, singing religious chants; a French officer, Ramballe, takes them for priests and orders that, in accordance with Napoleon's edict that services be restarted, they be taken to the cathedral, but he is stopped by his colleauge, Bonnet. Then some French actresses appear, fleeing from the theatre. As fire increasingly takes hold of the city, Napoleon enters, baffled at the hollowness of his victory and the courage of the people. Again the voices of the people are heard, vowing vengeance on the invaders.

Scene 12: In a village outside Moscow, Prince Andrey, in a fever, is lying on a bed in a hut. He can hear the beating of his heart ('Piti, piti') as he lies there, dying and thinking of the past, longing to see Natasha again. When she enters, he at first thinks her a product of his delirium; but she comes to his side and asks his forgiveness. They express their mutual love; but he is weary, and is overtaken by pain, sleep and – as the insistent 'piti, piti' comes to a sudden stop – death.

Scene 13: The French troops are in retreat, in November 1812, along the road to Smolensk; a blizzard rages. Ramballe and Bonnet bewail their failure. Among the prisoners are Pierre and Karatayev; Karatayev weakens, falters and falls, and is shot as a straggler. But then a group of partisans, led by Dolokhov and Denisov, swoop on the French; shots ring out as the French column is harried. Kutuzov arrives and thanks God and the soldiers for saving Russia; the people hail him.

★ ★ ★

Peace and War: the two parts of the opera share some of their material but are separated in their basic idiom by their subject matter. 'Peace' is dominated by two elements: on the one hand the love music, on the other the spectacular dance music for the ball scenes, which reminds us not only that Prokofiev was a great ballet composer but also that he allowed himself to be influenced by Tchaikovsky's *Eugene Onegin* with its mixture of public revelry and private drama. The dance music itself often recalls Tchaikovsky's; and in fact Prokofiev drew on themes he had composed a few years before for a stage version of Pushkin's drama (his ideas portraying Natasha's and Andrey's love were originally written for Lensky and Tatyana respectively). The formal and the intimate come together most tellingly in the theme of the waltz danced by Andrey and Natasha in Scene 2, capturing the tenderness of their mutual feelings (ex. 1); it recurs poignantly, as a distant memory, in the scene of Andrey's death.

Ex. 1

In the 'War' music, Prokofiev calls on two familiar veins: for the French, a crisp, staccato 'wrong-note' style with a hint of scherzo-like parody, shot through with bitter and sardonic feeling. For the Russians he called on the tone of the 'official' heroic Soviet cantata, with its rousing call to patriotic duty. This appears in the Epigraph, in the music for the peasants and the soldiers, and perhaps reaches its acme in the hymn-like utterance of Kutuzov at the end of Scene 10, as he apostophizes Moscow (just as it is about to be relinquished and fired); music such as this (ex. 2) has been greeted by cynical Western commentators as banal, but in the theatre it arouses an undeniable fervour.

Ex. 2

Voice

KUTUZOV

Migh-ty Mos-cow, il-lu-mined by the sun, mo-ther of our Rus-sian

land, With what fer-vent love we sa-lute you to-day!

Must you know now a time of bit-ter pain, When the Rus-sian ar-my

leaves And with-out a fight shall a-ban-don your walls?

KURT WEILL

1900–50

In the years preceding Hitler's fateful seizure of power (1933), Berlin was a centre of radical adventure in music and the theatre. It was there, at the State Opera, that Berg's *Wozzeck* was launched – after 100 rehearsals! – in 1925. At a subsidiary theatre of the State Opera, the 1927 season introduced a 'ballet-opera' called *Royal Palace* by a composer still in his twenties. This was Kurt Weill. With *Die Dreigroschenoper* ('The Threepenny Opera'), produced at another Berlin theatre in 1928, he secured a firm place in the history of musical theatre in the twentieth century.

Here, as in *Aufstieg und Fall der Stadt Mahagonny* ('Rise and Fall of the City of Mahagonny', 1930), and in other works, Weill's collaborator was the celebrated Marxist playwright and poet, Bertolt Brecht (1898–1959). *The Threepenny Opera* gathered satirical force from an English work of precisely two centuries before, *The Beggar's Opera* (see page 42). *Mahagonny* also flirted with the English language, but this time it was transatlantic English – the imaginary scene being get-rich-quick, cutthroat-capitalist America. By a bitter irony of history, it was in America that Weill later found himself as a Jewish refugee from Hitler's Germany and from war-torn Europe. In the United States he collaborated with such writers as Maxwell Anderson, Moss Hart, Ira Gershwin and S. J. Perelman in stage works now almost forgotten.

DIE DREIGROSCHENOPER
The Threepenny Opera
Libretto by Bertolt Brecht

First performed: Berlin, 1928
Prologue and Three Acts

Cast in order of singing or speaking:

A BALLAD-SINGER	[*tenor*]★
JENNY DIVER, A WHORE	[*mezzo-soprano*]
JONATHAN JEREMIAH PEACHUM, ORGANIZER OF A GANG OF	
BEGGARS	[*bass*]
FILCH, A BEGGAR	*spoken role*
MRS PEACHUM	[*contralto*]
MATT OF THE MINT, ONE OF PEACHUM'S GANG	*spoken role*
MACHEATH, CHIEF OF A GANG OF HIGHWAYMEN	[*baritone*]
POLLY, DAUGHTER OF THE PEACHUMS	*soprano*

JAKE
BOB
NED } MEMBERS OF PEACHUM'S GANG   *spoken roles*
JIMMY
WALT

THE REVEREND KIMBALL	*spoken role*
BROWN, CHIEF CONSTABLE OF LONDON	[*bass*]

DOLLY
BETTY } WHORES   *spoken roles*
VIXEN

TWO WHORES	*spoken roles*
SMITH, A CONSTABLE	*spoken role*
LUCY, BROWN'S DAUGHTER	[*soprano*]

Beggars, whores, constables
The action takes place in Victorian London

★Note: No specification of voices is given in the score; the parts are intended for actors who can sing, rather than operatically trained singers, and so are of a middle and rather narrow range. We give in square brackets a probable voice-casting in operatic terms. The characters listed above are anglicized from the German vocal score published at the time of the original production. The listing in the definitive English edition of Brecht's plays (Eyre Methuen, 1979) is slightly different. In it, Brown is not the Chief Constable of London but the High Sheriff.

★   ★   ★

PROLOGUE: At a fair in Soho, beggars, thieves and whores pursue their trades as a ballad-singer tells the audience of Mac the Knife (in German, Mackie Messer), a murderer who contrives to conceal his crimes. Jenny Diver, a whore, points him put.

ACT I: Mr Peachum, organizer and outfitter of beggars, is seen in his shop. He sings his Morning Hymn, an exhortation to get on with the dirty work. For a fee he consents to take a newcomer, Filch, into his gang, but to his wife he shows himself more concerned with the alarming likelihood that their daughter Polly has fallen to the allurements of Macheath the highwayman – the notorious Mac the Knife.

In the next scene Polly and Mac are celebrating their marriage – in a stable, to which his gang has brought stolen furniture. The Reverend Kimball pays a social call. Polly sings for the company the song of 'Pirate Jenny' – a barmaid who, apparently meek and uncomplaining, has it in her power to have everyone destroyed – and does so.

'Tiger' Brown, chief constable of London, comes – unofficially, of course – to congratulate his old comrade Mac. They join in a reminiscence of their army days ('The Cannon Song').

Back in Peachum's shop, Polly sings 'The Barbara Song', explaining to her parents why she yielded to and married Macheath. Peachum, afraid that he will be professionally damaged by Polly's revealing secrets to her new husband, plans to have Mac arrested and hanged.

In a 'Threepenny Finale', Polly and her parents lament over this miserable, distrustful world.

ACT II: Polly enters Mac's hideout in Highgate to warn him that her father and the police have set up a trap for him. He decides to 'disappear' and insists that she stops weeping and listens to his instructions on how she should run the business while he is away. As they part they sing – but not together.

Mrs Peachum steps in front of the curtain with Jenny Diver, one of the whores from a house Mac frequents. As Mrs Peachum sings ('Ballad of Sexual Obsession'), a man will not give up his habits, so that is where the police will succeed in finding him.

In a brothel at Turnbridge, Macheath sings with Jenny of the happiness he used to enjoy with her. But she betrays his presence to Constable Smith and Mrs Peachum, waiting outside. He is arrested.

In the next scene, at the prison, Macheath ignores the tearful Brown (who hoped his friend would have escaped arrest) and writes a cheque to the warder to get himself released from handcuffs. He sings the 'Ballad of Good Living': this simple life in jail is not to his taste. Lucy, Brown's daughter, whom Macheath has previously jilted, enters and storms at him. He softens her with an assurance that he loves her and is not really married to Polly. But Polly now enters: the two women sing a 'Jealousy Duet'.

Mrs Peachum enters and drags Polly away. Mac, with the help of the impressionable Lucy, escapes from his cell. Brown sees what has happened and feels relief – until Peachum enters to remind him that the public will take vengeance on Brown instead. Brown realizes he must have Mac arrested again.

The curtain falls. In front of it, to sing the 'Second Threepenny Finale' come Macheath and Jenny. They proclaim the hard facts: 'Erst Kommt das Fressen, später die Moral' ('Eating comes first, morality afterwards').

ACT III: In Peachum's shop the beggars are being outfitted for a special event, the Coronation. The whores who enter to collect money from Peachum for betraying Macheath are refused, because he has escaped. But Jenny now gives him away again – he is at the house of another whore, Suky Tawdry. (Mrs Peachum moralizes by singing a further verse of the 'Ballad of Sexual Obsession', Act II.)

Brown enters to arrest Peachum and stop the beggars infesting the streets for the Coronation. Peachum defies him with the 'Song of Human Insufficiency' and deflects him into pursuing Macheath at Suky Tawdry's. As Brown leaves, Peachum adds a further verse to his song; then Jenny, in front of the curtain, sings the 'Solomon Song' – even mighty men like Solomon are brought low, and now it is Macheath's turn.

To spy out where Macheath may be, Polly comes to pay a call on Lucy, with exaggerated politeness. A noise outside indicates that Macheath has been arrested and is here. Polly is dragged off by her mother to put on widow's clothes, since Macheath is to be hanged.

Macheath would like to bribe Constable Smith into releasing him but can raise no money. In his empty cell he sings the 'Call from the vault'. Brown comes in for a sentimental farewell: Macheath's insistence on discussing accounts with him makes him feel worse than ever. Macheath sings an 'Epitaph': in bitter mockery he begs everyone to forgive his sins.

But, as the hanging is about to take place, Peachum turns to the audience: as this is an opera (he explains), there shall be a happy ending. The crowd hails a royal messenger arriving on horseback (it is Brown) who proclaims that Macheath is not only freed as a Coronation gesture but raised to the peerage. 'Gerettet!' ('Reprieved!') sings Macheath, followed by Polly, in a parody of the attitudinizing of heroic opera. The last word is given to all the participants urging *us* to think of the dark and cold that befall mankind 'in this vale of sorrows'.

★　★　★

The warning which closes the last number is called a hymn-tune (*Choral* in German) and serves to remind us, in parody, of the moralizing hymn-tune setting at the end of many Bach cantatas. (Musically it also forms a clever contrast with the jigging rhythms of the previous song.) In a different sense, the opening number of Act I in which Peachum calls on the 'Corruptible Christian' to stir himself is similarly called 'Peachum's morning hymn': far from summoning a Bach-like solemnity, however, it is the melody of 'Through all the employments of life' from the original *Beggar's Opera* (ex. 1). The

rest of the score, however, is Weill's original, its modernity (of its own period) being emphasized by its instrumental scoring. Instead of an operatic orchestra, a pianist-director leads a team of eight who command a range of instruments including two saxophones, banjo, guitar and bandoneon (a small accordion).

The ballad-singer's introductory presentation of Mac the Knife is done in a cunningly droning fashion (ex. 2: 'like a barrel organ', the stage direction says).

The tenderness of Macheath's and Jenny's duet in Act II is ironic, since she will twice betray him. They dance to the tango rhythm of the accompaniment as they recall 'the time that has now gone by' (ex. 3) when he obligingly made way for her clients, 'in that brothel where we made our home'.

Ex. 3

DMITRY SHOSTAKOVICH

1905–75

Unlike Prokofiev, Shostakovich lived all his creative life as a Soviet citizen. Two years after the Bolshevik revolution of 1917, he was admitted in his early teens to the Conservatory of Music in Petrograd (soon to be renamed Leningrad). His First Symphony, heard in 1926, was a young man's triumph; it was followed by fourteen more symphones which, in their differences of style and their differing reception, chronicled the composer's uneasy relationship with the Soviet cultural officialdom.

The constraints exerted by the Soviet regime on its creative artists were also responsible for the drastic changes in the fate of his celebrated opera. It was produced in Leningrad on 22 January 1934 as *Lady Macbeth of the Mtsensk District* and in Moscow, two days later, as *Katerina Izmailova*. Much praised at first, performed 180 times in the two Soviet cities and also produced in other countries, it was then suddenly denounced in the official newspaper, *Pravda*, as 'chaos in place of music' – that is, as an example of deliberately ugly modernism. Not until 1963, ten years after Stalin's death, was the opera welcomed back in a slightly revised version which then achieved a new international fame. It is this version which is described here.

Interest has also been revived in an earlier (1930) opera, *The Nose*, a satirical comedy after a story by Gogol (almost in the vein of Gogol's celebrated play, *The Government Inspector*). A streak of biting humour is common to both operas and belongs also to some of the fast, scherzo–like movements in Shostakovich's orchestral compositions.

KATERINA IZMAILOVA
Libretto by A. Preys and the composer, after a story by Nikolai Leskov

Original version first performed: Leningrad, 1934
Revised version first performed: Moscow, 1963
Four Acts

Cast in order of singing:

KATERINA LVOVNA IZMAILOVA	*soprano*
BORIS TIMOFEYEVICH IZMAILOV, A MERCHANT, HER FATHER-IN-LAW	*bass*
ZINOVY BORISOVICH IZMAILOV, HER HUSBAND	*tenor*
A MILL-WORKER	*baritone*
SERGEY, AN EMPLOYEE OF THE IZMAILOVS	*tenor*
COACHMAN	*tenor*
AKSINYA, AN EMPLOYEE OF THE IZMAILOVS	*soprano*
A RAGGED PEASANT	*tenor*
CARETAKER	*bass*
CLERK	*bass*
TWO MILL-WORKERS	*tenors*
PRIEST	*bass*
POLICE SERGEANT	*bass*
A NIHILIST	*tenor*
AN OLD CONVICT	*bass*
SONYETKA, A CONVICT	*contralto*
A FEMALE CONVICT	*soprano*
A SENTRY	*bass*
A SERGEANT	*bass*

Chorus of workpeople, wedding guests, policemen, convicts
The scene is laid in and around a Russian mill-house, and later in a prison-camp in Siberia, in the nineteenth century

A murderess as heroine? A strange idea, and it is the only one which gives some justification for calling the heroine 'a Lady Macbeth'. There are no other parallels to Shakespeare. Katerina poisons her father-in-law and helps her lover to strangle her husband. The comic, oafish tone of the surrounding action in some way softens the theatrical impact of the crimes, for which Katerina could claim slight pretext in the brutal way she was treated. She pays the penalty in Siberian exile and suicide. As in Janáček's opera *From the House of the Dead* (after Dostoevsky's novel) the general oppression of the Siberian prison-camp frames the plight of the individual.

★   ★   ★

ACT I: Married for five years but still childless, Katerina finds life boring. Her father-in-law, the mill-owner Boris Timofeyevich Izmailov, reproaches her. Zinovy Borisovich, her husband, arrives but is urgently called away to attend to a dam-burst: her father-in-law forces Katerina to take a humiliating farewell at Zinovy's feet. In the courtyard of the mill the workmen are ragging one of the womenfolk, Aksinya: Katerina comes out to reprimand the principal tormentor, Sergey, but lets herself be tempted into a wrestling match with him. Boris Timofeyevich enters suddenly, sizes up the situation and threatens to report it to her husband on his return. In her bedroom, Katerina is wakeful; her father-in-law, at the door, tells her to stop wasting the candlelight and go to sleep. A knock: Sergey enters. Without much effort he seduces Katerina. Her father-in-law again calls from outside but does not see within.

ACT II: Later that night, Boris Timofeyevich walks the courtyard with a lantern. Katerina is beautiful, he muses: if only he himself were ten years younger . . .! But her open window reveals what has been happening in her room. When Sergey climbs down from the window, Boris grabs him and raises the alarm. As some of the workers gather, Boris takes a whip and flogs Sergey, then has him locked up in the store-room. Katerina, apparently docile, offers Boris a dish of mushrooms: they are poisoned. A priest arrives in time to take his confession, in which he accuses Katerina: but the priest takes little account of it and Katerina responds to Boris's death with a fine display of distress.

Katerina and Sergey are once more in bed together. Katerina resolves that he will be her new husband. The ghost of the murdered Boris appears (vocally represented by the chorus basses) – or so Katerina imagines. The ghost disappears, but Zinovy arrives. His suspicions of his wife are aroused, though Katerina has hidden her lover. When her husband starts to beat her, Sergey emerges and the two of them kill Zinovy. They carry the corpse downstairs, return to the bedroom and continue their lovemaking.

ACT III: Some time later, Katerina's wedding to Sergey is taking place. A ragged peasant (who previously appeared at the baiting of Aksinya) celebrates drunkenly. In search of liquor he investigates a cellar – and runs out announcing in horror that the corpse of Katerina's first husband, which had never been discovered, is there.

The scene changes to a police station: the sergeant and his men bewail their miserable, unprofitable lot. A local nihilist has been arrested and is brought in. His babbling about the souls of frogs fails to amuse the constabulary, but when the ragged peasant rushes in with news that they are needed at the Izmailov wedding party, they need no second bidding to leave for some exciting action.

In the Izmailovs' garden the wedding celebrations are at their height, the priest leading the toasts. Katerina and Sergey realize that the cellar has been broken into and their murder of Zinovy Borisovich discovered. They cannot escape and are led away in handcuffs by the gratified, chortling police.

ACT IV: At a temporary prison-camp in Siberia, Sergey and Katerina are among the convicts marching to a further destination. All are in fetters; the men are separated from the women. An old convict, with others joining in, laments their hardships. Bribing a sentry, Katerina approaches Sergey, but he has tired of her. Leaving her to pour out her dejection, he in turn bribes his way to the younger, prettier Sonyetka. Sonyetka demands he prove his love by getting her some new stockings. He persuades Katerina, on the plea that his own legs are sore, to give him her stockings – which he then presents to her rival while a furious Katerina is mocked by the other women. Katerina pushes Sonyetka into the river and then throws herself in. The bodies are not recovered. The other convicts are ordered to march on, their mournful song dying away in the distance.

★　★　★

Crime and punishment, indeed. For the purposes of operatic sympathy, Katerina's fate is absorbed in the fate of thousands of prisoners, and the heavy-trudging song of the old convict ends the work. But before that Katerina sings (ex. 1) of a far-away lake which

Ex. 1

she imagines – 'black (*chorniya*) as my conscience'. This bleak line is
characteristic of the composer's most intense utterance: the accompaniment is a single low note on cellos and double-basses, with the
rolling of kettledrum and bass-drum. At the other extreme of
expression are cameos of sheer entertainment, particularly at the
beginning of Act III. Here the drunken peasant sings in celebration of
liquor, and then the bored policemen burst out in operetta-like
strains (in waltz-time!) to complain of how scant are the available
bribes while they are 'fishing in troubled waters' (ex. 2). This is in
fact a score of much more variety and richness than its rather sombre
and nasty tale might suggest.

Ex. 2

The coachman who, in the opening scene, announces that 'the horses are ready' (only two words in Russian: 'Loshadi gotovy') does so with a deliberately wrong stress on the second instead of the first syllable of the first word. This, says a Russian commentator on the opera, is to express the coachman's wilful, devil-may-care nature – making this, with its two words and nothing more, the shortest real operatic role in existence!

HANS WERNER HENZE

born 1926

The most important and prolific opera composer in post-war Germany has undoubtedly been Hans Werner Henze. He was a pupil of Wolfgang Fortner, then of Schoenberg's French disciple René Leibowitz at Darmstadt, and as a young man held a number of posts in theatres. His operatic interest extends to staging as well as music and he himself translated into German the original English of *Elegy for Young Lovers* (see below). Like many Germans with theatrical leanings, he went to Italy, and in 1953 he settled there.

By that time his first major opera, *Boulevard Solitude* (first given in Hanover, 1952), was behind him; but the South left its mark on the operas he composed there in the next dozen years – *König Hirsch* (1956, revised in Italian as *Il re cervo*), *Der Prinz von Homburg* (1960, on a militarist theme after a famous nineteenth-century German play by Kleist), *Elegy for Young Lovers* (1961, to an English text by W. H. Auden and Chester Kallman) and *Der junge Lord* (1965). In these Henze's tender, glittering orchestral palette of his Italian period finds admirable outlets (indeed he specifically asked Auden and Kallman to provide scope for such writing in *Elegy for Young Lovers*), but in several there is a clear political content too – opposition to Prussian militarism in *Der Prinz von Homburg*, black-comedy parody of the aristocracy and people's reaction to it in *Der junge Lord*, for example. *The Bassarids* (1966), he has said, was his last formal opera; since then his only original operatic work has been *We Come to the River* (1976), to a play by Edward Bond, an experimental piece embodying ritual and violence. *The Bassarids*, widely acclaimed when first given and several times revived, has been reckoned the most substantial and greatest of his major operas.

THE BASSARIDS
Libretto by W. H. Auden and Chester Kallman, after Euripides

First performed: Salzburg, 1966
One Act with Intermezzo

Cast in order of singing:

DIONYSUS, VOICE AND STRANGER	*tenor*
TIRESIAS, AN OLD BLIND PROPHET	*tenor*
CADMUS, FOUNDER AND FORMER KING OF THEBES	*bass*
AGAVE, HIS DAUGHTER, MOTHER OF PENTHEUS	*mezzo-soprano*
BEROE, AN OLD SLAVE, ONCE NURSE TO SEMELE AND PENTHEUS	*mezzo-soprano*
CAPTAIN OF THE ROYAL GUARD	*baritone*
PENTHEUS, KING OF THEBES	*baritone*
AUTONOE, DAUGHTER OF CADMUS	*soprano*
A FEMALE SLAVE IN AGAVE'S HOUSEHOLD	*silent*
HER DAUGHTER	*silent*

Chorus of Bassarids (Maenads and Bacchants),
citizens of Thebes, guards, servants
The scene is laid in mythological times, in Thebes and on Mount Cithaeron

The title of the opera needs explanation: *bassarids* are followers of Dionysus, the Greek deity whose cult involves intoxication and violence. Bacchus is his more familiar Latin equivalent: perhaps *bassarids* was preferred to the more familiar *bacchantes* because the latter is usually taken to represent only females. The opera was composed to a text written in English by W. H. Auden and Chester Kallman, and first performed (at Salzburg Festival) in a German translation. In it Henze showed, it has been said, that he 'made his peace with Wagner', and though the composer by no means uses Wagnerian methods in this work he did cast it as continuous music drama, departing from his previous preference for 'number opera'. It is also possible to regard it as partaking of the Wagnerian tradition in its theme: for this is an opera about Man, about what happens to a person if he denies the sensual, Dionysian side of his nature and represses its demands. The opera is continuous, about the length of *Das Rheingold* but cast in four 'movements'.

⋆　⋆　⋆

First movement: The citizens of Thebes are formally gathered in the courtyard of the royal palace to pay tribute to Pentheus, their new king, who has just succeeded his grandfather Cadmus. As their hymn breaks off, a haunting voice is heard in the distance: it says that the god Dionysus has entered Boeotia. The people succumb at once to the enchantment the voice seems to offer; they take up the cry of 'Ayayalya', and go off to celebrate Dionysian rites.

Cadmus, Agave and Tiresias appear, with Beroe. Tiresias resolves to join the Dionysians. Cadmus is alarmed, for doubt and controversy surrounds this young 'god': is he truly a god, or an impersonator? – Dionysus is said to be the son of Semele (Cadmus's dead eldest daughter) by Zeus, but his divinity is doubted by those who hold that Semele's lover was a mortal. Moreover, Pentheus, the king, passionately denies Dionysus. Tiresias, who enjoys the gift of seeing the future, warns Cadmus of the danger of denying Dionysus; he goes off. In the background the Bassarids (the worshippers of Dionysus) are assembling; their songs of praise to him are heard. The Captain enters, followed by Autonoe. He has to read out a royal proclamation: in it Pentheus bans the cult of Semele. Now Pentheus, severe and ascetic looking, enters, ridicules the Semele cult and extinguishes the flame on her tomb, to Cadmus's dismay but Agave's delight. But he is infuriated to learn that the Theban populace had danced off to Cithaeron, and returns to his palace. Again the seductive voice is heard from afar, and this time Agave and Autonoe are overcome by it and dance away to Cithaeron.

Second movement: Pentheus returns to the courtyard; he and Cadmus discuss the divinity of Dionysus. He sings of killing and of the harder rule he intends to impose as the singing of the Bassarids is heard in the background. At the end he declaims his determination to abstain from wine, meat and sexual love. His guards return with prisoners – Agave, Autonoe, Tiresias, a Stranger (Dionysus), some bacchants and slaves. Some of them, clearly in a state of trance, are humming soft, sensuous music. Pentheus determines to find out where the so-called Dionysus is and questions his mother about events on Cithaeron, to which Agave replies in a visionary description: 'On a forest footpath'. Beroe points out the Stranger to Pentheus and identifies him as Dionysus. The Captain returns, but even torture has provided no information about the god. Pentheus dismisses his mother and Autonoe into the palace to be held captive and orders that Tiresias's house be razed. Then he cautiously starts questioning the Stranger, whom he taken to be a Dionysian priest; the Stranger tells a story about an event on a ship, where he was captured by pirates, but vines grew up the mast at Dionysus's bidding and wild animals appeared on board. The terrified pirates leapt into the sea and became dolphins.

Third movement: While the Bassarids' ecstatic song persists in the background, Pentheus orders the Stranger to be taken away and scourged. Then there is an earthquake and the prisoners (Agave, Autonoe, Tiresias and a bacchant) escape to Cithaeron; Pentheus orders his guards to Cithaeron to kill the people under Dionysus's spell, though the Stranger warns him that this is fruitless. Gradually Pentheus weakens and comes under the Stranger's spell and when the Stranger invites him to see, through his mother's mirror, an enactment of the Dionysian rites, he agrees.

The scene changes to a painted, Boucher-like garden, with statues and shrubbery in which are seen nymphs and satyrs. Agave and Autonoe appear, dressed as Rococo shepherdesses; they are talking amorously about the Captain, and when he enters wearing vine-leaves they compete for his caresses. Now Tiresias appears and suggests that they enact a charade. 'The Judgment of Calliope' – Agave will play Venus, Autonoe Proserpine and the Captain Adonis, while Tiresias himself will take Calliope. They do so: the tale of the birth of Adonis, the love of Venus and Proserpine for him, and his death at Mars's hand is told, in a decadently *risqué* manner.

The garden disappears and the characters resume their own identities. Pentheus expresses his disgust and loathing at the spectacle. He resolves to go to Cithaeron to observe the rites for himself; on the Stranger's urging, he consents to go in women's clothes (an ill-fitting dress of his mother's), to avoid recognition. Before they go Beroe begs Dionysus – for that, of course, is the Stranger's identity – to spare Pentheus, but he refuses. Dionysus leads off the half-bewitched Pentheus to Cithaeron by the blood-red light of the setting sun as the Bassarids' songs to Dionysus are heard. Beroe, left alone, bewails the impending fate of her king; and Cadmus enters to mourn the inevitable fall of the city he founded.

Night is falling as the revels continue on Mount Cithaeron. Pentheus is crouching on a branch of a tree, watching them. The revellers call on Dionysus; but he warns them that a stranger is spying on their rituals and they must rout him out. Frenetically, they seek him; then a light from Agave's mirror falls on him and he is surrounded. He utters a plea, finally to his mother to recognize him, but the Bassarids tear him apart and Agave decapitates him.

Fourth movement: The Bassarids are singing in triumph, particularly of Agave's prowess. Agave proclaims that she is holding the head of her prey, a young lion; she asks to see the king. Cadmus reminds her of who she is and compels her to look at what she is holding: she is appalled and incredulous to find that it is her own son's head. The Captain tells Cadmus that Pentheus's body, torn apart, has been found. Beroe and Agave express their grief; the others dissociate themselves from what has happened. Agave mourns her son. Now Dionysus appears, smartly dressed; he orders the palace to be fired, then calls on Persephone, the underworld goddess, and Zeus to release his mother Semele, and names her a goddess, Thyone. Two huge fertility idols spring up, and the people worship them.

★   ★   ★

The theme of the opera – the contrast between the Apollonian and the Dionysian, the intellectual and the sensual, the repressive and the free, the austere and the luxuriant – offers Henze just the kinds of musical opportunity he relished. The music for Pentheus is harsh, dissonant, severe, cast in dark colours, vocal and orchestral. That for Dionysus is soft, beguiling, full of the glittering timbres (flutes, harps, high violins) that characterize the works of his Italian period. While Pentheus speaks in jagged lines and abrupt rhythms, Dionysus's utterings are smooth and flowing, his vocal line favouring the consonant intervals (thirds and sixths) – as, for example, in his ecstatic opening song (ex. 1). The score is coloured too by the omnipresence of the chorus, the people of Thebes, changed into Bassarids (bacchants and maenads), whose song echoing from

Ex. 1 DIONYSUS

Mount Cithaeron serves as a constant reminder of the power of Dionysus's divinity and also its threat.

Lest, however, the grim theme and weighty matter of this opera should become oppressive to listen to, its authors – Auden and Kallman as well as Henze – devised an ingenious way of introducing contrast: the inclusion of the pseudo-Rococo intermezzo in which Pentheus's fantasies are exposed to him. Here the textures are light and brittle (coloured by the use of a pair of mandolins and a guitar) and the rhythms metric and crisply enunciated, as ex. 2, from Venus's song about Vulcan's and Mars's revenge on Adonis, shows. Although the device is an artificial one, it carries strong symbolic meaning and thus does nothing to lessen the impact of this exceptionally powerful opera.

GEORGE GERSHWIN

1898–1937

There might seem little to connect George Gershwin with the other American composer considered below, Gian-Carlo Menotti; but that little is perhaps the most significant thing about them, namely the fact that their theatrical work was delivered to the public through channels other than that of the established opera-house.

Opera in the United States has mainly meant the import of European successes, often with European stars. The process was well in train by the 1860s, and in 1873 Verdi's *Aida* reached New York before it reached London. Indigenous American opera had been rare, though it began as early as 1845 in Philadelphia with a *Leonora* (on the same plot as Beethoven's *Fidelio*) composed by William Henry Fry (1815–64). Neither in opera nor in the concert-hall did any American composer establish a world reputation, or, indeed, even a national reputation, before 1914. Then, when the vigour of the newer American composers insisted on a hearing, opera was not their preferred form. Even that startling surrealist stage-piece, *Four Saints in Three Acts* (1934), composed by Virgil Thomson to a text by Gertrude Stein, was a kind of mockery of opera and was independently presented. Though the Metropolitan Opera in New York and major companies in other cities have felt duty-bound to give American composers an occasional hearing, almost the only major composer to favour such a channel and to find a measure of success in it has been Samuel Barber (1910–81) with *Vanessa* (1958) and *Antony and Cleopatra* (1966).

Gershwin turned to opera after enjoying a twenty-year reputation in the world of the 'musical'. Jazz rhythms in the written music and jazz intonations in the manner of performance (both vocal and instrumental) were a feature of the universally conquering American popular music, and Gershwin brought them into his opera *Porgy and Bess* – not as a decoration, but as a fulfilment of his choice of subject, the story being set among the poor Black maritime community in

Charleston, South Carolina. The composer's score specifies a piano on stage, to be played 'in a jazz manner'. A black cast presented the opera in the production by the Theatre Guild in New York in 1935, and the opera was given on successive nights (like a play or musical), not as one of several works in a repertory season at an opera-house. It is a work which has been welcomed in many revivals and more than one complete recording, while a jazz-influenced American opera produced at the Metropolitan (Louis Gruenberg's *Emperor Jones*, 1933, on the play by Eugene O'Neill) appears to have passed harmlessly into history.

Gershwin also wrote, on an episode of Black life, a one-act opera called *Blue Monday*, produced as part of a revue in 1922 but withdrawn after one performance. It was later revised but still found no success.

PORGY AND BESS
Libretto by Du Bose Heyward, with lyrics by
Du Bose Heyward and Ira Gershwin

First performed: New York, 1935
Three Acts

Cast in order of singing:

CLARA, JAKE'S WIFE	*soprano*
MINGO	*tenor*
SPORTIN' LIFE, A DOPE PEDDLER	*tenor*
JAKE, A FISHERMAN	*baritone*
SERENA, ROBBINS'S WIFE	*soprano*
ROBBINS	*tenor*
PETER, THE HONEY MAN	*tenor*
LILY, PETER'S WIFE	*mezzo-soprano*
MARIA, KEEPER OF THE COOKSHOP	*contralto*
PORGY, A CRIPPLED BEGGAR	*bass-baritone*
CROWN, A STEVEDORE	*baritone*
BESS	*soprano*

Tradesmen, fishermen, policemen, undertaker, etc.;
chorus of residents of Catfish Row (including children)
The scene is laid in Charleston, South Carolina, in the 1930s

In 1926 Gershwin read the novel *Porgy* by Edwin du Bose Heyward
which was first to become a play and then, eight years later, to be
made into the libretto of his opera. In the Black community of a
tenement called Catfish Row, in Charleston, South Carolina, Porgy
is a familiar and constantly identifiable figure – a beggar and a cripple
who gets about in a goat-cart. Operatically he is a bass-baritone – a
voice inevitably associated in that time and in that context with the
Black singer, Paul Robeson, though it was not he but Todd Duncan
who took the role. The libretto uses Black (or, as it was then termed,
Negro) dialect. The language is colloquial, but there is fervent
prayer too, forming part of the large choral element in the score. The
executors of the Gershwin estate have insisted that performances in
English should retain a casting of black singers, though foreign-
language performances are permitted without that restriction. The
opera has been normally cut in performance, particularly because of
the strain in Porgy's role if sung (as it was) by the same singer on
successive nights. The story as narrated below covers the uncut text
of the published vocal score.

★   ★   ★

ACT I: It is Saturday night. The fisher-folk and others are relaxing
outside their dwellings. Jake's wife, Clara, sings a lullaby to her baby
('Summertime, an' the livin' is easy'). Men play a crap game, calling
out their wishes to the dice – against which the 'Summertime' lullaby
is heard again. The baby is still wakeful, so Jake takes it and sings a
song of his comic warning, with the refrain 'A woman is a sometime
thing'. Peter, a honey-seller, comes crying his wares, then Porgy in
his goat-cart ('Evenin', ladies, hello, boys!'). He has some money in
hand and enters the crap game. He mentions Bess, Crown's woman,
but says he himself 'ain't sof' on no woman', adding in a phrase
which contains his principal musical motive:

> When Gawd made cripple, he mean him to be lonely,
> Night-time, day-time, he got to trabble dat lonesome road.

Crown comes in, a tough stevedore, accompanied by Bess. Already
drunk, he buys a small packet of dope from Sportin' Life, the
drug-seller. The drug inflames his temper: quarrelling over the crap
game, while the crowd grows alarmed, he fights with Robbins
(*orchestral passage*). Crown hits Robbins with his cotton-hook and
kills him. When Crown leaves in haste, Sportin' Life offers to take
Bess to start a life of criminal adventure in New York, but she

replies: 'I ain't come to that – yet'. Where else is she to turn? Doors slam in her face. Only one person will give her shelter: Porgy.

The scene changes to Serena's room. The body of her murdered husband lies on the table. The chorus mourns him – the mourning ceremony being also the occasion at which money must be raised for the burial. Bess enters with Porgy. Serena at first refuses Bess's offering, but she explains that it is not Crown's money: it is Porgy who provides her money now. The chorus takes on a quicker, more agitated strain: 'Fill up de saucer till it overflow'. It ceases suddenly: a detective and a policeman (white men) enter. They arrest Peter on the ground that he will be a useful witness against Crown when Crown is caught. Serena bursts out in lament ('My man's gone now'). The undertaker agrees to bury Robbins for the meagre sum that has been collected. Bess suddenly jumps up and leads everyone in singing hopefully about the train 'leavin' for the Promise' Lan'.'

ACT II: A month has passed. The fishermen are preparing to take their boats out. Porgy, now a happy man living with Bess, leans out from the window and sings 'I got plenty o' nuttin'.' Sportin' Life attempts to peddle his 'happy dust', but Maria threatens him with a knife. A so-called lawyer enters who charges a dollar and a half for a 'divorce' (even though Bess was not actually married to Crown) which changes her from 'woman to lady'. Archdale, a friendly white man, enters to say he will provide bail-money, so Peter will return home shortly. A buzzard flies overhead – a bad omen, as Porgy dramatically tells (the 'Buzzard Song'). Sportin' Life sidles up to Bess again offering 'happy dust' and promises of big money in New York, but Porgy frightens him off. After a reminder from Jake that there is to be a picnic that day, Bess and Porgy express their newfound happiness in duet: 'Bess, you is my woman now'. A band marches on: everyone is making ready for the picnic. Porgy, crippled and unable to take part, smilingly urges Bess to go, and again sings happily of his 'plenty o' nuttin' '.

The scene changes to Kittiwah Island, the place of the picnic. Sportin' Life sings his sly, cynical song, 'It ain't necessarily so'. When it is time for the boat to return, Bess who is the last to go, is suddenly confronted by a figure emerging from the thicket. It is the fugitive Crown. She tries to resist his brutal ardour ('What you want wid Bess?') but he hurls her, hardly protesting, into the thicket.

The scene changes once more to Catfish Row, before dawn, a

few days later, Jake, despite the warning of a hurricane, prepares to put to sea in his boat. Bess, who stayed away two days, is a sick woman. Peter advises Porgy to send her to hospital. Porgy is alarmed at losing her and Serena prays over her ('Oh, doctor Jesus') to make her well. The street-cries of the Strawberry Woman, the Honey Man (Peter again) and the Crab Man are heard. Bess, recovering, feels unworthy of Porgy and fears that Crown will come and force her to leave with him. Porgy reassures her: 'You goin' stay'. A hurricane breaks [orchestral passage].

The scene changes back to Serena's room. All are huddled in terror of the storm and join in prayer. At the height of the storm Crown bursts through the door: he mocks their terror and prayer with a jazz song ('A red-headed woman'). After uttering more threats, he leaves. The praying – now a multiple babble over an insistent beat – is resumed and continues even after the curtain falls.

ACT III: Next night, the storm is no longer raging. But Jake was drowned in his boat and his wife Clara, who went out after him, is missing too. The others mourn for them: ' . . . Jesus is walkin' on de water,/Rise up an' follow him home'). Sportin' Life forecasts trouble for Bess, who now appears: she is looking after Clara's baby and sings (as Clara did) the 'Summertime' lullaby. The courtyard empties; Crown suddenly appears, determined to take Bess from Porgy. He passes under Porgy's window, an arm emerges, and a knife is plunged into his back (*orchestral passage*). Crown falls but staggers to his feet; Porgy gets a grip on his throat and kills him. Porgy laughs: 'Bess, you got a man now!'

Next afternoon, the Coroner arrives with policemen. They interrogate Serena but she claims to know nothing about Crown's death. They carry off Porgy to identify the body; he is terrified. Sportin' Life seizes his chance, pressing some of his dope on Bess, persuading her that Porgy may never return. He sings his song about the life of luxury to which he is beckoning her: 'There's a boat dat's leavin' soon for New York . . .'. Bess at first repels him and goes to her room. But she takes more dope and Sportin' Life knows she will follow him.

One week later, on a sunny day when people are walking happily through the streets and children are dancing, Porgy returns. He managed to win money by playing crap in jail. Now, released, he has brought gifts for his friends and for Bess. As he sings with plaintive urgency, 'Bess, oh where's my Bess?', they can hardly bear to tell him she has left. The song becomes a trio with Maria and Serena attempting to comfort him. When he hears where she is, he calls for his goat-cart; he will set off for New York and find her. No one can dissuade him. 'Oh Lawd, I'm on my way', he sings. His friends join in, caught up in his fervour, as the opera ends.

★ ★ ★

A banjo (prominent in 'I got plenty o' nuttin''') and two African drums are the only unusual instrumental touches in Gershwin's orchestral score. But the music itself – orchestral, choral, and the solo vocal roles – is full of the syncopations and 'blue notes' typical of jazz. In the most famous number in the score, 'Summertime', the orchestral accompaniment puts the flattened seventh of the scale, E natural (a 'blue note' in this context) against the 'regular' E sharp of the key (ex. 1). A similar effect is heard as Porgy first enters – the

Ex. 1

'blue' D natural against the 'regular' D sharp. Here the orchestra has the main tune but Porgy's own line coincides with it on the 'blue note' itself (ex. 2).

Ex. 2

That orchestral tag is similar in rhythm to the central words of
Porgy's 'creed' (as we may call it), heard a little later: when a man is a
cripple, 'Night-time, day-time, *he got to trabble* dat lonesome road'.
Moreover the tag itself often recurs to denote Porgy in his various
moods – for instance, just before the carefree song, 'I got plenty o'
nuttin'', and again as the opera ends.

When Porgy and Bess share their happiness, the 'creed' is recalled
in the orchestra, but is 'dismissed', as it were, by the love-duet that
follows. This duet, 'Bess, you is my woman now', is a high point of
an opera full of songs which have deservedly become famous on
their own. The choral writing is equally remarkable, often in the
characteristic vein of Black spirituals, with the displaced accent (here
on the word 'home') written into the music itself (ex. 3).

Ex. 3

GIAN-CARLO MENOTTI

born 1911

By birth Menotti is an Italian, and he must be ranked as the most successful Italian composer since Puccini. But he completed his education in Philadelphia and settled in the United States. After his first opera, *Amelia al ballo* ('Amelia goes to the ball'), all his operas have been in English. Uniquely among successful composers, he has been regularly his own librettist and his own producer (stage director), usually working with his own choice of singers outside the constraints of an opera-house. He became the central figure of a music festival at Spoleto, Italy, but unlike Britten's festival at Aldeburgh it did not revolve round the performance of his works. Like Britten, he has shown a special aptitude in the use of child characters and child performers in his works. His most widely diffused opera, written for television and proving capable of modestly scaled, inexpensively financed performances, was *Amahl and The Night Visitors* (1951), which has a crippled boy as its hero.

His gift for finding ingenious, taut plots and for an effective relationship between words and music was shown in two sharply contrasted one-act pieces of 1946 and 1947 respectively. *The Medium* is an opera of suspense and horror, *The Telephone* a witty comedy of two lovers. The operas since 1960 (they include *Help! help! the Globolinks!*, in which one female singer also plays the violin) have been less successful than Menotti's earlier ones. Of these *The Consul* has been produced all over the world; evidently its political implications were not always understood in the same way.

THE CONSUL
Libretto by the composer

First performed: Philadelphia, 1950
Three Acts

Cast in order of singing:

JOHN SOREL	*baritone*
MAGDA SOREL	*soprano*
THE MOTHER	*contralto*
SECRET POLICE AGENT	*bass*
THE SECRETARY	*mezzo-soprano*
MR KOFNER	*bass-baritone*
THE FOREIGN WOMAN	*soprano*
ANNA GOMEZ	*soprano*
VERA BORONEL	*mezzo-soprano*
THE MAGICIAN (Nika Magadoff)	*tenor*
ASSAN	*baritone*

[*The scene is laid in an unspecified country
in modern times*]

An empty stage – a political fugitive dashes in. To an earlier generation of opera-goers this could mean only Puccini's *Tosca*. But this is how Menotti also chooses to start his opera. The Consul is a character who never appears, though the power of saving human lives is apparently his. Why does he not appear? Has anyone *ever* seen him? That last agonized question is directly asked in this work, which brings on to the opera stage the mid-twentieth-century tensions of political tyranny, a secret resistance movement, would-be refugees and maddeningly slow bureaucracy.

In the mouths of the characters, colloquial language is used to convey what promises to be a wholly realistic drama until the final scene but is sharpened by two episodes lying on the plane of dream or crazed imagination. The everyday expressions and short sentences do not inhibit the building-up of long, thoroughly 'operatic' scenas for Magda, the heroine, and for the other main character, the Secretary in the Consul's office. In contrasting style is the passage of unaccompanied recitative between Magda and the glass-cutter who holds a position in the political resistance network. In the baby-talk of the grandmother, as in the banality of the song on the gramophone, the composer demonstrates a skill in dramatic irony: these, far from slackening the screws, turn them tighter.

★   ★   ★

ACT I: There is no overture. Through the window of a dark, empty room comes the sound of a record, with a voice singing 'Tu reviendras . . .' ('You will come back'). John Sorel, bloodstained, rushes in. His wife Magda and his mother move to his aid. The secret police are in pursuit. Wife and mother move him to a hiding-place in the roof as a police agent bursts in with two plainclothes subordinates. The agent questions Magda and remarks on her sickly-looking baby, but his men find nothing. When they have gone, John emerges. He must flee the country immediately and Magda must go to the Consulate and apply for a visa to leave with her mother and the baby. John instructs that when a stone from outside breaks a window-pane, Magda is to telephone Assan the glass-cutter, who will bring her news. Husband, wife and mother sing in trio: 'Now, oh lips, say goodbye'.

In the Consulate, later that day, a busy Secretary interviews in turn those waiting for visas. Elderly Mr Kofner with his slightly professorial air has applied many times before but has still not got his documents right and must come back 'tomorrow, and the day after tomorrow, and the day after every day . . .' (the music mirrors the repetitive process). Magda has already entered and Anna Gomez, a young woman with a nervous affliction, now joins those waiting. A Foreign Woman is next to be interviewed: she speaks only Italian, but Mr Kofner translates for her. She needs urgently to go to see her sick daughter and her daughter's newborn baby and is stunned to learn that the process of documentation may need months instead of days. Magda asks to speak to the Consul in person but is told that 'no one is allowed to speak to the Consul – the Consul is busy'. Instead she must follow the routine of form-filling as the Secretary instructs her: 'Your name is a number, your story's a case, your need a request'. Another hopeful, a theatrical magician called Nika Magadoff, passes time by practising a trick on a fellow-applicant, Vera Boronel. His professional patter, 'Now you see it – now you don't', threads its way into the ensemble in which all those waiting express their hope of release.

ACT II: A month later, the same record is heard through the window of the Sorels' room. The baby boy is too ill to respond to his grandmother, who attempts to play with him, then sings a lullaby. Magda, falling asleep with exhaustion, sees a vision of John entering the room in company with the Secretary, whom he calls 'my dear little sister'. When she wakes, a stone shatters the window. Acting on the signal, she telephones for Assan. But another visitor comes first: the police agent, who offers her freedom if she will name her husband's friends. She turns on him savagely. Assan enters and, when the police agent has left, discloses that John has not yet crossed the frontier and will not consent to do so unless he is reassured that Magda can follow. The Mother notices that Magda's baby, so still, is dead.

Back at the Consulate, it is Anna Gomez's turn to find frustration. Magda rushes in and attempts to jump the queue but the Magician insists on his place. He plies the astonished Secretary with flowers, a dove, one trick after another, a recital of his famous patrons' names. He even hypnotizes the others and makes them dance – but, unable to produce the requisite papers, he is turned away like everyone else. Magda, now that it is her turn, meets similar frustration. But she explodes with anger and an impassioned lament for man's inhumanity: 'To this we've come . . . Papers! papers!' As she finishes it seems that even the Secretary has been moved by Magda's reproaches. Maybe the Consul *will* see her when his present visitor has left. The visitor now emerges from the Consul's office: it is the secret police agent. Magda, overcome, faints.

ACT III: Several days later Magda again waits at the Consulate – uselessly. Her mother is now also dead. Vera Boronel enters and, amazingly, receives her permission to leave, singing happily with the Secretary as they complete the formalities. Assan enters and, despite the danger that they might be overheard, tells Magda that John is firmly resolved to get back to her – but if he does, 'it will be the end of us all'. Magda, possessed by the one idea that might stop him, departs in such a hurry that she leaves a pocket-book behind. The Secretary stores it away (after all, Magda may be relied on to come back next day) and, for the only time, gives vent to the stress of her job: 'Oh, those faces! . . . One must not think'. Suddenly John enters, on the run. Too late: the secret police are on his tail, and he consents to go with them, 'of my own free will', as he bitterly says. As the Secretary tries to telephone Magda (her first act of com-passion), the curtain falls.

When it rises again we watch Magda, in her room, shut off all ventilation and turn on the gas. Her fellow-applicants, her husband, her mother and the Secretary appear in a ghost chorus: 'Death's frontiers are open, all aboard!' The Magician again makes the others dance, then appears to be hypnotizing her. As the telephone rings, she is jerked back to reality. But her body falls slack, and in the room the telephone continues to ring, unanswered.

★   ★   ★

A musical stroke typical of operatic tradition – particularly favoured by Puccini – ends *The Consul*. A prominent theme from one of the opera's most emotional moments, in this case from Magda's soliloquy, returns in a poignant reminder. The soliloquy enshrines the heroine's 'creed', presented as the hope of every victim of a faceless political machine. Likewise in operatic fashion, the high note (B flat) associates the climax of the aria with the height of the singer's exertion as Magda foresees a day of deliverance (ex. 1). Menotti's

Ex. 1

skill contrasts such moments with others in which colloquial speech – its rapid delivery, its stresses, even its individual eccentricities – takes musical form. The Magician gives an empty, repetitive parade of the names of those celebrities for whom he has performed (ex. 2).

Ex. 2

The innocent–seeming duet (two voices moving conventionally in parallel) of the Consul's Secretary and the one successful applicant lends a cruel irony to the rest. 'Love may die and truth grow cold', they sing, 'but . . .' (ex. 3).

Ex. 3

One   must have one's   pa - pers,   pa - pers,   pa - pers.

MICHAEL TIPPETT

born 1905

Michael Tippett has a claim to be reckoned the most original and most visionary among British composers of this century. His idiom has continued to develop all his life, right into his seventies; and all he has composed has been actuated by his own passionately held views about man and society. He has used opera for the expression of those views, first of all in the best established of his operas, *The Midsummer Marriage* (1955), discussed in the following pages; then in the powerful *King Priam* (1962), concerned with the nature of human choice and the impossibility of trying to create a paradise; next in *The Knot Garden* (1970), which deals with the relationships between seven people and the self-knowledge they acquire through them; and fourth in *The Ice Break* (1977), in which a variety of archetypes are forced into confrontations in a brutal world and made to seek rebirth. These ideas are worked out through a variety of metaphors and symbols; and though Tippett has often been taken to task for the clumsiness and obscurity of his librettos – he writes his own – and the untheatrical complexity of certain of his scores, their power and their boldness in the exploration of the human psyche and the human situation are beyond question.

THE MIDSUMMER MARRIAGE
Libretto by the composer

First performed: London, 1955
Three Acts

Cast in order of singing:

MARK, A YOUNG MAN OF UNKNOWN PARENTAGE	*tenor*
TWO ANCIENTS, PRIEST AND PRIESTESS OF THE TEMPLE	*bass,*
	mezzo-soprano
JENIFER, MARK'S BETROTHED	*soprano*
KING FISHER, HER FATHER, A BUSINESSMAN	*baritone*
BELLA, HIS SECRETARY	*soprano*
JACK, HER BOY-FRIEND, A MECHANIC	*tenor*
SOSOSTRIS, A CLAIRVOYANTE	*contralto*
HALF-TIPSY MAN	*bass*
A MAN DANCING	*tenor*

[The role of Strephon, a dancer, is silent.]

Chorus of Mark's and Jenifer's friends,
dancers attendant on the Ancients
The scene is laid in modern times

The Midsummer Marriage is an opera of the 'quest' type, in which the central characters are seeking something – in this case a deeper self-understanding so that they can move towards a fuller and more profound union. It has often been paralleled, not least by the composer himself, with Mozart's *Die Zauberflöte*, though here the couple, Mark and Jenifer, move to their ultimate relationship through elopement, quarrels and the dispelling of illusion about themselves; like *Die Zauberflöte*, *The Midsummer Marriage* uses myth and ritual, as well as mysterious inner experience, towards the clarification of the characters and underpinning their union.

★   ★   ★

ACT I: The action takes place on Midsummer's Day, in a clearing in a wood, on a hill; there are trees and buildings, including one like a Greek temple, a cave, and staircases, one upwards, some leading down into the hillside. The friends of Mark and Jenifer are there as it grows light, then greeting the sun as it rises. Dancers appear, led by Strephon; the Ancients follow them. Mark enters and asks for a new dance on his wedding day, but the Ancients order the same one again and the He–Ancient trips and hurts Strephon. The Ancients retire, and Mark tells his friends about the Ancients and their dance before he expresses his joy at his forthcoming wedding.

Now Jenifer appears, dressed not for a wedding but for travel.

There will be no wedding today, she tells the uncomprehending Mark; she seeks not love but truth. The lovers quarrel, and Jenifer walks off to the ascending steps, climbs up them and vanishes. The voice of her father, King Fisher, is heard; Mark's friends urge him to go away, and he enters the cavern, whose gates close behind him. King Fisher enters, but has missed Mark; he tells his secretary, Bella, to inquire where he is, but the Ancients will not help her or admit anyone. King Fisher resolves to force the gates and sends Bella to fetch her boyfriend Jack, a mechanic. King Fisher addresses Mark's male friends, telling them that Mark is a rascal and that they should go off to work; he drives them off. Then he turns to the girls, assuring them that he is a good father to Jenifer and offering them money to find her; they refuse, and he drives them off too.

Jack arrives with tools to open the gates, and agrees to do as he is told; first, however, he and Bella sing of their courting. As he makes to open the gates a voice, that of Sosostris, calls out a warning to King Fisher. It is echoed by the girls, denied by the men, from offstage. Bella too warns Jack but King Fisher insists that he proceed. Now Jenifer reappears, altered by her experience; so too does Mark. She has an air of the 'starry heaven', he of the 'fruitful earth'. King Fisher's attempted intervention is silenced by the He-Ancient. Mark and Jenifer seem yet further apart, and go off again – this time he ascends and she descends. King Fisher's worldly utterances seem shallow, and the chorus urge him to let them go their ways.

ACT II: It is afternoon. Strephon is alone by the temple; he dances, then runs off, as the chorus come nearer. Bella and Jack enter, with the chorus. Bella tells Jack that the time has come for their marriage; they agree to have a home and family, and walk off into the wood. Now Strephon returns: the midsummer ritual is to be danced. The first dance is 'The Earth in Autumn'; it symbolizes the hound in pursuit of the hare (Strephon). The second, 'The Waters in Winter', at once follows; it is for the fish (Strephon) and the otter, and ends with the dancers sowing a field of spring corn. The third is 'The Air in Spring', in which a bird (Strephon) is chased, and ultimately caught, by a hawk. At its end Bella screams with fright and is comforted by Jack. She is restored, and prepares herself to return to King Fisher, despite Jack's misgivings. They go, as the chorus, offstage, sing of Midsummer's Day.

ACT III: It is evening, and the chorus celebrate the end of Midsummer's Day with food and wine; a half-tipsy man gets caught up in the dance. The chorus have been summoned by King Fisher, who now appears, with Bella: he is ready to challenge the Ancients with his clairvoyante, Sosostris. The Ancients are called: King Fisher charges them with catching his daughter, and challenges their power. A mysterious, oracular figure is borne in – but turns out merely to be Jack in disguise. But now a large and awesome figure appears, Sosostris herself. King Fisher tells her that his daughter has been kidnapped by these people and calls on her visionary powers to discover and free her. Sosostris utters a solemn warning and reluctantly applies her magic, looking into her bowl: she sees and describes an ancient marriage ritual, a girl yielding herself to a lion. King Fisher refuses to accept it and destroys the bowl.

Now King Fisher demands that Jack take a belt and holster and follow his commands. First he must unveil Sosostris; but Bella protests, and even Jack refuses – he will choose his own destiny – and leads Bella off. King Fisher starts to unveil Sosostris himself, in spite of the warnings of the Ancients. The final veil falls away, to disclose a huge, incandescent bud (it is now dark); the petals fall away, and within are Mark and Jenifer in mutual contemplation. King Fisher draws out his pistol, to (as he imagines) free his daughter, but as he raises it they look towards him and, clutching his heart, he falls before their power. He is dead, and the chorus bear him away.

Strephon emerges from the temple to execute the fourth dance, 'Fire in Summer'; during its final part the petals close over Mark and Jenifer, and Strephon too. This is a celebration of carnal love. The flames die down; in the moonlight the chorus contemplate what they have seen and call on the sun to return. The morning mist comes, and Mark and Jenifer meet one another, purified and enriched, ready for their union.

★   ★   ★

The score of *The Midsummer Marriage* is rich, sumptuous in its detail, sensuous in its sound. Its simplest parts are the scenes for Bella and Jack, straightforward, often conversational writing, with direct vocal lines and harmonizations; they talk in the tones of ordinary people. The parallel to Papageno and Papagena in *Die Zauberflöte* is obvious – here too is a couple who contemplate a marriage and family as their fullest realization. Mark and Jenifer are quite different, like Tamino and Pamina, altogether more exalted by their love and seeking for richer rewards from it; and this, too, is made plain by the complexity and indeed sometimes the tortuousness of

Ex. 1

the music assigned to them. One may, for example, compare the line
allotted to Mark in his first–act song looking forward to the marriage
(ex. 1) with the angry ranting of King Fisher (ex. 2) at the end of the

Ex. 2

act, or with the music assigned to the secondary lovers, like Bella's
lullaby as she envisages the simple domestic life she has chosen for
herself in Act II (ex. 3).

Ex. 3

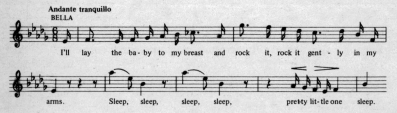

But in the last resort the impression left by *The Midsummer Marriage* – and this is its greatest strength – is of enriching mystery and ritual, represented in music by a score of rare floridity and elaboration, full of complex interwoven lines, sumptuous colours, rich harmonies: an opera remarkable and in its time unique for its sheer boldness and adventurousness of spirit.

BENJAMIN BRITTEN

1913–74

A leading composer of this century, and one who has enjoyed international success on a scale unprecedented for a British composer of opera, is Benjamin Britten. It was with *Peter Grimes* that he began his conquering operatic career in 1945. The astonishing thing about Britten as an opera composer was the degree to which he was self-made – with a great versatility of musical resources, with natural debts to some composers but chains to none, and showing very little connection with previous English opera.

At this point we may look over what might be justly called the pre-Britten century in English opera. Its two considerable international successes were *The Bohemian Girl* (1843) by Michael William Balfe (1808–70) and *The Mikado* (1881) by Arthur Sullivan (1842–1900). But·Sullivan failed with his one serious opera, *Ivanhoe* (1891), and of the composers coming after him only a few wrote works to which much interest attaches today, even in Britain. It is perhaps not invidious to pick out *A Village Romeo and Juliet* (originally in German, 1907) by Frederick Delius (1862–1934), *The Boatswain's Mate* (1916) by Ethel Smyth (1858–1934) and *Sāvitri* (1916), on an Indian legend, by Gustav Holst (1874–1934).

Ralph Vaughan Williams (1872–1958), like his teacher, Charles Villiers Stanford (1852–1924), wrote operas persistently but not very successfully: perhaps the best is *Riders to the Sea* (1937). Another Stanford pupil, Arthur Benjamin (1893–1960) showed a surer theatrical flair in *Prima Donna* (composed 1934, performed 1949) and *A Tale of Two Cities* (radio 1953, staged 1957). Composers who are older than Britten, but who began their operatic careers after he did, include Arthur Bliss (1891–1975), with *The Olympians* (1949); William Walton (1902–83), with *Troilus and Cressida* (1954, revised 1976) and the one-act 'extravaganza' *The Bear* (1967); Lennox Berkeley (born 1903), whose most successful opera is the witty one-act *A Dinner Engagement* (1954); and Michael Tippett.

Britten's own operas defy simple classification. Some were written for large theatres: *Peter Grimes* (1945), the all-male *Billy Budd* (1951), after Herman Melville, in which the action takes place on board ship, the coronation opera *Gloriana* (1953), which had a mixed reception on its first appearance but was more warmly received on its 1966 revival, and *Death in Venice* (1973), after Thomas Mann. *Owen Wingrave* (1971), after Henry James, might be placed in that category, though it was composed for television and only given in the opera-house two years later. Britten's chamber operas, using small instrumental forces, include *The Rape of Lucretia* (1946), the comedy *Albert Herring* (1947), *The Turn of the Screw* (1953) and *A Midsummer Night's Dream* (1960) – this last was rescored for full orchestra and given at Covent Garden in 1961. There are several other, miscellaneous works: *Paul Bunyan* (1941), a 'ballad opera' about the American folk hero, which Britten suppressed after its early performances, then revised and allowed to be staged in 1976; a very free adaptation of *The Beggar's Opera* (1948; see also page 42); children's operas, including *The Little Sweep* (1949), which is part of *Let's Make an Opera!*, and the miracle play *Noye's Fludde* (1958; for church performance with audience participation); and a triptych of 'parables for church performance': *Curlew River* (1964), after a Japanese Nōh play, *The Burning Fiery Furnace* (1966) and *The Prodigal Son* (1968), all three presented as if enacted by medieval monks, with small instrumental ensembles.

PETER GRIMES
Libretto by Montague Slater, after George Crabbe

First performed: London, 1945
Prologue and Three Acts

Cast in order of singing:

HOBSON, A CARRIER AND VILLAGE CONSTABLE	*bass*
SWALLOW, A LAWYER AND CORONER OF THE BOROUGH	*bass*
PETER GRIMES, A FISHERMAN	*tenor*
MRS SEDLEY, A RENTIER WIDOW OF AN EAST INDIA COMPANY'S FACTOR	*mezzo-soprano*
ELLEN ORFORD, A WIDOW, SCHOOLMISTRESS OF THE BOROUGH	*soprano*

AUNTIE, LANDLADY OF THE BOAR INN   *contralto*
BOB BOLES, A FISHERMAN AND METHODIST   *tenor*
BALSTRODE, A RETIRED MERCHANT SKIPPER   *baritone*
THE TWO 'NIECES', 'MAIN ATTRACTIONS' OF THE BOAR   *sopranos*
NED KEENE, APOTHECARY AND QUACK   *baritone*
THE REV. HORACE ADAMS, THE RECTOR   *tenor*
[The parts of John, Grimes's new apprentice, and the Doctor
are silent.]

Chorus of townspeople and fisherfolk
The scene is laid in the Borough, a small fishing
town on the East Coast of England about 1830

Like *Wozzeck, Peter Grimes* has a persecuted misfit for its protagonist
– a characteristically twentieth-century post-Freudian operatic
choice, we may think. Thus, beyond the multiplicity of individual
tensions, the opera presents a conflict between the lone fisherman
and the community in which he works. The moral scales are not, as
usual in opera, tilted conveniently in the hero's favour. When the
villagers recoil from Grimes's cruelty, we do so too; but such is the
illumination afforded by the music that we sympathize with him as
well. We feel (to quote the libretto itself) 'the pity and the truth'.

'The Borough', the setting for this opera (and for Crabbe's poem
of 1810 on which it is based), is a thinly disguised form of
Aldeburgh, the Suffolk fishing village where Britten made his
home. 'I am native, rooted here,' declares Grimes, and we may
perhaps imagine the composer – born not far away, at Lowestoft –
speaking through him.

★   ★   ★

PROLOGUE: The villagers are assembled in the Borough's Moot
Hall for an inquest on Peter Grimes's apprentice, who has died at sea.
Hobson calls Peter Grimes, who is questioned by Swallow, acting as
coroner. Grimes explains the circumstances of the death and of his
return with the boy's body (there is a brief intervention from Mrs
Sedley, one of the leading gossips, and the mutterings of the villagers
are heard, silenced by Hobson). Swallow advises Grimes to manage
without a boy apprentice in future and returns a verdict that death
was due to accidental circumstances. Grimes, suspected of treating
the boy brutally, asks to be confronted by his accusers, but Hobson
clears the court and Grimes is left alone with the schoolmistress,
Ellen Orford, who gently tries to console him.

ACT I: As dawn rises, the Borough's men and women set to work preparing the nets. A fisherman calls to Auntie, landlady of the Boar, who beckons some of them to the inn despite the protestations of Bob Boles, a Methodist. The retired skipper, Balstrode, comments on the approach of a storm. The Rector and Mrs Sedley pass, greeted by Auntie's two 'nieces', to whom the apothecary Keene calls out jocularly. Swallow, too, passes by.

From a distance, Grimes's voice is heard asking for help. At first nobody moves, but then Keene and Balstrode haul at the capstan for him while Boles talks to Auntie of Grimes's sinfulness. Keene tells Grimes that he has obtained an apprentice for him, and asks Hobson to fetch the boy in his cart. Hobson at first refuses, to the approval of the people assembled, but when Ellen Orford offers to look after the boy on the journey he agrees, and they depart. After asking Keene for a supply of the laudanum to which she is addicted, Mrs Sedley goes off.

Balstrode draws attention to the gathering storm, and he, Keene, Auntie, the nieces, Boles and the chorus sing of its approach and the rising of the tide. The fisher-folk fasten their boats and go into the Boar for shelter, leaving Balstrode and Grimes alone. Balstrode advises Grimes to leave the Borough, but despite the malice of the people Grimes finds the ties too strong. As the winds become fiercer, he describes to Balstrode the scene of the boy's death, and goes on to tell of his dreams of becoming wealthy, marrying Ellen and winning the Borough's respect. Balstrode leaves Grimes as the storm breaks.

The scene changes to the interior of the Boar. Mrs Sedley is there, waiting for Keene. Balstrode, then Boles and other fishermen arrive, struggling with the door in the fierce wind as they enter. The nieces come down, frightened, from their bedroom. More people enter with news of the storm's ravages. Boles, unaccustomed to drink, becomes tipsy; he behaves importunately to one of the nieces and is dealt with by Balstrode.

Keene and others come in (Keene mentioning a landslide on the cliff near Grimes's hut), soon followed by Grimes. Mrs Sedley faints, and the others mutter 'Talk of the devil', in a general unease. To the puzzlement of the others, Grimes philosophizes: 'Now the Great Bear and Pleiades where earth moves are drawing up the clouds of human grief.' To break the tension Balstrode calls for a song. Keene obliges, and soon all are singing a round, 'Old Joe has gone fishing'. Its liveliness is shattered when Ellen, Hobson and the new apprentice enter, soaked and storm-beaten. Auntie tries to make them warm and comfortable, but Grimes is in a hurry to be off. Ellen hands the boy over and, to the disapproval of all but her, Grimes takes him off into the howling storm.

ACT II: It is Sunday morning. Villagers are moving towards the church as the bell sounds, and Ellen comes in with the boy. She decides to stay on the beach rather than go to church, and sits knitting and talking to the boy as the voices of the congregation and the Rector are heard from the church. She suddenly sees that the boy's clothing is torn and that his neck is bruised. The suspicion that Grimes is ill-treating the boy is not lost on Mrs Sedley, who is passing.

Grimes enters excitedly. He has seen a large shoal and wants the apprentice to come, despite Ellen's reminder that it is the boy's day of rest. She reproaches Grimes, wondering whether they were right to plan a future together. Grimes cannot suppress his fury: he strikes her and goes off with the boy, seen by Auntie, Keene and Boles. Keene observes that 'Grimes is at his exercise', and as the people leave the church (among them Balstrode, who tries to calm the angry Boles and Mrs Sedley) they join in the angry buzz of conversation about Grimes 'at his exercise'. Swallow, the Rector and others join in. Eventually Boles starts haranguing the crowd against the apprentice system, against Grimes and against Ellen ('She helped him in his cruel games').

Ellen explains that she and Grimes planned to care for the boy's welfare but the crowd is in a jeering and angry mood, and Auntie leads Ellen off. The Rector proposes a deputation of the village men to Grimes's hut, to find out the truth about Grimes's suspected cruelties once and for all. Led by Hobson, beating his drum, and watched by the women, they go off. Ellen, Auntie and the nieces ponder upon the bitterness of woman's lot.

The scene changes to Grimes's hut. Grimes enters, pushing the boy before him; he throws the boy's sea clothes to him and shouts at the sobbing lad to prepare himself quickly. Seeing the sea seething with fish, he again dreams of a less troubled future with Ellen, then recalls the last apprentice. Sounds of the approaching procession are heard; realizing that the villagers are coming, he thinks the boy has been talking and becomes angry, telling him to hurry and get ready to go down by the cliff. Grimes warns his apprentice to take care. The boy goes first: he slips and, screaming, falls down the cliff to his death. Grimes goes out.

The villagers, led by the Rector, Swallow and Keene, enter the

hut. They are surprised to find it empty and well-kept; Swallow says
that there seems no cause for alarm, and that they should no longer
interfere. They all go, except Balstrode, who looks around the hut,
sees the precipice outside, and follows the route Grimes took down
the cliff.

ACT III: From the beach, in the evening, the distant sound of a Barn
Dance is heard from the Moot Hall. Swallow comes out of the hall,
tipsily bantering with the two nieces. Keene follows a little later and
is accosted by Mrs Sedley; she tells him that Grimes and his
apprentice have not been seen for two days and she feels sure Grimes
has killed the boy. He takes little notice and soon eludes her. The
rector and others come out of the Moot Hall – the time has arrived
for the older people to leave the festivities and go home to bed.

Mrs Sedley broods on the situation, concealing herself when Ellen
and Balstrode pass by. They are talking of Grimes: his boat is in but
they have not seen him, though they have found the boy's
embroidered jersey by the sea. They go off, full of foreboding,
hoping they can help Grimes.

As they disappear, Mrs Sedley runs off to the Boar, asking for
Swallow. Auntie tries to send her away but Swallow hears the
commotion and comes out. Mrs Sedley tells him that Grimes is back
and he promptly orders Hobson, as village constable, to organize a
search for him. The people, angry and suspicious, assemble, crying
'Peter Grimes! Peter Grimes!'

Some hours later, Grimes enters, weary and half-demented.
There is a thick fog: in the distance the cries of the villagers are still
audible. Grimes's thoughts are a jumble as he recalls the fate of the
apprentices (he repeats the Coroner's verdict of 'Accidental circumstances!') and other events which have driven him to his present
crisis. The voices grow nearer. Ellen and Balstrode arrive. She wants
to lead Grimes home, but Balstrode tells him [*spoken*] to take his boat
out to sea and sink it. He helps Grimes to put out, then leads Ellen
away.

For a moment the beach is deserted. Then, as another day dawns,
the people come out to start their work. Swallow reports to some
fishermen that a boat has been seen sinking out at sea beyond the
reach of help. The other villagers come out too. They sing of the
inexorable tides, for the life of the Borough in joy and sorrow is
governed by the sea.

* * *

Peter Grimes derives its characteristic and powerful musical shape
from Britten's use of orchestral interludes which not only indicate
the passage of time but serve as comment and convey atmosphere.
The sequence is: Court-room – *Interlude 1* (*Dawn*) – Beach – *Interlude
2* (*Storm*) – Inn – *Interlude 3* (*Sunday morning*) – Beach – *Interlude 4*
(*Procession to hut*) – Hut – *Interlude 5* (*Moonlight*) – Beach at night –
Interlude 6 (*Peter's disturbed mind*) – Beach, just before dawn. The titles
we have given to Interludes 4 and 6 are our own; those of the others
are Britten's own, not from the opera itself but from the suite called
'Four Sea Interludes' (in the order 1–3–5–2) published for orchestra
alone.

There is, however, no overture, and almost as soon as the curtain
rises Britten begins to differentiate Grimes from his fellow villagers.
Swallow reads out the formula for taking the oath ('I swear by
Almighty God', etc.) punctuated by heavy staccato brass discords;
Grimes not only alters the rhythm but also sings it more slowly,
refusing to rattle it off emptily, and is accompanied by sustained
strings.

Peter's only friend in the court-room is Ellen Orford; they are
finally left alone together and at the end of their duet, singing
unaccompanied and in unison, they sing a phrase (ex. 1) marked by a
distinctive upward leap which is a kind of motive representing
Peter's striving for a happier life and also representing the compassion Ellen offers.

Ex. 1

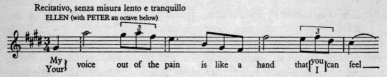

The chorus in the role of 'the people' plays a major part in the
opera, at two points joining in with the soloists in big, cumulative
set-pieces: the round 'Old Joe has gone fishing' (Act 1) and the
derisive 'Grimes is at his exercise!' – first heard as ex. 2. Note the
'chiming-in' of the second voice as if gossip were spreading. This
musical phrase is actually sung first of all to different words by
Grimes himself ('God have mercy upon me') and is afterwards
carried over into the Passacaglia which joins Interlude 4 as the men
are marching towards Grimes's hut: it may be called a 'persecution'
theme.

Ex. 2

The chorus also utters the menacing cries of 'Peter Grimes! Peter Grimes!' which are still heard, off-stage, in the final scene as Grimes recalls the past – and, musically, recalls the previous music of the opera. Ex. 3 shows the passage where he quotes his own philosophizing (from Act I, in the inn) and then quotes the round that was also sung in the inn; in between comes the distant shout of the chorus and the dull yet alarming note of the foghorn (played in the operahouse by an offstage tuba).

Ex. 3

Ellen is denied the tragic farewell aria which an earlier type of opera might have given her; instead the other villagers (soloists and chorus) remind us that fishermen's work goes on though this man or that boy be lost. The final bars recall the first orchestral interlude – dawn recalls dawn.

THE TURN OF THE SCREW
Libretto by Myfanwy Piper after the story by Henry James

First performed: Venice, 1954
Prologue and Two Acts

Cast in order of singing:

THE PROLOGUE	*tenor*
THE GOVERNESS	*soprano*
MILES	*boy treble*
FLORA	*soprano*
MRS GROSE, THE HOUSEKEEPER	*soprano*
MISS JESSEL, A FORMER GOVERNESS	*soprano*
PETER QUINT, A FORMER MANSERVANT	*tenor*

The scene is laid in an English country house, Bly, in the mid-nineteenth century

Not many operas are based on ghost stories as such, though aspects of the supernatural have attracted composers from the early Romantic era onwards. Henry James's ghost story has many ambiguities; reading it, one is never sure whether the ghosts are 'real' or figments of the Governess's overwrought imagination. In the opera, however, the ghosts actually speak, not only to the Governess but also to the children, which means that they must exist in their imagination, too. Moreover, in one scene they speak only to each other, implying an objective existence for them. There are other areas of mystery, or uncertainty, in the opera, too: for example, in just what does the evil or the corruption of the children reside? Is it sexual (as Miles's expulsion from school and Quint's words in the first scene of Act II might suggest)? Or is it a generalized loss of childish innocence, of the kind that so fascinated Britten, to judge by how often it served as the basic subject matter of his works?

The Turn of the Screw is a chamber opera, intended not for a full-size opera house, but for a modest, intimate one, where the sound of its thirteen-strong orchestra and the force of its emotions can come clearly across. Each scene has a title (shown in *italics* in the synopsis).

★   ★   ★

In the Prologue, a narrator introduces the story as if it were read from an old, faded book written by the governess. He tells how the young, inexperienced young woman had been appointed by the children's only relative, their uncle and guardian, a gallant, busy, offhand young man, to educate the children and care for them – the one condition being that he was not to be troubled over them.

ACT I: *On the Journey*   The Governess is travelling down to Bly for the first time, in a stage-coach, eager to take on her new job, anxious about it, hoping that the children and the old housekeeper will take to her.

The Welcome   On the porch at Bly, the children, Miles and Flora, and the housekeeper, Mrs Grose, are waiting for the Governess. She arrives and is warmly greeted by Mrs Grose and spiritedly by the children, who ask to show her around the house and park. She is sure she will be happy in her new home.

The Letter   It is some time later. Mrs Grose brings the Governess a letter: it is from Miles's school, saying he has been dismissed. Is he a bad boy, she asks? Mrs Grose reassures her: he can be wild, like most boys, but not bad. Miles and Flora enter, singing a nursery song, 'Lavender's blue': how, the women wonder, could such a boy be bad? They determine not to trouble his guardian.

The Tower   On a summer evening, the Governess is strolling in the grounds. She is thinking affectionately of the children and of her early anxieties, now happily passed. But then she looks up at the tower, and sees a man looking down at her: not a servant, but some sinister stranger. She is disturbed and puzzled.

The Window   In the hall, Flora and Miles are at play, riding a hobby horse and singing 'Tom, Tom, the piper's son' and chasing one another. The Governess enters, and calls them. For a moment she is alone, and she sees a man at the window; he quickly disappears. Mrs Grose enters and asks what is amiss; the Governess describes the man she has seen, whom Mrs Grose identifies as Peter Quint. The Governess asks who he is. Mrs Grose tells her: he was the master's valet; he used to spend hours with Miles, and he 'made free with' the former governess, Miss Jessel, who went away and died. The Governess asks what happened to Quint: he died too, Mrs Grose tells her. The Governess senses the evil in the house, left by Quint, and fears for Miles.

Lessons   In the schoolroom, the Governess is giving Miles a Latin lesson; Flora expresses a preference for history. Miles sings a strange song, 'Malo', which he claims he found.

The Lake Flora is walking with the Governess in the park, by
the lake; she is having a lesson about the seas, hesitating briefly
over the Dead Sea. They sit down, and Flora sings a lullaby to her
doll. At the end of it a woman's figure appears on the opposite
side of the lake: Flora turns round to face her. The Governess
looks up and sees her, and she disappears. Miles is heard, and
Flora runs off. The Governess realizes with alarm that this must
be Miss Jessel; the situation is worse than she had imagined.

At Night It is nighttime. Miles is in the garden, below the tower,
from which Quint is singing to him – strange songs, about heroism and wealth, deceit and secrets. Then Miss Jessel's voice is
heard: she is by the lake, and Flora at the window. The two spirits
sing enticingly and mysteriously to the children, who promise
them their loyalty. But then the Governess and Mrs Grose appear,
and lead them off. 'I am bad, aren't I?' says Miles.

ACT II: *Colloquy and Soliloquy* Quint and Miss Jessel are
together. She reproaches him for calling on her and betraying her;
he charges her with self-deception. He talks of the need of a friend
to ease his haunted heart; she too calls for a soul to share her woe.
They each end: 'The ceremony of innocence is drowned' (W. B.
Yeats). They disappear, and we see the Governess, confused, fearful, lost.

The Bells The children are in the local churchyard, singing: 'O
sing unto them a new song', a pseudo-Benedicite. Mrs Grose
greets the Governess, who cannot share in the housekeeper's
pleasure in Sunday morning or her assurance that all is well with
the children. Mrs Grose leads Flora into church; Miles stays
behind and questions the Governess about going back to school,
and about her thoughts, before he follows them. She takes this as
a challenge and talks of leaving 'this poisoned place'.

Miss Jessel The Governess enters the schoolroom, to find Miss
Jessel at the desk, bewailing her situation. She challenges her, but
is unheard. Miss Jessel vanishes, and the Governess sits down to
write to the children's uncle, asking if she can see him, his injunction of silence notwithstanding, as there are things he must be told
of.

The Bedroom Miles is sitting on the edge of his bed, singing the
'Malo' song. The Governess enters and questions him about his
thoughts, and tells him she has written to his guardian. He is
uneasy; the voice of Quint is heard, proclaiming his presence,
saying that he is waiting. Eventually Miles shrieks, and the candle

goes out. Quint is heard, talking of her letter, saying that it would be easy to take.

Quint Quint tells Miles to take the letter; he creeps across his room to the schoolroom and takes it.

The Piano Miles is practising the piano while Flora plays cat's cradle. The Governess tells Mrs Grose that she has written to the children's uncle. Mrs Grose dozes, and Flora slips out of the room. The Governess notices, wakens Mrs Grose and goes off with her to find the girl – she leaves Miles, who had helped Flora's escape from them, reckoning him already lost to Quint.

Flora Flora is by the lake; the Governess and Mrs Grose come out in pursuit of her. Miss Jessel appears, calling on Flora; but Mrs Grose cannot see her, and Flora denies her presence. Flora turns violently on the Governess, calling her cruel and hateful; Mrs Grose takes her away as the Governess contemplates her failure.

Miles Mrs Grose is taking Flora away, after (as she tells the Governess) a night in which the child has poured out horrors in her dreams. She mentions as she leaves that the Governess's letter was never sent. Miles and the Governess are alone; she tells him of her concern for him and urges him to tell her what is on his mind. But he is searching for help from Quint; and Quint's voice is heard, uttering warnings, and he is seen on the tower, then approaching them, as the Governess presses Miles to tell her what is afoot and to say why he took the letter. Miles can bear no more: 'Peter Quint, you devil!', he screams, and collapses in the Governess's arms. She thinks him saved, as Quint bids him farewell; then realizes the truth – he is dead. She echoes his 'Malo'.

★   ★   ★

None of Britten's operas is more closely organized, in terms of thematic structure and its dramatic significance, than *The Turn of the Screw*. Between its scenes, a musical design – a theme and variations – unfolds, serving as a commentary on the drama. Its theme is stated as the Prologue finishes, with the Governess's acceptance of the post (ex. 1). It is a 'twelve-note' theme, made up of all twelve notes of the chromatic scale without any being repeated (except immediately) before all are sounded; it is not, of course, used according to the Schoenbergian rules of twelve-note composition, to which Britten never subscribed. Its structure is simple: three identical sets of four notes (allowing for inversions by an octave), in which the interval of a fourth is specially prominent – as it is throughout the opera, for in a

Ex. 1

sense the entire score is composed of variations, or perhaps a fantasy, on this theme.

No less significant is the way that themes, or motifs, are used allusively. Flora's lullaby to her doll recurs when Mrs Grose goes to sleep, making it clear that Flora wanted her to sleep so that she could escape to Miss Jessel. Miles's haunting 'Malo' jingle (ex. 2), too, recurs, not only at the end but also in a scene where Flora refers to him (she mentions that she and he would not go into the Dead Sea as nothing can live in it) and in the scene where Miles takes the Governess's letter. Here as elsewhere the librettist has quoted the rhyming couplets and other aids to memory which generations of British schoolboys absorbed from Latin grammars. Four different senses of the Latin *malo* are conveyed in Miles's jingle, ending 'than a naughty boy . . . in adversity'. Such things are made to sound now sinister, now wistful, as are the English nursery-rhymes also quoted.

Ex. 2

Perhaps this musical corruption is most powerful of all in the piano-playing scene, where Miles plays Mozartian phrases with a dark, disjointed twist, and does so with especial spirit when the triumph of Flora's escape and the adults' pursuit of her – leaving him alone – is accomplished. Not only intervals and motifs and themes are used to draw this score together (to turn the screw more tightly, one might say), but also colour: the disembodied sound of the celesta is heard when Quint appears, the gong when Miss Jessel does. All this may help explain why this troubling opera appeals so powerfully on so many levels.

EPILOGUE:
THE MODERN SCENE

That Britten wrote operatic works which are not for the opera-house at all – and in this he is only one among many – is symptomatic of the suspicion with which many composers of different countries have viewed the traditional operatic form and its accoutrements. In the twentieth century, opera has become a kind of 'classic' theatre, in which interest is concentrated on the modes of performance (by the producer and designer just as much as the singers or the conductor) of a more or less static standard repertory. The reasons for this, as much economic as to do with taste or social factors, are complex, and not susceptible of full discussion here; but there is a case for saying that such genres as the Broadway musical have inherited the theatrical aliveness and the novelty-hungry audiences that once belonged to opera.

It is significant that the most successful of Italian-born opera composers since Puccini, Gian-Carlo Menotti, established himself more through 'theatre' than through 'opera' channels, and that he made his career chiefly in America. In Italy itself, considerable esteem is given to Ildebrando Pizzetti (1880–1968), whose works include an operatic version (1958) of T. S. Eliot's *Murder in the Cathedral*. The modern Italian opera that has won most notice elsewhere is *Il prigioniero* ('The Prisoner', 1950), in one act, by Luigi Dallapiccola (1904–75). Its story of 'torture by hope', particularly relevant to the crisis of human freedom in the twentieth century, is handled with an unsensational, oratorio-like seriousness. His *Ulisse*, a philosophical rather than a graphic treatment of the wanderings of Odysseus, so that it is a 'quest' opera about the human condition, was produced in 1968. Luigi Nono's *Intolleranza 1960* (1961) attracted considerable attention as a forceful political statement.

Among German composers, Hans Pfitzner (1869–1949) is deeply

respected for the spiritual qualities of his *Palestrina* (1917). Paul Hindemith (1895–1963) retained a largely traditional approach to opera after some early flirtations with the experimental; his *Cardillac* (1926), *Mathis der Maler* ('Mathis the Painter', 1938) and *Die Harmonie der Welt* ('The Harmony of the World', 1957) are all concerned with aspects of the artist's role in society. A composer who typified the experimental spirit of the 1920s in Germany (apart from Kurt Weill: see page 502) was Ernst Krenek (b. 1900), whose great success *Jonny spielt auf* (1927) contrasts the traditional artist's role with that of the free-and-easy Black American jazz musician.

Radical in quite a different way was Carl Orff (1895–1982). Leaving aside those of his stage works that are really cantatas mimed by dancers, we may note *Die Kluge* ('The Clever Girl', 1943) with its deliberately simple tunes, repetitive rhythms and artless, fairy-tale atmosphere, and *Antigone* (1949), a German setting of Sophocles' play which gives complete sovereignty to the words, the voices mainly reciting on one or two notes and the orchestra mainly punctuating – with impressive musical effect. Among younger Germans, Bernd Alois Zimmermann (1918–70) made an especial mark for his *Die Soldaten* ('The Soldiers', 1965), with its political message and its novel stage technique, with different layers of both action and music functioning simultaneously; Giselher Klebe (born 1925) should also be noted for his several operas with a strong literary basis (Schiller, Shakespeare and others) and a more traditional approach. The leading Austrian opera composer is Gottfried von Einem (born 1918), whose *Der Besuch der alten Dame* ('The Visit of the Old Lady', 1971), after Dürrenmatt, has enjoyed considerable international success.

In France, Maurice Ravel (1875–1937) shred the addiction of his elder contemporary, Debussy, and of other French composers to Spanish themes. He wrote a one-act comedy, *L'heure espagnole* (1911 – an ambiguous title, probably best rendered as 'Spanish Time') in which clock-chimes enter the score as a naturalistic element. A similar naturalism shows in the cries of the various creatures in *L'enfant et les sortilèges* ('The Child and the Spells', 1925), but here the grotesqueness is subordinated to a human tenderness not always evident in Ravel.

Among other Frenchmen Francis Poulenc (1899–1963) explored two extremes – tragic, Musorgsky-influenced chronicle opera (yet not without a hint of Gounod and Massenet too) in *Dialogues des Carmélites* (1957) and near-operetta in his comic treatment of myth,

Les mamelles de Tirésias ('The Breasts of Tiresias', 1947). The operas of Darius Milhaud (1892–1974) are sometimes revived; they include a treatment of the Orpheus myth, *Les malheurs d'Orphée* (1925), a historical work, *Christophe Colomb* (1928), with a text by Claudel and highly adventurous dramaturgy, and a setting of the third play in the Beaumarchais Figaro cycle, *La mère coupable* (1965). Some success has been won by *Jeanne d'Arc au bûcher* ('Joan of Arc at the Stake', 1938), a semi-opera by Arthur Honegger (1892–1955) in which the heroine does not sing.

Manuel de Falla (1876–1946), the most notable Spanish composer of the early twentieth century, employed a device of deliberate artificiality in *El retablo de Maese Pedro* ('Master Peter's Puppet Show', 1923), based on an episode from *Don Quixote*: there is an inner play, enacted by puppets, commented on by the other characters (who may be bigger puppets or live actors). The artificiality is admirably set off by the stylized music, which includes a part for harpsichord.

In Hungary, Béla Bartók (1881–1945) wrote, for only two characters, *Duke Bluebeard's Castle* (1918): its mixture of scenic demands and symbolic meaning makes it difficult to stage but it has both pathos and a sense of theatrical climax. Zoltán Kodály (1882–1967) had some success in his attempt to introduce folksong into the opera house in his 'Singspiel' *Háry János* (1926), really a play with songs. A more recent Hungarian (though *émigré*) to enjoy operatic success is György Ligeti, whose *Le grand macabre* (1978), a parody work about life and death, sex and politics, has been widely produced since its first production in Stockholm in 1978. Opera from Soviet Russia, Shostakovich and Prokofiev apart, has travelled little to the West, but at home *The Decembrists* (1953) by Yuri Shaporin (1887–1966) and *The Taming of the Shrew* (1957) by Vissarion Shebalin (1902–63) won places in the repertory; so, later, did *Not only love* (1961) by Rodion Shchedrin, a much younger composer (born 1932). In Poland, there have been few operatic developments of international importance since *King Roger* (1926), a vivid and rich treatment of the Bacchae myth by Karol Szymanowski (1882–1937), though *The Devils of Loudon* (1969) by Krzysztof Penderecki (born 1933) has had some impact for the force of its treatment of a mystical–religious subject. In Czechoslovakia two Slovak composers have had considerable success with operas: Eugen Suchoň (born 1908), with *The Whirlpool* (1949) and *Svätopluk* (1959), and Ján Cikker (born 1911), with *Resurrection* (1962).

In Sweden – where in 1959 *Aniara* by Karl-Birger Blomdahl (1916–68) had brought the modernity of a space-navigation plot and a partly electronic score into opera – a challenge to the conventional theatrical 'spacing' of opera was successfully issued by Lars Johan Werle (born 1926); in his *The Dream about Thérèse* (1964), the audience encircles the stage and the orchestral players (who change positions during the course of the work) encircle the audience. More recently, a Finnish composer, Aulis Sallinen (born 1935), has had considerable impact with his operas, especially *The Red Line* (1978), where the lot of the poor in the icy north is compellingly conveyed.

In Britain, a number of younger composers have made promising contributions to the opera literature. The most notable are Peter Maxwell Davies (born 1934), whose *Taverner* (1972), treating the self-destructive religious mania of the sixteenth-century composer John Taverner, was succeeded by a much more accessible work, *The Lighthouse* (1980), and Harrison Birtwistle (born 1934) whose one-act *Punch and Judy* (1968) embodies violence and ritual in highly arresting and dramatic ways. Davies has also written *The Two Fiddlers* (1978) for child performers.

Alexander Goehr (born in Germany, 1932) wrote his *Arden must Die* (1967) to a Hamburg commission (as *Arden muss sterben*); it embodies Brechtian morality-play elements. Goehr, like Davies, has worked in experimental music theatre, as seen in such works as his *Naboth's Vineyard* (1968), which owes something to Japanese theatre. More conservative in approach are Richard Rodney Bennett (born 1936), who, however, has never quite followed up the success of his impressive *The Mines of Sulphur* (1965), and the Australian Malcolm Williamson (born 1931), whose *The Violins of St Jacques* (1966) showed a richness of invention that he has not recaptured. Iain Hamilton (born 1922) won attention with his operatic transformation (1967) of Peter Shaffer's play *The Royal Hunt of the Sun* but of recent British works in the tradition of spectacular, political opera perhaps the most notable has been *Toussaint* (1977) by David Blake (born 1936).

In America, no native-born composer has enjoyed success equal to Menotti's (see also page 520). A brand of 'folky' operas, not readily exportable, is exemplified by *Ballad of Baby Doe* (1956) by Douglas Moore (1893–1969) and by *The Tender Land* (1954) by Aaron Copland (born 1900), the latter being one of several American operas designed for college performance.

Among the next generation of Americans, Carlisle Floyd (born

1926) impressed with *Wuthering Heights* (1958) and *Susannah* (1955), the latter of which has had numerous revivals. Of the younger, more radical generation, influenced by John Cage, few have attempted opera; one exception is Philip Glass (born 1937), whose *Einstein on the Beach*, in a single act of more than four hours, was given at the Paris Opéra-Comique in 1975 and later had something more than a cult-following in New York. Others, however, see the future of opera developing through an integration with the traditions of the musical. Leonard Bernstein (born 1918) brought out his *Candide* (1956) as a musical, though it is near-operatic in resource – as indeed he recognized when adapting it (1982) for performance at a major New York opera-house. Its commercial failure seemed to indicate that it was too light for opera-goers, too heavy (and too detached in spirit) for those who flocked to the composer's *West Side Story* (1958). Doubtless there is a moral to be drawn here.

BIBLIOGRAPHY

The literature of opera is large and various. There are histories, total or partial; there are dictionaries and other reference works; there are studies of individual composers, studies of individual works. And there are books of synopses, of which the most comprehensive in English is *Kobbé's Complete Opera Book* (first published in London in 1922; the ninth edition, revised and enlarged by the Earl of Harewood, appeared in 1976). Of this genre are Ernest Newman's two *Opera Nights* volumes (London, 1943, 1954) and his *Wagner Nights* (London, 1949).

Edward J. Dent's *Opera* (Harmondsworth, 1940, rev. 1949) is a brilliant one-man survey of the subject, though inevitably it has now dated. A careful, scholarly history is Donald J. Grout's *A Short History of Opera* (New York, 1947, rev. 1965); another important American book, critical rather than historical in approach, is Joseph Kerman's provocative and illuminating *Opera as Drama* (New York, 1956). A more popular approach is found in Wallace Brockway and Herbert Weinstock's *The World of Opera* (New York, second edition 1962) which quotes many other authorities and pursues the history of opera into the 1960s, not always quite dependably. Patrick J. Smith's *The Tenth Muse: A Historical Study of the Opera Libretto* (New York, 1970) is uneven in scope but gives valuable insights. Gary Schmidgall's *Literature as Opera* (New York, 1978) looks at the subject from a different standpoint, as its title suggests. Other recent books to essay new kinds of critical and aesthetic approach include Robert Donington's *Opera* (London, 1978) and John D. Drummond's *Opera in Perspective* (London, 1980).

Three useful series should be noted. The ENO Guides (published by English National Opera and John Calder, and edited by Nicholas John), each include a libretto, an English translation and essays on the work; they are also being issued in collected form. The Cambridge Opera Handbooks (Cambridge University Press) each offer a series of fairly detailed studies of aspects of the work. A series (published by John Calder) called 'The History of Opera' was inaugurated in 1981 with a volume by T. J. Walsh on the Paris Théâtre Lyrique, 1851–70, and is intended to comprise some twenty-six volumes covering the entire history of the genre in a social context.

A useful and wide-ranging reference work on opera is Leslie Orrey's *Encyclopaedia of Opera* (London, 1976); a smaller but very valuable one is *The Concise Oxford Dictionary of Opera* (London, 1964, rev. 3/1978) by Harold Rosenthal and John Warrack.

Of books about composers treated in the present volume, those listed below are recommended to general readers as the best available in English in 1983. All are published in London unless otherwise stated. Several are included as 'New Grove' biographies: that is, they are extracted from *The New Grove Dictionary of Music and Musicians* (1980) and like the other articles on composers and on opera itself in that volume, may be commended as methodical, authoritative studies. The dates of publication should be noted: these are of the most recent editions, and in some cases include changes and new material as compared with earlier ones. Printed librettos and record-album notes are not cited here, though these may often provide useful background information on the works concerned: for 'early' operas and other rarities, the record-album notes may indeed provide the best available and most up-to-date information on individual works and the problems arising in performing them.

Monteverdi
Denis Arnold: *Monteverdi* (Master Musicians), 1963
Denis Stevens: *Monteverdi: Sacred, Secular and Occasional Music*, Rutherford, 1978

Purcell
Robert Etheridge Moore: *Henry Purcell and the Restoration Theatre*, 1961
J. A. Westrup: *Purcell* (Master Musicians), 1980
Franklin B. Zimmerman: *Henry Purcell, 1659–1695: His Life and Times*, 1984

Rameau
Cuthbert Girdlestone: *Jean-Philippe Rameau: His Life and Work*, 1969

Handel
Winton Dean: *Handel and the Opera Seria*, Berkeley and Los Angeles, 1969
Winton Dean: *Handel* (The New Grove), 1982

Gluck
Alfred Einstein: *Gluck* (Master Musicians), 1936
Patricia Howard: *Gluck and the Birth of Modern Opera*, 1963

Mozart
Arthur Hutchings: *Mozart: The Man, the Musician*, 1976
William Mann: *The Operas of Mozart*, 1977
Charles Osborne: *The Complete Operas of Mozart*, 1978
Stanley Sadie: *Mozart* (The New Grove), 1982

Beethoven
Denis Arnold and Nigel Fortune, eds.: *The Beethoven Companion*, 1971
Maynard Solomon: *Beethoven*, New York, 1977
Alan Tyson and Joseph Kerman: *Beethoven* (The New Grove), 1983

Weber
William Saunders: *Weber* (Master Musicians), New York, 1970
John Warrack: *Carl Maria von Weber*, 1976

Rossini
Philip Gossett: 'Rossini', in *Masters of Italian Opera* (The New Grove), 1983
Francis Toye: *Rossini: A Study in Tragi-Comedy*, 1963

Donizetti
William Ashbrook: *Donizetti and his Operas*, Cambridge, 1982
William Ashbrook and Julian Budden: 'Donizetti', in *Masters of Italian Opera* (The New Grove), 1983

Bellini
Friedrich Lippmann: 'Bellini', in *Masters of Italian Opera* (The New Grove), 1983
Leslie Orrey: *Bellini* (Master Musicians), 1969

Verdi
Julian Budden: *The Operas of Verdi*, 3 vols., 1973, 1978, 1981
Spike Hughes: *Famous Verdi Operas*, 1968
George Martin: *Verdi*, New York, 1964
Andrew Porter: 'Verdi', in *Masters of Italian Opera* (The New Grove), 1983

Frank Walker: *The Man Verdi*, 1962
William Weaver and Martin Chusid, eds: *The Verdi Companion*,
  New York, 1979

Wagner
Carl Dahlhaus: *Richard Wagner's Music Dramas*, Cambridge, 1979
John Deathridge and Carl Dahlhaus: *Wagner* (The New Grove), 1984
Robert Donington: *Wagner's 'Ring' and its Symbols*, 1963
Ernest Newman: *The Life of Richard Wagner*, 1933–47
Ernest Newman: *Wagner Nights*, 1949
George Bernard Shaw: *The Perfect Wagnerite*, 1972
Curt von Westerhagen: *Wagner: A Biography*, Cambridge, 1979

Berlioz
Jacques Barzun: *Berlioz and the Romantic Century*, 1950
David Cairns, ed. and trans.: *The Memoirs of Hector Berlioz*, 1970
Hugh Macdonald: *Berlioz* (Master Musicians), 1982

Gounod
James Harding: *Gounod*, 1973

Offenbach
Alexander Faris: *Jacques Offenbach*, 1980

Saint-Saëns
James Harding: *Saint-Saëns and his Circle*, 1965

Bizet
Mina Curtiss: *Bizet and his World*, New York, 1958
Winton Dean: *Georges Bizet: His Life and Work*, 1975

Massenet
James Harding: *Massenet*, 1970

Debussy
Edward Lockspeiser: *Debussy: His Life and Mind*, 2 vols, 1962–5
Edward Lockspeiser: *Debussy* (Master Musicians), 1980
Roger Nichols: *Debussy*, 1973

Smetana
John Clapham: *Smetana*, 1971

Borodin
Serge Dianin: *Borodin*, 1963

Musorgsky
M. D. Calvocoressi: *Modest Mussorgsky: His Life and Works*, 1956

J. Leyda and S. Bertensson, eds: *The Musorgsky Reader*, New York,
    1970
Victor I. Seroff: *Modest Mussorgsky*, New York, 1968

Tchaikovsky
David Brown: *Tchaikovsky: A Biographical and Critical Study*, 4 vols,
    1978, 1982–
Edward Garden: *Tchaikovsky* (Master Musicians), 1973
John Warrack: *Tchaikovsky*, 1973

Rimsky-Korsakov
Gerald Abraham: *Rimsky-Korsakov: A Short Biography*, 1945

Puccini
Mosco Carner: *Puccini: A Critical Biography*, 1974
Spike Hughes: *Famous Puccini Operas*, 1959
Charles Osborne: *The Complete Operas of Puccini*, 1982

Strauss
Norman Del Mar: *Richard Strauss: A Critical Commentary on his Life
    and Works*, 3 vols., 1978
Michael Kennedy: *Richard Strauss* (Master Musicians), 1976
William S. Mann: *Richard Strauss: A Critical Study of the Operas*, 1964

Janáček
J. M. Ewans: *Janáček's Tragic Operas*, 1977
Ian Horsburgh: *Leos Janáček*, 1981
Jaroslav Vogel: *Leos Janáčeck: A Biography*, 1981

Stravinsky
Roman Vlad: *Stravinsky*, 1979
Eric Walter White: *Stravinsky: The Composer and his Works*, 1979

Berg
Mosco Carner: *Alban Berg*, 1975
Douglas Jarman: *The Music of Alban Berg*, 1979

Prokofiev
Israel V. Nest'yev: *Prokofiev*, 1961
Victor Seroff: *Sergei Prokofiev: A Soviet Tragedy*, New York, 1968

Weill
Kim Kowalke: *Kurt Weill in Europe*, Ann Arbor, 1979
Ronald Sanders: *The Days Grow Short: The Life and Music of Kurt
    Weill*, 1980

Shostakovich
Boris Schwarz: *Music and Musical Life in Soviet Russia, 1917–70*, 1983

Gershwin
I. Goldberg: *George Gershwin: A Study in American Music*, New York, 1958
E. Jablonski and L. D. Stewart: *The Gershwin Years*, Garden City, New York, 1973

Menotti
John Gruen: *Menotti*, 1981

Tippett
Meirion Bowen: *Michael Tippett*, 1982
David Matthews: *Michael Tippett, An Introductory Study*, 1980
Eric Walter White: *Tippett and his Operas*, 1979

Britten
Peter Evans: *The Music of Benjamin Britten*, 1979
Patricia Howard: *The Operas of Benjamin Britten*, 1969
Michael Kennedy: *Britten* (Master Musicians), 1981

Non-fiction

☐	**The Money Book**	Margaret Allen	£2.95p
☐	**Fall of Fortresses**	Elmer Bendiner	£1.75p
☐	**The British Way of Birth**	Catherine Boyd and Lea Sellers	£1.50p
☐	**100 Great British Weekends**	John Carter	£2.95p
☐	**Last Waltz in Vienna**	George Clare	£1.95p
☐	**Walker's Britain**	Andrew Duncan	£4.95p
☐	**Travellers' Britain**	Arthur Eperon	£2.95p
☐	**The Tropical Traveller**	John Hatt	£2.50p
☐	**The Lord God Made Them All**	James Herriot	£1.95p
☐	**The Neck of the Giraffe**	Francis Hitching	£2.50p
☐	**A Small Town is a World**	David Kossoff	£1.00p
☐	**Prayers and Graces**	Allen Laing illus. by Mervyn Peake	£1.25p
☐	**Kitchen & Bathroom Book**	Jose Manser	£5.95p
☐	**Best of Shrdlu**	Denys Parsons	£1.00p
☐	**Dipped in Vitriol**	Nicholas Parsons	£1.75p
☐	**The Bargain Book**	Barty Phillips	£1.95p
☐	**Thy Neighbour's Wife**	Gay Talese	£1.75p
☐	**Just off for the Weekend**	John Slater	£2.50p
☐	**Dead Funny**	Fritz Spiegl	£1.50p
☐	**The Third Wave**	Alvin Toffler	£2.75p
☐	**The World Atlas of Treasure**	Derek Wilson	£6.50p
☐	**Shyness**	Philip Zimbardo	£1.95p

All these books are available at your local bookshop or newsagent, or can be ordered direct from the publisher. Indicate the number of copies required and fill in the form below   10

....

Name..

(Block letters please)

Address..

_____

Send to CS Department, Pan Books Ltd, PO Box 40, Basingstoke, Hants
Please enclose remittance to the value of the cover price plus:
35p for the first book plus 15p per copy for each additional book ordered
to a maximum charge of £1.25 to cover postage and packing
Applicable only in the UK

While every effort is made to keep prices low, it is sometimes
necessary to increase prices at short notice. Pan Books reserve
the right to show on covers and charge new retail prices which
may differ from those advertised in the text or elsewhere